OBSESSIVE-COMPULSIVE DISORDER

The Wiley Series in

CLINICAL PSYCHOLOGY

Titles published under the series editorship of:

J. Mark G. Williams   *School of Psychology, University of Wales, Bangor, UK*

A list of earlier titles in the series follows the index.

OBSESSIVE-COMPULSIVE DISORDER
Theory, Research and Treatment

Edited by
Ross G. Menzies
*School of Behavioural and Community
Health Sciences, University of Sydney, Australia*

and

Padmal de Silva
*Institute of Psychiatry, King's College,
University of London, UK*

WILEY

This publication is designed to provide accurate and authoritative information in regard to the
subject matter covered. It is sold on the understanding that the Publisher is not engaged in
rendering professional services. If professional advice or other expert assistance is required, the
services of a competent professional should be sought.

Other Wiley Editorial Offices

John Wiley & Sons Inc., 111 River Street, Hoboken, NJ 07030, USA

Jossey-Bass, 989 Market Street, San Francisco, CA 94103-1741, USA

Wiley-VCH Verlag GmbH, Boschstr. 12, D-69469 Weinheim, Germany

John Wiley & Sons Australia Ltd, 33 Park Road, Milton, Queensland 4064, Australia

John Wiley & Sons (Asia) Pte Ltd, 2 Clementi Loop #02-01, Jin Xing Distripark, Singapore 129809

John Wiley & Sons Canada Ltd, 22 Worcester Road, Etobicoke, Ontario, Canada M9W 1L1

Wiley also publishes its books in a variety of electronic formats. Some content that appears in
print may not be available in electronic books.

Library of Congress Cataloging-in-Publication Data

Obsessive-compulsive disorder : theory, research, and treatment / edited by Ross G. Menzies
and Padmal de Silva.
       p.   cm.—(The Wiley series in clinical psychology)
    Includes bibliographical references and index.
    ISBN 0-471-49444-5 (hbk. : alk. paper)—ISBN 0-471-49445-3 (pbk. : alk. paper)
    1. Obsessive-compulsive disorder.   I. Menzies, Ross G.   II. De Silva, Padmal.   III. Series.

RC533 .O2745   2003
616.85'227–dc21   2002033137

British Library Cataloguing in Publication Data

A catalogue record for this book is available from the British Library

ISBN 0-471-49444-5 (hbk)
ISBN 0-471-49445-3 (pbk)

Typeset in 10/12pt Palatino by TechBooks, New Delhi, India
Printed and bound in Great Britain by TJ International, Padstow, Cornwall
This book is printed on acid-free paper responsibly manufactured from sustainable forestry
in which at least two trees are planted for each one used for paper production.

For Margot and Rachel (RGM),
Vasantha, Vin and Hesha (PdeS)

CONTENTS

Section V   Professional Issues

ABOUT THE EDITORS

Ross G. Menzies, a clinical psychologist, is Associate Professor and Head of the School of Behavioural and Community Health Sciences at the University of Sydney. He is also Head of Sydney University's Anxiety Disorders Clinic and Anxiety and Stress Research Group. He was a founding member of the Anxiety Disorders Foundation of Australia (NSW Branch), serving on the Board of the Association for 2 years. He is the past National President, and current NSW President, of the Australian Association for Cognitive Behaviour Therapy. Professor Menzies holds several other honorary appointments, including Honorary Associate of the Department of Medical Psychology at Westmead Hospital, Honorary Associate of the Sydney Clinic, member of the Advisory Board of the Sydney Anxiety Disorders Practice and Clinical Director of Anxpsych, an organisation bringing anxiety management skills to the corporate sector. He has been the overseas expert trainer in cognitive behavioural therapy at the National University of Singapore. In addition to his university and hospital commitments, he has run a private clinic specialising in OCD for the past 15 years. He continues to attract patients from across metropolitan Sydney, rural NSW, interstate and from overseas to this unit. His recent research has focused on the origins and cognitive mediation of OCD. He is the co-developer of the Danger Ideation Reduction Therapy (DIRT) package for compulsive washing. He is a member of the Obsessive Compulsive Cognitions Working Group and is the Founder of the Australian and New Zealand OCD Research Alliance, a co-operative of leading Australasian psychologists and psychiatrists researching in this area.

Padmal de Silva is Senior Lecturer in Psychology at the Institute of Psychiatry, King's College, University of London, and Senior Clinical Tutor for the Institute's doctoral training programme in clinical psychology. He is also Consultant Clinical Psychologist at the South London and Maudsley National Health Service Trust. He has been involved in clinical and research work in obsessive-compulsive disorder and other anxiety disorders for many years. He is the co-author, with Stanley Rachman, of *Obsessive-compulsive Disorder—The Facts*, and *Panic Disorder—The Facts*, both published by Oxford University Press.

LIST OF CONTRIBUTORS

Michael Bruch *Royal Free and University College Medical School, Dept of Psychiatry and Behavioural Sciences, 2nd Floor, Wolfson Building, Riding House Street, London W1N 8AA, UK*

Graham C. L. Davey *Psychology Group, School of Cognitive and Computing Sciences, University of Sussex, Falmer, Brighton BN1 9QH, UK*

Padmal de Silva *Department of Psychology, Institute of Psychiatry, King's College, University of London, De Crespigny Park, Denmark Hill, London SE5 8AF, UK*

Danielle Einstein *School of Behavioural and Community Health Sciences, University of Sydney, PO Box 170, Lidcombe, NSW 2141, Australia*

Andy P. Field *Psychology Group, School of Cognitive and Computing Sciences, University of Sussex, Falmer, Brighton BN1 9QH, UK*

Ian Frampton *Psychology Department, Dolphin House, Royal Cornwall Hospital, Treliske, Truro, Truro TR1 3LJ, UK*

Randy O. Frost *Department of Psychology, Smith College, Northampton, MA 01063, USA*

Lynne M. Harris *School of Behavioural and Community Health Sciences, University of Sydney, PO Box 170, Lidcombe, NSW 2141, Australia*

Tamara L. Hartl *University of Connecticut, Storrs, CT 06269, USA*

Mairwen K. Jones *School of Behavioural and Community Health Sciences, University of Sydney, PO Box 170, Lidcombe, NSW 2141, Australia*

Annette Krochmalik *School of Behavioural and Community Health Sciences, University of Sydney, PO Box 170, Lidcombe, NSW 2141, Australia*

Michael Kyrios *Department of Psychology, University of Melbourne, Parkville, VIC 3052, Australia*

Alison M. Macdonald *Department of Psychology, City University Northampton Square, London ECIV OHB UK*

Melanie Marks *75 Harley Street, London, W1N 1DE, UK*

Michael McDonough   *Wickham Park House, Bethlem Royal Hospital, Monks Orchard Road, Beckenham, Kent BR3 3BX, UK*

Joy McGuire   *King's College London, Department of Psychology, Institute of Psychiatry, De Crespigny Park, Denmark Hill, London SE5 8AF, UK*

Ross G. Menzies   *School of Behavioural and Community Health Sciences, University of Sydney, PO Box 170, Lidcombe, NSW 2141, Australia*

Antonio Prioglio   *Royal Free and University College Medical School, Dept of Psychiatry and Behavioural Sciences, 2nd Floor, Wolfson Building, Riding House Street, London W1N 8AA, UK*

Stanley Rachman   *Department of Psychology, University of British Columbia, Vancouver, BC V6T 1Z1, Canada*

Tamsen St. Clare   *School of Behavioural and Community Health Sciences, University of Sydney, PO Box 170, Lidcombe, NSW 2141, Australia*

Paul M. Salkovskis   *King's College London, Department of Psychology, Institute of Psychiatry, De Crespigny Park, Denmark Hill, London SE5 8AF, UK*

Roz Shafran   *Department of Psychiatry, University of Oxford, Warneford Hospital, Headington, Oxford OX3 7JX, UK*

Helen M. Startup   *Psychology Group, School of Cognitive and Computing Sciences, University of Sussex, Falmer, Brighton BN1 9QH, UK*

David Veale   *The Priory Hospital North London, The Bourne, Southgate, London N14 6RA, UK*

PREFACE

This book is set out in five sections. The first, consisting of two chapters, explores the nature of obsessive-compulsive disorder (OCD). In Chapter 1, Krochmalik and Menzies examine the history of descriptions of the disorder, from the earliest references right through to contemporary accounts. Considerable attention is given to current classificatory and diagnostic criteria, with an examination of the differences between obsessive thinking, general worry, overvalued ideation and delusions. In Chapter 2, de Silva provides an exploration of the phenomenology of the condition, with multiple case descriptions that help capture the essential features of the disorder. It is hoped that a careful reading of the two chapters of Section 1 will provide clinical trainees, beginning practitioners and researchers with a solid foundation for the theoretical chapters that follow.

Section II considers various conceptual and theoretical aspects of the disorder. The Section opens with Frampton's review of neuropsychological models (Chapter 3). Much of the experimental work in this area is shown to suffer from crippling methodological weaknesses, including the failure to control for multiple comparisons, co-morbid depression, medication and general speed deficits. In addition, there has been a general lack of underlying theory to guide experimentation. However, on a positive note, Frampton concludes that recent studies have begun to address these weaknesses and structural and functional neuroimaging have begun to strengthen theory and experimental design.

Frampton's chapter is followed by Salkovskis and MacGuire's review of higher-level cognitive models of the disorder (Chapter 4). Considerable emphasis is given to the way in which contemporary cognitive models may explain all of the symptomatology of the condition, rather than simply accounting for anxiety and avoidance. There can be no doubt that, in terms of the ability to account for the broad range of symptoms seen in OCD, cognitive models are well advanced on current neuropsychological explanations.

In Chapter 5, Davey, Field and Startup detail the way in which mood and cognitive decision rules may combine to produce perseverative, debilitating and ever-worsening rumination. Their thorough review of novel, laboratory studies on the topic adds much to our understanding of obsessive thinking. It is our view that the future application of this material may substantially advance treatment procedures for OCD and related disorders involving worry.

In the last chapter in Section II (Chapter 6), Macdonald examines research on individual differences in search of an explanation for why some individuals develop OCD whereas others do not. After all, as Macdonald and several other authors in this volume point out, nearly all members of the community experience intrusive thoughts with content related to OCD themes. After a thorough examination of family and twin studies (with all of their methodological inadequacies), Macdonald concludes that biological factors provide only a small part of the susceptibility to the condition. Importantly, from a familial transmission perspective, she urges a further exploration of psychological/developmental pathways to the emergence of biased reasoning styles (see also Chapter 4).

Section III of the book describes the clinical presentations and subtypes. Seven chapters cover washing and cleaning, checking, hoarding, obsessive slowness, ruminations, atypical presentations and the spectrum disorders (with particular emphasis on body dysmorphic disorder). Each of the chapters provides a detailed description of the clinical presentation, supplemented with extensive case examples. A brief summary of the content and orientation of each of these chapters is provided below.

In Chapter 7, Jones and Krochmalik take us through a close analysis of the presenting features of compulsive washers and describe the new Australian treatment program designed to target exaggerated disease expectancies in this subtype. On the basis of available data, Danger Ideation Reduction Therapy (DIRT) appears a viable alternative to standard interventions for compulsive washers. In Chapter 8, Rachman seamlessly combines 40 years of theory with clinical case descriptions and treatment recommendations for compulsive checking. He applies the general cognitive model of OCD to checking, emphasising the role of perceived responsibility in this subtype. In Chapter 9, Frost and Hartl describe the intriguing characteristics of hoarding, a behaviour that does not always appear to be driven by the popular constructs of threat expectancy and inflated perceived responsibility. The need to distinguish compulsive hoarding from appetitive collecting is stressed in this chapter. Rachman returns in Chapter 10 with an insightful coverage of primary obsessive slowness. Like hoarding, this OCD subtype presents some challenges to responsibility-based and threat-based models of the disorder. Rachman describes a raft of differences between this condition and more common presentations (i.e. washing, checking) that have led many to question whether primary slowness is best considered a form of OCD at all. In Chapter 11 de Silva presents an overview of the nature and management of the various cognitive components of the disorder, namely ruminations, obsessions and covert compulsions. Cases with predominantly cognitive symptomatology have not routinely been included in randomised controlled trials, and so relatively little is known about the efficacy of treatment procedures for these problems. De Silva's chapter makes a nice clinical companion to the earlier theoretical chapter of Davey, Field and Startup. Chapter 12, by Einstein and Menzies, presents a summary of the atypical presentations of OCD (including cases with sexual and aggressive compulsions, and counting rituals). The treatment recommendations of Einstein and Menzies centre on reducing threat expectancies, regardless of the idiosyncratic nature of a given client's symptoms. Case illustrations demonstrate the way in which behavioural experiments may be applied in such cases. Finally, in closing Section III, Veale critically examines the notion of OCD spectrum disorders and, more particularly, body dysmorphic disorder. The epidemiology, aetiology, clinical assessment and treatment of this condition are described.

Section IV, covering approaches to assessment and treatment, opens with McColl's review of the psychometric properties of the major measures of OCD (Chapter 14). McColl emphasises the need for the further development of reliable and valid instruments to assess the cognitive underpinnings of the disorder. The absence of such measures has limited the theoretical usefulness of treatment outcome research in the past.

In Chapter 15, Kyrios provides a detailed examination of the principles and practice of exposure and response prevention (ERP). Designing effective ERP programs is not as straight forward as many clinicians think, and Kyrios provides much advice on the many challenges facing the behavioral therapy (BT)-oriented clinician. Kyrios also reviews the outcome literature on this procedure, showing it to be the most established treatment for OCD. However, in Chapter 16, Marks begins her review of cognitive therapy (CT) by pointing to the limitations of ERP. There can be no doubt that the intense level of anxiety generated by ERP in many sufferers is largely responsible for the high drop-out rates associated with ERP programs. Effective alternatives to ERP are clearly needed. Marks' provides a thorough review of the practical aspects of CT. The chapter covers a range of procedures that arise from Beckian models of anxiety and the writings of Salkovskis. Although outcome research on CT (from a Beckian perspective) for OCD is limited at present, existing data do suggest it to be a viable approach to the condition.

In Chapter 17, McDonough reviews the effectiveness of medical-based approaches to OCD. He opens with clear statements about the superiority of current psychological treatments compared to all available physical treatments. At no point does he deviate from this position, suggesting that medication should ideally be reserved for ERP failures, drop-outs or refusers, or those with co-morbid conditions that clearly respond to medical interventions. As others in the book have argued (see chapters by Rachman, de Silva, Salkovksis and MacGuire, Einstein and Menzies, Jones and Menzies, and Marks), other cognitive-behavioural alternatives to ERP are also available, which further limits the usefulness of current medications. MacGuire provides a thorough review of the comparative data on the available serotonergic drugs in terms of efficacy, tolerability, safety, side-effects and management. Indications for neurosurgery are also described.

In Chapter 18, Shafran reviews the nature and management of OCD in children and adolescents. The phenomenology of the disorder in these groups is shown to be very similar to the phenomenology of OCD in adults. However, Shafran demonstrates that the cognitive-behavioural theories that dominate the adult literature (e.g. Salkovskis et al., 1998) are not those that underpin the most widely used cognitive-behavioural treatments for children with the disorder (March & Mulle, 1998). She calls for an increased cohesion between the science and practice of treating childhood OCD.

In the final chapter of Section IV, Bruch points to the high rate of ERP drop-outs and the inadequate treatment response to cognitive-behavioural therapy (CBT) in OCD as reasons to pursue more detailed examinations of the management of treatment-resistant cases. The clinical features of difficult clients are reviewed, including lack of motivation, the use of subtle avoidance strategies, and lack of understanding of the treatment rationale. In addition, Bruch considers the role of the therapeutic relationship and the critical importance of adequate case formulation in managing treatment-resistant presentations.

The final section of the book concerns professional issues. It consists of a single chapter by Harris and Menzies on training, resources and service provision. In Chapter 20, a number of issues that restrict access to effective treatment for those with OCD are explored. The chapter also covers the growth of support groups and computer-delivered treatment packages. The cost-effectiveness of these programs is reviewed. As the authors state, there can be little doubt that the computer age offers great opportunities for the cheaper delivery of effective psychotherapy. However, more RCTs will be needed before computer-based treatment becomes widely accepted as an alternative to individual, face-to-face psychotherapy for OCD.

Our book can be read as a single coherent volume, or as a set of five monographs, or even as 20 independent papers. Indeed, the chapters in Section III are intended to represent stand-alone guides to the major presentations of the disorder. The clinician confronted with a given case can simply turn to the relevant subtype chapter in order to gain a quick (but thorough) coverage of the state of knowledge in the area. Although Section IV is completely dedicated to treatment, we have allowed (indeed encouraged) the contributors in Section III to provide coverage of the contemporary management of the subtypes they are describing. In this way, the stand-alone status of these chapters is achieved. If more formal (and lengthy) instructions in specific treatment procedures are required, the reader may turn to the relevant chapters in Section IV.

Finally, it should be noted that close and careful readers of this volume will no doubt identify several apparent inconsistencies across chapters. In regard to the relative importance of one cognitive construct over another, or the relative effectiveness of cognitive and behavioural procedures, or the explanatory power of a given theoretical position, or the merits of a particular series of studies, authors in our book may take differing positions. As the editors of the volume, we see this as a strength rather than a weakness. We have not attempted to force agreement between leaders in the field where it does not exist. Rather, we have allowed our contributors to defend their positions with reference to the extant literature and their clinical experience. In this way, the true state of knowledge and opinion on a given question is clear for all to see. Clearly, many issues remain to be resolved.

Ross G. Menzies
Padmal de Silva

ACKNOWLEDGEMENTS

We would like to acknowledge the hard work of several individuals whose assistance was invaluable in producing this book. We offer our sincere thanks to Tamsen St. Clare, Annette Krochmalik, Celia Khoo, Peter Callow and the staff of John Wiley & Sons, Ltd.

SECTION I

THE NATURE OF OCD

Chapter 1

THE CLASSIFICATION AND DIAGNOSIS OF OBSESSIVE-COMPULSIVE DISORDER

Annette Krochmalik and Ross G. Menzies

This opening chapter will endeavour to provide an historical account of obsessive-compulsive disorder (OCD), and will also examine contemporary diagnostic and classificatory issues. The similarity of OCD to a number of other disorders, including the degree of co-morbidity with these, will also be addressed. Finally, a close examination of the epidemiology of the condition will be provided.

HISTORICAL OVERVIEW

The symptoms of OCD have been identified, with some consistency, from as early as the seventeenth century. At this time, obsessions were considered to exist purely within a religious framework and sufferers were considered to be possessed by outside forces, such as the devil (Salzman & Thaler, 1981). Not surprisingly, the most popular treatment method was exorcism, which, by all reports, resulted in some cases of therapeutic success. While little is known about the type of compulsive behaviour that dominated clinical presentations in this period, it is noteworthy that washing/cleaning behaviours have been clearly described from the earliest literature. Perhaps the first fictional portrayal of OCD is Shakespeare's illustration of Lady Macbeth in the sixteenth century. As we all know, this character, in an attempt to rid herself of guilt, repeatedly engaged in hand washing, a behaviour which continues to dominate much of the contemporary literature on the condition.

Obsessive-Compulsive Disorder: Theory, Research and Treatment.
Edited by Ross G. Menzies and Padmal de Silva. © 2003 John Wiley & Sons, Ltd.

By the early part of the nineteenth century, OCD had moved from the spiritual to the medical field of enquiry. The condition was considered to be a variant of 'insanity', a construct earlier introduced and defined by a number of French psychiatrists. Esquirol (1838) was the first to argue that, since his patients were aware that their obsessions were irresistible, they possessed a certain degree of insight. Thus, the emergence of 'neurosis' began during the early 1800s, a notion further developed when Morel described OCD as a 'disease of emotions'. He used the word 'delire' to allow for the unconventional reference to the presence of insight. Towards the end of the nineteenth century, Legrand du Saulle described OCD as an insanity with insight, but suggested that psychotic symptoms could be present (an issue that was later to become a contentious one in differential diagnosis). Of course, at this time, OCD, phobias, panic and other somatic symptoms were not well differentiated, further confusing the definition and description of OCD.

Across Europe, these early descriptions of OCD focused on differing aspects of the disorder, and were dependent largely on prevailing cultural issues in the homeland of the writer. While the English concentrated on the religious perspective of OCD and viewed the disorder as a melancholic illness, the French stressed the loss of will, or volition, and identified anxiety at the heart of the disorder. German writers, such as Westphal (1878), identified irrational thoughts as neurological events that had a cognitive representation.

These early European descriptions of OCD, especially the French and German perspectives, paved the way for the psychological perspective that was to emerge from the beginning of the twentieth century. Until this time, OCD was considered a medical condition, which warranted treatment within a medical framework (Rachman & Hodgson, 1980). It was only when clinical psychology emerged from the existing framework of clinical psychiatry that a non-pathological, non-religious view of OCD was clearly offered. Drawing on the research by Legrand du Saulle, Janet (1903) was the first to put forward the psychological view of obsessive-compulsive neurosis. He proposed that all obsessional patients possessed an 'abnormal' personality, with features such as anxiety, excessive worrying, lack of energy and doubting, and described successful treatment of compulsive rituals consistent with the later development of behaviour therapy (Jenike et al., 1998a; Rachman & Hodgson, 1980).

At around this time Freud (1896) proposed a revolutionary theory for the existence of obsessional thinking in which he defined obsessional ideas as 'transformed self-reproaches which have re-emerged from repression and which always relate to some sexual act that was performed with pleasure in childhood' (Freud, 1896, p. 169). This suggestion was formulated predominantly from his experience with patients at the turn of the nineteenth century. Although Freud saw a number of patients whom he considered to be suffering from obsessional neurosis, much of his thinking (and writing) on OCD was based on the now famous 'Rat Man', a case which will be briefly outlined below.

The patient, a youngish man of university education, told Freud that he had suffered from obsessions since early childhood. As a child, he had experienced an unnatural obsession about the death of his father (having believed that he had the power to control his father's general well-being). Without apparent questioning, the patient proceeded to discuss his infantile sexuality. From an early age, he expressed the wish to see girls naked and had a desire to touch them. Accompanying this desire was the feeling that if he did not prevent such thoughts, his father might die. The patient subsequently developed certain impulses that he believed would be effective in warding off the impending evil. These 'impulses' are now more commonly known as compulsions that serve to reduce the anxiety associated with his obsessive thinking.

Later in this patient's life, he came across a senior officer who conveyed a form of punishment that was extremely unnerving to him. This particularly horrendous method of torture involved the criminal being tied up and then having rats placed under a pot, which was turned upside down on the man's buttocks. The rats, having no means of escape, slowly bore their way into the man's buttocks (Freud, 1909). Although the patient expressed horror as he conveyed this story to Freud, Freud interpreted it as one of 'horror at pleasure of his own of which he himself was unaware' (p. 167). The precipitating cause of this man's obsessional thinking was never clearly identified by Freud or by the patient himself. Freud (1909) argued that the 'infantile preconditions of the neurosis may be overtaken by amnesia . . . though the immediate occasions of the illness are . . . retained in the memory' (pp. 195–6).

In a second illustrative example of OCD from the dynamic perspective, Freud (1909) described the symptoms of a patient who displayed an obsession with cleanliness. This particular individual was a government official who always presented crisp paper notes as payment. Freud remarked that that they were distinctive because they were always clean and smooth. The patient replied that he had ironed them at home for fear of contracting an illness from the bacteria on the notes. Because of Freud's suspicion of a link between the neuroses and infantile sexuality, he enquired about the patient's sexual life. The patient replied that he found it gratifying to masturbate a number of young women with his hands. To this Freud replied, 'but aren't you afraid of doing (them) some harm, fiddling about in (their) genitals with your dirty hand?' (p. 197). The patient was horrified and re-marked that it had never done any of the girls harm. On the contrary, he claimed, they had enjoyed the activity. Freud believed that this patient was able to justify his inappropriate sexual behaviour by the displacement of his self-reproach and, in line with his theory, assumed that the patient's sexual gratification was 'probably impelled by some powerful infantile determinants' (p. 198).

Instead of a medical treatment regime typical of the late nineteenth cen-tury, Freud opted for psychoanalysis, an attempt to resolve past conflicts in the afflicted individual by appealing to the unconscious. However, this form of treatment did little to improve the outcome of OCD patients (Jenike et al., 1998a). An important distinction was also made. Freud believed that obsessive-compulsive neurosis existed as a syndrome separate from the 'anal-erotic' character. The latter syndrome, according to Freud, predis-posed an individual to the development of OCD. It is this distinction, as discussed later in this chapter, that (in part) led to the present-day differ-entiation of OCD and obsessive-compulsive personality disorder (OCPD).

The most significant theoretical developments in the period since Freud are undoubtedly the emergence of the neurobiological and psychological/ cognitive perspectives. Since they, along with the treatments that stem from them, will be described in detail in various chapters that follow, they will not be dealt with here. Instead, attention will turn to the classification of the disorder, which, along with improvements in assessment, may be regarded as the other significant development in the area in the twentieth century.

CLASSIFICATION OF OCD

Contemporary attempts at the classification of OCD are now governed by two systems, the *International Classification of Diseases*, 10th Revision (ICD-10) and the *Diagnostic and Statistical Manual of Mental Disorders*, 4th edn (DSM-IV; APA, 1994). Although the ICD-10 (WHO, 1992) is regarded as the official coding system in many countries, the DSM-IV (APA, 1994) is the more popular amongst mental health professionals (Andrews et al., 1999).

Current Classification According to DSM-IV

The DSM-IV (APA, 1994) describes OCD according to five diagnostic cri-teria. The principle features of the disorder are: (a) recurrent thoughts, or images (termed 'obsessions') that are considered intrusive and that cause significant distress; and (b) ritualistic behaviours (termed 'compulsions') typically engaged in to rid or neutralise obsessive thoughts. Although it may be difficult to ascertain the degree of distress, the DSM-IV maintains that an individual must experience a significant disturbance in normal functioning, or engage in obsessive-compulsive activity for at least 1 hour/day, to be given a diagnosis of OCD. Further, the individual must, at some point during the course of the disorder, recognise the irrationality of his/her thoughts and behaviour. A specification of poor insight may be added to the diagnosis of OCD when an individual does not currently recognise that the obsessions and compulsions are excessive or unreasonable.

Previously, a diagnosis of OCD implied that the individual could generally recognise that his/her fears were irrational or unreasonable throughout the life of his/her disorder (Enright & Beech, 1997). It was only in DSM-IV that a 'poor insight' specification was added in order to account for a number of individuals who appear to fail to accept the senselessness and futility of their obsessive and compulsive behaviours. The addition of this category in the diagnosis of OCD may be considered favourable from a treatment perspective, since it is well established that individuals with a strong conviction that their fears are realistic have poor outcomes in behavioural programs (Foa, 1979). However, a number of writers have argued that the added specification of 'poor insight' does not help to clarify the distinction between OCD and other disorders. In fact, it may further complicate classificatory difficulties as it introduces a new problem. OCD sufferers with poor insight, or overvalued ideas, must now be distinguished from individuals with delusional beliefs. DSM-IV dictates that OCD should be diagnosed when 'an individual whose extreme preoccupation . . . although exaggerated, is less intense than in a Delusional Disorder' (APA, 1994, p. 422). But what is 'less intense' and how may it be defined?

In sum, the addition of 'poor insight' to the diagnosis of OCD brings about a number of difficulties that render the differential diagnosis of this disorder problematic. In order to establish a clear-cut definition of OCD, these concerns need to be considered. The following section will address: (a) the question of the classification of OCD as an anxiety disorder; and (b) the significant degree of overlap with a number of other disorders, e.g. the obsessive-compulsive spectrum disorders, the mood disorders, the personality disorders, and the schizophrenic disorders.

OCD AND THE ANXIETY DISORDERS

Ever since the introduction of the DSM-III, OCD has been classified amongst the anxiety disorders. However, the substantial overlapping features and high co-morbidity rate of OCD with other anxiety disorders complicates the diagnosis of OCD.

Distinctions between OCD and GAD

First and foremost, the greatest difficulty in the differential diagnosis of OCD and generalised anxiety disorder (GAD) lies in the distinction between worry and obsession. A number of researchers have attempted to clarify this distinction but there is little evidence to suggest that worry and obsessions do not simply reflect the same mental process (Turner 1992). The only distinguishing feature between these concerns offered by the DSM-IV (APA,1994) appears to rest on the consistency or duration of distress for sufferers of the two conditions. Worry appears to be a more drawn-out or consistent concern in GAD than does obsession in OCD, in that the former must 'occur more days than not for at least 6 months'. Descriptions of obsession imply a recurrence and persistence in thought but do not include any given time duration. In terms of the level of disturbance, there appears to be no distinction. Andrews et al. (1994) argue that the most important distinguishing feature is that the *content* of worry/obsession may be regarded as different in these two disorders. These authors argue that individuals suffering from GAD are primarily concerned with everyday issues (e.g. family, health or occupational issues that may be deemed 'appropriate'), whereas OCD sufferers frequently report unusual themes concerning dirt and contamination, aggression, hoarding and religion.

But is a distinction based simply on 'content' areas adequate? Is it possible (and clinically valid) to distinguish between everyday worries and other concerns? For example, if an individual expresses worries about the possible contamination of her child, is this concern different from a 'family or health concern' frequently reported by patients with GAD?

Important also is the notion of 'rumination' and its distinction from typical obsessional activity in OCD and worry amongst patients with GAD (see further discussion in Chapter 11). De Silva & Rachman (1992) have noted that the content of ruminatory thoughts tend to concern religious, philosophical or metaphysical subjects, which, once again, may tend to prove difficult to distinguish from obsessive thoughts or generalised worry. However, de Silva & Rachman (1992) have noted that, unlike obsessions, ruminations do not intrude into the patient's consciousness in a well-defined form or with a clear or repetitive content. In fact, some have argued that ruminations appear to be more frequently 'cognitive compulsions' because of their ability to briefly ameliorate anxiety (Foa et al., 1985). However, not all agree, with several authors arguing that rumination (somewhat like worry), may not always reduce anxiety in the way that compulsions (whether behavioural or cognitive) reliably appear to (see further discussion in de Silva & Rachman, 1992; Chapter 11, this volume).

Andrews et al. (1994) state that individuals with OCD regard their thoughts as 'unacceptable', whereas those with GAD are more likely to consider their issues realistic (since they focus on common fears/issues in the community). However, this statement is debatable. Although some individuals with OCD might agree that their thoughts are unacceptable, there are a number who argue that their beliefs are completely reasonable, as described earlier in this chapter. The added inclusion of the 'poor insight' subgroup in OCD in the DSM-IV (APA, 1994) clearly clouds the distinction between certain presentations of OCD and GAD.

Distinction between OCD and Phobias

Rachman & Hodgson (1980) have suggested that OCD and the phobic disorders share a number of similar features. These include avoidance behaviours, fear reactions in response to specific stimuli or situations, and a particularly successful response to behaviour therapy. In fact, it is clear that exposure with response prevention for OCD and graduated exposure for phobias are essentially the same treatment. The treatment method for the phobic disorders involves confrontation of the eliciting stimulus and also prevents the response, i.e. escape behaviour. In addition to these similarities, Rasmussen & Tsuang (1986) found that a substantial proportion of individuals with OCD had a history of simple phobia.

Despite these similarities, Enright & Beech (1997) have identified a number of distinguishing features between these two disorders. First, individuals with OCD will have persistent and recurrent thoughts about a feared stimulus/situation in the absence of this feared image/event. Phobic patients typically do not experience any distress in the absence of phobic stimuli. Second, and more important to the distinction, is the absence of ritualistic behaviour in the phobic disorders. Phobic patients routinely avoid their feared stimulus, whereas individuals with OCD are not confined solely to avoidance. More common is the ritualistic behaviour displayed in response to an obsession, which is triggered internally. However, if one considers the 'rituals' in OCD and 'escape-avoidance' in phobias as the same in terms of their purpose (i.e. removing an aversive stimulus), then a distinction between these disorders (in this regard) becomes less clear.

OCD AND OBSESSIVE-COMPULSIVE SPECTRUM DISORDERS

There are many disorders categorised in the DSM-IV that share close phenomenological similarities to OCD, and they have become popularly known as the obsessive-compulsive spectrum disorders. This approach, as discussed at length by Veale (see further, Chapter 13), is somewhat problematic, since almost a half of the DSM-IV may be viewed in this way. It is questionable whether the notion of OCD spectrum disorders has advanced our understanding of the conditions concerned. However, for completeness, some coverage of these conditions is warranted in the present chapter.

Lists of OCD spectrum disorders typically include Tourette's syndrome, hypochondriasis, body dysmorphic disorder (BDD), the impulse control disorders (e.g. trichotillomania, kleptomania) and the eating disorders. A number of these will be outlined in an attempt to clarify the distinction between OCD and these related disorders. As the spectrum disorders (and particularly BDD) are covered at length in Chapter 13, relatively little attention will be given to them in the following section. In the present chapter, only sufficient coverage of these disorders will be given to identify relevant diagnostic issues.

OCD and Tourette's Syndrome

OCD and Tourette's syndrome share a number of similarities including a high co-morbidity rate and a substantial overlap of clinical features (Hollander & Benzaquen, 1997; Steingard & Dillon-Stout, 1992). On the surface, it may appear that overt rituals in individuals with Tourette's syndrome resemble compulsive rituals in OCD. However, the nature of these behaviours can be differentiated. Stereotyped motor behaviours associated with tic disorder and Tourette's syndrome are involuntary and unintentional behaviours. These may be clearly distinguished from the ritualistic behaviours that an individual with OCD is compelled to perform in order to reduce the threat associated directly with his/her obsessions.

OCD and Hypochondriasis

Clinical experience and research suggests that there may be a subgroup of hypochondriacal individuals who seem more aligned to the anxiety disorders than to the somatoform disorders (Barsky, 1992). Indeed, hypochondriasis and OCD appear to share a number of similar features. The DSM-IV

(APA, 1994) defines hypochondriasis as a 'preoccupation with fears of having, or the idea that one has, a serious disease based on the person's mis-interpretation of bodily symptoms' (p. 465). This definition appears some-what consistent with the OCD subtype involving contamination/illness concerns. A number of similarities have been identified by Barsky (1992), including: (a) the content of the preoccupation; and (b) the similar nature of reassurance-seeking behaviours in hypochondriasis and compulsive rit-uals in OCD. Several distinguishing features, however, are apparent on closer examination. First it must be recognised that the main reason for the inclusion of hypochondriasis amongst the somatoform disorders is that so-matic, or physical, sensation must be experienced. OCD, in contrast, does not typically involve abberant bodily sensations. Second, the interpersonal dimension of these disorders differs substantially. Individuals with OCD are generally secretive about their disorder and tend to conceal it from pub-lic knowledge. Hypochondriacal patients will often vocalise their distress in an attempt to justify the seriousness of their perceived illness. Finally, no attempt is made to neutralise or resist thoughts about disease and illness among hypochondriacal patients. In stark contrast, individuals with OCD fiercely attempt to ignore, suppress and resist their obsessional beliefs.

OCD and Body Dysmorphic Disorder (BDD)

Since BDD forms the basis of Chapter 13, we will restrict our comments here. The disorder is categorised by a preoccupation with an imagined defect in one's physical appearance, which causes marked distress to an individual that subsequently impairs social and occupational functioning. Hollander & Benzaquen (1997) have found a 37% co-morbidity of OCD with BDD, suggesting some degree of overlap amongst these disorders. Although not formally necessary for a diagnosis, compulsive checking is typically found amongst BDD patients. Furthermore, these disorders share the same structure, in that individuals with either disorder experience intrusive thoughts that cause anxiety and distress (Goldsmith et al., 1998). Given that the symptom profile of these disorders is similar, BDD is often misdiagnosed as OCD.

Despite this similar symptom profile, however, Hollander & Benzaquen (1997) have identified a number of distinguishing features between these disorders. These include the ideational content, complexity and frequency of beliefs. Most importantly, BDD preoccupations typically revolve around self-appearance, whereas OCD concerns generally involve the overestima-tion of threat or harm. However, as argued earlier, one must be cautious when distinguishing between disorders on the basis of ideational content.

For example, it may be possible to interpret BDD as an obsessional over-estimation of threat or harm (i.e. in the form of social threat). These and related issues are examined at length in Chapter 13.

OCD and Impulse Control Disorders (e.g. Trichotillomania)

It may be tempting to classify the impulse control disorders under the category of OCD, given their similarity with respect to subjective urges and subsequent anxiety relief upon completion of relevant behaviours. However, Andrews et al. (1994) argue that they may be differentiated, since the behaviours employed in OCD are not ego-syntonic (i.e. the rituals *per se* are not considered to be gratifying in any way). Hollander & Benzaquen (1997) have provided a similar distinction between compulsivity and impulsivity. These authors maintain that compulsive activity is the means by which discomfort is decreased, whereas impulsivity involves the eliciting of pleasure. Trichotillomania, for example, is an impulse control disorder where an individual typically derives some pleasure or gratification from the activity of hair-pulling. In contrast, sufferers of OCD typically report that the only relief or satisfaction felt from compulsive activity arises from the elimination of any associated anxiety. Stein et al. (1995a) propose an added distinction between these disorders. OCD patients often describe that their compulsive behaviour is a direct response to their obsessions. However, these authors argue that individuals with trichotillomania do not appear to have a clear obsession that precedes their hair pulling (although in our clinical experience, these individuals may occasionally harbour threat-based beliefs about the colour, shape or feel of particular hairs). Finally, in our clinical judgement, trichotillomania is easier to stop, the hair pulling often ceasing in 1 or 2 sessions of behavioural monitoring (perhaps because it lacks the clear, overvalued obsessional component of OCD).

OCD and Eating Disorders

Eating disorders are regarded as part of the obsessive-compulsive spectrum disorders, due to their core abnormal thoughts and behaviours (Goldsmith et al., 1998). The excessive fear of gaining weight and the preoccupation with food and weight are obsessional and compulsive features that are reminiscent of those displayed in OCD. Furthermore, both these disorders possess a similar course, substantial co-morbidity and a similar response to medication-based treatment (Goldsmith et al., 1998). However, many authors argue that the eating disorders may be distinguished from OCD on a conceptual level. They suggest that thoughts regarding food or weight gain in the eating disorders are not ego-dystonic and the be-haviours are selectively purposeful (i.e. to lose weight or avoid gaining weight), rather than simply anxiety-reducing (see further, Andrews et al., 1994).

OCD AND DEPRESSION

There is no doubt that there is an overlap between OCD and depressive rumination (Rachman & Hodgson, 1980). First, there are certain abnormali-ties that are sometimes common to both, e.g. sleep disturbance, anxiety and guilt (Edelmann, 1992). Second, 17–70% of OCD patients are typically de-pressed (Miguel et al., 1997). As a result, the high co-morbidity of OCD with depression often renders differential diagnosis difficult. (Edelmann, 1992; Freeman, 1992; Rachman & Hodgson, 1980). Riggs & Foa (1993) attempted to draw a distinction between depressive rumination and obsessions. First, they argued that, as in GAD, depressive individuals ruminate about every-day, real-life events whereas obsessive-compulsive individuals will tend to have obsessions about unusual and clearly defined topics (e.g. contamina-tion concerns, aggressive thoughts, sexual thoughts). However, as outlined previously in this chapter, a distinction between disorders on the basis of content of thought may be insufficient. Miguel et al. (1997) propose a somewhat clearer distinction. First, they note that obsessive thoughts tend to centre around a current or future event, whereas depressive rumination typically involves a past incident. Second, obsessive compulsive individ-uals often describe their thoughts as intrusive, senseless and unwanted, and often report an attempt to resist them. In direct contrast, depressive ruminators maintain that their thoughts are non-intrusive and are rarely resisted. Third, OCD thoughts typically (although not always) engender anxiety, whereas depressive rumination produces dysphoria. Thus, despite some overlapping features, there are several reasons to identify OCD and depressive rumination as separate entities (see Chapter 5 for further dis-cussion of this distinction).

OCD AND OBSESSIVE-COMPULSIVE PERSONALITY DISORDER (OCPD)

The essential feature of OCPD is a preoccupation with orderliness, perfec-tionism and mental and interpersonal control. The relationship between this disorder and OCD has been the subject of a great deal of discus-sion for some time. As noted previously, as early as the beginning of the twentieth century, Janet (1904) had proposed the notion of the obsessive personality: an individual described as rigid, inflexible, overconscientious and persistent (Salzman & Thaler, 1981). Freud (1908) went on to suggest that this characterisation (which he labelled the 'anal-erotic' character), predisposed an individual towards the development of OCD. As such, it would be assumed that OCD would be more aligned to OCPD than any of the other personality disorders. An investigation of this question was conducted by Gibbs & Oltmanns (1995). Using a non-clinical sample of individuals exhibiting obsessive-compulsive symptomatology, these researchers found an association between checking behaviour and OCPD traits, suggesting that there may be a relationship between the checking subtype of OCD and OCPD phenomenology. Certainly the clinical descriptions of OC checkers and individuals with OCPD provided by Nestadt et al. (1991) suggest that they share a common theme, focusing on future orientation.

However, some studies have found that relatively few OCD patients have symptoms of OCPD. Perhaps surprisingly, avoidant personality disorder, dependent personality disorder, histrionic personality disorder, and paranoid personality disorder have been found to be more frequently present than OCPD in some groups of OCD subjects. Further, it should not be forgotten that true obsessions and compulsions are not found in OCPD. Patients with OCPD do not have obsessive-compulsive activity that interferes with their lives to the extent that OCD does (see further discussion in Jenike, 1991). As a number of researchers have pointed out, OCD symptoms are ego-dystonic, whereas OCPD traits are ego-syntonic and do not involve a sense of compulsion that must be resisted (Miguel et al., 1997; Rasmussen & Eisen, 1992). Finally, Jenike (1991) argues that the two disorders respond differently to standard treatments; for example, there is little research showing that behaviour therapy alone is effective in alleviating the symptoms of OCPD.

OCD AND THE PSYCHOTIC DISORDERS

The earliest clinical literature generally made no distinction between OCD and schizophrenia. Nineteenth century accounts suggested that OCD was a variant of schizophrenia, and it was classified at the time within the spectrum of psychoses. Westphal (1878) argued that OCD and schizophrenia shared a number of features, including a similar age of onset, a reduced rate of marriage and fertility, an increased incidence of other disorders, and a poor response to psychological and somatic treatments (Enright & Beech, 1997). Over time, as previously described, OCD came to be regarded as a neurotic disorder, given the absence of irrational beliefs in line with delusional states. However, more recently it has been argued that not all patients with OCD display rational belief systems with regard to their obsessions. As previously suggested in this chapter, the introduction of the 'poor insight' category in DSM-IV (APA, 1994) somewhat clouds the distinction between OCD and psychosis. How are we able to distinguish between overvalued ideas, poor insight and delusions?

De Silva & Rachman (1992) have attempted to differentiate these phenomena. They argue that, despite the strength of 'overvalued ideas' or delusion-like beliefs exhibited in a minority of OCD cases, 'many of these patients can ultimately be persuaded to concede that they may be mistaken' (p. 22). Of course, this argument is problematic for the many remaining patients who do not make such concessions. Other theorists point to the additional features typically found in the psychotic disorders as a means of differentiating them from OCD. Riggs & Foa (1993) propose that although some individuals with OCD may share a similar degree of poor insight with the schizophrenic constellation of disorders, they may be distinguished by the absence of hallucinations, flat or inappropriate affect and thought insertions that are exclusive to psychotic conditions. Further, it is important to remember that nothing precludes a dual diagnosis of OCD and schizophrenia if an individual does indeed display clear features of both disorders. Indeed, Enright & Beech (1997) have concluded that, although such a comorbidity is infrequent, this dual diagnosis is a powerful predictor of poor prognosis.

A number of studies have been conducted in order to investigate the proposition that some of the processes that underlie schizophrenia may also be evident in OCD. Enright & Beech (1990) demonstrated that OCD subjects exhibit significantly greater schizophrenic-like (schizotypal) features than subjects with other anxiety disorders (see also Chapter 12). Norman et al. (1996) investigated the relationship between OC symptomatology to anxiety and schizotypy in a clinical population of 117 psychiatric outpatients. The results revealed a higher correlation for OCD with schizotypy ($r = 0.60$, $p < 0.001$) than with anxiety ($r = 0.42$, $p < 0.001$). In addition, results from laboratory studies of information processing suggest that OCD subjects exhibit differential effects of negative priming that are more similar to those found in schizotypal and schizophrenic subjects than in the other anxiety disorders (Enright & Beech, 1997). The implication of all of these findings is that schizotypal, schizophrenic and OCD subjects share a common global deficit of cognitive inhibition that may not be evident in any of the other anxiety disorders. Further research on these issues is clearly warranted.

SHOULD OCD BE CLASSIFIED AS AN ANXIETY DISORDER AT ALL?

Ever since the introduction of the DSM-III (APA, 1980), OCD has been classified among the anxiety disorders. However, the inclusion of OCD in this category has not been universally accepted. Treatment failures, inadequate theoretical models, complex association with other disorders and clinical intuition have led many to suggest that OCD must be considered a distinct disorder, qualitatively different from other anxiety disorders (Edelmann, 1992; Enright & Beech, 1990). However, despite these arguments (and the research findings described above), it must still be recognised that anxiety is the most notable presenting symptom of OCD. Individuals suffering with OCD, like the other anxiety disorders, experience fear in the presence of specific stimuli and make efforts to avoid these stimuli. Moreover, little difference has been found between OCD and other anxiety disorders on measures of neuroticism and general measures of trait anxiety or specific fears (Steketee et al., 1987). It is the present authors' view that, in the absence of more compelling data to the contrary, and within the general framework of current classificatory systems, OCD is still best considered an anxiety disorder.

OCD: ONE DISORDER OR MANY?

Ever since its introduction in the DSM (APA, 1952), OCD has been regarded as an homogeneous disorder. Over the last few decades, however, attempts have been made to identify subtypes within the broad domain of OCD (Rasmussen & Eisen, 1992; Summerfeldt et al., 1999). Researchers have endeavoured to classify OCD into groups based on their demographics, phenomenology and symptomatology. One broad approach is the classic distinction between obsessions and compulsions. For example, the ICD-10 (WHO, 1992) has divided this disorder into three main categories as follows: (a) predominant obsessional thoughts or ruminations; (b) predominant compulsive acts (obsessional rituals); and (c) mixed obsessional thoughts and acts. These distinctions, although important, do nothing to classify the types of obsessions or compulsions seen across the many manifestations of the disorder. Given the diversity of presentations of OCD, considerable attention has recently arisen in more multidimensional representations (Summerfeldt et al., 1999). The most common approach appears to be the classification into subtypes based on manifest symptoms, such as washing/cleaning concerns, checking rituals, compulsive hoarding and so on (see Chapter 2).

Reflecting this move to symptom-based subtyping of OCD, prevailing assessment measures for the disorder are divided into subgroups based on presenting symptomatology (see Chapter 14 for a comprehensive discussion of OCD assessment measures). The Maudsley Obsessional Compulsive Inventory (MOCI; Hodgson & Rachman, 1977), for example, is able to determine a total score for OCD symptomatology, as well as scores on the subscales washing, checking, slowness and doubting. The Padua Inventory (PI; Sanavio, 1988) describes common obsessional and compulsive behaviour and identifies four factors underlying OCD: impaired control of mental activities, becoming contaminated, checking behaviours, and urges and worries of losing control over motor behaviours. The Y-BOCS (Goodman et al., 1989b), perhaps the most widely used instrument in the assessment of OCD, is essentially a symptom checklist of an individual's obsessions and compulsions, which is divided into categories based on the content of the obsession/compulsion. These scales suggest that distinct categories exist within the domain of OCD, although these categories have generally been identified *a priori*, rather than on the basis of factor analytic/statistical approaches.

The identification of these categories within OCD might suggest that different theoretical models (or, at least, differing cognitive constructs) may underpin these various subtypes. For example, it has been shown that an expectancy of threat or danger (in the form of disease) appears to drive washing behaviour (Jones & Menzies, 1997a), whereas perceived responsibility (and other constructs) appear more important in the mediation of compulsive checking behaviour (Lopatka & Rachman, 1995; Overton & Menzies, 2001; Salkovskis et al., 1999). These theoretical differences have direct implications for treatment; for example, simply targeting threat expectancy seems sufficient to eliminate compulsive washing (Jones & Menzies, 1997b, 1998a; Krochmalik et al., 2001) but might not be viable as a comprehensive treatment for other subtypes.

EPIDEMIOLOGY

Estimations of the prevalence and incidence of OCD have been subject to considerable scrutiny in recent years. The earliest attempts at estimating prevalence rates for OCD date back to the early 1950s, when Rudin proposed that 0.05% of the general population suffered from the condition. Similar retrospective 'chart review' studies over the next two decades lent support to the impression that OCD was a relatively rare disorder (Black, 1974). It is important to note that these studies were based on clinical judgements of the percentage of inpatients who presented for treatment, and did not attempt to include any formal diagnostic measures. It was not until the 1980s that any studies using semi-structured interviews to estimate OCD prevalence rates were mounted.

The Epidemiological Catchment Area (ECA) program was undertaken in the early 1980s in an attempt to investigate the epidemiology of prevailing psychopathology in five communities in the USA. The aims of this project were two-fold: (a) to determine the lifetime and 6 month prevalence of OCD in the general population by randomly surveying over 30,000 people, and (b) to determine where patients sought treatment (Rasmussen & Eisen 1992). Lay interviewers were trained in the administration of the Diagnostic Interview Schedule (DIS), an instrument constructed to make DSM-III (APA, 1980) diagnoses.

Results from the ECA study suggested that OCD was more common than earlier reports indicated. The most surprising finding, however, was that lifetime prevalence rates for OCD ranged from 1.9% to 3.3% (Karno et al., 1988), making it 40–70 times as common as hitherto thought. Furthermore, it suggested that OCD was twice as common as schizophrenia or panic disorder. In fact OCD was found to be the fourth most common psychiatric disorder in the US population (Pigott, 1998).

A similar epidemiological study of 3258 randomly selected household residents using the same diagnostic instrument and methodology as the ECA study was conducted in Edmonton, Canada. The results from the ECA study in the USA were supported. Bland et al. (1988) found that the lifetime prevalence of OCD in the Canadian cohort was 3.0%, consistent with the findings from the ECA survey.

Given that these findings represent a major change in the estimated prevalence of OCD, it is important to ascertain whether they are replicable, particularly across cultural boundaries. The Cross-National OCD Collaborative Group study (CNCG study) (Weissman et al., 1994) assessed and compared the prevalence of OCD in six countries: Canada, Germany, Korea, New Zealand, Puerto Rico and Taiwan. Results revealed comparable prevalence rates of OCD as those from the ECA study in the USA. Taiwan was the only country to exhibit a substantially lower prevalence rate of OCD; however, this is consistent with the surprisingly low prevalence rates of other psychiatric disorders that were reported in the same research in this country (Pigott, 1998).

Why are the prevalence rates from these large-scale epidemiological studies so much higher than those in earlier reports? A number of reasons for the discrepancies have been suggested. First, as stated previously, early estimates were based on clinical judgements alone and neglected the use of diagnostic instruments to estimate prevalence. Given the inadequate level of knowledge about OCD at this time, it is not surprising that clinicians did not routinely consider a diagnosis of OCD when assessing their patients. In addition, with less community understanding of the condition in the past (and potentially greater social stigma), many individuals may have chosen to hide their disorder, lowering the number of presenting individuals with the condition. Further, it must be remembered that, until recently, OCD was considered a purely medical disorder, generally treated within a drug-based framework. There is no doubt that at least some sufferers sought help from relatives, friends, healers and priests, rather than requesting drug-based assistance from medical practitioners. This would further lower presenting patient numbers and affect early prevalence estimates.

Of course, just as it is possible that earlier studies tended to under-report the number of individuals suffering from OCD, it may also be the case that contemporary studies have tended to over-diagnose the condition. Given the level of interest in OCD, the number of available treatments for the disorder and current media attention, contemporary prevalence rates may reflect a bias towards over-reporting. Clinicians may over-diagnose the condition, at least in part, because individuals are now more likely to self-diagnose the disorder. In addition, given the difficulties with respect to differential diagnosis already described, there remains the possibility that the current estimates are an exaggeration of the true prevalence of the condition due to mistaken classification of other disorders as OCD.

Further, despite the fact that the more recent epidemiological studies represent a major advance in research design (compared to studies of the 1950s), a number of criticisms have also been raised about the large-scale population-based studies described above. First, the use of lay interviewers rather than trained clinicians to administer the DIS has been criticised. According to opponents of the ECA study, lay interviewers are likely to over-diagnose all disorders. Some evidence that this may have occurred comes from a series of follow-up studies that used semi-structured interviews administered by psychiatrists. The results suggested a lower OCD prevalence than was suggested in the earlier ECA study (see further, Antony et al., 1998a). Over a decade later, a similar large-scale epidemiological study was conducted in Canada. Not surprisingly, given that this study once again employed lay interviewers to administer the DIS, the results obtained were similar to the pioneering, large-scale epidemiological studies conducted in the 1980s (Stein et al., 1997b).

Second, the use of the DIS itself has been criticised. Antony et al. (1998a) have argued that the DIS: (a) is neither a reliable nor a valid method of diagnosing OCD, and (b) leads to a general over-diagnosis of anxiety disorders. Nelson & Rice (1997) conducted a study in order to assess the stability of the diagnosis of OCD in the ECA study. Their results concluded that the DIS diagnosis of OCD possessed extremely limited validity and temporal stability, leaving the true incidence and prevalence of the disorder unknown. However, as Nestadt et al. (1998) have pointed out, the instability of DIS/DSM-III (APA, 1980) OCD diagnoses may be the result of a number of possible factors. These may include reduced recall of symptoms, decreased relevance of symptoms to patients whose symptoms change over time, and the reluctance of patients to admit potentially embarrassing symptoms.

In sum, it must be acknowledged that current estimates may, in the fullness of time, be shown to overstate the community OCD prevalence rate. However, when taken together, it seems safe to suggest that recent findings show the prevalence of OCD to be considerably higher than once assumed. When these epidemiological studies are further replicated, with contemporary diagnostic criteria and better-trained interviewers, more definitive conclusions will be possible (see Chapter 6 for further discussion of the problems of current epidemiological research and their relevance to interpreting available familial/genetic studies).

CONCLUDING COMMENTS

OCD is best conceived of as an anxiety disorder and is currently classified as such, despite the continuing debate over its differential diagnosis. It consists of obsessions, defined as intrusive recurrent thoughts or images that cause a significant degree of distress to the individual, and compulsions, overt or covert rituals that alleviate the associated anxiety that is generated from obsessive activity. Although once believed to be extremely rare, the general consensus is that a relatively high rate (2–3%) of OCD exists in the community. While once in the religious domain, OCD has moved from the psychiatric, medical/structural to the psychological field of investigation, where most modern advances continue to be made.

Chapter 2

THE PHENOMENOLOGY
OF OBSESSIVE-COMPULSIVE
DISORDER

Padmal de Silva

INTRODUCTION

This chapter deals with the phenomenology of obsessive-compulsive disorder and its impact on sufferers and others. As detailed in Chapter 1, the disorder has been described in the literature for over a century. Descriptions have been based on clinical observations and, in more recent times, experimental investigations. The impact of the disorder has also been looked at, although the literature on this is more limited.

THE PHENOMENA

The phenomena that constitute obsessive-compulsive disorder have been detailed by various authorities, including classical writers such as Janet (1903), Jaspers (1913) and Lewis (1936), as well as more recent investigators, such as Emmelkamp (1982) and Rachman & Hodgson (1980). The current position with regard to obsessive-compulsive phenomenology is reflected in the American Psychiatric Association's *Diagnostic and Statistical Manual* (DSM-IV; APA 1994). The widely agreed criteria for a diagnosis (see Chapter 1 for full description) require that the person must have either obsessions or compulsions or both. Thus, the essential features of the disorder are these two phenomena. *Obsessions* are recurrent, persistent ideas, thoughts, images or impulses that intrude into consciousness and are experienced as senseless or repugnant. They form against one's will and the person usually attempts to resist them or get rid them. The person recognizes that they are his/her own thoughts. They also cause marked anxiety or discomfort. *Compulsions* are repetitive, purposeful forms of behaviour

Obsessive-Compulsive Disorder: Theory, Research and Treatment.
Edited by Ross G. Menzies and Padmal de Silva. © 2003 John Wiley & Sons, Ltd.

that are carried out because of a strong feeling of compulsion to do so. The behaviour is not an end in itself, but is designed to prevent or reduce anxiety or discomfort or to prevent some dreaded event or situation. However, the activity is not connected in a realistic way with what it is designed to prevent, or it is clearly excessive. The individual generally recognises the senselessness of the behaviour and does not derive pleasure from carrying out the activity, although it provides a relief from tension (see further discussion in Chapter 1). Compulsions are usually performed according to certain rules or in a stereotyped fashion.

It is stressed that these features should not be secondary to another mental disorder, since similar phenomena can sometimes occur in certain other disorders. It is also stressed that the obsessions and/or compulsions need to cause distress to the person and/or interfere with his/her life and activities, in order for them to be treated as clinically significant.

Diversity of the Phenomena

It is important to recognize the diversity of the phenomena that occur in obsessive-compulsive disorder (cf. de Silva, 1986; de Silva & Rachman, 1998; Rachman, 1982).

First and foremost, it needs to be stressed that, while related, obsessions and compulsions are not the same phenomenon. This is clearly recognized in the DSM-IV definition but not in many others, including the World Health Organization's *International Classification of Diseases* (ICD 10; WHO 1992). Indeed, some authors have maintained that there is no essential difference between compulsions and obsessions (Cooper, 1983; Reed, 1985). Others have argued that the cardinal phenomenon, regardless of the manifestation, is essentially one of compulsion (Carr, 1974). Related to this, it has also been argued that the inconsistent and confusing uses of the two terms 'obsession' and 'compulsion' in the terminology of English psychiatric writing is due to the faulty way in which the original German and French terms were translated (Reed, 1985). The history of the terms and the concepts covered by them, and of how the various terms were understood and translated, is indeed fascinating (see Berrios, 2000; Spitzer & Sigmund 1997) but is beyond the scope of this chapter.

The clearing of the said inconsistency and confusion is not too difficult, and can be accomplished by a close analysis of the clinical phenomena. The DSM-IV explicitly recognizes the distinction between obsessive and compulsive phenomena, and the research of contemporary investigators, particularly Rachman and his associates, provides the necessary empirical and experimental basis for a full analysis (Rachman & Hodgson, 1980).

The experience of an obsession is essentially a *passive* one, with the person being the passive recipient or victim of it. A not uncommon clinical example, which is typical of this phenomenon, is the repeated intrusion of a thought such as, 'I must have killed someone', or 'I may strangle a child'. A *compulsion*, on the other hand, is an active phenomenon. It is brought about actively by the person. Consider, for example, someone touching the door handle three times in a particular way on every occasion he/she closes a door. This is not, in contrast to an obsession, a passive occurrence; it is something in which the person engages actively. It is caused by a strongly felt subjective urge, usually referred to as a 'compulsive urge', and for this reason it is unlike a muscle spasm or a tic. This urge is often resisted and the person may fight hard not to carry out the act; but the act is voluntary.

It is important to recognize that both obsessions and compulsions can take a variety of forms. An obsession can be a thought, image or impulse and is often a combination of two, or even all three of these (de Silva, 1986; de Silva & Rachman, 1998; Rachman & Hodgson, 1980). Some clinical examples are as follows:

1. Thought that he/she has a terminal illness.
2. Thought plus visual image that he/she may have knocked someone down while driving.
3. Thought, 'I am a Lesbian'.
4. Impulse to shout obscenities during prayer or a church service.
5. Image of corpses rotting away.
6. Thoughts of serious accident or harm occurring to his/her family.
7. Thought that he/she would not survive beyond the age of 28.
8. Thought that he/she may strangle, or may have strangled, children and pets.

A compulsion can be an overt and motor behaviour, like checking a door handle and washing hands repeatedly, or covert and cognitive in nature, as in the silent utterance of words in a certain fixed sequence.

Examples of compulsions are:

1. Repeated and extensive washing of hands to get rid of contamination by germs.
2. Checking gas taps, door handles and electric switches three times each time he moves past them.
3. Imagining in sequence the photographs of his spouse, children and parents, pictures of Jesus Christ and the Virgin Mary, and then photographs of two other persons.
4. Saying silently a string of words whenever he hears or reads of any disaster or accident.

5. Cleaning and washing around bed and nearby wall to get rid of germs and dirt.
6. Visualizing everything that was said to him in conversations, and what he/she was going to say in response.
7. Collecting and hoarding various useless items.

Constituent Elements of Obsessive-Compulsive Experiences

In clinical cases an obsession may occur without an associated compulsion, as when a young woman had intrusive thoughts and images of her wedding reception, which she found distressing, but which led to no active compulsion. Akhtar et al. (1975) found, in a large series of patients, that 25% had obsessions and no related compulsive behaviour. Similar findings were reported by Wilner et al. (1976). More often, obsessions lead to related compulsive behaviour, for example an obsessional thought of contamination by germs or dirt, leading to extensive washing of hands and body each time the obsession is experienced. In such cases the individual feels a strong need to wash and an inability to relax until this has been accomplished. Compulsions without obsessions are very rare but they do occur. An example is a man who had a compulsion to imagine each car number plate he saw with the numbers transformed in a certain way (e.g. multiplied by two, or squared). Wilner et al. (1976) reported that 6% of their series of 150 patients had compulsions only. Rachman & Shafran (1998) have recently pointed out that occasionally the compulsive behaviour can give rise to an obsession; repeated checking of the gas cooker, for example, can be followed by the obsessional thought that one's mental stability and reliability are impaired. Such instances, however, are rare.

The relationship between the obsession and the compulsion is perhaps best understood in the context of all the key variables that are associated with an obsessive-compulsive experience. These are presented schematically in Table 2.1. In the following paragraphs, these elements will be briefly described.

Trigger

A trigger is an event or a cue that sets off an obsession, a feeling of discomfort or, indeed, a compulsive urge. A trigger may be external, i.e. something in the environment, or internal. For example, a young woman had the obsession 'Did I stab someone?' or 'Will I stab my children?' each time she saw a knife or any other sharp object; the knife was thus the external trigger that provoked her obsession. Internal triggers are mental events that lead to the same result. A young man complained that every time he remembered a friend who had died in an accident, he experienced disturbing obsessions

Table 2.1 Elements of an obsessive-compulsive experience

Trigger	External/internal/none
Obsession	Thought/image/impulse/none
Discomfort/anxiety	+
Compulsive urge	±
Compulsive behaviour	Motor/cognitive/none
Discomfort reduction	+/?
Fears of disaster	±
Inflated responsibility	±
Reassurance seeking	±
Avoidance	±
Disruption	External/internal/none
Resistance	±

about death. The memory of the friend was the internal trigger for his obsessional thoughts. As indicated in Table 2.1, triggers are not invariably present in all obsessive-compulsive experiences.

Obsession

Since obsessions have been discussed in some detail already, there is no need to dwell on them here. Suffice it to say that there can be obsessive-compulsive experiences without an obsession as a part of them, although this is uncommon. A trigger, e.g. seeing the picture of a family member, may lead directly to a compulsive urge, e.g. to touch the picture and say a string of words silently.

Discomfort

The occurrence of the obsession usually leads to a feeling of discomfort. It may also, less commonly, be generated simply by exposure to the trigger, or by the emergence of the compulsive urge. For many this feeling is best described as anxiety, but some patients report that what they feel is not anxiety but general unease, tension or even a sense of guilt. 'Discomfort' is thus a better term to use here, because it encompasses all these emotions. Note that Table 2.1 suggests that obsessive-compulsive experiences always include discomfort; this may, however, not be so for non-clinical instances.

Compulsive Urge

This is the urge, or drive, that the person feels to carry out a particular behaviour, usually in a particular way. As Table 2.1 shows, not every obsessive-compulsive experience has this element.

Compulsive Behaviour

This is the behaviour, which can be either overt or covert, that results from the compulsive urge. When the term 'compulsion' is used, it usually refers to the compulsive urge and the compulsive behaviour taken together.

Discomfort Reduction

When the compulsive behaviour is executed in the required manner, the patient normally feels relieved; the discomfort (or anxiety) caused by the obsession (and/or the trigger, and/or the compulsive urge) is eliminated or reduced. In Table 2.1, a question mark has also been included against this element of obsessive-compulsive experience; this is because there are instances, admittedly few in number, where carrying out the compulsive behaviour does not lead to discomfort reduction. Indeed, in a small number of cases the discomfort may even increase. Moreover, even when the compulsive behaviour reduces the anxiety or discomfort, the person may be left feeling frustrated and demoralized (see Beech, 1971).

Fears of Disaster

These are found frequently: the patient feels that a certain disaster will happen unless he/she wards it off by engaging in his/her compulsive behaviour. For example, an elderly man had the very strong fear that, if he did not check the gas taps in his house a certain number of times, the house would explode and go up in flames. The relationship between the specific disaster feared by the patient and the compulsive behaviour is, of course, not always logical; a young man felt that his hand-washing rituals protected his mother from accidents when she was flying in aircrafts. Similarly, patients who are troubled by obsessive fears, such as that of developing cancer, may wash excessively, even though they know that washing one's hands is irrelevant and ineffective as a precaution against cancer.

Inflated Responsibility

Many patients experience an inflated sense of responsibility, even for events over which they have no control. Indeed, some authorities consider an exaggerated sense of responsibility to be a cardinal feature of the disorder (e.g. Salkovskis, 1985). Salkovskis (1998) stresses that obsessive-compulsive patients also feel responsibility for not preventing, or not trying to prevent, harm to others or self—in other words, responsibility for inaction (see Chapter 4). Clinical observation shows that an inflated sense of responsibility is particularly common among those whose main problem is excessive checking. This inflated responsibility also tends to generate intense guilt.

Reassurance Seeking

Many obsessive-compulsive patients resort to seeking reassurance from others, usually members of their families. Often, obsessional thoughts such as 'Will I go insane?' 'Did I do it properly?' and 'Do I need to check the taps again?' lead to the patient asking for reassurance. When reassurance is received, the patient feels some relief from his/her discomfort. Reassurance seeking is often done repeatedly, much to the exasperation of friends and family. At best, the provision of such reassurance provides only brief relief. Sometimes reassurance seeking is an undisguised attempt to enlist someone else to help in one's checking (Rachman & Shafran, 1998).

Avoidance

Avoidance can be a significant feature in the clinical picture, although it is not part of the obsessive-compulsive experience itself. The avoidance behaviour commonly concerns stimuli and situations that, potentially, can trigger the obsession or the compulsion. For example, those with obsessions about contamination by dirt or germs and associated washing or cleaning rituals usually strive to avoid what they believe to be dirty or contaminating; and those with checking rituals may avoid situations that demand checking. Some patients with severe and extensive fears of contamination confine themselves to their bedrooms; the rest of the world is seen as not clean and has to be avoided. A woman who had the obsessional thought that she might stab her children went to great lengths to avoid contact with knives, scissors and other sharp objects. A young man who feared that he might catch venereal disease totally avoided certain areas of the city he lived in. Sometimes, it is not places or things that are avoided, but behaviour. A patient may not wash in the morning, or at all, for several days because this behaviour requires a long and complicated ritual. An example of the avoidance of both objects and behaviour is given by de Silva & Rachman (1998):

> A married woman in her late 20s had the obsessional thought that she had cancer. After several years of checking for cancer symptoms, she began to avoid any situation where she might discover she had signs of cancer. Thus, she could not make her bed in the morning, or look at her used underwear, for fear of discovering bloodstains which, to her, would be a sign of the dreaded illness. She even stopped looking at herself in the mirror or at her own body. She began to wear blouses and jumpers with long sleeves so that she could

not see her arms, and trousers to that she could not see her legs. She stopped washing herself properly, as she feared that she would discover lumps and such like on her body.

In some cases, certain numbers are avoided because the patient feels that such avoidance is needed in order to avert some disaster, usually to a loved one. An illustration of this found in the following example, again from de Silva & Rachman (1998):

> A young married woman began to avoid the number four. Her husband's birthday was on the fourth day of a month and her obsessional logic dictated that, if she did not avoid the number, she would cause some great harm to him. She went to great lengths to achieve this; for instance, she would skip the fourth page of books and magazines she was reading, would never write the number four, never eat four of anything (e.g. potatoes or slices of toast) and so on. Life became impossible when this gradually extended to all numbers beginning or ending with four, multiples of four, those that were adjacent to four, and so on, at which point she sought help.

Disruption

When an obsessive-compulsive patient engages in his/her compulsive behaviour, the patient needs to carry it out precisely as he/she feels it has to be done. If the behaviour is disrupted in any way, for many it is invalidated and needs to be restarted. For long and complicated compulsions this can be extremely time consuming and exhausting. The events that can act as disruptors vary from noise and other external disturbances to certain classes of experiences and thoughts (e.g. a 'sinful' thought; image of a disaster; thought of death).

The need to form a safe or suitable thought before carrying out a compulsive or other act is also common. If the action is disturbed or disrupted by an unacceptable thought, the compulsive sequence has to be repeated in full.

In some instances the person feels impelled to remove all other thoughts before attempting to carry out the compulsive activity, for example, removing distracting thoughts all the better to concentrate on making sure that one has checked gas taps correctly.

Resistance

It has already been mentioned that both the obsession and the compulsion may be resisted by the sufferer. In his much-quoted paper, Sir Aubrey Lewis (1936) argued that the central and indeed essential feature of obsessive-compulsive disorder was the strong resistance that the patient had. More recent studies (e.g. Rachman & Hodgson, 1980; Stern & Cobb, 1978) have shown that whilst resistance is very common, it is not found invariably. It is possible that in the early stages a patient may resist his/her obsessions and/or compulsive urges strenuously, but after repeated failures over a period of time may begin to show much less resistance. There are chronic obsessive-compulsive patients where resistance to symptoms is quite low (Rasmussen & Tsuang, 1986).

Other Key Phenomena

A few other aspects of obsessive-compulsive phenomena need to be mentioned. The term 'ritual' is often used to refer to a compulsive behaviour. A *ritual* in this context is a compulsive act, either overt or covert, which has specific features: a rigid set pattern or sequence of steps with a clear-cut beginning and end. An example is a checking ritual where a system of checks is carried out in an invariant sequence. Most compulsive behaviours have a ritualistic quality to them but some are very highly ritualised.

A *rumination* is a train of thoughts, usually unproductive and prolonged, on a particular topic. A young man had complicated and time-consuming ruminations on the question, 'Am I genetically flawed?'. He would ruminate on this for long periods of time, going over various considerations and arguments and contemplating what superficially appeared as evidence. A rumination has no satisfactory conclusion, neither is there a set sequence of steps with a clear-cut end point, so it is different from a cognitive ritual. Not surprisingly, ruminations are hard to classify as either obsessions or compulsions. The decisive issue is whether they come as an intrusive experience, in which case they would fall into the category of obsessions, or whether there is a compulsive urge to think through a topic, in which case they would be compulsions. Clinically, it seems to be the case that ruminations are compulsions and that they are usually preceded by an obsession. To illustrate this, the intrusive cognition 'Am I mad?' or 'Am I going mad?' would lead to the compulsive urge to think through the subject. The muddled 'thinking through' that follows is the rumination. These issues are discussed more fully in Chapter 11.

In recent years, a particular cognitive feature that is found in many obsessive-compulsive patients has been highlighted: *thought–action fusion*. This refers to a tendency to fuse thoughts and actions (Rachman, 1993). The fusion appears to have two components. One is the belief that thinking about a distressing or disturbing event, such as an accident to a loved one, increases the probability of that event actually occurring. The second is the interpretation of obsessional thoughts as equivalent, in a moral sense, to forbidden action. Thinking about something unacceptable is as bad as actually performing that action. To cite an example from Rachman & Shafran

(1998), if a mother experiences the intrusive thought that she is going to harm her child, she is likely to feel almost as morally responsible as if she had really harmed her child. Thought–action fusion is discussed further in Chapter 12, and also in Chapter 4.

CONTENT OF OBSESSIONS AND COMPULSIONS

The main defining features of obsessive-compulsive disorders are the formal characteristics of the phenomena rather than their content (see also Reed, 1985). However, it is clear that there are certain common themes that form the subject of these experiences. The data from empirical studies (Akhtar et al. 1975; Dowson, 1977; Rachman & Hodgson, 1980; Rasmussen & Tsuang, 1986; Reed, 1985) show that contamination and dirt, disease and illness, violence and aggression, and moral and religious concerns are amongst the most common. There are also symptoms related to order, symmetry, numbers and sequence. Sexually related themes are also found (detailed descriptions of common OCD themes are provided in Chapters 7–13). An investigation into the 'preparedness' (Seligman, 1970, 1971) of the content of obsessions (de Silva et al., 1977) showed that most of these were highly 'prepared' in the sense that they could be considered biologically relevant for humans in terms of their evolutionary significance. In this they are like most phobias. Thus, while obsessive-compulsive disorders are defined by their formal properties, their content is neither random nor widely diverse. Indeed, the commonality of content across different cultures is remarkable (Akhtar et al., 1975; de Silva & Rachman, 1998). On the other hand, some of the specific contents of the obsessions can reflect common concerns found in a particular culture or in an era. While many patients in the present-day Western world have obsessions related to a fear of AIDS, 20 years ago many had obsessions about possible contamination by asbestos. It is also known that culturally specific religious ideas and behaviours are sometimes incorporated into patients' obsessive-compulsive symptoms (Okasha et al., 1994).

THE QUESTION OF NORMALITY

An important issue is whether obsessive-compulsive disorders are a clinical entity entirely discontinuous from normal behaviour and experience, or whether they are only quantitatively different from the normal. The apparent bizarreness of many obsessive-compulsive symptoms has encouraged some writers to consider the disorder as very different from normal behaviour and experience. Some have taken the position that obsessive-compulsive symptoms are a defence against a psychotic break-down, and that many obsessive-compulsive patients may end up being schizophrenic (e.g. Bleuler, 1955). There is no clear evidence that this is the case (for a review, see Pollack, 1987; Rachman & Hodgson, 1980). Yet some features of the disorder certainly lend themselves to being seen as very abnormal and bizarre. Some findings on the strength with which some of these patients hold certain beliefs associated with their obsessions and compulsions, leading to these being described as 'overvalued ideas' and even 'delusional', serve to emphasize this point (Foa, 1979). While the behaviour and feelings of a phobic patient can be seen as an extreme manifestation of normal behaviour, at least some obsessive-compulsive symptoms seem qualitatively different from what is usually regarded as normal (see Chapter 1; Jakes, 1996).

However, much of the obsessive-compulsive phenomenology is not unique to the small number of persons who come for help and get diagnosed as having obsessive-compulsive disorder. The two main characteristics of the disorder, the obsession and the compulsion, are commonly found in normal persons. In a study designed to assess the prevalence and characteristics of obsessions in a non-clinical population, Rachman & de Silva (1978) found that a very large proportion of normals did have obsessions remarkably similar to their clinical counterparts. The figure was around 80%. Both in form and content, these obsessions were very similar to, and indeed indistinguishable from, those reported by clinical obsessive-compulsive patients. The main differences were in frequency, distress and degree of severity. These findings have been replicated by Salkovskis & Harrison (1984), among others. This is not a surprising finding when one considers the essential nature of an obsession. An obsession is an unwanted cognition that intrudes into consciousness, and there are many studies showing that certain experiences, usually stressful, tend to cause intrusive cognitions. A case in point is the impressive series of studies by Horowitz (1969, 1975), and comparable data come from the more recent literature on post-traumatic stress disorder (e.g. de Silva & Marks, 2001). Intrusive cognitions also arise in non-stress conditions; indeed, the intrusion of cognitions into consciousness in normal day-to-day life is well established (Salkovskis, 1989c). The main differences between clinical obsessions and normal intrusions are that the latter are more persistent, more repetitive, may cause more discomfort and are harder to remove. The content of some obsessions is also impersonal and sometimes senseless (de Silva, 1986).

As for compulsions, it is clear that many people do have superstitious and stereotyped behaviours that resemble clinical compulsive behaviour. More importantly, a significant number of people who never come to clinics or hospitals do have compulsive behaviours very similar, in both form and content, to those of their clinical counterparts, although not as disabling (Rachman & Hodgson 1980). A report by Frost et al. (1986) provides clear evidence of this. Nearly 10% of a sample of 384 people scored 5 or more (range of possible scores 0–9) on the checking subscale of the Maudsley Obsessional-Compulsive Inventory (MOCI). Only 34% were completely free of 'symptoms' (i.e. scored 0). In a second study of 148 female students, the proportion of checkers, as determined by the same criterion, was 12%, with only 19% being complete non-checkers. The typical checking behaviours that these non-clinical subjects engaged in were very similar to those of compulsive patients, e.g. checking to make sure that doors are locked, checking that appliances are turned off and checking clothing for dirt. An Italian study (Sanavio & Vidotto, 1985) using the MOCI showed checking, contamination and cleaning, doubts and intrusive thoughts and, in males, slowness in a large ($n = 868$) non-clinical sample. Muris et al. (1997), in their study of compulsions in a non-clinical group, found that 55% exhibited some form of ritualistic behaviour, while a figure of 10–27% was reported by Frost et al. (1988).

Clearly both obsessions and compulsions are common in the general population, although they are less frequent, less severe and less persistent than in those with obsessive-compulsive disorder.

CLINICAL PRESENTATIONS

Obsessive-compulsive phenomena manifest themselves in different clinical presentations. Patients may be categorized, for convenience, on the basis of the prominent aspects of the disorder that they present with. The main clinical presentations are:

1. Those with washing/cleaning compulsions as the prominent problem.
2. Those with checking compulsions as the prominent problem.
3. Those with other overt compulsions as the prominent problem.
4. Those with obsessions unaccompanied by overt compulsive behaviour.
5. Those with compulsive hoarding.
6. Those with primary obsessional slowness.

Those with Washing/Cleaning Compulsions

This is the most common clinical presentation. Typically, the patient has obsessions about dirt or germs, pollution from some specific substance (e.g. urine, seminal fluid, animal fur) and related washing or cleaning behaviour. They also tend to have excessive avoidance, out of fear of contamination. The late American millionaire industrialist Howard Hughes was known to have suffered extreme contamination fears and extensive avoidance. Washing and cleaning compulsions are explored in detail in Chapter 7.

Those with Checking

These are the next-largest clinical group. These patients engage in excessive checking rituals, repeatedly checking things such as gas taps, ovens, electrical appliances, door locks, windows, cabinets and so on. Checking compulsions are designed to ward off harm coming to someone and/or to prevent disasters. In this sense they are almost always future-oriented. Doubting is a major feature of checkers, as is indecisiveness. These patients also tend to show a highly inflated sense of responsibility. Compulsive checking is discussed in further detail in Chapter 8.

Those with Other Overt Compulsions

Some patients display a range of other (e.g. not washing/cleaning or checking) compulsive behaviours as their main problem. Some tend to repeat day-to-day behaviours several times, usually a fixed number of times. Some have to do things in a specific, sequential set of steps. Some may go for order or symmetry. Others have a compulsion to touch things. If one hand accidentally touches an item, the patient may want to touch the same item with the other hand. Unless the required behaviour is successfully completed, the person remains anxious or tense. Many of these idiosyncratic behaviours are explored in Chapter 12 on atypical presentations.

Those with Compulsive Hoarding

This group's main problem consists of collection and retention of large numbers of articles that are useless or are of limited value. This can result in the accumulation of piles of objects that occupy a steadily increasing amount of living space, often causing fire and health hazards. Sometimes the house is so cluttered with items that the person—and the family— have to navigate through them with great difficulty. Hoarders tend to fear that they may throw away something that may become needed in the future. They find it very hard to decide what to discard and what to retain (see Frost & Hartl, 1996). A detailed discussion of this phenomenon is given in Chapter 9.

Those with Obsessions Unaccompanied by Overt Rituals

As noted in an earlier paragraph, there are some patients who have distressing obsessions, with no overt compulsive actions. Some of these have obsessions only; others may have cognitive, or covert, compulsive behaviours, which are also referred to as 'covert neutralizations'. These covert compulsions are functionally equivalent to overt compulsions such as washing or checking, in that they are carried out in response to a strongly felt compulsive urge and, once carried out, lead to a reduction of discomfort. Some of these internal compulsions are simple and straightforward, such as uttering string of words silently, whilst others may be complex and lengthy (see Chapter 12).

Ruminations also come under this category of presentation. In a rumination, the person ruminates, or dwells lengthily, on a specific topic or theme. This phenomenon will be described more fully in Chapter 11.

Those with Primary Obsessional Slowness

While many obsessive-compulsive patients may be slow in their activities due to the time taken by repetitive compulsions, some are *primarily* slow (Rachman, 1974). They are excessively slow and meticulous in their activities, especially in the domain of self-care. This slowness can be extremely handicapping and in some cases drastically impairs the person's ability to work or engage in social activities. Primary obsessional slowness is considered more fully in Chapter 10.

THE IMPACT OF THE DISORDER

Obsessive-compulsive disorder affects the sufferers' lives to varying degrees—in many cases in a rather drastic way. Rachman & Hodgson (1980), in one of the most valuable discussions of this subject, have made the point that the disorder can be malignant or benign. They also coined the terms 'full-timers' and 'part-timers'. In the case of full-timers, life is distorted in serious ways and is taken over by the obsessive-compulsive symptoms. In some cases, there may be almost total immobilisation and/or inactivity. For example, a patient with severe contamination fears felt comfortable only in her bedroom and eventually stopped venturing out of this safe haven altogether. Another illustrative example, from Rachman & Hodgson (1980), is as follows:

...[A] severely disturbed woman was ...dominated by her obsessional fears and washing compulsions. Practically every action of every day was planned and assessed in terms of the probability of contracting cancerous contamination. It determined where she lived and where she moved (frequently), it determined what clothing she was free to wear (very few items indeed). It determined whom she could speak to and whom she could touch (practically no one). It determined the homes and public places that she could visit (very few). It determined the type of work she could undertake (very limited and always unsatisfactory). The risk of contamination precluded any form of social activity. She was unable to pick up any reading material except and unless she wore protective clothing. Her conversation was confined mainly to a discussion of her fears and the actions she was obliged to take in order to avert or escape from them. Ultimately, after 30 years of this form of existence, the obsessions and compulsions had become the core and substance of her entire life (p. 59).

In contrast, there are obsessive-compulsive patients who, while experiencing clear symptoms, lead reasonably normal and productive lives. Some of the patients who seek therapy in outpatient clinics continue to be employed in responsible jobs, including highly regarded professions. Samuel Johnson, the famous lexicographer, had clear obsessional symptoms, as noted by his biographer (Boswell, 1904). Frederick Toates, a highly regarded academic psychologist, has described the obsessive-compulsive problems he has had to grapple with in his life (Toates, 1990).

In many, some areas of life are affected while others are not. Many with contamination fears have unimpaired sexual contact with their partners, but some are severely affected in this domain. De Silva & Rachman (1998) have referred to a married man who insisted on his wife taking a thorough bath before he would let her join him in bed. 'He would sometimes send her back into the bathroom, saying that he did not think that she had washed herself well enough' (de Silva & Rachman, 1998, p. 54). Highlighting a different scenario, Helen Singer Kaplan (1995) has described the case of a married woman who sought help for a specific problem: she had become totally averse to being touched by her husband. In clinical assessment it emerged that her husband had severe obsessive-compulsive problems, which pervaded many day-to-day activities. He also insisted on her behaving in certain specific ways. Kaplan (1995) concluded that the woman's apparent sexual dysfunction was the result of the husband's problems, something that neither had recognized.

Several authors have discussed the wider effects of a patient's obsessive-compulsive problems on marriage and family. A good proportion of patients with the disorder do not marry (see Steketee & Pruyn, 1998, for a review). Of those who do marry, many suffer marital problems (e.g. Emmelkamp et al., 1990; Riggs et al., 1992). However, the figures vary widely between studies. There is also a tendency for them to marry late.

Family functioning is, perhaps predictably, impaired in many. The patient sometimes exercises an almost tyrannical control or power over the rest of the family (Rachman & Hodgson, 1980). Young patients with the disorder may regulate what all other family members should and should not do. Many families go along with these demands without protest. However, there is evidence that family members are emotionally affected by having to modify their routine as a result of the patient's obsessive-compulsive problems. In a recent empirical study, Amir et al. (2000) found increased depression in family members in these circumstances.

Livingston-Van Noppen et al. (1990) have given a perceptive analysis of family response patterns in obsessive-compulsive disorder. They refer to a continuum of behavioural response patterns, with two polar opposites: totally giving in (accommodating) and totally opposing (antagonistic). The latter is characterized by being rigid, demanding, intolerant, and high in expressed emotion; the former is characterized by being unemotional, lacking in boundaries, poor in limit setting, and avoidant of conflict. Livingston-Van Noppen et al. (1990) have also identified a third response pattern: the split family. This refers to the situation where some of the family accommodate and appease the obsessive-compulsive patient, usually a child or adolescent, in his/her demands or rules, while others show intolerance and defiance. Most commonly, it is the two parents who take these opposing attitudes. An example of this split-family scenario may be cited from de Silva & Rachman (1998). They refer to a teenage girl who always received reassurance from her mother about all sorts of doubts and worries. Her father, however, never gave her any kind of reassurance. The mother also complied with the numerous demands the girl made (e.g. keeping the kitchen door open in a certain way, keeping the clock facing a particular direction). The father, on the other hand, always refused to comply. This inevitably led to the girl's problems causing a major conflict within the family.

In sum, obsessive-compulsive disorder can have a significant impact on the life and functioning of the sufferer. In a proportion of cases, this impact is drastic, while in others there are more limited effects. Severe obsessive-compulsive problems also have a major impact on the families of many, including serious disruption of family functioning and overt conflict.

SECTION II

THEORETICAL ACCOUNTS OF OCD

Chapter 3

NEUROPSYCHOLOGICAL MODELS OF OBSESSIVE-COMPULSIVE DISORDER

Ian Frampton

INTRODUCTION

OCD as a Neuropsychological Disorder

The characteristic repetitive behaviours and intrusive thoughts character-istic of obsessive-compulsive disorder (OCD) make it a prime candidate for neuropsychological modelling. Such models aim to account for how the surface features of the disorder relate to underlying information pro-cessing deficits. Similarly, the emergence of obsessions and compulsions in the context of head injury (Ravi et al., 1996), localised lesions to the basal ganglia (Chacko et al., 2000) and autoimmune neuropsychiatric disorders (Giedd et al., 2000) begs the question of the potential role of an underlying neurological substrate in the generation and persistence of OCD. Recurring obsessions and compulsions often have the quality of a failure to inhibit an everyday intrusive thought or repetitive behaviour pattern that most of us discard without difficulty, and these types of problems have information processing parallels (e.g. in *perseveration* and *inhibition*). Modelling them in neuropsychological terms may help our understanding and treatment of this beguiling disorder.

Importance of a Developmental Perspective

Building neuropsychological models of OCD provides an opportunity to take a developmental perspective of the disorder, since there is a remark-able degree of continuity between childhood and adult forms of OCD. Studies have suggested that as many as 80% of adult cases have a childhood

Obsessive-Compulsive Disorder: Theory, Research and Treatment.
Edited by Ross G. Menzies and Padmal de Silva. © 2003 John Wiley & Sons, Ltd.

or adolescent onset (Pauls et al., 1995), although others have suggested that childhood-onset OCD should be viewed as a distinct subtype (e.g. Geller et al., 1998). In any case, taking a developmental perspective in models of OCD is sensible, given the similarities between obsessions and compulsions on the one hand, and developmentally-normal superstitious behaviours and magical thinking that all children engage in on the other (Bolton, 1996; Leonard et al., 1990).

Neuropsychological models aiming to account for the generation and maintenance of obsessions and compulsions should be able to explain how such normal rituals and ways of thinking relate to the development of the disorder. For example, Rapoport et al. (1992) contend that the presentation of childhood OCD is generally similar to adult-onset, but that compulsions may occur without obsessions, or at least that compulsions may emerge first developmentally. As Bolton (1996) suggests, this is challenging for psychological models of OCD that view compulsions as functioning to reduce anxiety associated with obsessional thoughts. In this way the natural history of childhood-onset OCD challenges the traditional formulation of:

$$\text{obsessional thought} \rightarrow \text{increased anxiety} \rightarrow \text{performance of compulsion} \rightarrow \text{reduced anxiety}$$

If compulsions do emerge first developmentally, it may be that the obsessional thoughts act as secondary sense-making phenomena as the developing child tries to understand why he/she feels compelled to engage in such senseless behaviours ('so maybe the reason why I am washing my hands all the time is because I must be frightened of getting contaminated'). As Schultz et al. (1999) point out, such an alternative formulation raises the possibility that compulsions in childhood OCD are like complex tics, and that this can account for the relationship between OCD and tic disorders such as Tourette's syndrome. Potentially, taking a developmental perspective might lead us away from viewing OCD as an anxiety disorder altogether (Montgomery, 1993; see further, Chapter 1).

Of course, both obsessions and compulsions could predominate at different stages of the disorder, and in any case the emergence of cognitions about the meaning of behaviour needs to be modelled in relation to the normal development of such abstract thinking skills in childhood and adolescence. Schultz et al. (1999) make the point that until studies routinely take age of onset into account, its contribution to neuropsychological functioning deficits will remain unclear. Similarly, Rosenberg et al. (1997) argue that studies in childhood OCD are critical in determining whether neurodevelopmental abnormalities contribute to the genesis of the disorder.

Constraints on Neuropsychological Models

Potential neuropsychological models can be evaluated against *a priori* constraints. For OCD these could include the following.

Theoretical Basis

Models implicating neuropsychological deficits should begin from a psychological theory generating testable hypotheses. This approach can be distinguished from a 'battery' approach to neuropsychological assessment, whereby a large number of assessments are made (frequently without statistical control for multiple comparisons) without *a priori* predictions about expected patterns of deficits. At the most basic level, Otto (1990) suggests at least two possible explanations for neuropsychological deficits in OCD: first, obsessions and compulsions could arise as a *consequence* of underlying neuropsychological abnormalities; secondly, OCD symptoms could themselves be the *cause* of disruption in neural mechanisms, subsequently leading to interference with mental functioning, and hence neuropsychological deficits.

In addition, theory underpinning neuropsychological models of OCD should be able to account for the developmental and natural history of the disorder. As Bolton (1996) suggests, OCD itself may be a final common pathway emerging from a variety of predisposing and precipitating factors, and models should encompass this broad heterogeneity.

Relationship with OCD Symptoms

Proposed neuropsychological deficits should correlate with symptom severity (unless the model predicts that the deficit reflects an underlying trait, Mataix-Cols et al., 1999a). Models should also be able to account for why cognitions and behaviours in OCD are relatively restricted (to checking, ordering, concern with contamination and so on): why these OC symptoms and not others? In this regard there have been some interesting suggestions about the evolutionary significance of obsessional thinking and checking behaviours in early parenting (Leckman & Mayes, 1998b).

Finally, proposed neuropsychological deficits should be specific to OCD, and so studies should control for intelligence, co-morbid depression and the presence of other anxiety disorders, which can impact on test results (Christensen 1992; Tallis, 1997). It is also important in experimental studies to eliminate potential effects due to medication, and trials of medication-naive participants may be very helpful (Beers et al., 1999).

VISUOSPATIAL DEFICIT MODELS OF OCD

Visuospatial skills are required to perceive and manipulate objects in two and three dimensions (Rauch & Savage, 1997) and to put visual information together to see the 'big picture' (rather than focusing on individual elements in a sequence, as in linguistic processing). Such skills are associated with the Performance Scale of IQ tests, such as the WAIS-III and WISC-III-UK. From the perspective of adult neuropsychological theory, deficits in Performance Scale relative to Verbal Scale tasks are suggestive of right hemisphere dysfunction, according to models of lateralisation (Bryden, 1982).

However, from a developmental neuropsychology perspective, so-called 'verbal-performance (V-P) discrepancies' are associated with range of neurodevelopmental disorders, including autism, Tourette's syndrome and Turner's syndrome. It has been argued that V-P discrepancies with 'P-down' relative to verbal skills illustrate how neuroplastic factors in the developing brain preserve verbal over non-verbal skills (Goodman & Yude, 1996). Brain areas (particularly in the right hemisphere in right-handed individuals) that are normally destined to subserve visuospatial functions may also have a 'shadow' potential to take on language functions; where early disruption forces reorganisation, areas destined for visuospatial functions can be 'colonised' by language processes, with the resulting crowding out of subtle visuospatial skills.

In the case of OCD, Boone et al. (1991) report a well-designed study comparing seven patients with OCD who also had a family history of OCD in first-degree relatives, 13 patients with OCD without a positive family history and 16 control subjects on a range of neuropsychological measures. All the patients had been medication-free for at least 4 weeks prior to testing (none had been on medication on a regular basis) and this study also excluded patients with significant depression. Having corrected for multiple statistical comparisons, results showed that both patient groups had significantly lower performance IQs than the control group; nine of the 20 patients had a verbal IQ minus performance IQ discrepancy of 10 points or greater.

Similar V–P discrepancies have been found in other early studies with adults (Insel et al., 1983a) and adolescents (Cox et al., 1989; Swedo et al., 1989b) and have typically been cited as evidence for a neuropsychological model of a hemispheric deficit in OCD. Insel et al. (1983a) and Behar et al. (1984) concluded that a primary deficit in right hemisphere functioning can account for impaired visuospatial skills. Conversely Flor-Henry et al. (1989) and Rapoport et al. (1981) concluded on the basis of their studies that the visuospatial deficit is secondary to dysfunction of the left (dominant) hemisphere.

In an attempt to evaluate these two models, Head et al. (1989) used the Block Design task from the WAIS-R and the Line Orientation Test as part of a study to explore whether patients with OCD do show an impaired performance on tests with a spatial component, or whether this deficit can be understood in terms of an inability to shift cognitive or motor set (an executive functioning deficit model of OCD). Fifteen adult patients with OCD participated prior to receiving any treatment, and were compared against control participants matched for age, verbal IQ, sex, years of education and handedness.

On the tests of visuospatial ability, the patient group performed significantly worse on the Block Design task, but not on the Line Orientation Test. However, the authors failed to correct for multiple statistical comparisons, and so the results must be viewed with caution. Taken together with their findings on the set shifting tasks, they concluded that the spatial deficit observed in previous studies may index a specific difficulty with non-verbal tasks that involve mental shifts, rather than a true spatial difficulty itself.

Christensen et al. (1992) began from the premise that previous neuropsychological studies had suffered multiple methodological flaws, including failure to match for IQ, making multiple statistical comparisons without correction, inclusion of patients with significant depression, and compiling experimental samples on the basis of individual obsessive and compulsive symptoms, rather than using diagnostic criteria. In their study, 18 patients and controls were matched for age, education and gender, and multivariate analyses were used to test individual hypotheses. All patients were off medication for at least 2 weeks prior to the study.

Their aim was to explore processing domains potentially compromised in OCD from a location–function model, including: verbal abilities (left hemisphere); visuospatial abilities (right hemisphere); recent verbal memory (left mesial temporal); recent non-verbal memory (right mesial temporal); and executive functioning (prefrontal). The investigators used the Block Design and Object Assembly subtasks from the WAIS to assess visuospatial abilities, and no significant main effect of group for this factor was identified in their multivariate analyses.

Similarly, Beers et al. (1999) found no differences in Block Design performance between 21 children with OCD and controls matched for age, sex, socio-economic status and intelligence. This study aimed to evaluate cognition with children with OCD early in their illness, and none of them had ever received psychotropic medication or were depressed.

Tallis (1997) points out that where V–P discrepancies have been identified, this could be accounted for by the fact that most Performance Scale tasks are timed, whereas Verbal Scale tasks are not. He concludes that slowness related to 'task-irrelevant processing and meticulousness may be the principal cause of depressed scores' and recommends that speed deficits should be taken into account in interpreting visuospatial performance. Christensen et al. (1992) did just this in their comparison of Block Design performance of 18 patients and matched controls, and found that what appeared to be a statistically significant difference between the groups disappeared.

However, Galderisi and colleagues have suggested that while reduced performance speed in OCD is often viewed as a confounding variable, relating to meticulous concern over getting the test right or intrusion of obsessional thoughts, it may itself be a core neuropsychological deficit. They speculated that slowness in OCD patients might be a result of a difficulty in suppressing intrusive and perseverative responses, an executive functioning deficit model of OCD considered in more detail below.

Taken together, these studies do not suggest a clear visuospatial deficit model accounting for OCD. Results have been inconsistent, marred by methodological weaknesses and perhaps indexing deficits in other areas, such as shifting mental set or processing speed rather than visuospatial processes themselves. In terms of theoretical models, few authors have attempted to account for how visuospatial deficits could contribute to the phenomenology of obsessions and compulsions. Insel et al. (1983a) speculated that obsessional thoughts might evolve as verbal strategies to compensate for a right hemisphere deficit in visuospatial skills, and it could be argued that checking compulsions might relate to visuospatial deficits in processing visual information ('I can see that the light switch is off, but can I really trust what I'm seeing?'), contributing to Rapoport's (1989) 'epistemological doubt' in OCD.

From a developmental perspective, subtle deficits in visuospatial processes may be indexing neurodevelopmental risk factors for OCD operating early in life, rather than the lateralising models of adult neuropsychology. Adopting a temporal (early vs. late) rather than localising (right vs. left) role for visuospatial deficits may help to clarify how subgroups with childhood-onset OCD differ from those with adult-onset OCD.

MEMORY DEFICIT MODELS OF OCD

Neuropsychological models based on deficits in aspects of memory functioning are potentially strong candidates to account for the phenomenology of obsessions and compulsions (doubting whether an action has been completed; being compelled to make a check). Studies in OCD have typically explored aspects of *general* memory, such as visual and verbal memory, or alternatively specific components such as memory-for-action and its relationship with checking.

In terms of general memory, Cox et al. (1989) compared a group of 42 children and adolescents with OCD with 35 normally developing controls (matched on age, sex, and handedness) on measures of visual and verbal memory. The OCD group showed impaired performance on the Rey–Osterrieth Complex Figure (ROCF), but not the Rey Auditory Verbal Learning Task (RAVLT), relative to controls. No significant relationships were found between memory performance and a range of self-report and clinician-rated measures of OCD symptom severity. These authors concluded that children with OCD show visual but not verbal memory deficits, which they concluded to be suggestive of subtle right hemisphere dysfunction.

However, in this study, children with OCD showed significantly lower mean verbal and performance IQ scores than controls, and the effects of medication, anxiety and depression were not reported. The authors also reported preliminary results from a 2–7 year follow-up study conducted to assess the stability of the above findings. At follow-up, no significant difference was found between children with OCD and normally developing controls on an alternative version of the ROCF.

Visual memory deficits have been reported among adults with OCD (e.g. Aronowitz et al., 1994; Boone et al., 1991; Christensen et al., 1992; Dirson et al., 1995; Hollander et al., 1990a; Martinot et al., 1990; Zielinski et al., 1991). These studies have used visual and visuospatial recall tasks such as the Rey–Osterrieth Complex Figure (ROCF), the Visual Reproduction subtest of the Wechsler Memory Scale (WMS), the Benton Visual Retention Test (BVRT) and Corsi's Blocks Task, and visual recognition tasks such as Kimura's Recurring Figures Test (KRFT), all tests described by Lezak (1995). Memory deficits on these tasks have been reported relative to non-clinical controls.

Some of these studies have tested for relationships between visual memory impairment and OCD symptom severity. Zielinski et al. (1991) reported no significant correlation between memory performance on KRFT and Corsi's Blocks Task, and measures of OCD symptom severity, anxiety and depression. However, Dirson et al. (1995) found that visual memory performance on a battery of tasks (Signoret's Memory Efficiency Battery) correlated significantly with OCD symptom severity and anxiety, but not with depression.

In contrast, other studies have failed to find visual memory deficits among adults with OCD. For example, Christensen et al. (1992) found no impairment on the Designs subtest of the Continuous Paired Associates Test (CPAT-D) among a group of patients with OCD relative to non-clinical controls.

A number of studies have also reported verbal memory deficits among adults with OCD (e.g. Martinot et al., 1990; Zielinski et al., 1991). These studies used tasks such as the California Verbal Learning Task (CVLT) and the Rey Auditory Verbal Learning Test (RAVLT). Memory deficits were reported relative to non-clinical controls. However, other studies have failed to find verbal memory impairments among adults with OCD (e.g. Boone et al., 1991; Christensen et al., 1992; Dirson et al., 1995).

Taken together, these neuropsychological studies have suggested that there is some evidence for visual and visuospatial memory deficits in adults with OCD, with less evidence for verbal memory deficits. The same pattern has been suggested for children and adolescents with OCD, although few studies are available. However, there are significant methodological limitations inherent in many of these studies, including the failure to control for the effects of IQ, attention and speed of information processing, medication and co-morbid anxiety and depression. Furthermore, the specificity of any memory impairments to OCD is unclear, given the lack of clinical control groups. Most studies have not tested for correlation between memory functioning and OCD symptom severity, and so it is not possible to clarify the relationship between memory deficits and symptoms in any case.

The visual and verbal tasks used in these studies test *declarative memory*, i.e. memory for information that can be consciously recollected and stated, thought to be subserved by the hippocampus and related medial temporal areas of the brain. In an elegant recent study, Savage et al. (2000) have shown that what appeared to be visual and verbal memory deficits in 33 OCD patients compared with 30 normal control participants were in fact mediated by impaired organisational strategies used during the learning trials. This suggests that the 'memory impairments' identified in earlier studies may actually be strategic processing deficits in executive functioning, discussed in more detail below.

Memory for Action

In contrast to these studies of general declarative memory functioning in OCD, other authors have begun from specific hypotheses about failure of *procedural memory* (remembering learned skills such as motor sequences, which cannot be directly accessed as facts). Sher and colleagues predicted that specific procedural memory deficits would be shown by individuals with checking but not other types of compulsive behaviour (e.g. washing) (Sher et al., 1983, 1984, 1989). They hypothesised that checking might reflect a deficit in memory for motor-based actions (which they termed 'memory-for-action', MFA), or alternatively a deficit in distinguishing memories of actual from imagined events (which they termed 'reality-monitoring', RM). Using college students with checking compulsions compared with students without compulsions or with cleaning rather than checking compulsions (based on scores on the checking and cleaning subscales of the Maudsley Obsessive Compulsive Inventory, MOCI; Hodgson & Rachman, 1977), Sher et al. (1983) reported impaired MFA and reduced confidence in RM in the former group. MFA was measured by the number of completed experimental tasks recalled at the end of the testing session, and RM was measured by the number of words correctly classified as seen or imagined following an experimental procedure.

Ecker & Engelkamp (1995) reported impaired MFA, increased RM confusion, and reduced RM confidence among a group of adults with OCD and frequent checking symptoms, compared with high-checking and low-checking psychiatric controls. Patients were assigned to groups according to their scores on the MOCI checking subscale and MFA was measured by the free recall of self-performed motor actions. Patients with OCD and checking compulsions recalled significantly fewer self-performed motor actions than low-checking controls. This finding was not explained by the effects of anxiety, depression or global OCD symptom severity.

These studies into procedural memory deficits are promising, not least because such tasks are known to rely on the functional integrity of basal ganglia nuclei, including the caudate, which has been implicated in OCD (see Structural and functional neuroimaging, below). However, there are obvious limitations in existing MFA studies, in particular their failure to use an OCD control group who do not check but rather display other compulsions, such as washing. Where other psychiatric or normal controls are used, it is not possible to conclude that there is a direct relationship between checking and memory-for-action. As Tallis (1995a) points out, memory models also fail to account for the restricted classes of events that are doubted (such as turning a light switch off) rather than others (such a remembering what you had for breakfast).

Also, neuropsychological models implicating memory in OCD have universally attempted to account for symptoms in terms of memory *deficits*. However, recent work by Radomsky & Rachman (1999) has shown that adults with OCD who have contamination fears demonstrate superior memory for 'contaminated' items compared with anxious controls. Models will need to be able to account for such areas of enhanced memory as well as deficits.

EXECUTIVE FUNCTIONING DEFICIT MODELS OF OCD

The term 'executive functioning' (EF) encompasses a wide range of skills needed to solve novel problems. These include goal-directed behaviour, maintenance of a cognitive set of representations of the problem to be solved, inhibition of automatic responding and sustained attention. Laboratory studies in the primate (Goldman-Rakic, 1988) and clinical studies of human subjects (Lezak, 1995) have localised these functions to the dorsolateral region of the prefrontal cortex.

From a developmental neuropsychology perspective, Pennington & Ozonoff (1996) have reviewed the potential contribution of executive functioning deficits to a range of disorders, including autism and hyperkinetic disorder. As Tallis (1997) points out, given the extensive range of cognitive functions subserved by the frontal lobes, it would be extraordinary if OCD were not related to this part of the brain in some way. However, it may be that evidence from studies of the normative development of EF can be integrated with our knowledge about how OCD emerges throughout late childhood and adolescence in developmental models of the disorder.

Several studies have explored the emergence of EF skills in normal (Welsh et al., 1991) and clinical populations of children following meningitis infection (Taylor et al., 1993) and girls with Turner's syndrome (Romans, 1997). These studies indicate that measures of EF can be separated into three factors representing *planning*, *fluency* and *set shifting*, presumably reflecting an underlying fractionation of these skills (Rado, 1999; Tallis, 1997).

Planning

The Tower of Hanoi or related Tower of London task is frequently used to assess planning processes. In this task, the participant has to plan a series of moves to transfer three coloured balls or disks on pegs from a fixed starting position to a goal state. As the Tower of London task becomes more difficult, interim steps need to be planned where the balls are moved *away* from their goal locations temporarily. Mataix-Cols et al. (1999a) demonstrated that subclinical subjects scoring more than one standard deviation above the mean on the Padua Inventory (a self-completion questionnaire for the assessment of obsessions and compulsions) needed significantly more moves than controls to reach the solution criteria on the Tower of Hanoi puzzle, and their performance on this test was positively correlated with total score and the Checking factor of the Padua Inventory.

However, a study by Beers et al. (1999) showed that medication-naive and untreated children diagnosed with OCD were no worse than matched controls on Tower of Hanoi performance (or any other measure of executive functioning). Their results suggest that information processing deficits may not become significant until later in the course of OCD, with important implications for developmental models of the disorder.

Fluency

Fluency has been explored by Head et al. (1989) using the Controlled Oral Word Association Task (COWAT), which requires the subject to generate as many words as possible beginning with the letters F, A and S, given 1 minute in each case. Studies looking at the normal development of executive functioning across childhood and adolescence (Welsh et al., 1991) have located this task as a key indicator of the *fluency* factor. Although Head et al. (1989) found a modest effect size for OCD patients vs. controls, they failed to control for multiple measures.

Christensen et al. (1992) found no significant main effect of group for 18 non-depressed adult patients with OCD and well-matched controls on a range of executive functioning measures including the COWAT, although the pairwise mean difference between the groups on this task alone did reach significance. Beers et al. (1999) found no difference between 21 children with OCD and matched controls on COWAT total score; the mean total score for the OCD group was higher than the control group.

Set Shifting

In the case of OCD, early studies modelled the repetitive nature of obsessions and compulsions as being 'stuck in set', preventing the patient from terminating the obsessional thought or repetitive behaviour. These models predicted that people with OCD should therefore perform poorly on neuropsychological tasks requiring a rapid switching of cognitive or motor set. Head et al. (1989) explored this possibility using the Money Road Map Test (Money, 1976), which requires shifting of directional orientation (the task is to trace a route map through a city, reporting whether one is turning left or right at each junction; as the route traces back down the map towards the subject, directions have to be reversed as left becomes right and vice versa). Although they found statistically significant group differences between 15 drug-free OCD patients prior to treatment and matched controls, they did not control for multiple comparisons.

Hymas et al. (1991) reviewed earlier studies and suggested that three distinct but related cognitive functions could be implicated in OCD: pure spatial ability, cognitive set switching ability, or a third hybrid skill requiring spatial and set-shifting abilities. Again using the Money Road Map Test and other tasks requiring switching spatial orientation, they demonstrated that set shifting and complex spatial-shifting abilities were impaired in a subset of their patients with marked obsessional slowness relative to normal controls. However, there was no positive correlation between the neuropsychological impairment scores and degree of OCD measured by the Maudsley Obsessive Compulsive Inventory, and so the authors concluded that the neuropsychological findings might not necessarily be specific to OCD.

Many early adult studies used the Wisconsin Card Sorting Test (WCST) to explore potential set shifting deficits in OCD. One of the many variables in this test, *perseverative responses*, records the extent to which subjects revert to a previous solution after the card sorting rules have changed. Evidence from acquired head injury studies suggests that patients with frontal lobe damage make significantly more perservative errors than matched controls. Head et al. (1989) showed that subjects with OCD made significantly more perservative errors than normal controls, although their study failed to control statistically for multiple comparisons. Hymas et al. (1991) similarly found a significantly increased rate of a range of WCST error scores and concluded that although their results might not necessarily be specific to OCD, the disorder could be associated with difficulties in suppressing perseverative behaviour during the course of goal-directed action.

Conversely Christensen et al. (1992) found no main effect for comparison between 18 non-depressed adults with OCD and carefully matched controls on a range of tests of executive functioning including the WCST. Boone et al. (1991) found no significant differences in perseverative errors for the WCST between subjects with OCD with or without a family history of the disorder and control subjects. In a recent study comparing 21 adolescents with OCD who have never received medication with matched controls, Beers et al. (1999) found no difference on WCST measures.

Thus, studies using the WCST have failed to demonstrate a robust increase in perseverative responding in adults or children with OCD using this measure. In any case, as Tallis (1997) points out, poor performance on the WCST might be attributed to a range of deficits and recent evidence suggests that card-sorting may not be as differentially sensitive to frontal lobe functions as had been suggested by the early studies.

Taken together, these studies suggest that there is little clear evidence for models implicating developmental failures in planning, fluency or set shifting abilities (thought to be subserved by regions of the dorsolateral prefrontal cortex) in OCD. However, more recently brain circuits encompassing the orbitofrontal cortex, basal ganglia and thalamus (Modell et al., 1989), as well as the cerebellum (Baxter et al., 2000), have been implicated in a different set of executive functioning deficits in OCD, reflecting impaired motor inhibition and response suppression.

Motor Inhibition and Response Suppression

The flip side of perseveration (getting stuck in making a certain kind of response) is the inability to inhibit or suppress a response, and neuropsychological models implicating failure to inhibit responses are attractive in terms of potentially accounting for the phenomenology of obsessions and compulsions. In an elegant study using laboratory measures of competitive information processing, Hartson & Swerdlow (1999) showed that, compared against controls, a group of 76 adult patients with OCD (most of whom were on medication) demonstrated an increased bias towards a previously primed visual target. They proposed a model in which inhibition deficits in OCD may prevent old or irrelevant information from being discarded from consciousness and speculated that this deficit may contribute to the automatic and self-perpetuating nature of obsessions and compulsions.

In an earlier study, Swerdlow et al. (1993) demonstrated that patients with OCD are deficient on laboratory measures that assess the ability to inhibit or gate motor responses to sensory stimuli and proposed that difficulty inhibiting irrelevant information may play a central role in OCD symptomatology.

Similarly, Rosenberg et al. (1997) suggest that the symptoms of OCD might be caused by a problem in the natural inhibition of repetitive thoughts and behaviours, implicating the key behavioural functions of the orbital prefrontal–striatal system in response inhibition, initiating delayed responses and the temporal integration of behaviour. They compared 18 psychotropic medication-naive, non-depressed patients with OCD and case-matched healthy comparison subjects on a range of oculomotor tasks, and demonstrated that a significantly higher percentage of response inhibition failures was observed in the patients. In addition, severity of OCD symptoms (based on total score on the child version of the Yale–Brown Obsessive-Compulsive Scale; Riddle et al., 1992) correlated significantly with oculomotor response suppression error rate.

In their oculomotor response suppression task, subjects were required to fixate on a central visual target and then look the same distance away *but in the opposite direction* to a peripherally presented target. This task requires the suppression of a powerful reflexive response to look toward a novel stimulus, as well as the ability to look away from a target when no cue exists to guide the eyes towards the peripheral target. This oculomotor response suppression paradigm is fascinating in the context of OCD, as control of eye movement is dependent on the integrity of frontostriatal systems (see Structural and functional neuroimaging, below).

Using a clinical measure, the Test of Everyday Attention, Clayton et al. (1999) compared 17 adult patients with OCD, 13 adult patients with panic disorder and 14 controls. Their results suggested that people with OCD may have a reduced ability to selectively ignore unimportant external (sensory) and internal (cognitive) stimuli. The authors speculate that if obsessional thinking has its origin in normal intrusive cognitions that we all experience, then individuals with a reduced ability to automatically and unconsciously disattend selectively to their own intrusive thoughts may therefore be vulnerable to developing OCD.

If difficulties in suppressing motor and cognitive responses are the core deficits underlying OCD, how can they be modelled neuropsychologically? Shallice (1988) has proposed a Supervisory Attentional System (SAS) model, which is very helpful in potentially accounting for obsessions and compulsions. The model proposes that human information processing is constrained by a limited capacity system. Routine activities (walking, opening doors, standing up) are coordinated by the *contention scheduler*, a module that orchestrates and schedules *fixed action patterns*. These are considered to be very simple behavioural macros which release innate or learned motor plans. Low level conflicts between competing macros (e.g. holding a cup of coffee and scratching your nose) are resolved by the contention scheduler. Because all this happens without conscious awareness, attentional resources are freed up for other functions, conferring obvious evolutionary survival benefits.

However, when input pattern matching processes detect potential threat and/or the contention scheduler can no longer resolve conflicts between competing fixed action patterns, the *supervisory attentional system* fires up. This is construed as the executive functioning module of the system; rather than smooth automatic processing, the novel situation triggering the SAS demands slow, effortful processing with novel goal planning and monitoring. The SAS has been identified with frontal brain regions (Shallice & Burgess, 1998); by implication, the contention scheduler and fixed action patterns occupy the basal ganglia end of frontal–striatal circuits (see Structural and functional neuroimaging, below).

In terms of a neuropsychological model of OCD, it could be that inhibition deficits are indexing the failure of mechanisms that regulate fixed action patterns, particularly evolutionarily conserved grooming and checking behaviours. In a developmental model, the release of these behaviours subsequently generates cognitions about the meaning of the behaviour, which then take on a life of their own to perpetuate OCD through the classical obsessions → compulsions model.

Recent attempts have been made to fractionate components of the SAS model (Shallice & Burgess, 1998) and further work would be helpful to relate these subprocesses to patterns of executive functioning deficits in OCD and other neurodevelopmental disorders. From a developmental perspective, more needs to be known about the emergence of SAS systems and how deficits in discrete models could contribute to the development of OCD.

STRUCTURAL AND FUNCTIONAL NEUROIMAGING

Traditional neuropsychological models attempt to make connections between the *functional* deficits revealed by neuropsychological assessment and *structural* areas of the brain thought to subserve them. Intensive studies of individual patients with known lesions are used to correlate patterns of deficits with damage to discrete brain areas. This approach can be contrasted with cognitive neuropsychology, where neuropsychological deficits are used to pinpoint errors in purported cognitive systems without reference to the brain areas thought to subserve them. Temple (1997) reviews the cognitive neuropsychology of a range of neurodevelopmental disorders.

In the case of OCD, Rapoport (1990) hypothesised a core dysfunction in basal ganglia structures on the basis of brain imaging studies, psychosurgery and neuropharmacology evidence. Similarly, Luxenberg et al. (1988) reported neuroanatomical abnormalities in obsessive-compulsive disorder detected with quantitative X-ray computed tomography, which implicate basal ganglia and ventral prefrontal cortex in OCD.

More recent studies have homed in on structural deficits in the orbitofrontal cortex (Zald & Kim, 1996) and parts of the limbic system, including the caudate and globus pallidus nuclei of the basal ganglia and the thalamus, the so-called limbic cortico–striato–pallido–thalamic (CSPT) circuitry

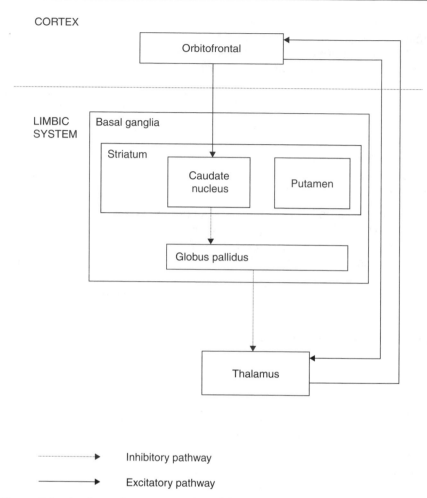

Figure 3.1   A schematic representation of the connections between the main basal ganglia nuclei implicated in OCD

(Modell et al., 1989; Swerdlow, 1995; Trivedi, 1996). Figure 3.1 illustrates a simplified schematic representation of the main basal ganglia nuclei implicated in OCD and the connections between them, based on the model described by Trivedi (1996).

Anatomy and Function of the Striatum in OCD

Rosenberg et al. (1997) found that medication-naive children with OCD had significantly smaller striatal volumes than controls, although they did not differ in prefrontal cortical, ventricular or intracranial volumes. Similarly, there are case reports of striatal lesions detected by structural imaging in patients presenting with the clinical features of OCD (Laplane et al., 1989; Weilberg et al., 1989) and acquired OCD associated with basal ganglia lesions (Chacko et al., 2000). Functional neuroimaging studies have detected increased local cerebral glucose metabolic rates in the head of the caudate nucleus in patients with OCD, compared with patients with unipolar depression and normal controls (Baxter et al., 1987).

How might the striatum be implicated in OCD? In a comprehensive review of neuroimaging and neuropsychology of the striatum, Rauch & Savage (1997) explore its role in mediating rule-based learning and memory for very simple associations. This type of non-conscious information processing is important in the acquisition of behaviours that are performed automatically (e.g. procedural learning). They present an interesting analogy, which casts the frontal cortex in the role of chief executive of a large company, mediating the executive functions. The striatum then takes on the role of PA to the boss, who can take control of simpler functions and regulates the flow of information to and from the CEO's office. Any disruption to either these functions (or the connections between them) will result in executive dysfunction.

Anatomy and Function of the Orbitofrontal Cortex in OCD

Zald & Kim (1996) describe the position of the orbitofrontal cortex (OFC) at the interface between sensory association cortices, limbic structures and subcortical regions involved in the control of autonomic and motor effector pathways. Numerous functional neuroimaging studies have detected hypermetabolism of the OFC in OCD, including Baxter et al. (1987) and McGuire et al. (1994); see also Zald & Kim (1996).

How might the OFC be implicated in OCD? Modell et al. (1989) suggest that disruption of the OFC's role in selecting and regulating input from the internal and external environment may be relevant in OCD. Primate studies reported by Zald & Kim (1996) suggest the involvement of the OFC in the recognition and processing of potentially aversive attributes of stimuli. The hypermetabolism of this region in OCD could then contribute to an increased fear response to innocuous stimuli.

Neuroimaging and Neuropsychology in OCD

In her model of OCD as a core dysfunction of basal ganglia circuits, Rapoport (1990) suggests that obsessions and compulsions might be genetically stored and learned behaviours, inappropriately triggered by the striatum without volitional control. Baxter et al. (2000) present a model in which the direct excitatory pathways between the cortex and thalamus tend to release *behavioural macros* (which they define as 'complex sets of interrelated behaviours choreographed for specific situations only'). Such behavioural macros could include the 'genetically stored and learned behaviours' proposed by Rapoport (1990), which encompass evolutionarily conserved behaviours such as grooming and checking.

There are striking parallels between this model and the neuropsychological supervisory attentional system SAS model described above, with the 'fixed action patterns' (or behavioural macros) released by the contention scheduler as a result of the failure of inhibitory mechanisms. In Baxter et al.'s (2000) model, the core dysfunction in OCD is the failure of inhibitory mechanisms that 'hold' rather than release these behavioural macros. These 'hold' mechanisms are implemented via inhibitory pathways projecting via the striatum and globus pallidius, regulating the mutually excitatory direct pathways between the cortex and thalamus.

Baxter et al. (2000) offer a wealth of neuroimaging and psychopharmacological data in support of their model; in the highly simplified version offered in Figure 3.1, the core proposed deficit in OCD is therefore the failure of inhibitory pathways projecting via basal ganglia structures to 'hold' the release of behavioural macros automatically triggered in response to specific patterns of internal and/or environmental stimuli. Returning to Rauch & Savage's (1997) analogy, in OCD the PA is frantically making responses to internal and external events from the restricted repertoire available in the absence of any novel response generated by the CEO.

This proposed neuropsychological model can account for the restricted classes of behaviours and thoughts involved in OCD, in so far as it draws on neuro-ethological theories of the conservation of fixed action patterns (Insel, 1988; Leckman & Mayes, 1998a, 1998b). However, it represents a profound oversimplification of the microstructure of basal ganglia nuclei and the connections between them, e.g. the 'direct' and 'indirect' pathways from the cortex through the striatum and globus pallidus en route to the subthalamic nuclei described in relation to OCD by Rauch & Savage (2000). In purely practical terms, imaging technologies currently lack the resolution needed to explore striatal substructures proposed by these models (Baxter et al., 2000).

Nevertheless, the development of such models demonstrates how neuroimaging and neuropsychological data can be brought together to generate testable hypotheses about OCD and how it responds to pharmacological and psychological treatments. As well as the development of neuroimaging technologies with increased resolution, neuropsychological models will need to similarly fractionate global executive functioning models into smaller component subsystems (Shallice & Burgess, 1998). More needs to be known about the normal development of executive functioning skills and the natural history of the everyday obsessions and rituals of childhood.

CONCLUSION

Neuropsychological models may be very helpful in developing our understanding of OCD. Repetitive behaviours and thoughts have obvious information processing parallels, and a strong neuropsychological theory would posit core processing deficits (e.g. in perseveration or inhibition), which can account for obsessions and compulsions. Weaker models might make comparisons between neuropsychological deficits and the phenomenology of obsessions and compulsions, without suggesting that they are somehow causal.

The development of neuropsychological models of OCD has tended to follow trends in neuropsychology research, beginning with a focus on lateralisation and visuospatial deficits, moving on to amnestic deficits and more recently encompassing executive dysfunction. Early experimental studies were flawed by design weaknesses including use of non-clinical control groups, failure to control for multiple comparisons, poor selection of clinical cases and lack of underlying theory guiding experimentation. More recent studies have addressed some of these weaknesses and links with other areas of neuroscience research, including structural and functional neuroimaging, has strengthened theory and experimental design.

One of the key areas where neuropsychological models may become increasingly helpful is in the delineation of subgroups within OCD. From the perspective of groups based on symptom subtypes (e.g. Leckman et al., 1997), age of onset (e.g. Schultz et al., 1999) and genetic characteristics (e.g. Pauls et al., 1995), neuropsychology may be helpful in defining subgroups within these based on common neuropsychological profiles (Alarcon et al., 1994). Functional neuroimaging tasks that include measures of specific neuropsychological functions may be particularly useful for detecting neuroanatomical characteristics that distinguish OCD subgroups (Hartson & Swerdlow, 1999).

Finally, taking a neuropsychological perspective may encourage the development of novel treatment strategies. Tallis (1993) has described a treatment intervention using visual cues to reduce checking, based on a memory-deficit hypothesis; Savage et al. (1999) describe 'cognitive retraining' approaches to treating OCD by targeting specific neuropsychological deficits, such as poor memory-encoding strategy. More recent neuropsychological models implicating executive dysfunction may encourage the adaptation of neurorehabiliation packages, devised to improve fluency and planning skills in schizophrenia (Wykes et al., 1999), for use in OCD. From a developmental neuropsychology perspective, early identification and intervention during childhood and adolescence, when these skills would normally be maturing, may provide new opportunities to prevent OCD growing into a chronic and debilitating disorder.

Chapter 4

COGNITIVE-BEHAVIOURAL THEORY OF OBSESSIVE-COMPULSIVE DISORDER

Paul M. Salkovskis and Joy McGuire

INTRODUCTION

Fundamental to cognitive-behavioural theories of obsessive-compulsive disorder (OCD) is the idea that obsessional problems occur as the result of a set of reactions which both stem from and intensify otherwise normal intrusive thoughts. Such obsessional (intrusive) thoughts in people who suffer from OCD are not qualitatively different from the intrusive thoughts experienced by people who do not suffer from clinical obsessive disorders. Intrusive thoughts, which were indeed indistinguishable in terms of content from clinical obsessions, were found to occur in almost 90% of the general population (Rachman & de Silva, 1978; Salkovskis & Harrison, 1984). Although the perception of threat arising from the occurrence and/or content of intrusive cognitions will give rise to anxiety, more is needed in an account of OCD. The perception of threat related to intrusions would give rise to generalised anxiety, and indeed there is evidence that this is what occurs in generalised anxiety disorder (GAD) (Beck et al., 1985; Freeston et al., 1994). Although overestimation of danger and threat is a necessary component of obsessional problems, intrusions in OCD are misinterpreted, not only as indicating danger to themselves or other people, but that the person could be responsible for bringing about and/or preventing this danger. Cognitive theories further indicate that behavioural responses are driven by threat appraisal, and that the aim of such responses is to seek safety (Salkovskis, 1991, 1996a, 1996c). In OCD, responsibility appraisal is crucial to the motivation of a range of safety-seeking behaviours, mostly reactions intended to prevent or otherwise neutralise harm or to diminish responsibility (Salkovskis & Freeston, in press). This theory is consistent

Obsessive-Compulsive Disorder: Theory, Research and Treatment.
Edited by Ross G. Menzies and Padmal de Silva. © 2003 John Wiley & Sons, Ltd.

with the full range of phenomenology of OCD, including the repetitive compulsive behaviours, reassurance seeking, the importance of 'just right phenomena', sensitivity to omission, prominence of thought suppression and the specificity of feared stimuli and situations (Salkovskis, 1996b).

The crucial difference between normal intrusive thoughts and obsessions thus lies in the meaning attached by obsessional patients to their intrusions, as an indication (a) that harm to themselves or to others is a particularly serious risk, and (b) that they may be responsible for such harm (or its prevention). The similarity between this theory and cognitive conceptualisations of other anxiety problems, such as the cognitive hypothesis of panic, (Clark, 1988; Salkovskis, 1988), health anxiety (Salkovskis & Bass, 1997), social phobia (Clark & Wells, 1995) and post-traumatic stress disorder (Ehlers & Clark, 2000) is not accidental. An overarching cognitive theory of anxiety has now developed, in which the specificity of the appraisals involved in particular anxiety disorders then drives particular combinations of reactions to such appraisals, including selective attention, safety-seeking behaviours, physiological responses, affective responses and so on (Clark, 1999). A key element in this approach is the idea that normal situations or stimuli, which often provoke some degree of anxiety and discomfort in people not suffering from anxiety disorders, elicit reactions in vulnerable individuals. It is these reactions that can then lead to negative effects on the situations or stimuli themselves, the way in which these are appraised, how preoccupied the person is with the negative appraisals, the extent to which they interfere with the person's life and the extent to which they diminish over time. For example, panic attacks are said to occur as a result of the misinterpretation of normal bodily sensations, particularly the sensations of normal anxiety (Clark, 1985). Most people experience such sensations, but only people who have an enduring tendency to interpret them in a catastrophic fashion will experience repeated panic attacks. By the same token, intrusive thoughts, impulses, images and doubts are normal, but only people who have an enduring tendency to misinterpret their own mental activity as indicating personal 'responsibility' will experience the pattern of discomfort and neutralising characteristic of OCD.

The specific *interpretation of* the occurrence and content of intrusions as indicating increased responsibility for threat or danger has a number of important effects in people suffering from OCD. These include: (a) increased discomfort, including but not confined to anxiety and depression; (b) the focusing of attention to both the intrusions themselves and to triggers in the environment which may increase their occurrence; (c) increased accessibility to and preoccupation with the original thought and other related ideas, and; (d) behavioural responses, including 'neutralising' reactions, in which the person seeks to reduce or escape responsibility (such behaviours can be overt or covert, and include compulsive behaviour, avoidance of situations related to the obsessional thought, seeking reassurance and thus diluting or sharing responsibility, and attempts to get rid of or exclude the thought from his/her mind).

Distress is therefore seen as a relatively automatic result of the person's interpretation of the content and occurrence of intrusive thoughts, whilst behavioural reactions are motivated reactions. Both types of reactions can have the effect of increasing the subsequent occurrence of intrusions and further enhancing the negative interpretations made. The inflated sense of responsibility which the sufferer attaches to his/her activities (including intrusive thoughts and memories as well as overt behaviour) leads him/her to attempt a pattern of mental and behavioural effort characterised both by *over-control* and preoccupation. In short, the sense of responsibility for potential harm leads sufferers to increasingly desperate efforts to avert it; *they try too hard* to keep themselves or others safe, and do this in a way that magnifies the perception of danger. Figure 4.1 shows the current cognitive-behavioural model of the development and maintenance of obsessional problems.

The immediate basis of obsessional problems is the occurrence of intrusive cognitions. Intrusions can be thoughts, images, impulses and doubts. Such intrusive cognitions mostly occur as an *automatic process*, but these are often linked to an individual's current concerns and probably play an important part in normal psychological mechanisms related to creativity and problem solving. Intrusive cognitions acquire emotional significance as a result of the way in which they are appraised. It therefore follows that intrusions are initially emotionally neutral, but can take on positive, negative or no emotional significance, depending on the person's prior experience and the context in which intrusions occur (Edwards & Dickerson, 1987; England & Dickerson, 1988).

If the intrusion is appraised as having no implications, further processing is unlikely. At least two aspects of the intrusion are subject to appraisal; the *occurrence* and the *content*. If appraisal suggests a specific reaction (including attempts to suppress or avoid the thought), *controlled processing* will follow. Behavioural reactions (overt or covert) to intrusive cognitions result in such cognitions becoming salient and therefore acquiring priority of processing. Thus, when an intrusive cognition or its content have some direct implications for the reactions of the individual experiencing it, processing priority will increase and further appraisal and elaboration become more likely. The deployment of strategic attention towards the control of mental activity (including attempts to be sure of the accuracy of

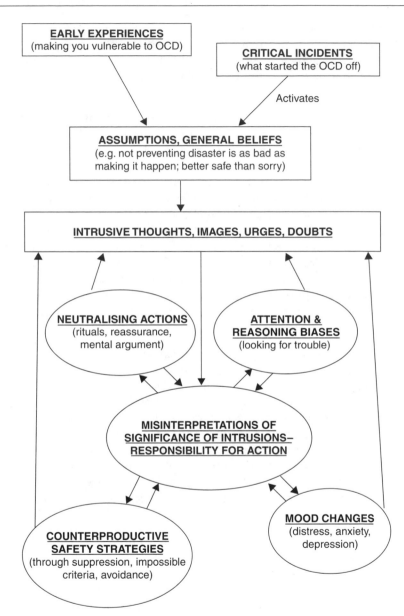

Figure 4.1 Cognitive model of OCD

one's memory, to take account of all factors in one's decisions, to prevent the occurrence of unacceptable material, to ensure that an outcome has been achieved when the difference between achieving it and not achieving it is imperceptible (e.g. getting rid of perceived contamination which cannot be seen or felt). Personally relevant ideas will therefore tend to persist and be the subject of further thought and action; irrelevant ideas can be considered but no further thought or action will ensue.

APPRAISALS AND ASSUMPTIONS IN OCD

Appraisal of responsibility and consequent neutralising can arise from a sensitivity to responsibility caused by a failure to control thoughts, and from an increase in the level of perceived personal responsibility. The majority of non-clinical subjects do not regard the occurrence of intrusive thoughts as being of special significance. Once neutralising responses to intrusive thoughts are established, they are maintained by the association with the perception of reduced responsibility and discomfort, whilst the recurrence of the intrusive cognitions becomes more likely as a result of the other processes described above. Thus, obsessional problems will occur in individuals who are distressed by the occurrence of intrusions and who also believe that the occurrence of such cognitions indicates personal responsibility for distressing harm unless corrective action is taken.

The appraisal of intrusive thoughts as having implications for responsibility for harm to self or others is therefore seen as important, because appraisal links the intrusive thought with both distress *and* the occurrence of neutralising behaviour and other deliberate responses to the intrusion. An obsessional pattern would be particularly likely in vulnerable individuals when intrusions are regarded as self-initiated (e.g. resulting in appraisals such as 'these thoughts might mean I want to harm the children; I must guard against losing control'). The importance of responsibility was clearly demonstrated by the experiments originally conducted by Rachman's research group (Roper & Rachman 1975; Roper et al., 1973) and continued more recently (Shafran, 1997). In these important experiments, situations that usually provoked checking rituals in obsessional patients (such as locking the door) produced little or no discomfort or checking when the therapist was present, in sharp contrast to the effects of having to deal with such situations when alone.

The central point of the model, and the element that marks the transition from 'normal' to 'abnormal' obsessions, is therefore to be found in responsibility appraisal, which is in turn linked to more general beliefs concerning responsibility for harm. 'Responsibility' appraisal as occurring in people suffering from obsessional problems has been defined as:

> The belief that one has power which is pivotal to bring about or prevent subjectively crucial negative outcomes (Salkovskis et al., 1996).

This means that the person believes that he/she may be, or come to be, the cause of harm (to self or others); implicit in this definition is the need to take some preventative or restorative action. It is this appraisal of the occurrence and content of intrusions as indicating personal responsibility that results in repeated 'neutralising' behaviour. Although it is not clear what the origins of OCD-related responsibility assumptions are, some preliminary theoretical work has been done (Salkovskis et al., 1999).

Neutralising is, of course, much better understood, as neutralising behaviours have formed the primary focus of a great deal of research into OCD. Neutralizing includes both overt compulsions (such as washing and checking), (Rachman, 1976a,b; Salkovskis, 1985, 1989b) and mental checking and restitution activity (such as 'putting right' by saying prayers, thinking 'good thoughts' in response to 'bad thoughts', repeatedly running over details of events in memory) (Rachman, 1971; Salkovskis & Westbrook, 1989). The problem behaviours in obsessions therefore include not only obvious compulsive activities, such as repeated checking and washing and their mental equivalents, but also attempts at thought suppression (which paradoxically may increase intrusions and preoccupation; see below). Neutralising is defined as voluntarily initiated activity, which *is intended to have the effect of reducing the perceived responsibility* and can be overt or covert (compulsive behaviour or thought rituals). These responsibility-motivated neutralising efforts reduce discomfort in the short term but have the longer-term effect of increasing preoccupation and triggering further intrusions. Attempts to both suppress and to *neutralise* the thought, image or impulse can be counterproductive, in that they can both sustain and/or increase responsibility beliefs and increase the occurrence of intrusive thoughts. As a consequence of neutralising activity, intrusive cognitions become more salient and frequent, they evoke more discomfort and the probability of further neutralising increases. By the same token, attempts to suppress the thought increase the likelihood of recurrence.

THE MAINTENANCE OF OCD BY REACTIONS TO THREAT AND RESPONSIBILITY APPRAISALS

OCD is therefore conceptualised as a problem, which arises because the patient *tries too hard* to prevent harm from occurring because of what they do or do not do. Such reactions can involve a range of activities, such as attempts to remember, to be clean, to be certain, to stop intrusive thoughts from occurring, to ensure that avoidable harm does not occur, to have no doubts and to feel that actions have been completed or done properly. People suffering from OCD try too hard to exert control over mental processes and activity in a variety of counter-productive and therefore anxiety-provoking ways. Efforts at overcontrol increase distress because: (a) direct and deliberate attention to mental activity can modify the contents of consciousness; (b) efforts to deliberately control a range of mental activities apparently and actually meet with failure and even opposite effects; (c) attempts to prevent harm and responsibility for harm increase the salience and accessibility of the patient's concerns with harm; and (d) neutralising directed at preventing harm also prevent disconfirmation (i.e. prevent the patient from discovering that the things he/she is afraid of will not occur); this means that exaggerated beliefs about responsibility and harm do not decline.

The Basis of Responsibility Beliefs in Threat Appraisal

Cognitive theories specify that both anxiety and avoidant/escape behaviours, including attempts to (over)control mental activity, arise from threat beliefs (Beck et al., 1985); emotional reactions as an involuntary response, behaviours as a motivated response. The perception of threat leads both to anxiety and to active attempts to achieve safety. In anxiety, appraisal is not confined to the perceived probability of danger, but can be represented as:

$$\text{Anxiety} = \frac{\text{Perceived likelihood of anticipated danger} \times \text{Perceived awfulness/cost of anticipated danger}}{\text{Perceived ability to cope with danger} + \text{Perceived external factors that would assist ('rescue')}}$$

Despite being virtually instantaneous, the appraisal of threat in a particular situation is clearly a complex process, based on a combination of past experience, present context, mood state and so on. Although not truly mathematical, this 'equation' neatly summarises the idea that very low probabilities of danger may become very anxiety provoking if associated with very high cost, and that efforts to control and cope with danger are part of the overall perception of threat.

The cognitive theory proposes that people are predisposed to making particular appraisals because of assumptions which are learned over longer periods from childhood onwards, or which may be formed as a result of unusual or extreme events and circumstances. These assumptions result in negative appraisals when intrusive thoughts occur. Some assumptions that apparently characterise OCD patients are:

- Having a thought about an action is like performing the action.
- Failing to prevent (or failing to try to prevent) harm to self or others is the same as having caused the harm in the first place.

- Responsibility is not reduced by other factors such as something being improbable.
- Not neutralising when an intrusion has occurred is similar or equivalent to seeking or wanting the harm involved in the intrusion to happen.
- One should (and can) exercise control over one's thoughts.

Thus, the person who believes that thinking something is the same a doing it (a 'thought–action fusion' assumption) has no problems as long as any intrusive thoughts remain relatively benign. However, if the person were to experience a thought such as 'I would like to kill my baby', it would be expected that he/she would become much more distressed than someone who does not have the thought–action fusion assumption.

The effects of these type of assumptions are often described in terms of 'thinking errors' (Beck, 1976); thinking errors are characteristic distortions which influence whole classes of reactions. Thinking errors are not of themselves pathological; in fact, most people make judgements by employing a range of 'heuristics', many of which can be fallacious (Nisbett & Ross, 1980). The cognitive hypothesis suggests that OCD patients show a number of characteristic thinking errors which link to their obsessional difficulties; probably the most typical and important is the idea that:

Any influence over outcome = responsibility for outcome.

The belief that 'ANY influence over outcome = responsibility for outcome' could be expected to increase concern with *omissions*. Consideration of the phenomenology of obsessional problems suggests several ways in which omissions may become relatively more important. An important factor in judgements concerning responsibility is the perception of 'agency', meaning that one has chosen to bring something about. Particular importance is usually given to *premeditation*, in the sense of being able to foresee possible harmful outcomes. Thus, if a person can anticipate a real possibility of causing harm, and does not act to prevent it, the act or the omission would be regarded as blameworthy. In addition, responsibility tends to be linked to the idea that one *should* be aware of the possibility of harm. Clearly, this everyday notion leads to the conclusion that one has a duty to anticipate harmful outcomes (Salkovskis, 1996b). Unfortunately, it is in the nature of obsessional problems that patients are troubled by intrusions, which appear to represent foresight of a range of possible negative outcomes. That is, the intrusive thoughts often concern things that could go wrong unless dealt with (such as passing on contamination, having hurt someone accidentally, having left the door unlocked or the gas turned on). As described above, some people consider it their duty to try to foresee negative outcomes. However, if in any case a negative outcome *is* foreseen, even as an intrusive thought, responsibility is established, because to do nothing the person would have to decide not to act to prevent the harmful outcome. That is, deciding *not* to act despite being aware of possible disastrous consequences becomes an active decision, making the person a causal agent in relation to those disastrous consequences. Thus, the occurrence of intrusive/obsessional thoughts transforms a situation where harm can only occur by omission into a situation where the person has 'actively' chosen to allow the harm to take place. This might mean that the apparent absence of omission bias in obsessionals is mediated by the occurrence of obsessional thoughts. There is now some evidence supporting such a view (Wroe & Salkovskis, 2000; Wroe et al., 2000).

Deciding not to do something results in a sense of 'agency'; thus, a patient will not be concerned about sharp objects he/she has not seen, and will not be concerned if he/she did not consider the possibility of harm. However, if something is seen and it occurs to him/her that he/she could or should take preventative action, the situation changes because NOT acting becomes an active decision. In this way, the actual occurrence of intrusive thoughts of harm and/or responsibility for it come to play a key role in the perception of responsibility for their contents. Recent research from our group has found evidence consistent with this, in that it was noted that the inclusion of an intrusive thought in a situation increased the person's distress and involvement in it, whether or not he/she suffered from OCD, and that obsessional patients show a heightened sensitivity to omission bias in those areas most directly related to their problems, relative to both non-clinical and anxious controls (Wroe & Salkovskis, 2000).

Responsibility, Decision Making and Elevated Evidence Requirements in Criteria for Stopping an Action

Many of the areas problematic for obsessional patients concern activities which are, in others, usually relatively automatic, in that no particular conscious effort is devoted to them. For example deciding when to stop washing, recalling what has been said during a conversation, deciding whether a door is locked or the gas has been turned off. When such things are the focus of their obsessional problems, patients suffering from OCD appear to be trying too hard in ways that actually interfere with the decision-making process itself. This problem may again be mediated by the occurrence of intrusions; to disregard intrusions concerning harm would be to actively disregard threat, as described above. Obsessionals tend to use two main solutions to the problem of how to decide when to stop or when they have done enough. These are: (a) they repeat the action until it they are sure that it 'feels right'; or (b) they conduct the activity in such a way as to ensure some feeling or token of 'completeness'.[1]

In the first instance, obsessionals use their affective state to confirm their decision to stop neutralising activity. The basis for such judgements vary from person to person, but most commonly involves feeling 'comfortable' to a particular level, having 'the right attitude' or carrying out the neutralising without experiencing the obsessional thought. In the first two of these instances, pre-existing mood disturbance (depression or anxiety) makes finishing particularly difficult, as the obsessional needs to achieve the sense of rightness regardless of general mood. Trying not to have the obsessional thought whilst ritualising is a particularly difficult version of thought suppression, in that there is almost invariably a link between the obsession and the neutralising activity. If someone washes because they think they may be contaminated, terminating washing without thoughts of contamination presents special difficulties.

Work carried out by our group (particularly by Karina Wahl) has highlighted the impact of using internal and subjective criteria in the decision to stop an activity (i.e. to stop checking, washing and so on). Preliminary evidence has been obtained which suggests that obsessional patients make simple decisions (such as whether or not the light switch is off, or whether or not one's hands are clean), using the type of criteria that would be typical of non-obsessionals *when they are making a particularly important decision*. For example, when trying to decide whether or not to marry a particular person, one would tend to consider how that person looks and sounds, how tall he/she is, whether he/she shares interests and tastes with you, and so on. Having considered all such factors available to us, it is still likely that we would finally interrogate our feelings. Does it feel right to spend the rest of your life with this person? How do you feel about him/her in general? Such emotionally based criteria will sway the decision. The stronger our 'just right' feeling, the less we would subsequently doubt our decision. Interestingly, most people would also continue to consider information (and mentally work with it) about what they felt *until they had achieved some emotional closure of this kind*. Similarly, if they had to make the decision despite feeling that *it might not be right*, they are much more likely to be beset by doubts about the correctness of their decision. How can a

---

[1] There is an additional set of strategies available for use to ensure completeness. These involve introducing some distinctive sequence that ensures that the neutralising is recalled clearly enough 'to be sure'. Unfortunately, the frequency with which ordinary activities are carried out tends to result in difficulties in remembering any particular instance. The greater the repetition, the less distinctive any particular instance becomes. Patients adopt sequences to overcome this, but these become subject to the same doubts.

set of phenomena which apply to 'life-and-death' decisions be applied to the kind of decisions OCD patients make, such as whether or not the gas is off, whether their hands are sufficiently free of contamination? The cognitive theory suggests that, for the obsessional patient, such decisions have taken on the proportions of life-or-death decisions (or at least having more serious implications than they actually have).

Thus, OCD patients misinterpret the gravity of certain decisions they have to make, often because they have experienced an intrusion concerning the possibility of negative consequences in a situation which would otherwise not have involved any decision. For the obsessional patient, stopping a compulsive behaviour can become the type of important decision that is usually made on the basis of as wide a range of evidence as is available. Given that the evidence may be relatively complicated (and possibly even somewhat contradictory), they are more likely to use difficult to achieve internal states (being sure of something, feeling certain and so on) as the criteria for ceasing repetition (see also Salkovskis, 1998; Salkovskis et al., 1998b, p. 50). They therefore set 'elevated evidence requirements' for their decision, most commonly the decision that they have done enough to ensure that they are making the correct decision (to stop washing, that they do not need to check something). The 'elevated evidence requirement' means that the otherwise automatic decision would become a strategic one, and that multiple criteria have to be fulfilled in order to stop the compulsive activity. Initially *multiple external criteria* (where these are available) would have to be fulfilled and towards the end of the compulsion, if the person continues to be troubled by ideas of severely negative outcomes, *additional internally referenced criteria* become the criteria required for the decision. Note also that, when a decision is regarded as extremely important (such as a stop decision, with high perceived negative consequences of being mistaken) and there are few or no external criteria available, then internal criteria and 'just right' feelings may be the only way available to the person to make a strategic decision. There is one further instance in which internal criteria are likely to be deployed. Some decisions that enough has been done are made on the basis of one's memory of how much has in fact been done. If one (a) makes efforts to try to recall what one has done (mental checking) and (b) either cannot clearly recall this, or is not confident in the memory, then repeating may again become important. In other words, the pattern we expect to find in obsessionals could be a hierarchical one, with external criteria being important most the time and internal criteria becoming more and more important when the compulsion progresses. For each of these criteria it is assumed that they have to meet an increased threshold compared to thresholds involved in decision making for non-compulsive behaviour.

The decision-making process involved in compulsive behaviour is therefore not necessarily qualitatively different from the decision-making processes in non-compulsive behaviour, if the full range of decisions are considered. Under certain conditions every decision-making process can be based on 'elevated evidence requirements'. An analysis derived from the cognitive theory suggests that these conditions may be characterised by the perception of harm threatening yourself or others and the belief that by acting in a certain way you can prevent or reduce this harm. OCD patients thus make use of *strategic* decision-making processes in order to stop a compulsion. These processes are assumed to require mental capacity and conscious awareness, and they can be voluntarily started and finished. By contrast, in order to initiate or terminate brief non-compulsive behaviour, less mental effort is spent on it, and it can occur without awareness (but we assume it is subject to voluntary control).

RESPONSIBILITY BELIEFS: EVIDENCE

Rachman et al. (1995) conducted two psychometric studies in non-clinical participants to develop a reliable self-report scale for measuring responsibility, and found four factors: responsibility for harm, responsibility in social contexts, a positive outlook toward responsibility, and thought–action fusion (TAF). Rhéaume et al. (1994) developed a semi-idiographic questionnaire measuring responsibility and found satisfactory reliability and validity using non-clinical participants. Freeston & Ladouceur (1993) developed a questionnaire about beliefs concerning intrusive thoughts and responsibility; the control of such thoughts and their possible consequences; and appropriateness of guilt and neutralizing behaviour as a response. A significant relationship between obsessive-compulsive symptoms and beliefs about obsessions were found in 87 non-clinical participants and 14 patients. Bouvard et al. (1997) also found responsibility beliefs, as measured by a French translation of the Responsibility Attitude Scale, to be important in a comparison between obsessionals and non-obsessionals. These researchers also found that the consequences imagined by the two groups were similar, differing in terms of the evaluation of severity and probability of the consequences and the influence they can have on them.

In another study, which included both OCD patients and anxious controls, Frost et al. (1998) used several belief measures, including one of those used here (the RAS) and Freeston et al.'s Inventory of Beliefs Related to Obsessions (IBRO). The findings were consistent with the hypothesis that obsessional problems are associated with beliefs, including responsibility, control, threat estimation, tolerance of uncertainty, concern about anxiety and coping. However, there was very little evidence of specificity in the beliefs measured, e.g. threat estimation was elevated in OCD but not in anxious controls, an extremely surprising result. However, the results of that study are difficult to interpret for a number of reasons. Items for all scales on the beliefs measure devised for this study were selected specifically because they correlated with the Y-BOCS, a specific measure of obsessional symptoms. There was considerable criterion contamination in many of the items used (Steketee, personal communication, 18 January 1999). For example, at least 10 of the threat estimation items (from a total of 16) referred to risk associated with obsessional symptoms, accounting for the specificity of this scale to OCD. We understand that there were similar problems in the other scales. There was also a problem in the way participants were diagnosed (self-report of having a particular diagnosis).

Salkovskis et al. (2000a) recently reported studies which investigated responsibility assumptions and appraisals in OCD patients, patients suffering from other anxiety disorders and healthy controls. The measures of inflated responsibility were found to have good test–retest reliabilities and internal consistency. The results of these studies were consistent with the hypothesis that people suffering from obsessional problems are characterised by, and experience, an 'inflated sense of responsibility' for possible harm, linked to the occurrence and/or content of intrusive cognitions. Obsessional patients were found to be more likely to endorse general responsibility beliefs and assumptions than were non-obsessionals and were also more likely to make responsibility-related appraisals of intrusive thoughts about possible harm. There was also evidence of an association between responsibility cognitions and the occurrence of compulsive behaviour and neutralising. The data suggest specificity of responsibility cognitions in OCD, as obsessional patients differed not only from the non-clinical group, but also from the clinically anxious comparison group, who had very similar levels of anxiety and depression.

There was evidence of a strong association between the measures of responsibility and of obsessionality. Multiple regression analyses indicated that both types of responsibility measures make unique and substantial contributions to the prediction of scores on measures of obsessional symptoms. Further analyses indicated that the responsibility measures were less strongly associated with measures of symptoms of depression and anxiety. As depression and anxiety symptoms are themselves associated with obsessional symptoms, this result suggests that the responsibility measures used may be tapping something other than general dysfunction and dysphoria. Consistent with this view, it was found that responsibility measures did not make a unique contribution to the prediction of depression symptoms, and only a very minor contribution to clinical anxiety symptoms.

In that study, the SCID-defined clinical groups had demonstrably comparable (high) levels of anxiety and depression, and were currently patients. The inclusion of such 'anxious controls' in the analyses tests the possibility that any difference between obsessionals and non-obsessionals is a general effect of either anxiety, depression or the fact that an individual is currently seeking or undergoing treatment. The differences found between OCD patients and both non-clinical controls and anxious patients suggest specificity to OCD.

EXPERIMENTAL EVALUATION OF ASPECTS OF THE COGNITIVE BEHAVIOURAL THEORY OF OCD

Most aspects of the cognitive behavioural theory of OCD have now been subjected to experimental evaluation. Such research has, for example, established that beliefs directly and indirectly related to responsibility are elevated in obsessional patients relative to both non-clinical and anxious controls (Freeston & Ladouceur, 1993; Rhéaume et al., 1994; Wilson & Chambless, 1999). In a large study conducted by our group, responsibility assumptions and interpretations in obsessional patients, anxious controls and community volunteers found not only that responsibility beliefs were higher in obsessional patients than in controls, but also that these were also strong predictors of obsessional symptoms (Salkovskis et al., 2000a).

The finding that responsibility assumptions and appraisals are significantly elevated in obsessionals compared to controls is consistent with cognitive-behavioural theory. However, the presence of such an association could also be interpreted as indicating that such beliefs might arise as a *consequence* of having OCD. The impact of responsibility appraisals has been shown experimentally in the effect of responsibility manipulations on systematically increasing and decreasing obsessional behaviours (Bouchard et al., 1999; Ladouceur et al., 1995b, 1997; et al., Lopatka & Rachman, 1995; Shafran, 1997) and on intrusive thinking (Rassin et al., 1999), e.g. evidence consistent with a causal role for responsibility beliefs comes from experimental studies on the impact of the manipulation of responsibility. Ladouceur et al. (1995b) asked non-clinical participants to complete a manual classification task and manipulated responsibility by giving participants different reasons for the study. The 'high responsibility' group were informed that the research group was 'specialised in the perception of colours and had recently been mandated by a pharmaceutical company for a project concerning the explorations for medication for a virus which was presently very widespread in a South-East Asian country'. The 'low responsibility' group were told that the researchers were 'only interested in the perception of colours and that this was only a practice before the real experiment began'. There were found to be differences between the groups in perceived severity of the outcome. Lopatka & Rachman. (1995) tested 30 obsessive-compulsive checkers and 10 obsessive-compulsive cleaners and demonstrated that a decrease in perceived responsibility was followed by decreased discomfort and by a decline in the urge to carry out compulsive checking. Shafran (1997) found that these effects were not confined to checkers, but occurred in obsessional patients with a range of symptoms.

The parallel between covert neutralising and overt rituals has been established (Rachman et al., 1996), as has the effect of neutralising on increasing discomfort and decreasing resistance to further neutralising (Salkovskis et al., 1997). Numerous studies have demonstrated the 'paradoxical' effect of thought suppression on the occurrence of intrusions in both the short term (Clark et al., 1991; Salkovskis & Campbell, 1994; Wegner et al., 1987) and the long term (Trinder & Salkovskis, 1994). Our group has found that a major component of the effects seen in suppression studies may be related to the effects of self-monitoring; this is an important observation, as it is clear that obsessional patients tend to become highly focused on their own thought processes, particularly to the occurrence of intrusions.

TREATMENT IMPLICATIONS
OF THE COGNITIVE THEORY

Cognitive theory indicates that successful treatment requires modification both of beliefs involved in, and leading to, the misinterpretation of intrusive thoughts as indicating heightened responsibility, and of the behaviours involved in the maintenance of these beliefs. Prior to treatment, obsessional patients are distressed because they have a particularly threatening perception of their obsessional experience; for example, that their thoughts mean that they are child molesters, or that they are in constant danger of passing disease on to other people, and so on[2]. The essence of treatment is helping sufferers to construct and test new, less threatening models of their experience. Obsessional washers are helped to shift their views of their problem away from the idea that they might be contaminated and therefore must ensure that they do not pass this on to someone else or come to harm themselves, onto the idea that they have a specific problem which concerns their *fears* of contamination. That is, patients are helped to

---

[2] This is similar to the treatment of a panic patient believes that his palpitations mean that he is dying. Therapy is intended to help him to form and test a psychological model of his problem as arising from his misinterpretation.

understand their problem as one of *thinking* and deciding, rather than the 'real-world' risks that they fear. Therapists and patients work to construct, agree and actively test a coherent alternative and less threatening explanation of their problems. This shared understanding of the mechanism of obsessional problems is directly and explicitly contrasted with the beliefs they had previously held and which had motivated their obsessional and avoidance behaviour. Thus, the mother who has intrusive ideas about harming her children is helped to consider that this may be because she loves her children so much that she dwells on and worries about the worst thing imaginable. This explanation is clearly quite different from the idea that she has these intrusions because she is a wicked person and a bad mother who is in imminent danger of harming her children.

Treatment therefore involves a number of interlinked and interwoven cognitive and behavioural components, all of which relate to, or reinforce, the formulation that has been agreed as part of the shared understanding. Discussion techniques help patients to understand better how the problem works, drawing upon their existing experience in order to help them make sense of what is happening to them. Behavioural experiments then flow from the discussion, and are usually derived from the shared understanding in order to generate new experience which can help to make sense of their problems. The principal components of treatment are therefore the following:

1. Working with patients to develop a comprehensive cognitive-behavioural model of the maintenance of their obsessional problems as an alternative to the fears that they have. This process involves the identification of key distorted beliefs and the collaborative construction of a non-threatening alternative account of their obsessional experience to allow the patients to evaluate the validity of this alternative.
2. Detailed identification and self-monitoring of obsessional thoughts and patients' appraisal of these thoughts, combined with strategies designed to help patients to modify their responsibility beliefs.
3. Discussion techniques and behavioural experiments intended to challenging negative appraisals and the basic assumptions upon which these are based. The aim is modification of the patients' negative beliefs about the extent of their own personal responsibility (for example, by having a patient describe all contributing factors for a feared outcome and then dividing the contributions in a pie chart).
4. Behavioural experiments to test directly appraisals, assumptions and processes hypothesised to be involved in patients' obsessional problems, e.g. demonstrating that attempts to suppress a thought leads to an increase in the frequency with which it occurs, or showing that beliefs

such as, 'If I think it, I therefore want it to happen' are incorrect. Each behavioural experiment is idiosyncratically devised in order to help a patient to test his/her previous (threatening) explanation of his/her experience against the new (non-threatening) explanation worked out with his/her therapist.

5. Helping patients to identify and modify underlying general assumptions (e.g. 'not trying to prevent harm is as bad as making it happen deliberately') which give rise to their misinterpretation of their own mental activity.

It is necessary not only to tailor treatment to the specific shared understanding reached between therapist and patient concerning the particular idiosyncratic pattern of maintaining factors, but also to follow well-defined general principles concerning the way therapy is conducted. A number of sources provide further details of these and other techniques in the treatment of obsessional problems (Salkovskis, 1989a; Salkovskis et al., 1998b; Salkovskis & Kirk, 1997; Salkovskis & Warwick, 1985, 1988; Salkovskis & Westbrook, 1987, 1989). Approaches to treatment of OCD are further described in Chapters 15–19.

Although the effectiveness of therapeutic interventions based on a particular theory does not provide evidence in support of that theory, the failure of such interventions, assuming that they were properly conducted, would call the theory into serious question. Thus far, the results of treatment studies have consistently demonstrated the effectiveness of cognitive interventions.

EFFECTIVENESS OF COGNITIVE-BEHAVIOURAL STRATEGIES

Cognitive treatment without the incorporation of exposure has, surprisingly, been shown to be at least as effective as behavioural treatment (van Oppen et al., 1995a). It has also been shown to be as effective as a combination of cognitive treatment with fluvoxamine or behavioural treatment with fluvoxamine (van Balkom et al., 1998). A number of studies are now under way in which cognitive-behavioural therapy (CBT) is compared with behavioural therapy; the results of these should illuminate the relative contribution of explicit cognitive elements.

Whilst some indication of the contribution of cognitive as opposed to purely behavioural treatments is of academic and theoretical interest, clinical interest has tended to focus on the issue of drug vs. cognitive-behavioural treatment, and whether it is likely to be helpful to combine these. Over the last few years, it has often been suggested that pharmacotherapy and psychotherapy operate through different mechanisms. It would therefore follow that their effects would be additive in combination. On the basis of this, combination therapy has been proposed as the treatment of choice. Kozak et al. (2000) have recently reported preliminary results of a particularly well-conducted two-centre study investigating this issue. CBT, pharmacotherapy, placebo and their combination are evaluated. In the short term, CBT adds to the effectiveness of pharmacotherapy but not vice versa. In the longer term, pharmacotherapy is associated with a high relapse rate, with a very low relapse in both CBT and combination treatments. If the results of this interim analysis prove to hold on completion of the study, they suggest that the mechanisms of action may be more similar than had previously been thought. This raises the interesting prospect of investigations involving a microanalysis of the cognitive and behavioural changes which occur in pharmacotherapy and which are reversed by medication cessation. Such an analysis could lead to more efficient combinations, in which pharmacotherapy is used for brief periods in order to enhance psychological changes, which would be expected to be more enduring, once established, and when medication were withdrawn.

FUTURE DIRECTIONS: COGNITIVE APPROACHES WILL ENHANCE NEUROSCIENCE

The next decade will see the completion of a substantial number of individual difference and experimental studies designed to investigate the contribution of cognitive factors in OCD, particularly studies emanating from the international obsessive-compulsive cognitions working group, and randomised controlled trials systematically investigating the contribution of cognitive components in the treatment of OCD. An important question remains in terms of the extent to which CBT in OCD simply represents the addition of cognitive restructuring elements to behaviour therapy (Foa, 2000), or whether the use of cognitive elements constitutes a set of guiding principles resulting in a substantially different and more cognitively elaborated treatment, as described here. Better understanding of the cognitive mechanisms involved in the maintenance of OCD should lead to better treatment and possibilities for prevention, particularly in vulnerable groups who have not yet developed obsessional problems.

Perhaps surprisingly, the biggest challenge for cognitive-behavioural theories is posed by the almost complete failure of biological theories to provide any coherent account of the mechanisms involved in OCD. There has been, for some time, considerable tension between biological and psychological understandings of OCD. Although a variety of biological mechanisms have been proposed to account for obsessional problems, none have received consistent experimental validation. It has been suggested (Salkovskis, 1996b) that this problem at least in part arises from the type of theories of OCD currently used in biological psychiatry, which tend to rely on overly simplistic 'lesion'- or 'biochemical imbalance'-type models. Most commonly, there is a failure of such theories to account for the *phenomenology* of OCD, i.e. there is little correspondence between the pattern of symptoms which patients report and the biological mechanisms which are supposed to account for them. By contrast, the main psychological theories adopt a continuum/normal processes-type approach to OCD, explicitly specifying that there is no distinctive pathophysiology involved. However, even from such a normalising perspective it could be argued that identifying brain mechanisms involved in the key psychological processes, particularly in the way OCD-relevant stimuli are processed, would have at least epistemological value. From such a perspective, it could be argued that a sensible (non-lesion-based) neuroscience approach should take as its starting point an understanding of the psychological processes involved in OCD. The limited success of pharmacotherapy and the extraordinarily high relapse rates suggest an important direction of such an approach. This type of approach would involve a 'microanalysis', in which OCD is not seen as a 'lump', but rather as a complex (but readily definable) interaction between cognitive processes and products. For example, it is possible to define separately the occurrence of intrusions, their vividness, the associated meaning, the strength of any urge to neutralise, the degree of resistance experienced, the intensity of any neutralising, and so on. The components of the model shown in Figure 4.1 can be characterised in terms of an assessment of at least 30 items. Based on such an approach, a microanalysis of the psychological changes associated with effective treatment with medication could be used to identify which components change in the course of successful treatment, and which revert to their original levels when medication is withdrawn and patients relapse. Such analyses should allow identification of a relatively smaller number of specific components of OCD, which could usefully be dealt with following effective pharmacotherapy and should reduce relapse rates. By the same token, a comparable microanalysis should allow the identification of patients in whom the response to CBT has been less than complete, and who are likely to benefit from the addition of medication. Although complex to implement, the results of such a programme of research would inform both theoretical and clinical issues. Clearly, for such a programme to become a reality, there is a need for some further elaboration of cognitive factors in OCD, although considerable progress has been made in this respect already. More problematic is the way in which biological theories have become both fragmented and have been built on the assumption that OCD must involve some fundamental disturbance of brain functioning. Paradoxically, then, helping biological researchers to achieve a more sophisticated view of OCD is probably the greatest challenge facing those working from a CBT perspective (see also Chapter 3).

Chapter 5

REPETITIVE AND ITERATIVE THINKING IN PSYCHOPATHOLOGY: ANXIETY-INDUCING CONSEQUENCES AND A MOOD-AS-INPUT MECHANISM

Graham C. L. Davey, Andy P. Field and Helen M. Startup

A notable feature of many psychopathologies is the tendency of the individual to engage in repetitive types of thought or behaviour. What the disorders have in common is that the individual is seen to persist at an activity, way beyond its utility, be that a cognitive activity, such as catastrophising in generalised anxiety disorder (GAD; Davey & Levy, 1998a), a behavioural activity, such as compulsions in obsessive-compulsive disorder (OCD; Turner et al., 1992), or ruminative thoughts in depression (Martin & Tesser, 1989, p. 307). As well as their repetitive nature, what these thought styles and behaviours have in common are their negative emotional consequences. Ruminative thoughts typically focus on failed attempts to reach some goal, and so invariably yield negative emotional reactions (Martin & Tesser, 1996); catastrophic worriers report a significant increase in subjective discomfort as catastrophising unfolds (Vasey & Borkovec, 1992) and both the appraisal of obsessive thoughts and the compulsions themselves are associated with increases in negative mood (Frost et al., 1986; Gershuny & Sher, 1995; Steketee et al., 1998a).

In theoretical terms there are at least two important issues: first, what effect does this repetitive thinking have on the individual; and second, what mechanism causes individuals with psychopathology to persist at generating iterative steps when non-pathological individuals will terminate such activities at a significantly earlier stage? This chapter is an attempt to

Obsessive-Compulsive Disorder: Theory, Research and Treatment.
Edited by Ross G. Menzies and Padmal de Silva. © 2003 John Wiley & Sons, Ltd.

investigate these issues by presenting current research that both demonstrates the anxiety-inducing effects of a repetitive thinking style and explains this process in terms of a mood-as-input mechanism.

RUMINATION AND OCD

Rumination has been characterised as a class of conscious thoughts that recur in the absence of environmental demands requiring such thoughts and that revolve around a common instrumental theme (Martin & Tesser, 1996). A detailed description of this phenomenon is provided in Chapter 11. These ruminations typically engender failed attempts to reach some goal and so invariably evoke negative emotional reactions (Martin & Tesser, 1996), which in turn should motivate people to stop the process to avoid the negative emotions that it evokes. Most theories of rumination share the common assumption that some degree of ruminative thought is a normal and adaptive process (either as a response to stress, a means of goal attainment, or both) but that if this thinking process fails to reach a natural closure, it can be maladaptive (Field et al., 2000). This idea fits well with research in both clinical and non-clinical populations that shows that high levels of rumination are an integral cognitive process in psychopathology, e.g:

1. Sufferers of OCD frequently report unwanted, repetitive and intrusive thoughts, images and impulses (Foa & Kozak, 1995; Salkovskis, 1999).
2. Sufferers of GAD typically suffer repetitive and uncontrollable ruminations about the sources of anxiety (Marks, 1987; Mathews, 1990).
3. Contemporary models of anxiety-acquisition incorporate rumination as a contributing factor (e.g. Davey, 1997; Field & Davey, in press).
4. Rumination might be an important trait vulnerability characteristic in dysphoria (Roberts et al., 1998).
5. Rumination is associated with cortisol secretion during stress (Roger & Najarian, 1997).
6. Rumination can enhance the retrieval of negative memories in depressed samples (Lybomirsky & Nolen-Hoeksema, 1995).

SIMILARITIES BETWEEN RUMINATIONS, OBSESSIONS AND WORRIES

Rumination as a process has much in common with the type of obsessions found in OC sufferers. OCD has been shown to be co-morbid with Axis I and II disorders, anxiety disorders in general (Crino & Andrews,

1996) and specific disorders such as GAD (Abramowitz & Foa, 1998). The terms 'obsessions', 'worry' and 'ruminations' have been used interchangeably within the clinical literature because they all refer to repetitive unwelcome thoughts. Turner et al. (1992), however, distinguished obsessions and worry in three respects: worries typically focus on daily concerns; obsessions may be more intrusive than worries; and obsessions lead to compulsions (see also Chapter 1). Like worry, rumination is a repetitive, iterative and somewhat uncontrollable thought process and is similarly associated with anxiety (Davey & Tallis, 1994) and depression (Borkovec, 1994). However, ruminations and worries can be distinguished in terms of their frequency, duration, ratio of verbal to visual image content, interference, ego-dystonic nature and elicited emotions (Langlois et al., 2000); worry is typically expressed verbally, is more distracting, more realistic, more voluntary and is associated with a stronger urge to act, whereas ruminations are typically ego-dystonic, can occur through images and impulses as well as verbal thought, and are more intrusive (Turner et al., 1992). Worry also appears to focus on future events (Borkovec, 1994), whereas rumination typically focuses on past events and experiences (Martin & Tesser, 1989). Like ruminations, the obsessions of OC sufferers engender thoughts, impulses and images that are highly intrusive (Rachman & Hodgson, 1980; Salkovskis, 1999).

Although the distinctions between obsessions, ruminations and worries are, at best, fuzzy, they engender iterative thinking, and obsessions and ruminations in particular seem difficult to distinguish, as both need not centre on daily concerns and are highly intrusive. The only clear distinction between ruminations and obsessions, *prima facie*, is the behavioural outcome: obsessions lead to compulsions (Turner et al., 1992). However, if the function of compulsions is examined, then this distinction becomes less clear. The relationship between obsessions and compulsions in OCD centres on anxiety reduction (Hodgson & Rachman, 1972; Rachman et al., 1976). OCD is currently classified as an anxiety disorder in DSM-IV (APA, 1994), primarily because of the anxiety and distress that obsessions cause. Once an obsession has occurred, or has been triggered by some external cue, it has been argued that the misinterpretation of this event (in terms of perceived responsibility for an outcome and feelings that such obsessions should be controlled) leads to anxiety that is reduced through acting out an associated compulsion (see Rachman, 1998; Salkovskis, 1999; Salkovskis & Kirk, 1997). The connection between the obsession and compulsion can be completely logical (checking a locked door to relieve anxiety about the obsession that the door is unlocked) or can be in some sense magical (tapping the wall 14 times to prevent someone's death). This model shares much in common with theories of rumination in which rumination is seen as potentially self-ceasing because people should be motivated to carry out behavioural or cognitive acts to reduce or avoid the negative emotions associated with rumination (Wegner & Gold, 1995). As such, ruminations, like obsessions, are not only intrusive and not focused on daily concerns but also evoke acts designed to reduce or avoid anxiety. As such, there is little to differentiate the two processes. The assumptions in theories of OCD are that: (a) obsessions and ruminations increase anxiety; and (b) compulsions reduce it. Although there is clinical evidence that compulsions reduce anxiety (Rachman et al., 1976; Hodgson & Rachman, 1972), there is, at present, little experimental evidence to verify that obsessions and ruminations increase anxiety.

WHAT IS THE EFFECT OF RUMINATION?

Does Rumination Increase Anxiety?

Davey (1995), amongst others, has suggested that rumination about the outcome of an interaction with a fear-evoking stimulus should enhance fear about that stimulus (see also Harvey et al., 1993). Indeed, initial laboratory studies have shown that: (a) rehearsing the possible outcomes of a phobia-related encounter can exacerbate anxiety towards the fear-evoking stimulus (Davey & Matchett, 1994; Ehlers, 1993; Jones & Davey, 1990); and (b) rumination about an anxiety-provoking event maintains anxiety, compared to a distraction task (Blagden & Craske, 1996). Furthermore, two experiments by Davey et al. (2000a) have shown that the content of rumination is key to enhancing fear. In their first experiment, Davey et al. showed that rumination about the consequences of an encounter with an anxiety-evoking stimulus increases subsequent anxiety significantly more than rumination about the physical properties of the stimulus. In the second experiment, rumination about the participant's emotional reaction to the consequences of an interaction enhanced fear, whereas rumination about physical threat or no contact with the stimulus did not.

Field and colleagues (Field, 1999; Field et al., 2000) have recently extended this work to look at the connection between rumination, anxiety and catastrophic thought. Although past research has shown that rumination about the outcomes of anxiety-related encounters can inflate self-reported anxiety, no research has investigated whether rumination actually leads to a magnification of the severity of the outcomes imagined. In two experiments, Field et al. (2000) looked at the effects on catastrophic thought of ruminating about the consequences of interacting with an anxiety-evoking stimulus. Their basic paradigm involved showing a picture of a spider both to a group of analogue arachnophobic participants (whose scores on the Spider Phobia Questionnaire, SPQ, were equivalent to clinical samples) and a group of non-fearful participants. Participants then rated their subjective anxiety on a visual analogue scale. Half of each group then thought of a consequence of interacting with the spider in the picture and ruminating about that consequence for 2 minutes, whereas the other half ruminated about the consequences of interacting with a pet or a non-threatening animal. Following rumination, the picture of the spider was shown again and subjective anxiety was re-rated. In Experiment 1 of Field et al. (2000), rumination was looked at on a between-group basis (participants only ruminated about interactions with a spider or pet) whereas in Experiment 2 rumination was investigated on a within-subject basis (participants repeated the procedure once for a spider and once for a non-threatening animal in counterbalanced order). In Experiment 2, rumination was specifically manipulated to focus either on an actual past experience (past-based rumination) or a possible future interaction (future-based rumination).

The results of these experiments are shown in Figure 5.1. In terms of anxiety, rumination about a fear-evoking stimulus (i.e. a spider to arachnophobic participants) increased both self-report measures of anxiety and heart rate upon subsequent presentation of that stimulus. In participants fearful of spiders, initial presentation of the spider picture increased anxiety (as shown by the heart rate data); during rumination about interacting with that spider anxiety increased slightly (so rumination maintained the levels of anxiety elicited by the picture) but more interesting was that subsequent presentation of the spider picture increased anxiety above and beyond the level that the picture initially elicited. In non-fearful participants this was not the case, with heart rates remaining relatively stable across the experimental procedure. In fearful participants, rumination about a non-threatening animal reduced anxiety. Field et al. also found that these effects occurred both when rumination was past-based (i.e. related to an actual past encounter with a spider/non-threatening animal) and when it was future-based (i.e. related to a hypothetical, as yet unexperienced, encounter).

These results show that if anxious individuals ruminate about the source of their anxiety, then anxiety increases even more upon subsequent experience of the source. This finding seems to be the result of ruminative thinking in general, because ruminating about real-life past experiences or concerns (which would be an analogue of the rumination and 'post-mortem' characteristic of social phobia: Clark, 1997; Rachman et al., 2000) produces similar results to ruminating about hypothetical future concerns (which mimics the worry process: Borkovec, 1994).

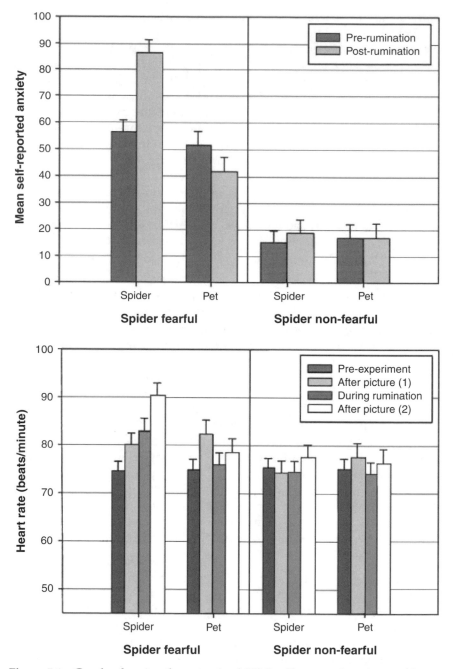

Figure 5.1   Graphs showing the mean (and SEM) self-reported anxiety and heart rate towards a picture of a spider, both before and after rumination about the spider or a non-threatening animal (pet) (data from experiment 2 of Field et al., 2000)

Does Rumination Increase Catastrophic Thought?

Rumination is also implicated in catastrophising, which has been characterised in the pain literature as a multidimensional construct comprising rumination (thoughts and images about the pain itself), magnification (thinking about whether something serious might happen) and helplessness (feeling overwhelmed by thoughts) (see Sullivan et al., 1995; Sullivan & Neish, 1998). The implication in this model is that rumination leads to a catastrophic magnification in negative thought content. In the worry literature, catastrophising is similarly seen as the tendency to iterate negative outcomes to a potential worry (e.g. Davey & Levy, 1998a). It is a notable feature that catastrophic worry tends to focus on future, potential catastrophes and that such potentials are presented and represented into awareness through the adoption of a 'what if . . . ?' questioning style. Rather than bringing the problem to a satisfactory close, however, this process usually leads the worrier to perceive progressively worse and worse outcomes to the worry topic (Davey & Levy, 1998a; Kendall & Ingram, 1987; Vasey & Borkovec, 1992).

To make catastrophising thoughts overt, Vasey & Borkovec (1992) designed the catastrophising interview: the interviewer begins by asking the participant what is the focus of his/her current main worry. The participant then writes down or verbalises his/her worry (e.g. 'exams'). The interviewer then asks, 'What is it that worries you about X?', where X was the worry that the participant had just reported (e.g. 'what is it that worries you about exams?'). The participant then writes or verbally reports this new worry (e.g. 'because I might fail them'). The interviewer then asks 'What is it that worries you about X?', where X is the new worry, and so on. Often worriers will continue this interview until they reach a point of utter catastrophe, such as saying 'life just wouldn't be worth living' (Davey & Levy, 1998a). Thus, what begins as a mid-term concern for the individual becomes an exacerbated nightmare, through the process of perseverative iteration.

Field et al. (2000) looked at the effect of rumination on catastrophic thought by conducting catastrophising interviews after each of the rumination procedures previously described. Participants engaged in two catastrophising tasks (counterbalanced): in one, participants catastrophised a negative outcome of interacting with a spider, and in the other they catastrophised a negative outcome of interacting with a non-threatening animal. The catastrophising measure was adapted from the interview described above, but with the experimenter beginning the interview with the question 'What is it that worries you about interacting with the spider (or pet)'?

The results of Field et al.'s experiment 2 are shown in Figure 5.2. Rumination about an anxiety-evoking stimulus resulted in significantly more

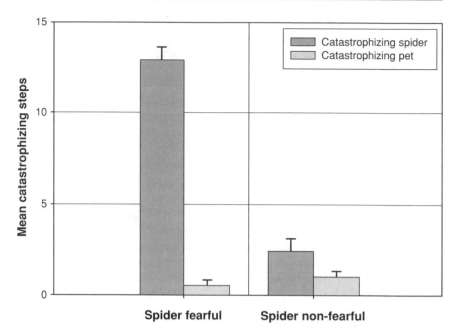

Figure 5.2 The mean (and SEM) number of catstrophising steps generated about future interactions with either a spider or a non-threatening animal (pet), after rumination about either the spider or the non-threatening animal (data from experiment 2 of Field et al., 2000)

catastrophising steps about a future encounter with that stimulus than in people not anxious of that stimulus. However, both anxious and non-anxious groups produced similar numbers of catastrophising steps when asked to catastrophise a future encounter with a non-threatening animal. These effects were virtually identical, both when rumination was past-based (i.e. related to an actual past encounter with a spider/non-threatening animal) and when it was future-based (i.e. related to a hypothetical, as yet unexperienced, encounter).

The catastrophising in this experiment is not simply the result of spider-fearful individuals possessing a 'data bank' of negative outcomes that are accessed during the catastrophising interview, because in Experiment 1 spider-fearful participants catastrophised future interactions with a spider after ruminating about a non-threatening animal, and produced the same number of catastrophising steps as non-fearful participants. Davey & Levy (1998a) showed that individuals scoring high on trait worry possess a general iterative style that they apply to novel situations (see later): it seems that rumination about interacting with an anxiety-evoking stimulus triggers a similar thinking style.

Implications for OCD

The main findings from this work are that repeated thought about the consequences of an anxiety-evoking event can both (a) increase subjective and physiological anxiety and (b) produce perseverative, iterative thought about possible catastrophic outcomes resulting from future events. This occurs only in already anxious individuals. In terms of OC sufferers, if intrusive thoughts or external events trigger ruminative thoughts, as suggested by Rachman (1998) and Salkovskis (1999), then these thoughts are indeed likely to increase their anxiety. The fact that obsessions increase anxiety is an assumption that has received little experimental support; the body of work described here (Davey et al., 2000a, 2000b; Field, 1999; Field et al., 2000) is some of the first laboratory-based work to demonstrate this relationship. In addition, the work described here clearly shows that an important feature of rumination in anxiety is that to enhance fear the thoughts must be directed at the *consequences* of an anxiety-evoking event. The misinterpretations of obsessions in OCD usually relate specifically to the negative or catastrophic consequences of the obsession and are driven by an inflated sense of responsibility over those consequences (Rhéaume et al., 1994; Salkovskis & Kirk, 1997). As such, these consequence-based obsessions are likely to inflate anxiety and catastrophic thought in much the same way as shown by Field et al. (2000).

A number of factors could help explain why ruminating about the consequences of an anxiety-evoking event leads to catastrophic thought about future events. First, given the emphasis on imagery in rumination (Langlois et al., 2000; Turner et al., 1992) one possibility is that individuals with anxiety-related psychopathology possess greater imagery ability or can become more absorbed in the ruminative process than non-anxious people. However, Davey et al. (2000b) found no effects of visual imagery or absorption on the anxiety-enhancing effects of rumination, and so this explanation seems unlikely. Anxious individuals might also attend to and interpret threatening information differently to non-anxious individuals during rumination. Indeed, Davey et al. (2000b) reported that rumination significantly affected self-reported anxiety in a non-anxious sample only in individuals that had high levels of interpretive bias. This suggests that interpretive bias is an important mediating variable in the enhancement of anxiety through rumination. Perhaps rumination enhances fear only in anxious individuals because they have a greater sensitivity to processing threat-related information. A final possibility is that the fear-enhancing process is mediated by negative mood. Rumination has been shown to exacerbate naturally occurring depressed mood (Nolen-Hoeksema & Morrow, 1993) and can maintain anxious mood (Blagden &

Craske, 1996). In addition, laboratory-induced negative mood significantly increases both catastrophising about personal worries (Johnston & Davey, 1997; Startup & Davey, in press) and iterative thinking in general (Startup & Davey, in press) and depressed mood can create a tendency to catastrophise threats (Vasey & Borkovec, 1992).

The results presented thus provide some insight into the anxiety-inducing effect of consequence-based rumination. However, there is no mechanism to explain the perseverative thought induced by this rumination. The next part of this chapter describes some of what we now know about the complex contribution of negative mood to catastrophising and iterative thinking. In turn, a mood-as-input model is presented to explain the persistence of iterative thoughts and behaviours.

WHAT PROCESSES CONTRIBUTE TO PERSEVERATION?

A number of factors have been shown to be associated with perseveration across the various symptoms and disorders, e.g:

1. *Mood.*   Individuals in a negative mood have been shown to process more extensively than individuals in positive moods; thus, mood influences cognitive perseveration (Mackie & Worth, 1989; Schwarz & Bless, 1991).
2. *Perfectionism.*   There is a significant link between perfectionism and OC symptoms (Bouchard et al., 1999), particularly with the tendency to perform poorly at precision and decision-making tasks (Rhéaume et al., 1995, cited in Bouchard et al., 1999). There is also an association between perfectionism and worry (Pratt et al., 1997), such that worriers require additional information before they are able to reach closure on a problem (Tallis et al., 1991).
3. *Inflated responsibility.*   This is typically defined in terms of an individual's belief either that he/she has have power to cause harm should things not go as they should (Rhéaume et al., 1994), or that he/she has power that is pivotal to bringing about or preventing subjectively crucial negative outcomes (Salkovskis et al., 1996). This sense of responsibility is associated with both worry (Wells & Papageorgiou, 1998) and OC symptoms (Salkovskis et al., 2000a). Specifically, the lowering of responsibility is associated with a significant drop in discomfort and need to check (Lopatka & Rachman, 1995), whereas studies that have experimentally manipulated responsibility have shown that increases in self-reported responsibility result in more checking behaviours than in low-responsibility controls (Bouchard et al., 1999; Ladouceur et al., 1995a, 1997). Although such findings extend our understanding of

what variables may drive perseverative features of cognition and behaviour, they are devoid of a mechanistic framework. Exactly *how* these mood and person variables lead to perseveration has yet to be conceptualised.

THE MOOD-AS-INPUT APPROACH TO UNDERSTANDING PERSEVERATIVE PSYCHOPATHOLOGY

A new framework for understanding perseverative psychopathology has been offered in the mood-as-input hypothesis (Davey et al., 2002; Martin & Davies, 1998; Martin et al., 1993; Sanna et al., 1996; Startup & Davey, in press). This account attempts to place the findings described above within a single mechanistic framework, with the suggestion that perseveration is brought about via an interaction between mood states and the stop rules required by a particular task. Thus, rather that being intrinsically linked to certain default processing strategies (such as mood-congruent processing) (Mackie & Worth, 1989; Schwarz & Bless, 1991), the mood-as-input hypothesis proposes that it is an individual's interpretation of the mood, rather than the mood *per se*, that has particular performance implications. Mood, in this connection, assumes more of a secondary role, the function of which is derived from 'top-down', 'configural' interpretations based on the goal at hand (Martin & Davies, 1998).

The mood-as-input hypothesis can be described in the following way. When working on a task, people may ask themselves, either explicitly or implicitly, 'Have I reached my goal?' People in positive moods would tend to answer 'yes', whereas people in negative moods would tend to answer 'no'. That is, people in a positive mood are likely to interpret their positive affect as a sign that they have attained or made progress toward their goal (i.e. Hirt et al., 1996; Martin et al., 1993). In contrast, in a negative mood, individuals may interpret their negative affect as a sign that they have not attained or made progress toward their goal and so continue to persist at the task (Frijda, 1988; Martin et al., 1993; Schwarz & Bless, 1991). If, however, the individual asked the question, 'Do I feel like continuing this task?', then mood provides very different information. People in positive moods would again answer 'yes' and people in negative moods 'no'. However, this different question or 'stop rule' in the context of the same mood informs different goal-directed behaviour, because in this case an answer suggesting that one is enjoying the task (positive mood) would motivate the individual to continue the task longer. On the other hand, an answer of 'no' (negative mood) provides information consistent with terminating the task sooner.

Many studies have lent support to this configurative view of how mood states are processed in the context of individual tasks (see Martin & Davies, 1998, for a review) and the following study is described to clarify both the methodological framework typically adopted and the pattern of results typically derived from mood-as-input studies.

Martin et al. (1993) induced either positive or negative moods in their participants and asked them to generate a list of birds' names. Half of the participants were told to stop generating the names of birds when they no longer felt like doing it (a 'feel like continuing' stop rule), whereas the other half were asked to stop when they thought they had generated as many as they could (an 'as many as can' stop rule). They found that the effect of mood on the generation task was dependent on the stop rule that the participant was asked to use: for those using the 'feel like continuing' stop rule, participants in the positive mood persisted at the task for significantly longer than those in the negative mood. However, for participants using the 'as many as can' stop rule, participants in a negative mood persisted for significantly longer than those in the positive mood. Martin et al. (1993) interpret these effects in mood-as-input terms. So, participants in a negative mood interpret their mood in relation to the stop rule: in the 'feel like continuing' condition their negative mood tells them to stop, but in the 'as many as can' condition their negative mood tells them they are not satisfied with the number of items they have generated on the task, and so they persist at the task for longer.

Catastrophic worrying and compulsive checking represent two forms of perseverative activity and will be described in more detail below. They offer useful examples of the applicability of the mood-as-input approach to perseverative activity because they share certain key features (such as their association with features of responsibility and perfectionism) but also differ usefully in that they represent one behavioural demonstration of perseveration (obsessive checking) and one cognitive demonstration (perseverative worry).

Mood-as-input Conditions Relevant to Perseverative Psychopathology

One particular combination of mood and task stop rules is particularly relevant to perseverative psychopathology. This is the combination of negative mood and 'as many as can' stop rules. Under this configuration, individuals will persist significantly longer at the task because the 'as many as can' stop rule motivates the individual to ask the question, 'Have I fully and successfully completed the task?', and the negative mood provides the answer 'no', thus leading to further perseveration.

This combination is particularly relevant to the psychopathologies of OC checking and pathological worry because: (a) both pathological worriers and OC checkers report chronic high levels of negative mood (Davey et al., 2002; Frost et al., 1986; Meyer et al., 1990; Steketee et al., 1998); and (b) there are certain characteristics of worriers and OC checkers that suggest that they will use fairly strict 'as many as can' criteria for terminating a worrying or checking task. For example, worriers hold dysfunctional views about worrying being a necessary and important activity for preventing catastrophes (Borkovec & Roemer, 1995; Davey et al., 1996), which would be consistent with the use of strict 'as many as can' stop rules. Similarly, worry concerns *potentials* of a largely non-concrete variety (Stober, 1998). There is, therefore, little opportunity for the worrier to draw on external markers to determine when the issue has been resolved. The worrier instead has to rely on subjective criteria to determine when to reach problem closure.

In addition, OC checkers are known to possess beliefs related to inflated responsibility (an exaggerated belief in an individual's power to cause harm; Rhéaume et al., 1994), and this inflated responsibility is likely to motivate the OC checker to use very strict 'as many as can' stop rules when indulging in a checking task. Similarly, using the Meta-cognitions Questionnaire (MCQ; Cartwright-Hatton & Wells, 1997), pathological worry was correlated (as measured by the Penn State Worry Questionnaire, PSWQ) with negative beliefs about worry (subscale 4), including themes of superstition, punishment and responsibility (e.g. 'if a bad thing happens which I have not worried about, I feel responsible'; Wells & Papageorgiou, 1998).

The following discussion examines some of the predictions from the mood-as-input hypothesis, in particular the view that perseveration is determined by the use of, and strictness of, the stop rules implicitly brought to the perseverative task in certain psychopathologies.

Mood-as-input and Obsessive Checking

Davey et al. (2002) have argued that the perseverative features of OC checking can be conceptualised in mood-as-input terms (Davey et al., 2002). In their first experiment, the authors successfully induced a positive, negative or neutral mood in a sample of non-clinical analogue participants using a manipulation of music and lighting. Participants were then required to perform an analogue checking task: 'imagine that you are leaving home to go on holiday for 3 weeks; list as many things in or around your home that you should check before you go away'. Half of the participants in each mood condition were instructed to continue until they felt they had 'recalled as many items as they could' and the other half until they 'no longer felt like continuing with the task'. The authors demonstrated that

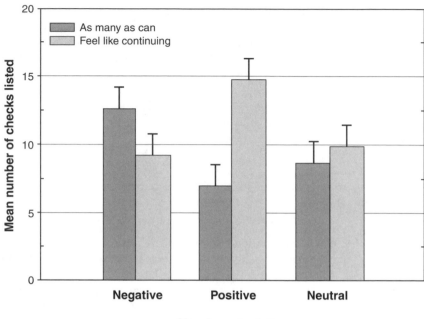

Figure 5.3   Mean number of checks listed for all six sub-groups in Davey et al. (2002), Experiment 1

persistence at generating items was dependent on a combination of mood state and stop rules required by the task. Specifically, participants in a negative mood generated more items and spent significantly more time on the task than individuals in a positive mood, but only when working within an 'as many as can' stop rule. When persistence at the task was governed by a 'feel like continuing' stop rule, participants in a positive mood persisted at the task for longer and generated more checking items than those in a negative mood (see Figure 5.3).

In a second study, the authors induced a positive and negative mood into a sample of analogue participants and required them to perform a check-recall task, i.e. participants recalled a previously learnt list of items under one of two stop rule conditions: half in each mood condition were required to recall items until they had recalled ' as many as they could' and half continued just as long as they 'felt like continuing'. Results again suggested that a combination of mood and stop rule influenced the pattern of perseveration: participants in the negative mood condition spent significantly more time recalling items following an 'as many as can' stop rule than those following a 'feel like continuing' stop rule. Conversely, in the positive mood condition, participants in the 'feel like continuing' condition

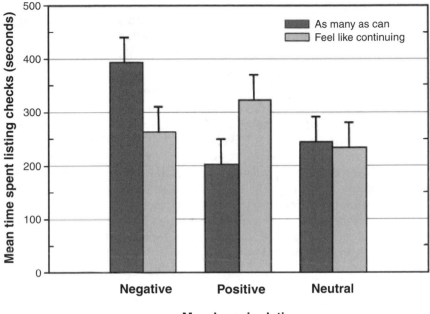

Figure 5.4   Mean time (in seconds) spent listing check items for all six sub-groups in Davey et al. (2002), Experiment 1

spent more time recalling than those in the 'many as can' stop rule condition (see Figure 5.4).

Thus, this study demonstrated that persistence both at generating items in an analogue checking task and in attempts to recall items in an analogue check-recall task were dependent on a combination of mood state and the stop rule required by the task. Most applicable to OC checking was the fact that persistence in these task was significantly enhanced when the participants were in a negative mood and operating under an 'as many as can' stop rule. Davey et al. suggested that these conditions are comparable to the pervasive negative mood that OC checkers experience, both dispositionally and in enhanced form when commencing checking tasks (Frost et al., 1986; Gershuny & Sher, 1995; Steketee et al., 1998a). They also suggested that the beliefs of inflated responsibility possessed by OC checkers is consistent with them performing under an 'as many as can' stop rules.

The Mood-as-input Account Applied to Catastrophic Worry

Using a similar method to the catastrophising procedure described earlier, Vasey & Borkovec (1992) found that chronic worriers generated significantly more catastrophising steps than non-worriers and reported a significant increase in subjective discomfort as catastrophising unfolded. Worriers also rated the events in the catastrophising sequence as significantly more likely to occur than did non-worriers.

Most recently, Davey & Levy (1998a) conducted a series of six studies, using the catastrophising interview procedure described above to investigate some of the characteristics of catastrophic worrying. They employed a non-selected sample of analogue participants and established their trait worry score by means of the PSWQ (Meyer et al., 1990). As well catastrophising their main worry topic (as described above), participants also catastrophised both a happy feature of their life and a hypothetical worry. For the 'happy topic', participants were asked to write down the feature in their life that currently made them happiest and then to imagine that this aspect of their life was actually worrisome to them in some way. When they felt able to do this, participant's catastrophised this topic using the interview described above. For the hypothetical worry, participants were asked to imagine that they were the Statue of Liberty standing in New York Harbour. They were asked to imagine that they were not happy being the Statue of Liberty, and were feeling very worried about it. Participants again catastophised this hypothetical worry using the catastrophising interview. Finally, participants were also required to 'reverse-catastrophise', or say 'what is good about . . . ' both a hypothetical worry (Statue of Liberty) and their main worry. The reverse-catastrophising procedure begins with the experimenter asking the question, 'What is it about being the Statue of Liberty (or main worry topic) that is good?'. If the participant's response is, for example, 'being famous', he/she is then asked, 'What is it about being famous that is good?.' If the participant replies, 'People will admire me', then the experimenter asks, 'What is it about people admiring you that is good?' and so on. This process continues until the participant can think of no more responses.

Davey & Levy (1998a) found that:

1. Worriers generated significantly more catastrophising steps than non-worriers for both their main worry topic and the hypothetical topic that they would never before have encountered. Therefore, it is unlikely that the greater catastrophising of worriers is due to them having thought more about the worry prior to the catastrophising interview. Specifically, both worriers and non-worriers are unlikely to have thought about being the Statue of Liberty before (see also Vasey & Borkovec, 1992).
2. Worriers were more likely to catastrophise a positive aspect of their life than were non-worriers.

3. Worriers were more likely to catastrophise a topic regardless of the subject-perceived valence of the task ('What is good . . . ?' about being the Statue of Liberty).

These experiments revealed that: (a) the persistent catastrophising style of worriers was readily transferred to new hypothetical worries that the individual had never thought about before; (b) worriers displayed a general iterative style that was independent of the valence of the iterative task (i.e. they would be equally likely to persist in elucidating what was 'good' about a topic as they would in elucidating what was 'bad' about it); and (c) worriers tended to couch their worries in terms of personal inadequacies, and personal inadequacy became a feature of their catastrophising, regardless of the worry topic (Davey & Levy, 1998b). However, although these features add to our conceptualisation of catastrophic worry and enable us to characterise the catastrophising process more clearly, it is a list of effects that does not point to a single mechanism or psychological process as being responsible for perseverative catastrophising.

In a subsequent series of studies, Startup & Davey (2001) have found that the length of bouts of catastrophic worrying can be explained in mood-as-input terms. They found that persistence in a catastrophising interview was determined both by the valence of the individual's current mood state and by the stop rules ('many as can' vs. 'feel like continuing') under which the interview was conducted. These findings provide a conceptual framework with which the catalogue of features identified by Davey & Levy (1998a) can be explained.

In their first stop rule manipulation study (Startup & Davey, 2001, experiment 2), groups of high and low worriers (defined in terms of a tertile split on PSWQ scores) performed one of two brainstorming tasks, differing only according to task valence. Participants were required to generate reasons why 'being the manager of a small hotel would be a good (or bad) thing'. Half of the participants were instructed to continue until they had 'generated as many reasons as they could' and they other half 'just as long as they felt like continuing'. Measures of state (as measured by 100-point visual analogue scales) and trait mood (as measured by the POMS) were also recorded. Results indicated that worriers were in a more inherent state and trait negative mood and that overall item generation was a function of worry status and stop rule condition. Under an 'as many as can' stop rule, worriers generated significantly more items than non-worriers, and under 'feel like continuing' stop rules, worriers generated significantly fewer items than non-worriers.

In their second experiment, Startup & Davey required worriers and non-worriers to catastrophise a hypothetical worry (being the Statue of Liberty)

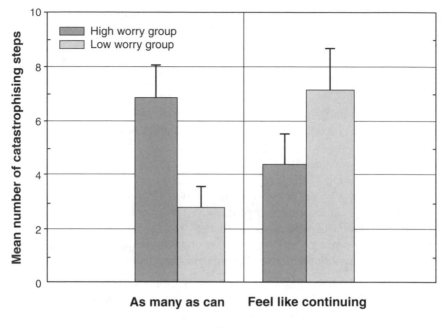

Figure 5.5   Mean (and SEM) number of catastrophising steps generated by high and low worriers within the two stop rule conditions. Adapted from Startup & Davey (2001)

under one of two stop rule conditions—either until they had 'reached the goal of sufficiently exploring their worry' or for 'as long as they felt like continuing with the interview'. Results indicated that high worriers generated significantly more steps than low worriers following an 'as many as can' stop rule but non-significantly fewer than low worriers following a 'feel like continuing' stop rule (see Figure 5.5).

These results indicated that the degree to which worriers would persist at any iterative task (whether it was a catastrophising task or not) was dependent on the configuration between their current mood state and the stop rules specified for the task. When these were systematically manipulated, worriers could be made to persist *less* than non-worriers during a catastrophising interview. These findings suggest that perseverative catastrophising is neither a function of the systematic processing of mood (such as a simple mood-congruency effect, e.g. Vasey & Borkovec, 1992), nor of a single dispositional feature of worriers (such as a generalised perseverative iterative style, e.g. Davey & Levy, 1998a), but is the result of the heuristic processing of mood within the context of the rules specified for the task (i.e. a mood-as-input explanation).

Responsibility and Perseveration—a Potential Mediating Variable

Although the mood-as-input hypothesis offers a useful explanatory framework for the patterns of perseveration exhibited by analogue catastrophic worriers and OC checkers, what remains to be elucidated are the mediating variables that lead these individuals to adopt an 'as many as can' stop rule during perseverative activities/tasks. In an earlier section, features of high trait worriers and of OCD sufferers were presented to specify reasons why these individuals might employ an 'as many as can' stop rule. One potential mediating variable, common to both worry and obsessive checking, is features of responsibility (Rachman, 1998; Salkovskis, 1985; Wells & Papageorgiou, 1998).

Whether features of responsibility *per se* engender the adoption of an 'as many as can' stop rule has been tested empirically by Startup & Davey (2002). Positive, negative and neutral moods were successfully induced in separate groups of analogue participants. Half of the participants in each mood condition were then required to catastrophise a hypothetical worry (a good friend suffering from dyslexia) under one of two responsibility conditions (high or low). High responsibility was induced by informing participants that their personal responses (from the catastrophising interview) might be used to compile a booklet for public distribution, the results of which could influence the budget received by dyslexic students. Low responsibility was induced by informing participants that their responses were of no real importance beyond the purposes of the experiment. The results indicated that the tendency to generate catastrophising steps for a hypothetical scenario was a function of mood state and perceived responsibility. Following the manipulation of high responsibility, individuals in an induced negative mood generated significantly more catastrophising steps than individuals in an induced positive mood and neutral mood. In contrast, following manipulations of low responsibility, individuals induced into a positive mood generated significantly more catastrophising steps than individuals in a neutral mood and non-significantly more than individuals induced into a negative mood (see Figure 5.6).

This finding that responsibility could lead to the adoption of an 'as many as can' stop rule has two implications: (a) there may be common variables (such as features of responsibility) across psychopathologies that might in part explain perseveration in terms of general rather than disorder-specific

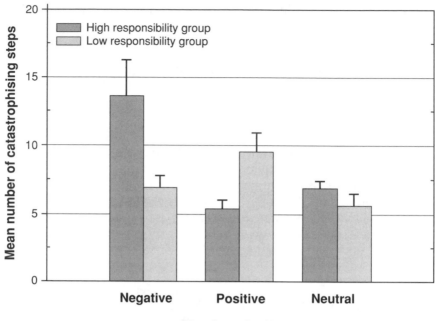

Figure 5.6   Mean (and SEM) number of catastrophising steps generated by high and low responsibility participants within the three mood conditions. Adapted from Startup & Davey 2002 (submitted)

phenomena; and (b) The adoption of an 'as many as can' stop rule may not be an inherent characteristic of the individual, but can be regarded as a state rather than trait factor. That is, situational variables such as variations in the degree of responsibility imposed by the situation may in themselves engender the adoption of a 'many as can' stop rule.

CONCLUSIONS AND IMPLICATIONS

The research discussed in this chapter has many implications for our understanding of perseverative psychopathology in a general sense:

1. Repetitive thinking about negative consequences of anxiety-evoking events can enhance subjective and physiological anxiety to subsequent encounters with that event in anxious individuals.
2. This form of rumination also leads to catastrophic iterative thinking. Important for OCD is that this evidence supports the idea that obsessions and ruminations do lead to anxiety.

3. Particular configurations of mood and task stop rule have been shown to consistently generate perseverative responding in analogue psychopathology tasks. This mood-as-input explanation provides a more parsimonious explanation of perseveration than explanations couched either in mood congruency terms (Davey & Levy, 1998a; Startup & Davey, 2001), or in terms of the individual having a generalised iterative or obsessive tendency.

4. Importantly, the mood-as-input hypothesis provides a mechanism by which known influential variables (such as responsibility) may have their effect. This moves beyond merely stating *what* variables are influential and offers a suggestion as to *how* these variables might exert their influence on perseveration.

5. The mood-as-input hypothesis also suggests that perseverative responding may not be an inherent characteristic of the individual, but can be manipulated using appropriate combinations of stop rules and mood.

6. So far we have focused on a conceptualisation of negative mood and 'as many as can' stop rules. It is clear that there are other combinations of mood and stop rule that will also generate perseveration. One of these is the combination of positive mood and a 'feel like continuing' stop rule (see Figures 5.1, 5.2 and 5.3 for examples of this). Such a combination may play a role in many addictive psychopathologies, such as alcoholism and bulimia. The present discussion has focused on a conceptualisation of perseverative responding in terms of the adoption of an 'as many as can' stop rule in conjunction with negative mood. What begs further research is the possibility that a positive mood in conjunction with a 'feel like continuing' stop rule may be more than just a suitable control condition, but may actually generate psychopathology in its own right.

Chapter 6

PERSONALITY AND INDIVIDUAL DIFFERENCES IN OCD

Alison M. Macdonald

INTRODUCTION

Current cognitive behavioural theories regard intrusive thoughts, impulses, images and doubts as 'an integral part of normal everyday experiences' (Salkovskis et al., 1998b). Evidence provided by a number of studies (Rachman & de Silva, 1978; Salkovskis & Harrison, 1984) indicates that some 98% of people experience a range of intrusive obsessional thoughts. It is less common to experience distress associated with these occurrences. When this does happen, and when efforts are made to neutralise the discomfort that arises, rituals, compulsions and obsessive patterns of thinking may develop and reach a level of interference with normal psychological functioning such that the person may be said to have obsessive-compulsive disorder (OCD) (see further, Chapters 1 and 4).

So why do some people develop OCD and not others? Why are obsessional thoughts, images and impulses so problematic for some people and yet not for others? Is there an inherited or genetic difference leading to vulnerability to OCD or does it result from some kind of environmental damage or disease process that affects the brain or other physiological functioning? On the other hand, is there some early developmental pattern of learning, perhaps common to members of a family, or some specific critical incident that leads to vulnerability or to the onset of OCD? Individual differences research has attempted to address some of these questions through a variety of methods. In the present chapter some of the findings will be reviewed and discussed.

Obsessive-Compulsive Disorder: Theory, Research and Treatment.
Edited by Ross G. Menzies and Padmal de Silva. © 2003 John Wiley & Sons, Ltd.

OBSESSIONAL PERSONALITY—HISTORICAL CONTEXT AND RELATIONSHIP TO OCD

One consistent thread in the literature on obsessionality over the last 100 years is that of the relationship between obsessional personality and OCD (see also Chapter 1). Many clinicians have viewed OCD as the result of breakdown in a vulnerable predisposed personality. The traits that form the obsessional personality have been variously described (Sandler & Hazari, 1960) and investigations have been conducted into the extent to which these traits are causal and overlap with OCD (Pollak, 1987).

The obsessional personality was originally a simple description of pre-morbid personality traits that supposedly occur in people with OCD. This restricted usage loosened and the term came to be applied, in common usage, to describe people displaying just a single characteristic, such as a concern for order. The term has subsequently become interchangeable with the psychoanalytic concept of anal–erotic character (see below), which did not originally imply a predisposition to OCD or obsessional symptomatology but was used to describe a particular character type that could function well.

According to Ingram (1961a), 'obsessional personality exists; it can be defined provisionally as what psychiatrists say it is'. Ingram was referring to the convergence of definitions in a number of textbooks of psychiatry available at the time. The consensus view prevailed that a cluster of traits observed in the premorbid personality of obsessional patients constituted the 'obsessional personality', as had been described by Kraepelin and by Janet (Pitman, 1984). Both Janet's and Freud's followers (Fenichel, 1946) saw the premorbid obsessional personality as a necessary and sufficient cause of OCD.

The obsessional traits included 'excessive cleanliness, orderliness, pedantry, conscientiousness, uncertainty, inconclusive ways of thinking and acting . . . a fondness for collecting things, including money' (Lewis, 1938). The psychoanalytic view of anal–erotic character is a 'triad of characteristics which are almost always to be found together—orderliness, parsimoniousness and obstinacy' (Freud, 1908). Ingram (1961a) further observed that the primary difference between these definitions of obsessional personality was in differences of emphasis in the language used, and in the elaboration of the theory of anal–eroticism as linked to infant bowel functions and toilet training. A number of studies have failed to demonstrate such links (reviewed by Pollak, 1979). Even if these could be shown, they could be interpreted as functions of childhood training in general as subject to the rigid, obsessional practices of a parent rather than due to specific repressive toilet training (Carr, 1974).

Nevertheless, the so-called obsessional personality became viewed as a precursor to the development of OCD. Lewis (1936) noted that while many patients with OCD did indeed show such traits, it was easy to confuse them with symptoms and, pre-empting more recent research, suggested that 'They are . . . just as commonly found among patients who never have an obsessional neurosis but who get an agitated melancholia . . . The traits are also, of course, common among healthy people. They are, conversely, sometimes undiscoverable in the previous personality of patients who now have a severe obsessional neurosis'. Lewis (1936) held the view that at least two different types of clusters of traits were characteristic of the premorbid personality of OCD sufferers, and moreover that such traits were not wholly maladaptive. He cites Samuel Johnson as an example of the 'obstinate, morose, irritable' obsessional and Charles Darwin as a 'vacillating, uncertain . . . submissive' obsessional. Both men substantially contributed to their chosen fields, and their 'obsessional' traits, which in both were resisted and periodically caused great distress, may have contributed to their success. Certainly, neither man failed to complete his great work.

Ingram (1961b) observed that, of 31 patients with severe OCD, not only did the majority (19) fit neither of Lewis' descriptions, but also they did not differ from other patients in the extent to which the character types were found. Further, only 32% of the OCD patients showed marked premorbid obsessional traits (more than five of the seven that Lewis, 1938, proposed) while 13% had none. The necessary and sufficient link between so-called obsessional personality and OCD is not substantiated, as others have repeatedly shown (Pollak, 1987; Rachman & Hodgson, 1980), albeit with the odd dissenters (Tallis et al., 1996).

The cognitive approach to OCD provides a different view of what earlier writers might have called 'obsessional personality'. In discussing the development of an overdeveloped sense of responsibility, Salkovskis et al. (1999) suggest that 'people suffering from obsessional problems appear to have an *enduring tendency* to make negative interpretations of intrusions . . . . *pre-existing general assumptions and beliefs* concerning such responsibility may be the basis of such tendencies' (italics added). They examine a number of factors that may predispose people to obsessional thinking and behaviour by leading them to formulate general assumptions and beliefs that increase their sense of responsibility. In the main, these derive either from childhood experiences of parents or other authority figures, or from critical incidents that influence learning (see further Chapter 4).

Alongside the development of cognitive models of OCD, individual difference research has begun to examine the correlation of phenomena such as responsibility and perfectionism with OC symptoms, primarily in nonclinical populations. Scarrabelotti et al. (1995) found that responsibility, together with Eysenckian N, predicted discomfort from OCs after controlling for mood, while Rhéaume et al. (2000) found that responsibility and perfectionism moderately correlate with OC tendencies, both seeming to be important. Bhar & Kyrios (1999) also found perfectionism to be related to OC phenomena. In each of these studies correlations are modest and no 'all-or-none' phenomena are present, indicating heterogeneous routes to susceptibility, an area in need of further research.

INDIVIDUAL DIFFERENCES IN OCD—THE SEARCH FOR A CAUSE

The findings that obsessions and compulsions are common in non-clinical populations (Rachman & de Silva, 1978; Salkovskis & Harrison, 1984), and that they differ from those in OCD mainly in frequency, intensity and consequences, rather than in form and content (Rachman & Hodgson, 1980), are at odds with a purely medical model of OCD as a disorder clearly separable from 'normal' healthy functioning. A number of studies have examined biological aspects of OCD, most recently using techniques of brain scanning, such as proton emission tomography (PET) and magnetic resonance imaging (MRI), and some have suggested the presence of abnormalities (see further, Chapter 3; McGuire, 1995). There have been no clear, and replicated, demonstrations of any such factors being implicated in the aetiology, either as all-or-none factors or with a major contributory role. Salkovskis (1996d) discusses the problems of such research and considers that most observations of differences in brain structure and function may equally be seen as secondary to obsessions and compulsions, i.e. they may be a consequence rather than a cause.

There have been many studies conducted that have addressed the idea that there is an inherited vulnerability to OCD. It is usually accepted that if a disorder clusters in the relatives of index cases, there is likely to be some familial, and possibly some genetic factor, in the aetiology. Twin, family and adoption studies are the traditional methods used (see Neale & Cardon, 1992; Sham, 1998). There are no adoption studies of OCD to date, but twin and family studies have been reported and are reviewed in the following sections. Some twin studies also examine the relationship of obsessional phenomena to anxious and depressive symptoms in nonclinical populations of twins. Twin and family studies can show whether or not there is a possible involvement of genetic factors, but not identify what genes may be involved. Over the last 5 years techniques of molecular genetics have begun to be applied to OCD, in attempts to demonstrate or to exclude the involvement of specific genes in the aetiology of OCD. In the main these studies focus on genes involved in two neurotransmitter pathways, serotonin and dopamine, and results from some of these studies and their implications for psychological theory and practice are discussed.

FAMILY STUDIES OF OBSESSIVE-COMPULSIVE DISORDER (OCD)

The interest in an inherited vulnerability to OCD has led a number of investigators to study the relatives of obsessional patients with regard to rates of OCD, as well as the occurrence of subclinical obsessional symptoms and obsessional personality traits which might be regarded as milder forms of expression of a common underlying liability. Early studies predated the use of structured interviews and diagnostic criteria. As a consequence, most involve non-blind diagnoses of relatives, often based on reports rather than direct interviews, and these have been reviewed and discussed extensively elsewhere (Carey & Gottesman, 1981; Macdonald et al., 1991). Across these early studies, rates of obsessional neurosis seemed to occur in 4.6–10% of parents of cases (a perhaps surprising level of agreement, considering the varying nature of the studies and methods used). Far more widely ranging assessments of the frequency of obsessional personality traits are found (3.3–37%). Broadly speaking, it seemed that rates of OCD and obsessionality were high in relatives of index cases, especially when compared with estimated prevalence rates for OCD available at this time, of around 0.05% (Woodruff & Pitts, 1964). More recent population-based epidemiological studies suggest higher rates (0.7–3%; Bebbington, 1998; Karno et al., 1988; see further, Chapter 1) but the familial rates are still higher.

More recent studies have used diagnostic criteria for both the index cases and assessment of relatives and so results are more readily comparable (Table 6.1). McKeon & Murray (1987) found rather different results from those of earlier reports. 0.7% of relatives of both OCD cases and controls were found to have OCD (just one relative in each group). In this, the first study in which relatives were systematically examined for other operationally defined diagnoses, the relatives of OCD cases were found to have high rates of neurotic disorders in general. McKeon & Murray (1987) found significantly more psychopathology among index relatives as compared with control relatives, largely accounted for by anxious, phobic and depressive disorders.

Black et al. (1992) conducted a family interview study with 32 probands with OCD recruited from a drug trial and a psychiatric clinic, together with 33 controls and their families. First-degree relatives were interviewed using the Diagnostic Interview Schedule (DIS) and comparable rates of OCD were found in both proband (2.5%) and control (2.3%) relatives. Few

Table 6.1 Family studies of obsessive-compulsive disorder*

Study	No. of index cases	Controls (n)	Type of relatives	Rates in relatives (%) (rates in relatives of controls)		
				OCD	Obsessive traits/personality	Any abnormality
McKeon & Murray (1987)	50	GP attenders (50)	All first-degree	0.7 (0.7)		27.5 (13.9)
Black et al. (1992)	32	33	120 First-degree (129)	2.5 (2.3)	18.0 (12.9)	54.2 (48.8)
			Parents		15.6 (2.9)	
			Sibs		20.4 (19.0)	
Bellodi et al. (1992)	92	None	370 First-degree	2.9–3.4		19.7–25.7
			Parents	3.0–3.4		
			Sibs	4.2–4.7		
Pauls et al. (1995)	100	33	466 First-degree (113)	10.3 (19)	18.2 (4.0)	
Nestadt et al. (2000)	80	73	343 First-degree (300)	11.7 (2.7)	10.4–24.8	
				Odds ratio 4.7	(2.4–12.2)	

*Studies shown are those since 1987; earlier studies are included in previous reviews (see e.g. Carey & Gottesman, 1981; Macdonald et al., 1991).

differences in the prevalence of disorders were found, apart from anxiety disorders, which affected 30% of relatives of probands and 17.1% of control relatives, and thus the authors considered their results partially consistent with McKeon & Murray (1987).

Another study conducted in Italy, using a combination of family interview (DIS) and family history methods with 92 consecutive patients at a university anxiety disorders clinic (Bellodi et al., 1992), found a morbid risk of 3.4% for OCD in families. While relatively low, this was a high rate when compared with lifetime prevalence in an Italian general population study of 0.72% (Faravelli et al., 1989).

The problem remains that, without reliable and comparable prevalence rates for OCD and obsessional personality in the general population or in a well-chosen large control sample, the figures obtained from assessment of relatives cannot be related to any particular genetic model. Carey et al. (1980) have shown how the widely varying assessments of prevalence rates for neurosis in the general population have dramatic effects on the results of quantitative analysis of familiality. For the relatively rare OCD, with prevalences differing between 0.01% and 2.5% in a range of studies examined, analysis using the 2.3% rate in siblings found in one family study (Rüdin, 1953) led to an estimation of sibling correlation for liability to OCD of between −0.02 and 0.51, with correspondingly wide-ranging estimates of heritability. In other words, depending on the prevalence rate used in comparison with the observed rate in relatives, OCD may appear to be either totally non-familial or entirely familial!

Thus, family studies conducted in the 1980s and early 1990s failed to support a strong familial component to OCD specifically, and pointed instead at a broad spectrum of anxiety disorders as familial, and hence possibly to a less specific inherited vulnerability. The two most recently reported family studies seem to provide data that contradict this view.

Pauls et al. (1995) examined relatives of 100 probands with DSM-IIIR OCD diagnoses recruited through specialist clinics, and treatment studies found a 10.3% rate of OCD in the first-degree relatives (by DIS interview and family history method), compared with 1.9% in control relatives. When a 'subthreshold' form of OCD was included, combined rates rose to 18.2% in relatives of probands and 4.0% in controls.

That this study should find rates that compare with those for 'obsessional traits' even in earlier studies must lead to examination of the sample and methods. The authors note that if they used only direct interview information, the rate of OCD in relatives would drop to 6.5%. Also, 82% of Pauls et al.'s probands had onsets before age 18, while in that of Bellodi et al.

(for example) the mean age of onset was over 20 years. Examination of the data provides some support for heterogeneity—rates of OCD being much higher among relatives of early onset cases than among those of probands with later onset. However, the recruitment of probands through a clinic specialising in OCD, the use of a small comparison group and the fact that only 39% of relatives were directly interviewed are considerable caveats to interpretation of this study as support for a specific genetic diathesis.

The most recent study of familiarity of OCD (Nestadt et al., 2000) compared 343 first-degree relatives of 80 probands recruited through specialty OCD clinics with 300 relatives of 73 matched non-OCD controls identified by random digit dialling. In this study, where 71% of relatives were directly interviewed using structured interviews and blind ratings, lifetime prevalence of OCD was 4.7 times higher in relatives of probands with OCD than control relatives, whose rates were comparable to population-based studies (Bebbington, 1998; Karno et al., 1988). Rates for obsessions and compulsions were also higher, but no details of other anxiety and mood disorders were given. The authors suggest that their findings indicate OCD is familial, a necessary but not sufficient condition for genetic aetiology, and recommend using molecular genetic approaches to identify 'a genetic aetiology for OCD'.

A number of interesting issues arise in this study. All the probands were cases in treatment in specialist clinics. The authors note that although cases and controls were matched for education, age, etc., the cases were less likely to ever have been married, or to have had children even if married, a common finding in studies of people with hospital-treated OCD (Macdonald, 1996). They also found that 90% of their cases had onset of symptoms by age 17 (75% by 14) and there were no cases of OCD in relatives of cases with an onset after age 17. These factors suggest that the case sample were people with an early onset and chronic morbidity. Treatment for OCD in recent years has become more readily available through both primary care and self-help groups and manuals. Stoll et al. (1992) showed that rates of diagnosis of OCD increased during the 1980s, when effective drug and behavioural treatments became available. People who find their way to specialist centres nowadays are likely to be more severely affected, as perhaps they might have been years ago when effective treatments were not available, and so only people with severely limiting OCD reached the attention of clinicians. It may also be that these people have a stronger biological or genetic vulnerability.

These issues are complex, resting on the categorisation of OCD within the medical model vs. the dimensional view of OCD commonly taken in psychological studies, as well as on epidemiological factors other than the presence or absence of a diagnosis. One recent study (Leckman et al., 1997) factor-analysed symptom clusters in OCD patients and extracted four factors (obsessions and checking, symmetry and ordering, cleanliness and washing, and hoarding) that bear strong parallels to non-clinical statistically derived clusters of OCs (e.g. Sanavio, 1988). They concluded that OCD is a multidimensional and heterogeneous condition and that genetic studies would do well to examine these factors.

TWIN STUDIES OF OBSESSIVE-COMPULSIVE DISORDER

Adoption and twin studies may be used to tease apart the effects of heredity and environment. The comparison of biologically related individuals with different proportions of shared genes, such as monozygotic (MZ) and dizygotic (DZ) twins or singleton sibling pairs, permits partition of the total variation into proportions of liability due to genetic and environmental factors. Relatives may be reared together or in adoptive families (adopted singletons and reared-apart twins). In adoption studies shared environmental factors are excluded from the correlations in liability and more accurate estimates of heritability can be made. Although adoption studies have not proved feasible in OCD, twins have been examined for this disorder.

Case Reports

Many reports of twins with OCD are based on one or two cases. Inouye (1972) provided a headcount of 27 concordant and eight discordant MZ pairs, against zero concordant and seven discordant DZ pairs in the literature. This had increased to 30 concordant and 13 discordant MZ pairs and zero concordant but 14 discordant DZ twin pairs in the world literature by the time of Carey's (1978) review. Most of these pairs have been discussed extensively by previous reviewers (Black, 1974; Carey & Gottesman, 1981; Emmelkamp, 1983).

OCD was thought to be a rare disorder. Some authors of OCD twin case reports (Marks et al., 1969; Woodruff & Pitts, 1964) have used the justification that on the basis of a 0.05% prevalence rate, the chance of finding a pair of concordant MZ adult twins would be one in 600–800 million if OCD arose independently in each co-twin, rather than due to some combination of shared genetic and environmental factors. Using Karno et al.'s (1988) maximum prevalence rate for OCD increases the probability of finding MZ twins concordant by chance to around one in 200,000. Rachman & Hodgson (1980) have argued that concordance is not only 'not random', but in such a rare disorder bias will inevitably occur in 'the se-lection, assessment and diagnosis of co-twins of monozygotic obsessional patients'. Other reviewers (Black, 1974; Emmelkamp, 1983) have not con-sidered the evidence to be sufficient, or sufficiently good, on the basis of early case reports to assess the contribution of genetic factors to OCD in MZ twins.

It has long been recognised that case reports are inadequate. Lewis (1936) noted that ' . . . a striking concordance in one or two pairs of monozygotic twins proves nothing: one needs a series and a control group of fraternal twins'. Nevertheless, when a disorder is apparently rare, often the only reports that prove feasible concern occasional pairs.

Table 6.2 shows the continuing addition of case reports to the literature. These continue frequently to cite the probabilities calculated by Marks et al. (1969) as a rationale, which is misleading, particularly as calculation of this figure was based on an erroneous transcription (Macdonald, 1996).

The quality of case reports is so variable that further discussion of those already done will serve to clarify the difficulties of conducting twin stud-ies of OCD and to indicate a 'good standard'. There does seem to be a common thread of authors following the trends of the times and report-ing only those details considered currently interesting. Older reports seem anecdotal and often lack rigorous diagnosis and zygosity testing but con-tain detailed descriptions of parenting and phenomenology. Recent ones focus on 'biological' measures and fail to report much about the familial background and 'non-genetic' details that might in part account for twin similarity. A number of the pairs in the literature are from a series of con-secutive admissions to the Maudsley Hospital in London, UK, and these are shown separately in the table. Some of these pairs have also been the subject of earlier case reports on Maudsley twins with OCD (Carey, 1978; Carey & Gottesman, 1981; Macdonald & Murray, 1989; Marks et al., 1969; Parker, 1964).

Tarsh (1978) has reported a concordant opposite sex DZ pair; the male twin suffered from obsessional ruminations about his sperm leaking and contaminating others, and developed checking and cleaning rituals, while his sister was said to ruminate about her physical appearance and checked her ribs. Both became depressed and both were given leucotomies in their early 20s. Hoaken & Schnurr (1980) described a discordant MZ pair. The twins (reported at age 20) had certainly not passed through the age of risk, and cannot therefore be described as definitely discordant. Furthermore, the proband's diagnosis is questionable in the light of possible organic complications and a lack of resistance to compulsions, which were largely ego-syntonic.

Table 6.2   Twin studies of OCD

Twin study	n, Sex and zygosity	Concordant or discordant	Comments
Case reports			
Tarsh (1978)	1 OSDZ	Concordant	Concordant for leucotomy
Hoaken & Schnurr (1980)	1 MZF	Discordant	Reported at age 20. No resistance, possible brainstem seizures
Mahgoub et al. (1988)	1 MZM	Concordant	Discordant for epilepsy. Minor symptoms in non-epileptic co-twin
Kim et al. (1990b)	1 MZF	Concordant	
Case reports of twins from the Maudsley Hospital			
McGuffin & Mawson (1980)	2 MZF	Concordant	
McKeon et al (1984)	1 MZM	Discordant	Onset following head injury
Lewis et al. (1991)	3 MZM	Concordant	Two pairs from previous reports, all discordant for schizophrenia
Series of twins			
Torgersen (1983)	3 MZ 9 DZ	Discordant	Part population-based. 1 MZ and 1 DZ co-twin had anxiety disorder (not OCD)
Andrews et al. (1990)	13 MZF 14 DZF 5 MZM 6 DZM 10 OSDZ	Discordant	Population-based. Four MZ and 11 DZ co-twins had other neurotic diagnoses, often multiple, but no OCD

There have been two additional recent case reports. Mahgoub et al. (1988) report a pair of Muslim MZ male twins said to be concordant for OCD. The twins were very close and the first-born, affected by grand mal epilepsy from age 5, experienced obsessions and compulsions from age 10 that came to psychiatric attention at age 24. These included obsessions and compulsions relating to cleanliness and prayers that form part of the Muslim religious rituals, but in his case caused some slowness that irritated his family. The co-twin, who knew of the other's problems and teased him for it, was said to have developed obsessions and compulsions at age 13. His problems were obsessive fears of disasters befalling his co-twin whenever they were apart, which was said to be infrequently. There were also some other obsessions and compulsions, similar to those of his co-twin, but less functionally intrusive.

Kim et al. (1990b) report a pair of MZ females concordant for OCD involving checking rituals and obsessional doubting, which caused subjective distress and led them to leave their jobs. There is little information given about the twins' backgrounds, but they seem to have married at a similar age and live nearby each other, so presumably remain in close contact. As Rachman & Hodgson (1980) concluded two decades ago, it is difficult to draw conclusions from the case reports, even where zygosity diagnosis is good and diagnostic details better, that such concordance might be 'genetic'. These newer cases appear simply to confirm the bias in reporting of MZ (three out of four when the expectation from birth rates for twins would be about one in three) and apparently concordant (three out of four) pairs, and the tendency to report this even where the co-twin (as in Mahgoub et al., 1988) is unlikely to have been considered alone to have any serious problems. None of the studies mention a 'twin effect', i.e. the influence that symptoms of one twin might have on the other, although they do sometimes note suggestive details like fears of disasters befalling a co-twin, which are regarded as obsessional rather than twin-specific.

Series of Twins with OCD

There have been few systematic studies of series of obsessional twins. Ascertainment would usually be through consecutive admissions to a hospital or other treatment facility, or through population- or other register-based screening. Reports of small series of twins prior to the use of diagnostic criteria have been reviewed elsewhere (Carey & Gottesman, 1981; Macdonald et al., 1991). In most cases, like the family studies of the same time, diagnoses in early reports are unreliable. Additionally the reported ratios of MZ and DZ twins suggest sampling biases and doubtful zygosity diagnosis. Carey & Gottesman (1981) reported 15 pairs of MZ twins and 15 pairs of DZ twins, ascertained through consecutive admissions of index cases to the Maudsley Hospital, and including some pairs previously reported (Marks et al., 1969; Parker, 1964), as well as those examined in more detail in Carey (1978). 33% of MZ co-twins had psychiatric or general practitioner treatment involving obsessional symptoms vs. 7% of DZ co-twins. Obsessional symptoms with or without treatment were observed in 87% of MZ co-twins and 47% of DZ co-twins. Unfortunately, no further analyses of these carefully collected data (and reliable diagnosis of zygosity), which include questionnaire measures of obsessionality and other traits, seem to have been published. This remains the only published study of a systematically ascertained series of twins where index cases had received hospital treatment for OCD. More recently published reports of series of twins are summarised in Table 6.2. Torgersen (1983) investigated three MZ and nine DZ twin pairs from the Norwegian population-based twin registry; in each case at least one twin had a diagnosis of OCD, and he found none of them to be concordant for OCD. One MZ co-twin was diagnosed agoraphobic (without panic) and one DZ co-twin had GAD; three other DZ co-twins had diagnoses of somatoform, conversion and pain disorder.

Andrews et al. (1990) report interviews with 446 pairs of adult twins from the Australian twin registry. The twins were interviewed using an interview scored according to the Diagnostic Interview Schedule (DIS; Robins et al., 1981) items and so the study is comparable with the large Epidemiological Catchment Area Study (ECA; Karno et al., 1988). The report provides information on six subtypes of neurotic disorder in twins, including OCD; 48 persons were found to meet criteria for OCD, an extraordinarily high prevalence rate of 5.4%. However, while 15 of these cases were from twin pairs concordant for a broad range of neurotic diagnoses (depression, dysthymia, social phobia, panic/agoraphobia, GAD) in not one case did a co-twin have a diagnosis of OCD. Information is not given about obsessions and compulsions separately but, as 7% of females and 3.4% of males overall were affected, the study seems, like the ECA study, to be picking up something different in the general population from the clinically defined OCD, or current DSM- or ICD-diagnosed cases.

It is thus of interest that the only two series of twins collected from population-based sources and rated according to diagnostic criteria, found no concordant pairs at all among the 60 pairs where one twin was said to have OCD. The co-twins did have other neurotic, especially anxiety, diagnoses, which is in keeping with the results from those family studies of OCD where the broader spectrum of anxiety disorders have been reported (Table 6.1). It also reflects observations made by Torgersen (1987) that concordance rates for twins seem to increase depending on sampling source—population based studies will have lower rates than primary care, with psychiatric hospital-based ascertainment of twins giving the highest rates.

MOLECULAR GENETIC STUDIES OF OCD

Since the mid-1990s a large number of molecular genetic studies of OCD have been reported, of which space prevents an extensive review. The search for specific genes for OCD has focused on genes involved in two neurotransmitter systems that have been hypothesised to be involved in OCD. Although there is some evidence of genetic influences on OCD, as described earlier in this chapter, little is known about the mode of inheritance beyond a likelihood that it is probably complex, and involving a number of genes of small effect interacting with environmental agents.

Some serotonergic reuptake inhibiting drugs (SSRIs) show selective anti-obsessional efficacy, leading to a hypothesis that there may be serotonergic (5HT) dysfunction of some kind in OCD. An alternative hypothesis is for the involvement of the dopamine system (DA), based on the 30–40% non-response of OCD sufferers to SSRIs, animal models of compulsive behaviour induced by dopaminergic agents, and drugs such as clomipramine and fluoxetine that have some efficacy in OCD and display antidopaminergic activity. Most molecular genetic studies examine associations between the frequency of particular alleles and OCD as compared with non-OCD controls, or use a family design of OCD cases and their parents to test for so-called linkage disequilibrium. This occurs when the usual chance transmission rate of an allele from a heterozygous parent to a child of 50% is found to be deviated from significantly, and suggests association of the allele and OCD.

While there are considerable numbers of negative reports (non-association) for genes in both 5HT and DA systems, a few studies now report positive findings. Bengel et al. (1999) reported an association of a functional polymorphism in the region of the 5HT transporter gene (5HTT) and OCD, where OCD patients were more than twice as likely to have two copies of a particular allele than controls. Another study of this region has shown a familial association between OCD and a functional polymorphism of the serotonin transporter (McDougle et al., 1998). Hanna et al. (1998) have found some relationship between blood levels of 5-HT in relatives of children with OCD and their 5-HTT genotypes.

Studies of the DA system show a similar pattern of negative reports of associations, as well as some positive findings that disappear after statistical corrections are made for multiple analyses (Billett et al., 1997). Some studies of genes for catechol-O-methyltransferase (COMT) and monoaminoxidase-A (MAOA) have reported familial associations with OCD, but with differing results in men and women (Karayiorgou et al., 1999), suggesting different genetic influences between the sexes.

Overall these studies are in their infancy, and results do not indicate any 'all or none' effects, which will probably be of little surprise to psychologists familiar with the heterogeneous presentations of OCD and wide-ranging individual differences in phenomenology, onset, chronicity and response to treatment. General reviews of this field conclude 'no significant linkage findings, although the search has included many neurologically relevant genes' (Alsobrook & Pauls, 1997).

QUANTITATIVE GENETIC STUDIES OF OBSESSIONALITY AS A COMPLEX DIMENSIONAL TRAIT

Twin and family studies of OCD rely on the assumption that the attainment of the diagnostic category of OCD (by people with a sufficient number and severity of symptoms to meet the relevant diagnostic criteria) is through passing a threshold on an underlying continuous distribution of liability (Falconer, 1965). An alternative approach to exploring the genetics of obsessionality is by assessment of obsessional complaint or symptom scores in a sample of twins unselected for OCD comparable to other individual differences research in OCD on non-clinical samples. In such a sample the application of biometrical genetic analyses (Neale & Cardon, 1992) is possible. Instead of relating diagnoses of OCD to thresholds on a hypothesised liability distribution, we may hypothesise that a score obtained from the reported number and severity of obsessional symptoms provides a more direct index of a continuously distributed liability to obsessionality. Such analyses are also theoretically possible in a diagnostic study of a complete population sample of twins, but this would require sampling very large numbers of twins to ascertain sufficient affected pairs and has not been attempted as yet.

In the study of neurotic disorders and traits in general, twin studies of the relationship between symptoms of anxiety and depression and the neuroticism personality dimension have been published in the last few years. These use increasingly sophisticated techniques that have become more accessible as computer technology has improved (Neale & Cardon, 1992). For obsessionality specifically, Clifford (1982) and Clifford et al. (1984) began to explore the relationship of obsessionality and neuroticism, work that has been expanded by Macdonald (1996).

Clifford (1982) and Clifford et al. (1984) examined the relationship between obsessionality and neuroticism as measured by the 42-item version of the Leyton Obsessional Inventory (LOI) and the Eysenck Personality Questionnaire (EPQ), in 419 pairs of adult volunteer twins. Using a maximum likelihood method on the between- and within-pair mean squares derived from the analysis of variance of the twins' scores on the LOI, Clifford et al. observed that the heritability estimates for trait and symptom scales of the LOI were so similar (47% and 44%, respectively) that they might both be measuring an underlying neurosis variable, so they examined the relationship of the scores on the LOI to the same twins' responses to the EPQ N score. (A more logical and parsimonious explanation for this observation is that, as the division of the LOI items into 'trait' and 'symptom' scores is essentially arbitrary, it is likely that both scores reflect a single dimension of obsessionality, hence the similar heritability estimates.)

Examination of the factor structure of the twin resemblance on the LOI and EPQN suggested two genetic factors. One factor was influencing a 'neuroticism' trait and accounted for a large part of the correlation between EPQN scores and LOI symptom scores, and an additional independent factor related to obsessional traits like 'incompleteness', 'checking' and, to an extent, 'cleanliness'. The influence of heredity, or 'h', on twin resemblance was greater than that of the environment, and the latter showed an absence of general factors and, in particular, of any noticeable effect from the non-genetic shared environment, or 'c2'.

This study also attempted further analysis of obsessionality by using four subscale scores from the brief LOI, and reflecting 'incompleteness', 'cleanliness and tidiness', 'gloomy thoughts' and 'checking'. There were genetic contributions to all the factor scores, and in each case common environmental factors were eliminated from the models without decrement of fit. Multivariate analysis of the four factor scores with Neuroticism revealed a general genetic factor contributing to all the factor scores but most strongly to 'incompleteness', 'gloomy thoughts' and N. A second genetic factor contrasted 'incompleteness', 'checking' and 'cleanliness and tidiness' with 'gloomy thoughts' (which had a negative loading) but was independent of N. The environmental factors appeared to be more specific, with a first factor mostly contributing to 'gloomy thoughts' and 'checking', a second factor to 'incompleteness' and 'cleanliness and tidiness', both of which were largely unrelated to N, the environmental contribution to N being largely due to specific effects.

A more recent study of OCs, assessed by using the Padua Inventory (PI; Sanavio, 1988) in a large sample of like-sex female volunteer twins aged 15–75 years, indicated that there are heritable influences on obsessionality (Macdonald, 1996). 49% of the co-variance among the twins was due to additive genetic influences '(h')' and 51% to specific environmental influences unique to the individual. When the PI sub-scales ('mental activities', 'contamination', 'checking' and 'motor control') were examined separately, the heritability varied from one to another, ranging from 33% for 'motor control' to 51% for 'checking'.

When multivariate models were tested on all four subscales, there appeared to be a common additive genetic factor influencing all four scales, but to differing extents. This influence was completely correlated for 'mental activities' and 'checking'; these in turn correlated strongly (0.6) with 'contamination'. The results suggested that similarity of checking and washing behaviours was influenced by the same genetic effects as on the other aspects of obsessionality, individual differences in these sub-scales arising from specific environmental effects, which were partly similar across the two scales but mainly differed.

The influence of unique environmental factors was substantial. Unique environmental factors were only partially correlated across subscales, (between 0.2 and 0.6). It seems that the environmental factors leading to particular subtypes of obsessions and compulsions in this female sample mainly differed, while the (smaller) additive genetic factors were broadly similar. Further analyses indicated shared additive genetic influences with symptoms of anxiety and depression and EPQN, again with differing environmental effects on the different symptom measures.

CONCLUSIONS

A large number of studies have examined many aspects of the individual differences in susceptibility to develop OCD, or to experience OCs. The results of family and twin studies, often provided as clear evidence that OCD has a strongly genetic aetiology, are equivocal and strongly affected by the sampling methods (cases from the general population or specialist treatment centres). Some studies point to a shared vulnerability to OCD, depression and anxiety disorders. Work from a variety of areas points to the heterogeneity of OCD as well as OCs and these findings need to be incorporated in future research using genetic methodologies, to begin to tease apart the multidimensional nature of OCD. Molecular genetic studies could be just as susceptible to such biases through population stratification—there may be a subgroup of people with severe OCD who are more biologically vulnerable, and selection of cases with early-onset, chronic morbidity may affect these studies. This may be appropriate—identifying people with particular biological vulnerability and targeting pharmacological treatments may then be possible—but as OCs are experienced by the majority of people while only some develop OCD, and many people with OCD are no longer treated in specialist centres, the vulnerability is likely to be more complex.

Salkovskis et al. (1999) raised questions about psychological/developmental pathways to development of inflated responsibility (see further, Chapter 4) and these deserve further study, perhaps from a familial transmission perspective. From the point of view of a practitioner, a working knowledge of the studies outlined in this chapter may prove useful in aspects of psycho-education and normalising in therapeutic work with people with OCD. Understanding that there seem to be many routes to OCs, that these may be biologically influenced, but in a way that probably infers susceptibility and depends on experiences of particular environments for expression, can be useful for patients. Some clients are resistant to undertaking behavioural work or CBT because of reading about biological studies using brain scans in OCD, or who hope for a drug or surgical solution to their problems. Such people may find it helpful to understand that OCD is not a unitary problem and that there is no 'all-or-none' explanation, that in the majority of cases biological factors may provide but a small part of the susceptibility.

SECTION III

CLINICAL PRESENTATIONS AND SUBTYPES OF OCD

Chapter 7

OBSESSIVE-COMPULSIVE WASHING

Mairwen K. Jones and Annette Krochmalik

In perhaps the most cited literary example of obsessive-compulsive disorder (OCD), contamination obsessions and handwashing rituals were depicted in the seventeenth century by Shakespeare in the character of Lady Macbeth, her 'mind diseased' and more in need of the 'divine than the physician'. The performance of frequent, repetitive cleaning/washing behaviours and excessive concerns about contamination are extremely common symptoms in OCD. This chapter will review what is currently known about the nature, prevalence, origin and treatment of OCD washing.

NATURE AND PREVALENCE

Washing and contamination concerns may occur quite early in the course of the disorder. It has been suggested that fear of contamination is one of the most common obsessions in childhood OCD, and washing and cleaning behaviours are one of the most prevalent compulsions in this group (March & Leonard, 1998); for example, Swedo et al. (1989b) identified washing rituals in more than 85% of a group of 70 childhood cases of OCD.

So common are these concerns across the age spectrum that it has been suggested that the majority of OCD patients have performed excessive, compulsive washing at some point in their illness (Levenkron, 1991; Rachman & Hodgson, 1980; Rapoport, 1989; de Silva & Rachman, 1992). Rasmussen & Eisen (1992) reported that over an 8-year period, 50% of the 560 subjects they saw had contamination obsessions. More recently, Summerfeldt et al. (1997) reported that of 182 patients with OCD, 105 (57.7%) had contamination obsessions and 116 (63.7%) had washing compulsions. Finally, according to DSM-IV (APA, 1994), 'almost 50% of OCD patients are washers' (p. 420). So typical are washing concerns in the

Obsessive-Compulsive Disorder: Theory, Research and Treatment.
Edited by Ross G. Menzies and Padmal de Silva. © 2003 John Wiley & Sons, Ltd.

histories of many OCD sufferers, that it has been suggested that washing represents a distinct subtype of OCD (e.g. Leckman et al., 1997; Marks, 1987; see further, Chapters 1 and 2).

The first detailed acknowledgement of the existence of subtypes or symptom clusters within OCD can be attributed to Marks (1969). He noted that while some sufferers have thoughts about contamination and may wash compulsively, others have thoughts of fire and thus check electrical switches compulsively. Recent research has provided support for the classification of OCD into distinct subtypes. Leckman et al. (1997) found cleanliness and washing (including contamination obsessions and cleaning compulsions) as one of four symptom factors identified from factor analysis of two large independent OCD samples ($n = 208$, $n = 98$). Khanna et al. (1990) and van Oppen et al. (1995c) have also noted that washing and checking can be categorized on different dimensions. Currently, however, no OCD subtypes have been formally identified in popular classificatory systems like the Diagnostic and Statistical Manual of Mental Disorders (DSM; American Psychiatric Association). Instead, informal labels such as 'washers', 'checkers' and 'hoarders' are used in these systems to indicate an individual's dominant presenting symptomatology.

While it is generally accepted that OCD occurs in as many males as females, a higher ratio of females has been identified for the washing subtype, e.g. Stern & Cobb (1978). Analysing 307 OCD cases, Marks (1987) identified more women than men with compulsive washing (66% vs. 54%) and avoidance of contamination (47% vs. 40%). Other researchers have also identified a gender disparity for washing/cleaning concerns (e.g. Castle et al., 1995; Dowson, 1977; Khanna & Mukherjee, 1992; Noshirvani et al., 1991; Rapoport, 1989; Stern & Cobb, 1978).

It has been noted that even in cultures that are arguably less concerned with cleanliness, e.g. rural Nigeria and rural India, OCD sufferers will still experience contamination concerns and associated washing behaviours (Rapoport, 1989). Additionally, a high frequency of OCD washing has been consistently found across time (Akhtar et al., 1975; Okasha et al., 1968). However, the particular content of the obsessions experienced by OC washers may vary. When potentially life-threatening infectious diseases are dominant at a particular period in history, the primary obsessional concerns and subsequent washing rituals among OCD sufferers are said to reflect these dangers (Jenike et al., 1998a; Rachman & Hodgson, 1980). For example, it is argued that through the later part of the twentieth century, fears of HIV and cancer increased and obsessions in OCD sufferers regarding these phenomena began to appear (e.g. Bruce & Stevens, 1992; Rachman & Hodgson, 1980; see also Chapter 2).

Table 7.1   Number and type of contamination-related obsessions among a group of 44 obsessive-compulsive washers

Contamination-related obsessions	Current	Past
Concern or disgust with bodily waste or secretions (e.g. urine, faeces, saliva)	27	27
Concern with dirt or germs	27	27
Excessive concern with environmental contaminants (e.g. asbestos, radiation)	6	8
Excessive concern with household items (e.g. cleaners, solvents)	9	9
Excessive concern with animals (e.g. insects)	19	20
Bothered by sticky substances or residues	19	19
Concerned will get ill because of contaminant	13	15
Concerned will get others ill by spreading contaminant	9	9
No concern with consequences of contamination other than how it might feel	4	4

While the degree of concern with particular diseases or substances may change over time, a wide variety of substances, including toxic chemicals, poisons, radiation or heavy metals (e.g. Rasmussen & Eisen, 1992), seminal fluid, animal fur and asbestos, can feature in contamination concerns (e.g. de Silva & Rachman, 1992).

Researchers at the Sydney University Anxiety Disorders Clinic investigated the prevalence and nature of OCD concerns in a sample of 44 individuals with OCD whose washing/contamination concerns dominated their clinical picture. Krochmalik, Jones and Menzies (unpublished manuscript) examined the frequency and type of various contamination obsessions and related washing/cleaning compulsions using the symptom checklist from the Yale-Brown Obsessive-Compulsive Scale (Y-BOCS; Goodman et al., 1989a, 1989b). A summary of these findings are presented in Tables 7.1 and 7.2.

Table 7.2   Number and type of washing/cleaning compulsions amongst a group of 44 obsessive-compulsive washers

Washing/cleaning compulsions	Current	Past
Excessive or ritualised handwashing	26	26
Excessive or ritualised showering, bathing, toothbrushing, grooming or toilet routine	22	23
Involves cleaning of household items or other inanimate objects	15	16
Other measures to prevent or remove contact with contaminants	13	14

As can be seen in Table 7.1, the categories 'concern with dirt and germs' and 'concern with bodily waste or secretions' were the most common obsessions. At least 61% of the total sample of OCD washers reported concerns in each of these categories. The most frequently identified compulsive activity among this OC washer group was excessive or ritualised handwashing (59% of sample). Ritualised showering, bathing, toothbrushing, grooming or toilet routine was the second most frequently endorsed item. Follow-up interviews with these patients revealed common anxiety-provoking themes. Clients frequently mentioned that they believed certain parts of their body such as feet, hair, elbows and hands often become contaminated, since they regularly come into contact with the rest of the world. At least 30% of 20 OCD sufferers with washing/contamination concerns who presented most recently at our clinic reported that they considered their feet to be perpetually dirty or contaminated and felt the need to keep them at a distance from other parts of the body. One individual described how she would open doors with her feet rather than her hands since she believed her feet were already 'germ-ridden'. This behaviour enabled her to avoid touching door handles with her relatively clean hands, thus avoiding compulsive handwashing. Another individual described never sitting on, or picking up anything from the floor because 'feet have been there'. A number of others stated that they never washed their feet because they were too dirty to touch. Clearly it appears that a preoccupation with feet is a significant concern for a substantial number of individuals with OCD who display contamination fears and washing behaviours. This theme has also been noted by other clinicians (e.g. de Silva & Rachman, 1992; Rangaswamy, 1994; Rapoport, 1990).

Another feature of OCD illustrated in these descriptions is avoidance. While it may be assumed that 'washers' are fanatical about keeping things clean and tidy because of repetitive cleaning and washing rituals, this may not always be the case. Because these individuals are often so fearful of contamination, there may be certain places and objects that they refuse to confront. This type of avoidance is illustrated in the following descriptions of two recent cases:

Case 1: A 29-year-old male

I keep a very clean and orderly house. Everything has its place and I am proud to say that every room of my house is spotless. However, there is one thing that I never touch—the windows that look out to the garden. At one point I could see the garden, the shops up the road, and even the sea at a distance. Now, I cannot even see the house next door. The last time I remember those windows being cleaned was in September 1992 when my partner decided that they needed a clean. Since then, I have not been able to bring myself to go near them. They are simply too dirty to touch and I fear even getting too close to them because I might fall ill.

Case 2: A 35-year-old woman

> As a general rule, I cannot see things unless I am wearing my glasses. For most of my life, this has been a hindrance. However, having said that, there are some situations where I am so thankful for the fact that I can't see clearly. For example, I can't stand the sight of hair on the floor (or anywhere else for that matter). Obviously the place that you would see hair lying about would be the bathroom. I share a house with two other women so you can imagine that the bathroom is usually full of stray hair: on the tiles, in the shower, in the drain, in the sink. The easiest way I get around it is to take my glasses off whenever I enter the bathroom. That way I am able to avoid seeing any hair that might be around. It sounds silly but at least I feel less anxious when I don't see it.

Another theme that emerges from clinical interviews with OC washers concerns the importance of their sense of smell. For many washers, it seems that certain smells may signal the existence of germs. One young woman described a number of bodily smells that were distressing to her. 'Flesh odours and sweat both point to the existence of germs', she commented. Another woman compared the smell of her feet to a dog's breath. 'I know that a dog's breath smells bad and is highly contaminated, so (since my feet smell) there must be some degree of contamination that is associated with them'. Bodily smells are not the only odours that concern OC washers. One individual described fearing her kitchen sponge because of the unpleasant smell she associated with it. In order to alleviate this smell, she washed this sponge on at least 50 occasions during the day.

OCD washing can involve cleaning one's hands over 100 times a day, bathing or showering for several hours, washing and wiping household surfaces and furniture for long periods of time, rewashing clothing many times, using large quantities of cleaning products and hundreds of sheets of toilet paper. A 34-year-old female client with compulsive handwashing behaviours described the complex ritualised process she would go through when washing at a sink:

> After doing various things, such as taking out the rubbish, I have to wash my hands over and over in a special way so that I get rid of the germs that have transferred from the bin onto my hands. First I pick up the soap container that no-one else is allowed to use and take out the soap from inside. Before I start washing I wash the soap under the hot water so it is clean enough for me to wash my hands with. Then I start washing my hands over and over. First I rub my hands together, then I scrub away at my left hand, and then my right hand and then under my nails to get all the germs out from underneath them. The whole thing takes me about 10 minutes because I need to repeat the process three times. After I have carefully washed the soap again I put it back into the sealed container so I can use it next time. I especially make sure that, before I turn the taps off, I have a little bit of water left in one hand so I can wash away the germs I may have picked up from turning off the tap.

After I have finished at the sink, just to make sure there are no germs left on my hands, I put some antibacterial lotion on both my hands. The smell from the dettol is really strong so I have to disguise it by spraying some deodorant over my hands. I let my hands-drip dry, I never trust drying them on a towel. I know it sounds like a bit too much, my boyfriend tells me that I don't need to wash for so long, but if I don't go through the right process then I get really worked up and agitated and can't get on with anything else.

As can be imagined from this illustration, the performance of such rituals can be severely disabling and time-consuming, causing marked distress for the sufferer. OCD washing can permeate an individual's personal, social and working life and make even simple tasks of daily living difficult or impossible to complete (Perse, 1988). Two OC washers describe their condition and how it impacts on their lives:

Case 1: A 48-year-old male

I come from a very close family within a tight-knit community and I feel like I'm losing touch with everything because of my concern with contamination and my excessive washing behaviour. You see, I already feel cut off from my parents and I can't bring my children to see them either. They live in a house that is very dirty and I find I can't go there because of the smell. So my children rarely get to see their grandparents. Also, I find that I cannot take my children out on weekends because I am too afraid to enter public shopping centres. I consider those places to be really dirty and wouldn't dream of using a public toilet there. I also have trouble on the work front. My ritualistic behaviour involves extensively wiping down my suit with a damp cloth at least 40 times a day to get rid of any dust or dirt that may be present. I also have trouble handling money. This is a problem since I am in charge of the banking at the end of each day. After counting the money and then banking it, I have to wash my hands and under my nails for at least 15 minutes. Only then can I carry on with other activities. Handwashing is also a problem throughout the day. I find that at work I am washing more than 20 times a day and when I come home, I wash at least 10 times in the evening. All this time involved in washing leaves me limited time for work during the day and takes away from time with my family in the evenings, not to mention the fact that my children and wife have to be subjected to my problems and suffer as a result.

Case 2: A 32-year-old female

I was in a relationship for 2 years before my partner left me 2 months ago. I know why. He told me he couldn't cope any more with the endless hours of worry I had about germs and, well, actually, sperm, to be perfectly honest. It's understandable I guess, after all, what kind of a life did he have with a woman who was always worried about falling pregnant without having intercourse? I know it sounds crazy but I am really scared that somehow, if I'm not careful, I could fall pregnant. I avoid sitting on public benches where others have sat before me, or swimming in public pools, or using public toilets. I even feared lying next to my partner at night unless I was fully clothed for fear that somehow I would come into contact with sperm. I also have a lot of trouble with dirt and germs. Around the house, I spend a lot of time dusting ornaments and pictures in the living room and also spend a great deal of time in the laundry. I always wash my clothes more than once after I have been out to a public place, and used to always separate my clothes from my partner's clothes for fear that perhaps his underwear might contaminate my clothes. I guess it wasn't unreasonable for him to leave. I mean, who would want to be around someone who was spending unnecessary time cleaning things (that were of no harm to begin with) and avoiding reasonable activities because of a fear of falling pregnant? I'm pretty depressed about things at the moment, I really loved him and hoped that one day we'd get married.

THE ROLE OF DISEASE-EXPECTANCY IN OC WASHING

As well as significant interference in general functioning, a preoccupation with disease and danger also appears typical of OCD washers. Irrational beliefs about the dangers of certain stimuli have long been observed in clinical OCD patients with washing/contamination concerns (Jones & Menzies, 1997a, 1997b). Early last century Freud (1909) described how a patient with obsessional neurosis repeatedly ironed his money. According to Freud the patient believed the paper florins harboured all sorts of dangerous bacteria that might do harm. Emmelkamp (1987) argues that during the execution of washing rituals, cognitions about possible contamination play a prominent role. As such, rituals are provoked by ideas concerning harming oneself (and, less frequently, harming others). In several reports of OCD washers, sufferers have articulated a clear link between contamination and washing. That is, they claim to wash in order to prevent disease (Lelliott et al., 1988). Two OC washers discuss the basis of their fears and the reasons for performing compulsive washing:

Case 1: A 33-year-old female

I've read biology textbooks and I have seen those advertisements so I know that microbes are attacking everything. They're there, everywhere and you can't see them or get rid of them. And you can never be certain that they're gone. That's why it's really important to me to be perfectly clean at all times. Because if you're not, then germs will get into the body which can then lead to some terrible disease.

Case 2: A 32-year-old male

It's really important to me that my house is kept germ-free at all times. I have three young children who are the most important things to me in the world and I wouldn't want them getting sick or catching some disease just because I was careless about their hygiene. Each morning when I leave the house I have to walk to the train station, sit on the train seats on the way to work, walk into work, use the public toilets, take the train home and then walk home from the station. All these activities involve me having contact with different surfaces that are extremely dirty, especially my shoes, and I must not bring any of those germs into the house. When I return home each day after work, I wash the soles of my shoes with antibacterial soap before stepping into the house, then take all my work clothes off (down to my underpants) just inside the front

Table 7.3 Threat-based expectancies among a group of 41 obsessive-compulsive washers

	Feared event			
	Cannot occur	May occur	Will often occur	Certain to occur
Becoming contaminated after touching money	4	25	4	8
Contamination of clothing or other harm occurring after slight contact with bodily secretions (e.g. perspiration, saliva)	3	13	9	16
Becoming contaminated or harmed after touching an object that has been touched by strangers or by certain people.	2	24	9	6
Becoming contaminated or harmed after touching garbage or dirty things	1	13	6	21
Becoming contaminated or diseased after using public toilets	1	18	10	12
Becoming contaminated or diseased after using public telephones	3	26	8	4
Becoming contaminated or diseased after inadequate handwashing	0	13	12	16
Becoming contaminated or diseased after failing to wash when I think I might be dirty	3	10	12	16
Becoming contaminated or diseased by failing to wash or clean myself after touching something that I think is contaminated	1	6	9	25
Becoming contaminated or diseased by failing to wash myself or change my clothing after an animal has touched me	4	18	7	12

door and put them into a plastic bag. Then I go straight to the shower and make sure I wash till I'm clean. My wife immediately puts my clothes into the washing machine to soak overnight before being washed the next morning. The plastic bag then gets put into the rubbish bin.

These examples highlight the extent of threat-based beliefs among OC washers. Disease expectancies among 41 consecutive washers at the University of Sydney Anxiety Disorders Clinic are summarised in Table 7.3.

In general, it is clear from these data that OCD washers have strong (and clearly irrational) beliefs in the likelihood of becoming diseased from daily activities. Strongly held 'overvalued' ideas have long been known to interfere with behavioural approaches to this disorder. Two decades ago, Foa (1979) detailed how four treatment-compliant clients with contamination concerns failed to benefit from traditional exposure-based techniques. Common to all four cases was excessive threat-based expectancies. The first patient was afraid of inflicting mental retardation on his son by being in contact with retarded people, whereas the second feared contracting tetanus from contact with sharp objects. The third patient expressed fear of life-threatening contamination by 'male germs'. The last patient feared contact with leukaemia germs, believing that such contact would inevitably cause the death of her husband and children.

From these, and similar cases, it appears that some OCD patients with contamination concerns (a) have excessively high estimates of the probability of dangerous events occurring, and (b) think the cost or outcome of the dangerous event is particularly high (in terms of the severity of the disease/illness contracted). Recent research in our clinic bears strongly on this issue. A study conducted by Jones & Menzies (1998a) assessed the role of danger expectancies in OCD washing phenomena. The researchers experimentally manipulated the level of perceived danger in a behavioural avoidance task by modifying the instructions given to 18 undergraduate subjects (who had displayed washing/contamination concerns) at the task commencement. The results showed that for the two behavioural expressions of OCD (i.e. washing and avoidance) which could be accurately and objectively measured, there were large and significant differences found between subjects in the high and low danger conditions. The fact that a task perceived as more likely to contaminate could lead to significantly increased washing and avoidance was argued to be supportive of danger-based models of OCD washing (e.g. Beck et al., 1985; Carr, 1974).

In an earlier study by Jones & Menzies (1997a), the potential mediating role that danger expectancies and other potential cognitive mediators, including responsibility, perfectionism, anticipated anxiety and self-efficacy, have on obsessive-compulsive handwashing was examined. Ratings were obtained from 27 obsessive-compulsive washers before and during a behavioural avoidance test. In general, the results strongly suggested that, of the set of cognitive variables examined, danger expectancies were the most likely cognitive mediator of washing-related behaviour. According to Jones & Menzies (1997a, 1998a) these findings suggest that illness-related beliefs are the most prominent cognitive feature of the condition.

While the evidence to support this view is considerable, it has been suggested that other subtypes of OCD washing may exist (Rachman, 1994;

Tallis, 1996). Rachman (1994) proposed that cleaning compulsions may arise from a number of different underlying motivations, only one of which relates to illness. These are defined as (a) a fear of illness, (b) a sense of dirtiness or (c) a sense of mental pollution (defined as a sense of internal uncleanliness, which can arise and persist in the absence of observable external dirt). Tallis (1996) has since suggested that there exists a further class of washing behaviour attributable to the personality trait of perfectionism. Tallis suggests that some OCD washing individuals fail to exhibit concern in relation to contamination resulting in illness. Instead, they claim the motivation for their washing behaviour is to maintain a perfect perceived condition of their possessions. The following example demonstrates the notion that not all washing behaviour may be motivated by a need for cleanliness in the face of disease or illness.

Case 1: A 38-year-old female

I know it's not that I'm afraid that I'll get sick, it's just that I like everything to be orderly. For example, everything in my wardrobe is perfectly symmetrical, my pants are all lined up, my tops are all folded exactly right and my shoes are perfectly aligned on the floor. When it comes to the kitchen I have to make sure that the sink is wiped down completely after I have washed up all the dishes. I hate seeing any marks or drops of water after everything is clean. When I put anything back into the fridge, it has to be cleaned before I place it back on the shelf that is lined with a paper towel. Often I have thoughts that if I don't keep everything neat and orderly then somehow my partner or I will be punished.

Having described in detail the nature of OC washing, attention will now turn to the origins of the behaviour.

THE DEVELOPMENT OF COMPULSIVE WASHING

While sudden onset does not appear to be a typical experience for all OCD sufferers, it has been suggested that washers are more likely to have had a precipitating event than those with checking compulsions (Rachman & Hodgson, 1980). Khanna & Mukherjee (1992) conducted an investigation of 412 OCD subjects that spanned almost a decade. The researchers reported significant differences between OCD subtypes (washers, checkers, mixed) with regard to the onset of their OCD symptoms. The washer subgroup revealed both a later age at first consultation and a later age of reported onset than either the checker subgroup or mixed group. Consistent with the suggestions of Rachman & Hodgson (1980), washers were also found to be more likely to have acute development of symptoms following a triggering event. These findings may be seen as providing support for associative learning models of OCD origin.

However, while general learning theory has been proposed to account for both the onset of OCD and its maintenance via anxiety/discomfort reduction, there is a dearth of controlled research investigating the learning account of OC washing. Although the beginnings of this disorder have been argued to often occur after a stressor (see further Tallis, 1995a), there is little evidence to suggest a direct conditioning trial precedes OCD symptoms. In the study conducted by Tallis (1996) with four individuals displaying washing compulsions, none of the cases could describe specific learning experiences that would account for their obsessional features. Reports of patients who have experienced a traumatic (conditioning) experience as the starting point for their problem behaviours are scarce.

Prior to 1998 there had not been a single controlled study examining the relevance of associative learning pathways in the development of OCD in either a mixed group of OCD sufferers or in subgroups of sufferers, such as washers or checkers. It has already been suggested that there are important differences between these subtypes of OC ritualisers (e.g. Steketee et al., 1985). In particular, it has been argued that distinct forms of ritualistic behaviour may differ with respect to their aetiology (Rachman, 1976a, 1976b; Steketee et al., 1985). Accordingly, Jones & Menzies (1998c) set out to investigate the relevance of associative learning in the development of OCD in a sample of 23 OCD washers and 23 age- and sex-matched controls. The origins questionnaire developed by Jones & Menzies (i.e. the OCD Origins Questionnaire, OOQ) is currently the only retrospective instrument designed to systematically investigate the origins of OCD.

Using this instrument, the researchers attributed the development of OCD washing to an associative learning event in only three of the 23 washers investigated. One subject was classified into each of the three associative learning categories, accounting for 13% of the OCD sample. The direct conditioning case involved the contracting of an illness (UCS) following contact with an animal (CS). The vicarious conditioning case involved the repeated observation of a flatmate's compulsive washing/cleaning. The instructional onset occurred when a parent repeatedly instructed the patient that her cats were unclean. Nine of the 23 washers reported that they could not remember a time when they were not excessively fearful or anxious in the presence of the obsessive-compulsive thoughts, objects, situations or activities. This finding is consistent with the high frequencies reported in several reports of non-associative fear in the specific phobias (e.g. Jones & Menzies, 1995; Menzies, 1995, 1996, 1997a, 1997b; Menzies & Clarke, 1993a, 1993b, 1994, 1995a, 1995b, 1995c; Menzies & Harris, 1997, 2001; Menzies & Parker, 2001). In these papers, such findings were claimed to support ethological models of phobic onset. A further 13% of Jones & Menzies's (1998c) cases ($n = 3$) were found to have arisen following an unrelated traumatic experience (e.g. verbal harassment by a work colleague in the absence of contamination-related stimuli). Together, these non-associative pathways accounted for significantly more cases than direct conditioning alone, or the direct and indirect learning categories combined. Finally, 34.8% of subjects ($n = 8$) could clearly remember a time before their concerns developed in which they were not even mildly distressed by the presence of OC thoughts or activities but could not remember when their fear began or the events surrounding its appearance. These subjects were classified as 'can't remember' cases. No subjects gave inconsistent responses requiring the 'can't classify' category.

The Jones & Menzies (1998c) report also highlighted interesting relationships between depression, associative learning events and OCD washing onset. It has been widely accepted in some quarters that depression develops as a consequence of having OCD, rather than as an antecedent for the condition. Contrary to expectation, all of the subjects in the origins study who experienced either a direct conditioning event or a relevant vicarious event when *already* depressed subsequently developed OCD washing. In contrast, none of the subjects who experienced a direct conditioning event without concurrent depression became OCD sufferers. It was suggested that depression may facilitate associative learning in the development of OCD washing.

Alternative theoretical accounts of the origin of OCD washing have been proposed. Some researchers and clinicians have looked to ethology and its offspring, neuro-ethology, to explain the presence of excessive hand washing in OCD sufferers (e.g. Hollander, 1974; Stein et al., 1992; Swedo et al., 1989b). Rapoport (1989) argues that these behaviours have their counterpart in other species, e.g. washing is likened to the grooming seen in many animals. As such, washing is viewed as a fixed action pattern. Swedo et al. (1989b) described two childhood cases of OCD in which the children with compulsive hand washing also licked their hands in a ritualised manner. The relief provided by successful drug treatment, and the otherwise normal functioning of many of their paediatric subjects, led them to speculate that OCD is a set of species-specific adaptive acts, such as grooming or sensitivity to danger, that are released abnormally by an altered drive state (Swedo et al., 1989b).

It has been proposed that displacement activities seen in animals are a possible model for human compulsive behaviours (e.g. Hollander, 1974; Musaph, 1968). Canine acral lick dermatitis is characterised by excessive licking or biting of the extremities, which leads to localised hair loss and subsequent granulomatous lesions. Stein et al. (1992) argue that this condition is a particularly interesting animal model of OCD washing because it does not simply involve grooming, but rather a disorder of exaggerated grooming. Further, it has been found that following the intraventricular administration of a substance produced in the pituitary, adrenocorticotropic hormone (ACTH), rats will begin grooming excessively (Bertolini et al., 1988, cited in Winslow & Insel, 1991). Also, administration of certain drugs leads to a cessation of grooming. In another study the injection of amphetamine into the ventrolateral striatum of rats led to intense oral stereotypy, such as forepaw licking (Kelley et al., 1988). These behaviours have been shown to respond to medications commonly prescribed in the treatment of OCD (i.e. the selective serotonin reuptake inhibitors, SSRIs) (Goldberger & Rapoport, 1991). Swedo et al. (1989b) argue that the similar and apparently limited content and style of symptoms across subjects suggests an ethological model for OCD. Moreover, de Silva et al. (1977), judged the large majority of obsessions in 82 OCD patients to be biologically relevant. Certainly, on the surface, the potential benefits of excessive washing to the species seem obvious. Before the discovery of antibiotic treatment of bacterial infections, frequent washing/cleaning may have provided the best protection against infectious diseases. However, much of the support for an ethological model of OC washing is, of course, highly speculative. It depends on a series of assumptions, including: (a) excessive washing in the past reduced the frequency of infectious disease among our ancestors; (b) excessive washing increased reproductory opportunities, presumably by extending life in these ancestors and; (c) excessive washing is partly under genetic control. Each of these assumptions is open to question, even the superficially sound first assumption. It has been argued that vigorous washing can damage the integrity of the skin, causing cracks and fissures that can become the portal of entry for pathogens (see further, Jones & Menzies, 1997b). Therefore, claims of strong support for an ethological model in OCD washing are premature. Despite this, given the paucity of knowledge concerning the development of OCD, further research in this area may prove enlightening.

While our current knowledge of the aetiology of OCD washing is incomplete, research investigating the treatment of the condition is quite advanced. We will now present an overview of the treatment of the condition.

THE TREATMENT OF COMPULSIVE WASHING

If one excludes single case studies, there are relatively few treatment trials that have exclusively used subjects who present with washing/contamination concerns as primary OCD symptoms. A controlled trial assessing the effectiveness of exposure and response prevention (ERP) for five washers was conducted by Mills et al. (1973). They reported dramatic declines in washing for all subjects. Studies have also been undertaken which compare the effectiveness of exposure alone vs. response prevention (Foa et al., 1980a, 1984; Steketee et al., 1982). First, using a sample of washers, Foa et al. (1980a) reported that patients exposed to obsessional triggers, but not prevented from performing compulsive rituals, subsequently experienced less anxiety with contaminants but showed no reduction in the number of compulsive rituals performed. Alternatively, those allocated to the response prevention alone condition were permitted to avoid obsessional triggers but prohibited from performing compulsive rituals. These subjects showed a reduction in rituals but no reduction in anxiety. Similar findings were reported in a controlled study by Steketee et al. (1982). Finally, Foa et al. (1994) randomly assigned patients with washing rituals to treatment either by exposure only, response prevention only or a combination of exposure and response prevention. All participants received daily 2-hour sessions for 15 days over a 21-day period. When tested at post-treatment and follow-up it was found that participants who had received the combined treatment experienced greater OCD symptom reduction than those who had received single-component treatments. Therefore, the findings from studies conducted with OC washers clearly suggest the necessity for utilising *both* exposure and response prevention in the behavioural management of OC washers (see further, Chapter 15).

Compared to trials of behavioural procedures, there is a dearth of research investigating the effectiveness of cognitive therapy for OCD washing. A study by Ownby (1983) used both thought stopping and rational emotive therapy when treating a 13-year-old boy suffering from a fear of contamination and compulsive handwashing rituals. A large decrease in handwashing episodes following treatment was observed. Salkovskis & Warwick (1985) used cognitive therapy in the case of a woman with OCD contamination/cleaning concerns who had initially improved with behavioural therapy but subsequently relapsed. Typical exposure sessions had not resulted in within-session declines in anxiety. She had also failed to respond to medication and refused to take part in further behavioural therapy. The cognitive therapy involved the use of Beckian techniques to challenge negative intrusive thoughts. The patient expressed the strong conviction that she would contract cancer if she did not clean and avoid any form of ultraviolet light and appeared to have overvalued ideation. Following the commencement of cognitive therapy, Salkovskis & Warwick (1985) reported an immediate reduction in her belief ratings for the intrusive thought (from 98% to 40%). At the completion of cognitive therapy the client agreed to engage in behaviour therapy, with resultant within- and between-session anxiety reduction. At the end of treatment and at 6 month follow-up she was found to be almost completely recovered. However, once again treatment consisted of both cognitive and behavioural elements. In discussing the case, the researchers credited the cognitive therapy with changing the 'automatic thoughts' following the anxiety-evoking stimulus and making the patient more receptive to the reinstitution of the flooding programme. The authors claimed that following cognitive therapy she responded to the flooding session more like a 'typical obsessional' rather than in the style characteristic of patients with overvalued ideation. However, the importance of the exposure session following the cognitive therapy cannot be overlooked. It appears clear from this case that the flooding was necessary to achieve the meaningful reduction in symptoms.

Danger Ideation Reduction Therapy

In the mid-1990s a new cognitive, psychoeducational treatment package was developed by Jones & Menzies (1997b) specifically for OCD cases in which washing/contamination concerns dominate the clinical picture. This treatment, called Danger Ideation Reduction Therapy (DIRT), is solely directed at decreasing danger-related expectancies concerning disease. Components of DIRT include corrective information, cognitive restructuring, filmed interviews, microbiological experiments, attentional focusing and Hoekstra's (1989) probability of catastrophe estimation task (see further Jones & Menzies, 1997b, for a detailed description of the methods). The package is void of any exposure (in vivo, filmed or imaginal) and even behavioural experiments are not included. Given this, the package does not typically produce anxiety in participants. Anti-exposure instructions are given to ensure that participants do not attempt to confront OCD-relevant stimuli, unless no anxiety is experienced. The rationale of the program emphasises that when illness beliefs have been eliminated, participants will naturally engage with previously feared stimuli, without the need for fear. Accordingly, the entire program sets about to dismantle exaggerated threat-beliefs about disease. In the program, detailed information about the nature of the immune system, true disease rates and risk behaviours, the 'normal' behaviours of community members and the absence of disease-related consequences, is provided. Traditional restructuring of irrational beliefs forms the backbone of the treatment, although a variety of novel procedures are also employed. Much is made of the behaviours of individuals in various occupational groups who regularly, without disease-related consequences, confront money (e.g. bank tellers), garden soil (e.g. gardeners), toilets (e.g. cleaners), chemicals (e.g. laboratory workers) and other relevant stimuli. Filmed interviews with relevant workers challenge compulsive washers to re-evaluate their perceptions of risk.

Three subjects participated in the first evaluation of this treatment, which was conducted in individual, 1 hour weekly sessions over 6–10 weeks. All three subjects had presented with contamination/washing concerns but had refused to participate in exposure and response prevention. DIRT was found to be extremely effective in reducing OCD symptomatology in all three subjects. These improvements were maintained at 3 month follow-up. Not only was there a large reduction in OCD symptomatology, but post-treatment scores on the Mandsley Obsessional-Compulsive Inventory (MOCI) were similar to scores obtained by 'normal' or community control subjects in several studies (e.g. Sternberger & Burns, 1990a, 1991).

The second study evaluating DIRT was a controlled trial of 23 OCD sufferers with washing/contamination concerns. Twelve of the subjects received Danger Ideation Reduction Therapy (DIRT) over eight 1 hour weekly group sessions. Eleven subjects were placed on a wait list and did not receive DIRT or any other treatment. All subjects were assessed at pre-treatment, post-treatment and 3 month follow-up using a number of assessment measures. Once again, DIRT was found to be effective in reducing OCD symptomatology. Changes from before treatment to after treatment were significantly greater in the DIRT condition than in the non-DIRT condition for all measures.

In the third and most recent report on the effectiveness of DIRT, five intractable cases of OC washing were administered the package after failing to benefit from two serotonergic drug trials and up to 25 weeks of exposure and response prevention. All five cases exhibited poor insight (perhaps explaining the intractable nature of the symptoms). Within 14 sessions of DIRT, four of the five individuals had returned to normal functioning. These gains were maintained at a 4–6 month follow-up (Krochmalik et al., 2001).

In sum, DIRT appears to be a viable treatment option for individuals suffering from obsessive-compulsive washing. At present, a randomised controlled trial of DIRT and ERP is being conducted at the University of Sydney. Preliminary analyses suggest that DIRT, compared to ERP: (a) is associated with greater reductions in all symptomatology; (b) is associated with fewer drop-outs or treatment refusers; (c) produces greater changes in cognitive variables thought to underpin compulsive washing (i.e. disease expectancies).

CONCLUDING COMMENTS AND FUTURE DIRECTIONS

OC washing can occur in males and females across the age spectrum, with a range of stimuli triggering anxiety and avoidance in sufferers. The descriptions from OC washers presented earlier in this chapter illustrate how severe the condition can be. Clearly, disabling interference with the daily life of the sufferer and his/her family is a feature of the disorder. While our knowledge concerning the nature, origin and treatment of this condition has advanced in recent years it is far from complete. Future research investigating why individuals develop the disorder and how best to manage the condition needs to be undertaken. It is hoped that the development of new interventions will prove fruitful in alleviating this severe, complex condition. A new Australian program focusing on the reduction of disease expectancies continues to show promise as an alternative to traditional treatment approaches. Future research will determine whether DIRT represents a viable alternative to the traditional behavioural and pharmacological approaches to the disorder.

Chapter 8

COMPULSIVE CHECKING

Stanley Rachman

In the past 30 years considerable progress has been made in improving our understanding of the bewilderingly repetitive and self-defeating nature of compulsive checking. Why do they do it, over and over again? The first advance was accomplished when the compulsions were subjected to detailed behavioural analyses in the early 1970s, and the results of these experiments helped to consolidate the growing ability to modify this abnormal behaviour. The second advance came with the infusion of cognitive concepts and analyses, beginning with Salkovskis' remarkable paper in 1985. The second part of this chapter will trace the chronology of these advances.

Compulsions are the most common and most prominent feature of obsessive-compulsive disorders and in many cases they constitute the major problem. Two main compulsions have been identified: checking compulsions and cleaning compulsions. Clinical descriptions of these two types of compulsions were subsequently confirmed by factor-analytic studies (Hodgson & Rachman, 1977; Rachman & Hodgson, 1980). A psychometric scale, the Maudsley Obsessional Compulsive Inventory (MOCI), was developed to determine the structure of OCD and yielded two stable major factors, checking and cleaning (Hodgson & Rachman, 1977). Constructed in the behavioural era, the scale had good service (Taylor, 1998) but has been replaced by scales that are fuller and include more cognitive items (e.g. Foa et al., 1998b). These measures will be discussed more fully in Chapter 14.

As discussed in Chapter 2, compulsions are repetitive, stereotyped, intentional acts. The necessary and sufficient conditions for describing repetitive behaviour as compulsive are an experienced sense of pressure to act and the attribution of this pressure to internal sources. The occurrence of resistance is an important confirmatory feature, but it is not necessary or sufficient. The compulsions may be wholly unacceptable or, more often,

Obsessive-Compulsive Disorder: Theory, Research and Treatment.
Edited by Ross G. Menzies and Padmal de Silva. © 2003 John Wiley & Sons, Ltd.

partly acceptable, but are regarded by the person as being excessive, exaggerated and, when judged in calmer moments, senseless. The compulsive behaviour displayed by patients with OCD is motivated, purposeful behaviour, in contrast with the mechanical, robotic, repetitive behaviour observed in other disorders, notably neurological ones. Checking compulsions are carried out in order to prevent future misfortunes, and particularly to protect people from harm; they are a form of preventive behaviour. The compulsions are associated with indecisiveness and doubt. The checking can be overt and obvious or covert and inaccessible to an observer. It can be carried out by proxy, and in one version appears in the form of repetitive pestering requests for reassurance: 'Is it safe?'; 'Check it for me'. Checking behaviour can be protracted, thereby leading to intolerable slowness and poor timekeeping. It is rarely possible to achieve certainty that a future misfortune is completely ruled out, especially as most of the anticipated misfortunes are obscure. As it is carried out in an attempt to prevent obscure future misfortunes, the checking behaviour has no natural end point. So the checking must continue—checking sans frontieres. It remains incomplete.

Checking compulsions, more often than cleaning compulsions, are associated with doubting and indecisiveness, take a long time to complete, evolve slowly, evoke some internal resistance, and tend to be accompanied by tension and/or anxiety (Rachman, 1976a). The repetitive, intentional execution of these purposeful but irrational actions is within the person's voluntary control but the urge to carry out the acts can become so strong that they are executed against one's rational inclinations. The urges tend to provoke subjective resistance, particularly in the early evolution of the disorder, but gradually the person comes to yield to the urges, and the checking becomes stylized and streamlined. In specifiable circumstances, checking can be delayed, extended, postponed, reduced—or even carried out for the affected person by a friend or relative. Patients are driven to repeat their behaviour, such as checking a lock over and over again, almost always with the purpose and expectation of gaining some relief from their discomfort or anxiety. The compulsive behaviour is a source of considerable distress and people experience a sense of reduced volition, but the compulsive activity is repeatedly reinforced by its temporary anxiolytic properties. If the compulsive activities are particularly intense and/or extensive they can become disabling as well as distressing. These disabling/distressing qualities distinguish them from the so-called normal compulsions (see Frost et al., 1986; Muris et al., 1997; Sher et al., 1989).

The classical examples of compulsive behaviour are repetitive and excessive cleaning and comparably stereotyped checking, especially to ensure safety in the home and at work (e.g. by repeatedly checking the safety of the stove, doors, windows). Many people with obsessive-compulsive disorder have elements of both of these forms of compulsions; people who display cleaning compulsions often will have some stereotyped checking behaviour, but compulsive checking may occur in the absence of any compulsion to clean. Information about the relative frequencies of the main forms of compulsion is incomplete but it appears that compulsive checking may be more common than compulsive cleaning, perhaps in the ratio of 4:3 or 6:3 (Antony et al., 1998a; Henderson & Pollard, 1988). In a questionnaire study of OCD symptoms, nearly half of the OCD respondents reported compulsions without obsessions, and 32% reported obsessions without compulsions (Welkowitz et al., 2000). The results of a community study in central Canada produced comparable figures and it was also found that 'the most common compulsion was checking (15.1%)' (Stein et al., 1997b). Primary obsessional slowness, in which the person carries out everyday self-care activities in a meticulous and stereotyped sequence, is fortunately rare (see Chapter 10). It can take up to 6 hours or more to get dressed (Rachman, 1974; Rachman & Hodgson, 1980). Primary slowness is distinguished from the slowness that is secondary to the time-consuming repetitions of the same act, such as checking the stove over and over again.

OCD is strongly associated with depression (Antony et al., 1998a; Rachman & Hodgson, 1980) and a range of other anxiety disorders (Brown, 1998; Sher et al., 1991), such as social phobia, generalised anxiety disorder (GAD), health anxiety (formerly hypochondriasis) and with anorexia (Parkin, 1997; Welkowitz et al., 2000). In comparison with non-checkers, checkers are more anxious, depressed, introverted and inclined to perfectionism (Frost et al., 1986; Gershuny & Sher, 1995; Steketee et al. 1998a).

Clinical examples of compulsive checking include the following:

- A 28-year-old patient had checking compulsions that were precipitated by a fear of harming others. He was unable to drive his car, as this provoked intolerable thoughts and checking compulsions. He also avoided crowded streets for fear of causing harm to others. He repeatedly checked razors, pins, glasses and so on.
- A 34-year-old married woman had checking compulsions that were precipitated by contact with other people. Looking at or talking to people or giving them food led to checking behaviour in order to ensure that no harm came to them (providing food for other people to eat is a common source of anxiety for affected people, and in one instance we had a patient who was unable to even boil a kettle of water for tea unless she was accompanied by a trusted adult).
- A 36-year-old single man had checking compulsions that focused on excrement, and he engaged in prolonged and meticulous inspection of any speck of brown, particularly on his clothes and shoes.

- A 40-year-old nursery school teacher checked that all rugs and carpets were absolutely flat, lest someone trip over them, and spent long periods looking for needles and pins on the floor and in furniture. She repeatedly checked to ensure that all cigarettes and matches had been extinguished, and so forth.
- A 30-year-old male nurse was incapacitated by repeated checking behaviour. He had to ensure that no one had been inadvertently locked in a room, or trapped in a manhole, or that babies had not been dumped in the bushes, and so on.
- A 40-year-old man had to retrace many of his motor car trips in order to check that he had not injured anyone inadvertently.
- A 28-year-old woman teacher spent up to 3 hours each night checking the doors, gas taps, windows, plugs and switches before going to bed.
- A 45-year-old television technician spent up to 2 hours checking the taps, doors, windows, electrical plugs, etc. of his flat before he was able to leave for work.
- A 35-year-old married woman repeatedly checked with the police to ensure that she had not caused any accidents.
- A 19-year-old clerk carried out 4 hours of checking after other members of his family retired at night. He checked all the electrical appliances, doors, taps and so on and was not able to get to bed before 3 or 4 o'clock in the morning.

Some of the notable features of checking compulsions include the following: most checking occurs predominantly in the person's own home; most compulsive checks are carried out when the person is alone; the compulsions appear to intensify when the person is depressed, they are most intense when the person feels responsible for the act concerned or, put another way, if they feel they are not responsible they seldom engage in intense checking compulsions (Rachman, 1976a, p. 270).

In addition to the overt compulsive checking that people engage in, they are much inclined to avoid situations which are likely to produce the anxiety or discomfort that will trigger compulsive checking. Furthermore, many of the affected people engage in neutralizing activities, some of which are covert, in an attempt to put matters right. They attempt to reduce the subjective discomfort and/or reduce the likelihood of a nasty event occurring, or attempt to reduce the effects of any nasty event that might occur. Neutralizing acts often provide transient relief, but they are thought to make an unfortunate contribution to maintaining the problem. Neutralization is best regarded as a variant of compulsive checking, because both of them are aimed at cancelling the effects of the person's thought or action or, most commonly, an attempt to prevent the feared event from occurring. In his cognitive analysis of OCD, Salkovskis (1985,

1998) attaches considerable significance to the role and effects of neutralization and connects it to the concept of inflated responsibility and the need for reassurance (see further, Chapter 4). Neutralization, compulsive acts and reassurance seeking share some common features and all can be construed as attempts to reduce the probability of a nasty event occurring or to reduce the effects of such an event. They also serve to reduce one's responsibility for any such anticipated misfortune. The clinical implications of neutralization are fully described by Salkovskis & Kirk (1997).

PSYCHOLOGICAL EXPLANATIONS

Broadly, three psychological explanations for obsessive-compulsive disorders have been put forward: one based on psychoanalytic theory, a second on behavioural theory and therapy, and the third based on cognitive-behavioural theory and therapy. As the psychoanalytic theory in general has faded over the last few years, and indeed in the opinion of some critics is now discredited (e.g. Eysenck, 1985; Grunbaum, 1984), it is unnecessary to describe it in detail. Moreover, the theory had very little to offer in dealing with the specifics of compulsive checking as opposed to other manifestations of OCD. The inability of psychoanalytic treatment to cope with OCD and other disorders (e.g. Cawley, 1974; Rachman & Wilson, 1980) undermines the psychoanalytic theory in general (see Grunbaum, 1984). It has to be said that there have been no fresh contributions from that direction in a long while. Instead we have seen a massive shift, a virtual tidal wave, in the direction of biological explanations of psychological disorders, including OCD. Whatever their merits, however, the biological theories are content-less and thus far have been silent on the questions raised by the similarities and differences between the various kinds of compulsion. For example, there has been no attempt to explain compulsive checking as such, or why the patient checks rather than cleans; these content-type questions remain to be tackled. Neither do the biological explanations take account of the cognitive aspects of OCD, such as pure obsessions, the intentional motivated quality of compulsions, the role of responsibility and so forth. Interestingly, neuropsychological deficits bear no relation to the outcome of psychological treatment for OCD (Bolton et al., 2000).

Of the remaining two theories, the behavioural theory achieved considerable early success and was instrumental in the development of what proved to be a reasonably effective method for treating this disorder. Within the last 15 years, the infusion of cognitive concepts and methods into clinical psychology has led to a considerable expansion of our understanding of OCD and of compulsive checking in particular (see Freeston &

Ladouceur, 1997; Salkovskis, 1985, 1998, 1999). A detailed account of the earlier, behavioural approach to compulsive checking can be found in Rachman (1976a) and Rachman & Hodgson (1980). In keeping with the thinking at the time, researchers working on the subject in the early 1970s approached the problem of compulsive behaviour on the basis of Mowrer's (1939, 1960) two-stage theory of fear and avoidance. He argued that fear is a form of conditioned pain reaction and that, in addition to being a reaction, it is also a motivator. Organisms seek to avoid fear and if they are unsuccessful at avoiding, they then engage in escape behaviour. Mowrer argued that the puzzling persistence of neurotic behaviour (such as compulsions) can be explained precisely because such behaviour is successful in reducing anxiety. Any form of behaviour that achieves this end, whether it is adaptive or non-adaptive in the long run, will be reinforced and strengthened.

On this basis it was argued that checking compulsions are a form of active avoidance behaviour and cleaning compulsions are a form of passive avoidance behaviour (Rachman & Hodgson, 1980). It was argued that in passive avoidance you get punished if you do, but in active avoidance you get punished if you don't. It was assumed that in the case of passive avoidance, and indeed of cleaning compulsions, the person is suffering from fear of an object or a situation. In the case of checking compulsions, which implied active avoidance behaviour, it was argued that the person is motivated largely by a fear of criticism or guilt. It was also argued that most forms of phobia are best thought of as instances of passive avoidance, and hence there should be an affinity between phobias and compulsive cleaning. However, there should be less similarity between phobias and compulsive checking, which, according to behaviour theory, is best viewed as a form of active avoidance (see Figure 8.1).

The idea that compulsive behaviour persists because it reduces anxiety gathered some support and for a long while had a strong influence on the way in which the problem of OCD was construed. The reports given by people who have OCD can be accommodated with ease into Mowrer's view (they commonly report a partial relief after completing a successful cycle of checking; see below for experimental confirmations) and the theory served well for a period. However, the inadequacies of the theory gradually became apparent and it was concluded that it could not provide a comprehensive account of OCD, or of compulsive checking in particular (Rachman & Hodgson, 1980). Among other limitations, the behaviour theory had little to offer in explaining the genesis of OCD. Despite its considerable success in explaining maintenance, it rested on the untenable equipotentiality premise, encountered insuperable difficulty in coping with the cognitive features of OCD (especially obsessions) and was insufficiently

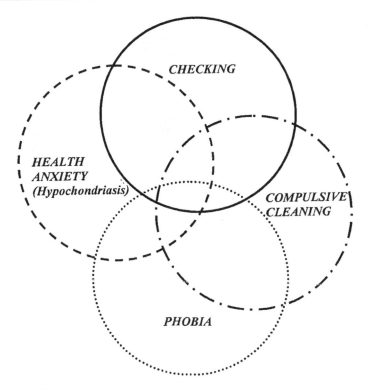

Figure 8.1 The relation between compulsive checking, cleaning, phobia and health anxiety (hypochondriasis)

discriminating. The inability of the theory to discriminate between OCD and other anxiety disorders was a weakness. For instance, why do certain people develop OCD and others develop social phobia? This very lack of discriminability was an important prompt for Salkovskis's attempt to find a superior explanation, one that started out from a cognitive perspective. 'The greatest limitation of the behavioural theory was its failure to differentiate between the theoretical conceptualisation of different anxiety disorders,' (Salkovskis, 1998, p. 36).

A combination of clinical investigations, psychometric studies and experimental analyses introduced a measure of clarity into the nature and function of compulsive acts such as checking. In a number of experiments it was found that when patients with OCD are deliberately stimulated by contact with one of their provocative stimuli (e.g. touching dirt), they almost always report a steep increase in anxiety and an accompanying urge to carry out the relevant compulsive acts, such as cleaning. If the compulsive

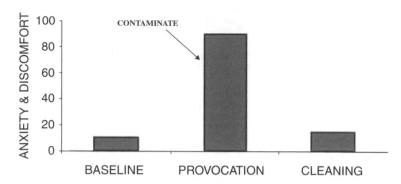

Figure 8.2   Anxiety/discomfort increases promptly and steeply after touching a 'contaminant', and decreases rapidly after appropriate cleaning

act is carried out, the anxiety declines promptly (see Figure 8.2). In other experimental conditions, patients were asked to delay carrying out the activity, such as checking, and it emerged that their anxiety persisted for a while and then gradually declined. The execution of the relevant compulsive act was followed by a quicker decline in anxiety than that observed during 'spontaneous' declines. This relationship is illustrated in Figure 8.3. These figures are schematic illustrations.

The initial experiments were carried out with patients whose main problem was compulsive cleaning and it was confirmed that the execution of the compulsive cleaning action was indeed promptly followed by a reduction in the strength of the urge to clean and the associated anxiety. Very few exceptions were encountered. The patients were asked to touch

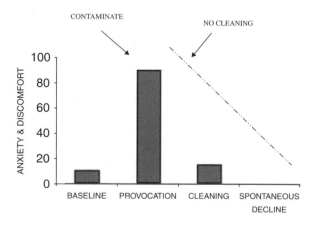

Figure 8.3   Anxiety/discomfort decreases rapidly after cleaning. The spontaneous decline of anxiety, shown by the dotted line, is slower

a 'contaminant' and then report their anxiety. Typically, it arose immediately and was accompanied by a strong urge to clean. The discomfort and urges remained high for 15–120 minutes. However, if the patients were asked to carry out their chosen method of cleaning directly after touching the contaminant, the anxiety and compulsive urges dropped sharply and promptly. These experiments etched out the connections between exposure to threat, the evocation of anxiety and the urge to escape by cleaning away the threat. The results were consistent with the idea that compulsive cleaning is an anxiety-reducing tactic, and also with the hypothesis that the dependable and swift reduction of anxiety achieved by compulsive cleaning serves to strengthen the compulsion and perhaps conserve the fear (of contamination and illness).

However, when comparable experiments were carried out on patients whose main problem was checking, a number of exceptions were observed. The same experimental technique of provocation, followed by permission to carry out the preferred compulsive actions, was used. Patients with OCD were asked to use a personally selected appliance (e.g. stove) or other selected task and report their anxiety (as numerous checkers said that they were not anxious but rather were uncomfortable, the designation was altered to anxiety/discomfort). In most instances the provocation was followed by an increase in anxiety/discomfort, but the group results did not reach the high levels of discomfort reported by the compulsive cleaners. Sometimes the completion of the compulsive checking left the anxiety/discomfort unchanged, and in exceptional circumstances it was even followed by a slight increase in anxiety (see Figure 8.4). Roper & Rachman (1975) had to resort to testing some of the patients in their own homes because they reported little or no anxiety/discomfort when asked

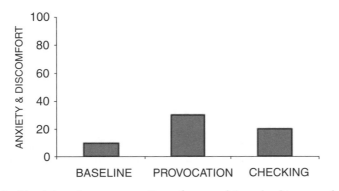

Figure 8.4   The laboratory provocation of compulsive checking produces less anxiety/discomfort than provocation of cleaning by touching a contaminant. Also, carrying out the appropriate checking action is less effective

to carry out the provoking tasks in the laboratory. The results from the two groups of patients, cleaners and checkers, were broadly similar, but the unexpected differences could not be ignored. The checkers reported discomfort more than they did anxiety, the amount of anxiety provoked under these experimental conditions was larger and easier among patients with cleaning compulsions than among those who engage predominantly in checking, some provocations left the checkers unmoved, and often the tactic failed to produce the usual reactions in the laboratory. The significance of these differences was missed at the time, only to emerge when Salkovskis (1985) drew attention to the important effects of inflated responsibility, as part of his cognitive account of OCD.

As discussed in Chapter 2, there is a close and probably causal relationship between compulsive urges and compulsive acts, with the former producing the latter. Using the same experimental methodology, the natural course of these compulsive urges and their relation to anxiety was mapped out (Rachman & Hodgson, 1980). It was found that the completion of the appropriate compulsion reduced the anxiety and the urges, leaving only a minimal amount of residual anxiety. After the anxiety and urges had been provoked, a 3-hour observation period was used in order to track the time course of the spontaneous decay of urges and anxiety. In most cases the urges and the anxiety had declined significantly by the end of the first hour, and by 3 hours almost complete dissipation had taken place. After repeatedly experiencing the spontaneous decay of anxiety and compulsive urges, patients had lasting decreases in anxiety and urges. These observations on the spontaneous decay of compulsive urges/behaviour were consistent with, and contributed to, the development of the behavioural techniques for treating OCD (see below).

Obsessions (recurring, intrusive, repugnant thoughts) and compulsions are closely related. Most often, the compulsions follow the obsessions. The experience of an obsession is almost always distressing and generally prompts the affected person to take steps to reduce the unease (Rachman, 1997, 1998). These steps can take the form of observable compulsions or avoidance behaviour, or attempts to neutralize the probability and/or anticipated effects of the thoughts and actions. Repeated requests for reassurance are usually regarded as a disguised form of compulsion, often a disguised form of compulsive checking (see further, Chapter 2). Salkovskis (1998) adds that these repeated requests for reassurance can also serve to diffuse responsibility. As an illustration, one of our patients who was fearful of inadvertently harming people by serving them unsafe food could overcome her inhibition only if she fully informed the recipient of the history of the food and the need for caution; 'Now that they know, the responsibility is theirs' (see also Chapter 4).

In summary, the behavioural approach succeeded in a number of ways. It provided a foundation for the experimental analysis of OCD and produced support for parts of the Mowrer theory. Most importantly, it demonstrated the anxiety-reducing effects of compulsive activities. It was shown that relevant anxiety is easily provoked in a laboratory setting, and that carrying out the relevant compulsive behaviour generally produces prompt and large reductions in anxiety. The research also led to the identification of a spontaneous decay of anxiety—in addition to the compulsion-induced declines. It was further shown that episodes of spontaneous decay are cumulative and can be lasting, thereby buttressing the emerging behavioural therapy for OCD. The behavioural approach also led to the identification of the two major—separable but related— forms of compulsion, checking and cleaning. It was also of great significance that the behavioural theory plus the supporting experiments contributed to the development of a demonstrably effective form of therapy, comprising the two elements of exposure and response prevention (ERP).

This thinking and research was productive and enlightening but fell short of providing a comprehensive psychological account of OCD. A major premise of Mowrer's theory, that fear/anxiety is acquired by a process of conditioning, was found to be an overgeneralization. There are at least two other pathways to the acquisition of fear, namely vicarious acquisition and informational acquisition (Rachman, 1977, 1990). The behavioural theory was weak on explaining the acquisition of specifically obsessive-compulsive disorders; no specific OCD pathway was found. The behaviour theory was better able to account for the maintaining factors than aetiological ones. The cognitive component of OCD, the obsessional thoughts, remained an aetiological and treatment puzzle. Behaviourally speaking, where do they come from and why are they so desperately recurrent? Is a thought a behaviour? The absence of a satisfactory conception of thought processes, and no respectable means of studying thoughts as behaviour, were insuperable obstacles. Behavioural theorists took the famous advice of a Scottish pastor: if you meet an insuperable obstacle, walk around it. Naturally, the treatment of obsessional thoughts was accordingly rudderless.

Despite the remarkable progress made in accounting for important aspects of compulsive behaviour, some features of checking were left unexplained. The qualities and dynamics of compulsive cleaning, as revealed in experiments, were regular and predictable, but compulsive checking was less stable and less predictable. As will be seen, some of the remaining puzzles were made more intelligible when cognitive analyses were introduced.

COGNITIVE APPROACHES

As discussed in Chapter 4, significant advances have been made in the cognitive analysis of various types of abnormal behaviour and experience, such as panic, and Salkovskis (1985) applied this approach to obsessional disorders. In the introduction to his cognitive analysis of OCD, Salkovskis (1985, p. 571) observed that 'obsessional thinking is the archetypal example of a cognitive disorder in the neuroses', and went on to propose that these thoughts 'revolve around personal responsibility, the possibility that if things go wrong it might well be the person's own fault' (p. 574). He went on to argue that a major factor in OCD is inflated belief 'in the responsibility of being the cause of serious harm to others or self' (p. 575). A second factor in OCD is that the person interprets the occurrence of intrusive thoughts, images, impulses and doubts as revealing and threatening (Salkovskis, 1998, 1999). This combination of OCD-related beliefs and maladaptive appraisals lies at the root of the disorder and gives OCD its distinctive qualities. Attempts are being made to establish the nature of these qualities, and the interactions of the beliefs and appraisals is a subject of current interest; an international working group has made good progress in defining and measuring these cognitions (Steketee & Frost, 2000). The absence of an explanation for the differences between disorders was a weakness of the behavioural approach, hence the current interest in distinguishing between and within anxiety disorders (for reviews of the cognitive approach in general and the available psychometric, experimental and clinical evidence, see Rachman, 1993, 1997; Salkovskis 1998, 1999; Chapter 4, this volume). The strategic shift from behavioural to cognitive theory also involves a change in emphasis, from behavioural maintaining factors to a focus on the person's beliefs and the associated appraisals of perceived threat. The shift towards cognitive explanations led to an accidental rediscovery of phenomenology.

Where does compulsive checking fit into all this? Analysing the experimental differences in the results obtained from patients with predominantly compulsive checking and those whose problem was predominantly compulsive cleaning, Roper & Rachman (1975, p. 32) noted that among the checkers, the experimental 'effects were more pronounced when the patient was alone. The presence of another person, in this study an experimenter, dampens the discomfort associated with checking compulsions. One reason for this effect may be the transfer of some responsibility from the checker to the other person'. It was speculated that 'the significance of the checker's feeling of responsibility can be accounted for by the fact that it is only those acts for which they can be held responsible that are liable to produce guilt or criticism. If the checker is not responsible for the act or its consequences then it relieves him of being criticized for the action and it also helps to avoid guilt... the fact that most checking is concentrated on the home can be attributed to the fact that it usually is the place of greatest responsibility' (Rachman, 1976a).

An exaggerated sense of responsibility can take various forms. It can be too extensive, too intense, too personal, too exclusive—or all of these. A feeling of responsibility can reach extraordinary extremes in which people 'confess' to the police that they have been responsible for crimes or accidents of which they have no knowledge. One such patient became so well known to nearby police stations that she was eventually obliged to take train journeys to other towns in order to confess. A sense of excessive responsibility usually is manifested at home and at work but can spread to any situation in which other people may come to harm—provided the affected person feels a sense of belongingness in that place. Affected people also have a tendency to experience guilt, not only for their own actions but also for those of other people. A person who has inflated responsibility will be inclined to be troubled by a wider range of his/her intrusive thoughts, in addition to any actions or omissions that might form the basis for compulsive checking, hence the exaggerated sense of responsibility that is particularly evident in compulsive checking can also be at play in obsessional thinking. When the affected person experiences an obsessional thought, he/she may feel unduly responsible for the thought and for taking action to prevent any misfortune that might arise from that thought. This phenomenon, described as 'thought–action fusion', is a cognitive bias in which a fusion or confusion between thought and action arises (Rachman, 1993). It takes one of two forms, probability bias and morality bias; in the first the person believes that having an unwanted thought concerning harm increases the risk of actual harm occurring to someone, and in the morality bias the person believes that having the unwanted intrusive thought is morally equivalent to carrying out the repugnant act (Rachman & Shafran, 1998). There is a high correlation between thought–action fusion and compulsive checking (0.41 in Shafran et al., 1996). Amir et al. (2000) recently confirmed the association between thought–action fusion and OCD, and concluded that 'The role of thought–action fusion in OCs may extend to exaggerated beliefs about thoughts regarding the reduction of harm'. Their subjects with OCD symptoms gave elevated ratings to the likelihood of negative events occurring as a result of their thoughts. In predictable circumstances, vulnerable people who experience thought–action fusion regarding harm coming to someone may feel compelled to carry out protective safety checks (including neutralization). The trigger for an episode of repetitive checking can be an external event/situation or an unwanted, intrusive and repugnant thought.

In addition to thought–action fusion, another and related bias also occurs in compulsive checking. Lopatka & Rachman (1995) found that for checkers, carrying out the action of checking can actually increase the sense of responsibility, thereby contributing to the self-perpetuating and self-defeating properties of compulsive checking. Further, they found a bias among checkers towards believing that the probability of harm occurring is elevated when they feel responsible. Another contributor to the self-perpetuating cycle was uncovered by Tolin et al. (2001), who found that episodes of excessive checking decrease the person's confidence in the accuracy of the relevant memory. Broadly, the more you check, the less sure you are that you have checked. So repeated checking can fuel a self-perpetuating cycle by inflating the person's sense of responsibility, increasing the perceived chances of harm and decreasing confidence in one's memory.

Most attempts at neutralization are covert and therefore difficult to access. For the purpose of experimentation, it is necessary to use a method for externalizing the act of neutralization and in this way make it accessible and open to manipulation. Rachman et al. (1996) carried out an experiment to test the hypothesis that neutralization resembles overt compulsive behaviour. In particular, it was predicted that neutralization reduces the anxiety that is evoked by unacceptable thoughts, and if neutralization is delayed, then the anxiety and the urge to neutralize will decay naturally. A total of 63 subjects selected because of their proneness to thought–action fusion were asked to write a sentence about harm coming to a relative or friend in order to evoke the necessary anxiety. This tended to provoke distress and many participants were loath to do the task. There was much hesitation and discomfort. After writing the message, they were asked to immediately neutralize, or in the second condition to delay neutralizing for 20 minutes, after which time anxiety and the urge to neutralize were re-assessed. They were free to use any method of neutralizing, and many changed the written message (e.g. by substituting the word 'not') or tore it up; some even burnt it. The participants who had neutralized were then instructed to delay and those who had delayed were now instructed to neutralize immediately, at which time the final assessments were taken. The results confirmed the prediction that neutralization resembles overt compulsions, in that they are followed by a prompt reduction in anxiety. There were no differences between the amount of anxiety reduction after an immediate neutralization or after a 20 minute delay (see Figure 8.1). This spontaneous decay of anxiety/discomfort after preparing a harm message resembles that observed in OCD participants after they had touched contaminants or used 'unsafe' appliances, etc., and is consistent with the idea that neutralization is functionally similar to overt compulsive behaviour.

An inflated sense of responsibility is a common characteristic of compulsive checkers and doubters, but may be less intense and less common among compulsive cleaners. Even within this broadened sense of responsibility, however, some curious features can be observed. The most dedicated adherents of elevated responsibility always acknowledge some borders. Characteristically, the affected people experience little or no responsibility in the homes or work places of other people. They feel responsible within their own psychological territory, and it can be fascinating to watch this sense of responsibility grow in a new situation. For example, after admission to hospital, patients initially feel relieved of responsibility, have little tension and display minimal checking behaviour. However, when they become accustomed to the ward and their sense of responsibility grows, the tension returns and they begin checking on the ward. A similar process of emerging responsibility can be seen when people go on holiday. As they start to feel comfortable on holiday ('at home'), a sense of territory emerges and this is followed by the growth of responsibility, and then tension. Some patients intertwine their feelings of responsibility with a strong desire to be compassionate, and may even come to interpret their extreme sense of responsibility as a necessary expression of compassion; to feel responsible means that one is considerate and compassionate, and vice versa; 'If I do not feel responsible for protecting my neighbours from misfortunes, it means that I don't care, that I am wanting in compassion'.

A range of psychometric and experimental evidence is consistent with Salkovskis' cognitive-behavioural analysis emphasizing the role of responsibility appraisals (e.g. Freeston et al., 1992; Lopatka & Rachman, 1995; Shafran, 1997) and its particular relevance for OCD (Salkovskis et al., 2000). For example, Lopatka & Rachman (1995) suggested that changes in perceived responsibility are followed by corresponding changes in the urge to check compulsively. In order to ensure ecological validity, the experiments were conducted in the homes of the OCD patients, using tasks and objects that played a part in their disorder (e.g. using the stove). For experimental purposes, the patient's sense of personal responsibility was manipulated and it was found that a decrease in responsibility was followed by significant declines in discomfort and in the urge to carry out the compulsive checking. It proved difficult to obtain the patients' agreement to transfer responsibility to the experimenter, even for the circumscribed short period of the experiment, but when accomplished this had a major effect on the checking. Similarly, Shafran (1997) manipulated responsibility by varying the presence and absence of the experimenter during a behavioural task. The manipulation was successful in that responsibility for threat was higher when the subject was alone than when the experimenter was present. In the high-responsibility condition, estimates of the urge to neutralize, of discomfort and the probability of threat were all significantly higher than in the low-responsibility condition. Research by Freeston along the same lines has produced comparable results. The experimental findings are consistent with clinical observations, which indicate that under natural conditions, increases in responsibility can provoke or exacerbate compulsions, especially checking. In a case-file study, Rasmussen & Tsuang (1986) identified two typical triggers of compulsions—loss or an increase in responsibility.

The cognitive approach has expanded the questions and provided some answers that have broadened our understanding of the disorder. It has gone part-way towards addressing the specific question that prompted Salkovskis (1985) to look for a fresh approach to OCD. How can the Mowrer two-stage theory of fear and avoidance explain the variations of anxiety disorders, and why do some people develop OCD rather than another disorder? What accounts for the specificity of OCD?

The introduction of cognitive concepts, particularly the emphasis on inflated responsibility, has improved the analysis of individual case problems and clarified the driving force that underlies certain compulsions, especially those in the realm of checking. Progress has also been made in answering the original question of why patients develop their particular anxiety disorder. Compulsive checking is now more intelligible and we have clues about the predisposing and precipitating factors. We also have a specific theory to account for obsessions (Rachman, 1997, 1998).

These clinical problems are now more easily treatable. Not least, the new understanding provides a basis for the therapeutic 'behavioural experiments' (e.g. Rachman, 2001) that are playing an increasing part in CBT. For example, patients are asked to test out the effects of suspended/transferred responsibility on their checking urges and compulsions. Consistent with the experimental findings, such transfers or suspensions can produce dramatic changes in checking.

A full account of the emerging cognitive theory of compulsive checking is provided in Rachman (2002) and for the sake of completeness an outline of this explanation is set out here. Compulsive checking is said to occur when people who believe that they have special responsibility for preventing harm coming to others/self feel unsure that a perceived threat has been adequately reduced or removed. In their attempts to achieve certainty that all is safe, they repeatedly check. Paradoxically, these attempts to check for safety can produce adverse effects, which fuel a self-perpetuating mechanism. So far, four elements of this mechanism have been identified. The first element arises from the person's inability to achieve certainty, to ensure safety, because the checking can have no natural terminus. It is rarely possible to achieve certainty that these future threats have been eliminated, and the checking has no natural end. Hence, it recurs. The second element is a deficit of memory, actually a deficit of confidence in one's memory. With repeated checking, the person's confidence in his/her recall of the checking (and its safety effects) declines (Tolin et al., 2001). The more persistently one checks, the less confidence one has in the memory of the checking. The third element is a cognitive bias in which people feel that the probability of harm occurring is elevated when they are responsible, when they are on duty (Lopatka & Rachman, 1995). The fourth element in the self-perpetuating mechanism is another cognitive bias, in which people experience an increase in responsibility after completing a check for safety (Lopatka & Rachman, 1995). In short, the checking sets off a self-perpetuating mechanism. The more you check, the more responsible you feel, the greater the perceived threat and the worse your memory gets. Hence, the more you check, the more you check.

The intensity and duration of the compulsive checking is determined by three 'multipliers'. As the person's perceived responsibility rises, the intensity and duration increase. The two other multipliers are the perceived probability of harm and the predicted seriousness of the harm, both of which increase the intensity and duration of the checking. The very worst set of multipliers comprises extremely high responsibility, high probability of harm and extremely serious 'costs'. The cognitive similarities and differences between compulsive checking and related disorders, such as obsessions, compulsive cleaning, and hypochondriasis (health anxiety), are delineated in the full theory (Rachman, 2002).

The two main maladaptive cognitions are the belief in one's special responsibility for preventing harm and the misinterpretation of the personal significance of the out-of-control checking behavioural and impaired memory confidence. Consequently, cognitive-behavioural therapy should be directed towards modifying these cognitions. In addition, attempts should be made to disrupt the self-perpetuating mechanism, predominantly by the institution of response prevention. Incidentally, the probable reason for the moderately successful early forms of behavioural treatment of compulsive checking can be traced to the disruption of the self-perpetuating mechanism by preventing the checking behaviour. It seems unlikely that exposure methods had much to add, but the introduction of more properly cognitive methods should help to raise the improvement rates.

Many problems remain. The nature and origins of inflated responsibility have been identified as important questions (Salkovskis, 1985, 1998, 1999). The interrelations between OCD beliefs and maladaptive appraisals need clarification. The derived treatment strategies and tactics need to be set out in full, evaluated and compared to the existing procedures. And most challenging of all, fresh efforts need to be directed towards explaining the aetiology of OCD. The traditional assumptions about conditioning effects, vicarious learning and so forth have not gained the necessary support. The results of a comprehensive longitudinal study of a cohort of children in Dunedin failed to produce any pointers to the development of OCD (Poulton, personal communication, 2000), and a study of OCD in children designed to examine the early origins (and possible causes) of the disorder was also disappointing (Shafran & Rachman, 2002).

MEMORY

The perplexing inability of many patients to remember whether or not they have checked to ensure that the the electrical appliances have been switched off, or locked the doors, or whatever, gave rise to the idea that people with this disorder suffer from a memory deficit (e.g. Brown et al., 1994b; Sher et al., 1984; Tallis, 1995a). Commonly they are unable to remember whether or not they have turned off the stove (for example), even after numerous repetitions, and even after the passage of mere seconds. This is troubling and frustrating for the affected person, and puzzling for the increasingly impatient observer. Some researchers are of the opinion that this curious inability to recall is evidence of a memory deficit which arises from a biological dysfunction or damage (e.g. Boone et al., 1991; Tallis, 1995a).

This memorial phenomenon is best approached within a broader context of studies of information processing in anxiety disorders generally (e.g. Barlow, 1988; Rachman, 1998). It is assumed that people vary in their proneness to experience anxiety, and that the vulnerable people become hypervigilant when entering the normal or potentially intimidating situation. Their hypervigilance promotes rapid and global scanning, which then turns to an intense and narrow focus if a threat is detected. The detection of the threat triggers an inhibition of ongoing behaviour (Gray, 1982), often characterized, by attentive stillness and high arousal. If the available information is interpreted as signifying safety, the person can then resume the ongoing behaviour. However, if the information is interpreted as signifying a danger of harm, then anxiety arises and this may be followed by escape, avoidance or coping. In the case of people with OCD it can give rise to compulsive checking behaviour.

Hypervigilance is especially obvious under stressful conditions. In clinical practice with patients suffering from anxiety disorders, the occurrence of hypervigilance and selective attention is an obvious and daily occurrence. In extreme cases the attentional processes are so distorted that the patient engages in rapid visual scanning in virtually all new situations. A remarkable example of this hypervigilance was encountered in a patient who complained of compulsive checking for signs of detonator caps or other potentially explosive materials whenever he went outdoors. He was a trained engineer and felt that it was his special responsibility to ensure that public places were kept safe from potentially harmful materials. When he did venture out he immediately engaged in rapid and intensive scanning of the environment, taking great care to check any object or item that seemed to him to be potentially dangerous. Comparably intense scanning can, of course, take place of one's internal environment as well as the outside world, most notably in panic disorder (see Clark, 1985, 1997).

Although a number of studies have shown that there are attentional and selective biases in anxious subjects, there is only weak and contradictory evidence of memory biases in these subjects. The studies showing memory bias in depressed patients have not been easy to replicate in people with anxiety. It has been suggested that these failures speak to the elusiveness of the phenomenon (Rachman & Shafran, 1998, p. 67). There is good reason to expect a memory bias in anxiety because one of the earliest and most prized examples of the operation of non-conscious processes in memory was provided by Claparede (1911) in a clinical anecdote that illustrated a memory bias for threat in a mist of amnesia (see Rachman, 1998). Claparede carried out a series of investigations into the memorial functioning of a 47-year-old woman residing in the Bel-Air asylum. Her memory for distant events was intact but she did not know where she was, or even that she had been in the asylum for 5 years. She did not recognise the physicians, whom she saw every day, or the nurse who had been caring for her for 6 months. She forgot from one moment to the next what she had been told, despite numerous repetitions. In a famous demonstration, Claparede pricked her hand with a pin held between his fingers. The mild pain that it produced was as quickly forgotten as all other new information, and seconds after being pricked she could remember nothing of the event. However, when he brought his hand close to hers a second time, she pulled back her hand. When asked why she did this, she replied: 'Well, don't I have the right to pull my hand away?' and 'Maybe there is a pin hidden in your hand'. When she was asked why she thought about a pin, she replied, 'It is just an idea which crossed my mind'. She never recognised the idea of being 'pricked' as a memory. Her avoidance behaviour indicates that she was responding to the threat of repeated pain, even though she could not recall the reason for her fear. A wider discussion of information processing in OCD is provided by Rachman (1998) and by Rachman & Shafran (1998).

One of the reasons for supposing that there is a memory deficit in OCD is that it has face validity, for many compulsive checkers complain that they cannot clearly recall whether or not they have carried out an act of checking, even when the action has been completed only moments before. The memory is elusive. In some studies non-clinical 'checkers' performed less well on tests of memory than did comparison subjects. Research by Sher and colleagues produced data showing that 'checkers' had poorer recall for past actions than non-checkers and the checkers obtained lower scores on the memory quotient of a standard scale for measuring memory (Sher et al., 1983, 1984, 1989). Comparable findings were obtained by Rubenstein et al. (1993), but two qualifiers are in order; first, the participants were non-clinical subjects; and second, their scores of memory were lower but not in the abnormal range.

Many patients with OCD have extremely well-developed or even enhanced memorial abilities for OCD-related events and can recall precise details of situations and experiences (e.g. contact with contaminating material) that were disturbing or threatening (Radomsky & Rachman, 1999). So, for example, a patient who was intensely frightened of disease-related contaminants, and consequently engaged in extensive avoidance behaviour, was able to recall in detail the types of blood stain and other threatening stimuli that he had encountered in particular places as far back as 12 years earlier! The same patient also had a milder fear of making errors and engaged in a certain amount of checking behaviour, especially to ensure that the stove had been switched off. He frequently had difficulty in remembering whether or not he had turned off the stove and on numerous occasions felt compelled to return to the kitchen to check his memory. This is a not uncommon example of a curious combination of excellent and precisely accurate memory relating to some threats and a patchy unreliable recollection of other activities. No biological explanation takes account of the evidence of enhanced memory in OCD patients, and certainly none of them would predict enhanced memory. In addition, there is evidence that, on standard tests of memory, people with OCD perform as well as non-OCD participants (McNally & Kohlbeck, 1993; Radomsky et al., 2001; Shafran, 1997). Memory for contaminated stimuli among OCD participants with a fear of contaminants was compared to memory in a group of anxious controls and a group of students (Radomsky & Rachman, 1999). All of the participants were shown 25 contaminated items and 25 clean items. They then completed a neuropsychological memory assessment, after which they were asked to recall the original 50 items. 'The OCD group had a better memory for contaminated items than for clean ones. Neither comparison group showed such a bias' (p. 605). There were no differences between any of the groups on the standard tests of memory.

The curious combination of excellent memory for some threats and poor recollection for other information, such as whether or not they have checked, may help to account for the inconsistencies in the results from studies of memory deficits (Rachman & Shafran, 1998). The phenomenon is an inconsistent one. It has been suggested that some of the inconsistencies arise not from actual deficits in memory but rather from patients' lack of confidence in their memory, in particular settings (see Brown et al., 1994b; Constans et al., 1995; McNally & Kohlbeck, 1993). In keeping with this possibility, Radomsky et al. (2001) reported that people who engaged in compulsive checking behaviour obtained memory scores on standardized tests that were average or above average and that, under specifiable conditions, their memory for checking activities could be increased or decreased by deliberate manipulation. They also found that the OCD participants had significantly lower confidence in their memory than did comparable non-compulsive subjects.

Following a confirmatory diagnostic interview, the participants were asked to carry out a relevant baseline check in their own homes. Then two additional checks were completed, one under conditions of high responsibility and one under low responsibility. 'After each check, participants completed a memory and confidence interview which assessed their memory for threat-relevant and threat-irrelevant aspects of the checks, and also confidence in memory for the check'. A week later the participants attended the laboratory to view a video made of their checks carried out at home.

The results showed a 'positive memory bias for threat-relevant information', and under high responsibility this bias was accentuated. In addition, it was found that high responsibility had an even greater influence on confidence in memory than on actual accuracy of the memory. This is consistent with the recent report that OCD subjects showed a progressive decline in memory confidence over repeated trials in which they were required to recall sets of safe and unsafe items (Tolin et al., 2001). The OCD participants had overall memory scores equal to anxious controls and to non-clinical participants.

Rachman & Shafran (1998) concluded their review of the subject: 'In summary, the results regarding memory deficits are inconsistent, and the conclusions are dependent on the paradigm used to test the hypothesis. However, at present, the hypothesis that patients with OCD may suffer from a lack of confidence in their memory in particular settings is gaining empirical support' (p. 68). Additionally, a positive bias for recalling threat-relevant information has been identified in OCD participants, as has an enhanced memory for such information. Theories of OCD-specific memory deficits, cast in a biological framework or not, need to accommodate the occurrence of a positive memory bias, and enhanced memory, in people with OC disorders.

The oddities of memory in compulsive checking are intriguing but their importance should not be exaggerated. There is no reason to believe that these vagaries of memory are central to an understanding of this phenomenon. And as mentioned earlier, there is no relation between neuropsychological deficits, including memorial deficits and response to psychological treatment (Bolton et al., 2000).

THE TREATMENT OF COMPULSIVE CHECKING

The effectiveness of behavioural treatment for OCD is attested to by randomised control trials (e.g. Foa et al., 1992; Rachman et al., 1979), by compilations and analyses of such trials by standard methods (see Foa et al., 1998a; Swinson et al., 1998) and by meta-analyses (e.g. Abramowitz, 1997). In light of the evidence and analyses, the technique has been endorsed by expert committees. Guideline 1 of the OCD Consensus of Experts (March et al., 1997a) reads: 'The experts usually prefer to begin the treatment of OCD patients with either CBT alone or with a combination of CBT and medication (CBT + SRI)'. Similarly, in 2000, a separate group of experts set out recommendations for primary care physicians (Evans et al., 2000). The 'first line' recommendation is for psychological therapy; 'cognitive behaviour therapy strategies may include exposure and response prevention' (p. 28). The best established psychological treatment consists of these two components, exposure and response prevention, often supplemented by therapeutic modelling (Rachman & Hodgson, 1980; see Chapter 15, this volume, for details). With the infusion of cognitive analyses and fresh experimental findings, the original behavioural treatment is undergoing refinement and extension. Considerable attention is now directed to ascertaining the patient's OCD beliefs and their interpretations of intrusive thoughts and perceived threats (e.g. Rachman, 1997; Salkovskis, 1999). Their appraisals include the role and effects of the compulsive activities; for example: 'What do you think would happen if you refrained from neutralizing?', 'What new information do you acquire when you check the lump on your breast 2 minutes after completing the previous 10 checks?'. Given the importance now attached to the role of inflated responsibility in OCD, especially in compulsive checking, cognitive-behavioural therapists assess the nature of this responsibility in each case and usually encourage the person to strive for a more realistic and benign sense of responsibility. The particular value of these cognitive additions remains to be established. To date there is insufficient evidence to conclude that the present versions of CBT produce superior results to the already effective BT techniques (van Oppen et al., 1995; Whittal et al., 2000). However, the cognitive additions do seem to clarify the problems facing particular patients and we are approaching the stage at which therapeutic analyses finally are able to accommodate the exact content of the patient's fears and associated compulsions. This is perhaps one of the reasons for the recent finding that, while BT and CBT are equally effective when delivered in groups of patients, CBT appears to have the edge when provided in individual therapy (Whittal et al., 2000).

In most treatment outcome studies, patients were included if they demonstrated compulsive activities of whichever type, and as a result there is little information about the comparative effectiveness of this treatment in respect of different types of compulsive activities. What indirect evidence we have provides little indication that exposure and response prevention is selectively effective with different types of compulsions. With the exception of a recent outcome study carried out in the Anxiety Disorders Unit of the University Hospital in Vancouver (Whittal et al., 2000), it appears that two main forms of compulsion respond equally well to this treatment. The Vancouver finding, that compulsive checkers made larger therapeutic gains than did the compulsive cleaners, especially when treated in individual rather than in group sessions, will need to be confirmed (one possibility is that there is a sub-group of compulsive cleaners who are 'treatment-resistant').

The original form of treatment was developed during the behavioural era and, like all of the behavioural techniques, took no heed of cognitive factors and ignored the specific content of the abnormal behaviour. Attention has now been turned to the specific nature of the compulsive activities and the presumed purpose for carrying out this activity (Salkovskis, 1999). Checking in particular is said to arise from a strong prior belief that one has particular and great responsibility for ensuring the safety of other people/self. Preliminary work on the modification of inflated responsibility, for therapeutic purposes, is encouraging but the reduction of perceived responsibility is no easy matter. Many patients will not agree even to a temporary transfer of responsibility. However, when the inflated responsibility can be brought down to more reasonable and realistic levels, remarkable improvements can occur. For example, a young woman who engaged in persistent and intense compulsive checking of the safety of her home, in order to prevent it from fire damage, eventually made a remarkable improvement when a large part of responsibility for the safety and security of the house was transferred to other members of her family. Once this was accomplished, her checking behaviour reduced to minimal levels, within normal parameters.

In summary, it now appears that when people who believe that they have special responsibility for caring for and protecting others/self enter situations in which they perceive a high probability of significant harm occurring, they will attempt to remove or reduce these risks and will repeatedly check to ensure that their attempts are sufficient. In order to ensure protection from harm they repeatedly check the safety of the situation, and while this frequently produces a slight but transient relief from anxiety, the repeated checks also have the paradoxical effect of perpetuating the compulsion because they increase the sense of responsibility and also decrease confidence in one's memory of the relevant checking activity. Given this construal, a combination of reducing responsibility and blocking the checking should do it. The tenacity with which patients cling to their inflated responsibility will emerge as a practical problem.

Building on the knowledge acquired during the behavioural period, the newer cognitive analyses have expanded our understanding of compulsive checking and laid a basis for improved treatment of this form of OCD. We are also moving towards a fuller analysis of the self-defeating and self-perpetuating qualities of compulsive checking. Beliefs, appraisals and especially the inflation of responsibility can be expected to play a prominent role in research and treatment of compulsive checking.

Chapter 9

COMPULSIVE HOARDING

Randy O. Frost and Tamara L. Hartl

INTRODUCTION

In Dante's *Inferno* (Alighieri, 1998), 'hoarders' and 'wasters' were sent to the fourth level of hell, where they would bash each other with heavy stones for eternity. The stones were burdens that symbolized their lives, having wasted their time caring too much for material things. Possessions provide convenience, comfort and pleasure for most people. However, when judgements about their value become distorted, possessions can become the heavy stones of Dante's hell. Only recently has hoarding become the focus of research, so we know relatively little about its prevalence or seriousness. We do know, however, that it can be associated with extreme incapacitation, and circumstances created by this behaviour can be unhealthy or even lethal (Frost et al., 2000b). In this chapter we will review the evidence regarding compulsive hoarding and current attempts to develop treatments for it.

DEFINITION

Early conceptualizations of hoarding derive largely from psychoanalytic theory. Freud (1908) viewed the hoarding of money as a feature of the 'anal triad', symbolizing faecal retention. Jones (1912) expanded this notion somewhat to include the hoarding of non-money and non-food items. Fromm (1947) suggested that acquisition of possessions was one way people related to the world, and further, that a 'hoarding orientation' was one form of non-productive character. He observed that hoarders depend on acquiring and saving things for their sense of security, and they use acquisition and saving as a mechanism to escape fear. More recently, Salzman (1973) discussed hoarding in the context of obsessional neurosis. For Salzman, the core of obsessional neurosis is a drive for perfection, and

Obsessive-Compulsive Disorder: Theory, Research and Treatment.
Edited by Ross G. Menzies and Padmal de Silva. © 2003 John Wiley & Sons, Ltd.

hoarders save things in order to avoid mistakes; because they are uncertain about what will be needed in the future, they take the safe route and save everything.

Hoarding appears in the DSM-IV only as a symptom of obsessive-compulsive personality disorder. Here it is defined as the inability 'to discard worn-out or worthless objects even when they have no sentimental value' (APA, 1994, p. 673). Recent findings suggest that this definition does not accurately reflect the phenomena, in that people who hoard frequently report sentimental attachments to their possessions (Frost et al., 1998). We (Frost & Gross, 1993) have suggested the following definition:

> 'The acquisition of, and failure to discard, possessions which appear to be useless or of limited value' (Frost & Gross, 1993, p. 367).

Furthermore, two additional criteria are necessary in order to define hoarding in a clinically significant context: cluttered living spaces that prevent appropriate use of the space, and significant distress or impairment caused by the hoarding (Frost & Hartl, 1996). The inclusion of clutter in the definition springs from several considerations. First, some people acquire and save large collections of things which they store or organize efficiently. These individuals typically do not have cluttered homes. Instead, their collections are neatly arranged in storage rooms or on display. Furthermore, collectors do not report interference or distress as a result of their collections. Clearly, collecting and hoarding are different at some level. Second, 'clutter' was the predominant response given when hoarders were asked how someone would know they were 'pack-rats' by looking at their home (Frost & Gross, 1993). A definition of hoarding that discriminates clinical hoarding syndromes from collecting and normal saving involves:

> '(a) the acquisition of, and failure to discard, a large number of possessions that appear to be useless or of limited value; (b) living spaces sufficiently cluttered so as to preclude activities for which those spaces were designed; and (c) significant distress or impairment in functioning caused by the hoarding' (Frost & Hartl, 1996, p. 341).

This definition is useful in identifying clutter as the significant problem and source of disruption in hoarders' lives.

MANIFESTATIONS OF HOARDING

Hoarding involves more than the inability to discard worthless or worn-out items. As emphasized in the definition above, part of this problem involves excessive acquisition of possessions. We have seldom seen people with serious hoarding problems who did not also have a problem with compulsive acquisition. These difficulties range from compulsive buying to the compulsive acquisition of free things. Some hoarders spend enormous amounts of time shopping in discount stores, while others cruise the streets on trash pick-up day looking for 'treasures'. Frost & Gross (1993) found that hoarders reported buying significantly more extra items in order not to run out than did non-hoarders. Frost et al. (1998) found that the Hoarding Scale (a measure of hoarding severity) was significantly and positively correlated with a measure of compulsive buying among college students. In a separate community sample, people who reported problems with compulsive hoarding scored significantly higher on compulsive buying than did a non-hoarding control group. Furthermore, in both samples (students and hoarding community), hoarding was associated with a tendency to acquire free things (e.g. collecting other people's trash). The latter findings suggest that compulsive buying may be part of a larger construct of compulsive acquisition. In a follow-up study, Frost et al. (2002) compared a group of compulsive buyers (based on criteria defined in Faber & O'Guinn, 1992) with an age-matched control group on levels of compulsive hoarding and related constructs. Compulsive buyers scored significantly higher on the Hoarding Scale and on a six item measure of compulsive acquisition of free things. They also showed a pattern similar to hoarders in that they had higher levels of perfectionism, indecisiveness and obsessive-compulsive symptoms, as measured by the Padua Inventory (Sanavio, 1988).

Compulsive buying has been conceptualized as an impulse-control disorder and hypothesized to be a part of a compulsive–impulsive spectrum (McElroy et al., 1994). The pattern of behaviour in compulsive buying (as well as compulsive acquisition of free things) resembles the sequence of experiences in OCD. Recurrent and intrusive urges to buy (or acquire) are accompanied by discomfort that is relieved by acquisition or avoidance of acquisition cues. For example, one of our participants could not walk past a news-stand because of her urge to acquire potentially important information in newspapers and magazines. She would cross the street and turn her head the other way to avoid looking at the news-stand. Additional evidence that hoarding is closely related to impulse-control problems was found in a recent study in which pathological lottery and scratch-ticket gamblers scored significantly higher on the Hoarding Scale, a new Yale–Brown Obsessive Compulsive Scale that measures acquiring and saving, and on a measure of compulsive buying (Frost et al., 2001). They did not score higher on a measure of the compulsive acquisition of free things, however.

The above evidence strongly suggests that compulsive acquisition is an integral component of hoarding. In talking with people suffering from compulsive hoarding, one gets the sense that once they see something they want it immediately becomes part of their world and they must acquire it, regardless of the practicalities involved. One of our participants already had 34 bottles of shampoo, but when she saw a sale on shampoo, she felt she had to buy more. Another participant felt compelled to acquire information and spent up to 10 hours each day attending lectures on almost any subject. The time spent on these activities prevented her from doing anything else, yet she felt obligated to do this or she would miss potentially important information.

Aside from acquisition, the most salient manifestation of hoarding is the inability to discard possessions. The behaviour can appear quite odd, and occasionally hoarders report saving things no-one else would save, such as fingernail clippings and rotten food. However, the types of things saved by hoarders are generally the same as the types of things most people save, such as clothing, papers and books (Frost & Gross, 1993). Furthermore, the reasons given for saving are the same as those given by non-hoarders. In seminal work on the nature of possessions, Furby (1978) suggested that the reasons for ownership can be classified by the type of value placed on the possession. Three types of value have been identified. *Instrumental* or practical value reflects the extent to which the possession is believed to have some present or future use. *Sentimental* value refers to the emotional meaning attached to the possession, usually as a result of its association with a particularly important time, event or person. *Intrinsic* value is sometimes given to possessions that have no practical or emotional importance, but to which an attachment forms. For example, one hoarder felt attached to a bag full of bottle caps. This was not because it had any practical or emotional significance, but simply because she liked the shapes and colours of the caps. The major difference between hoarders and non-hoarders is that their thresholds for each of these types of value are lower. Consequently, they assign more of each of these types of value to a broader array of things than non-hoarders do.

Acquiring and saving a large volume of possessions does not by itself reflect psychopathology. The number of possessions people acquire and how much they save varies considerably within and between cultures. The feature of hoarding that makes it pathological is the inability to organize possessions in such a way that they do not interfere with the ability to carry out necessary everyday activities (i.e. cooking, cleaning, hygiene, etc.). The inability to organize possessions creates extreme clutter and chaos in living areas and prevents the use of space for necessary life tasks. This manifestation is related to the volume of possessions acquired and saved, since organization becomes more complicated in small living spaces if there are lots of things that go into them. However, based on our observations, a great deal of the clutter found in the homes of hoarders appears to be associated with difficulties in organizing possessions. This is associated with the general indecisiveness demonstrated by compulsive hoarders (Frost & Gross, 1993). Decisions of any sort seem to be difficult for people who hoard. Therefore, creating and implementing an organizational plan is difficult. Another feature that may be related to organizational problems is the fear many hoarders have of putting things out of sight (Hartl et al., 2000). Because they believe they have a very poor memory, many hoarders believe they must keep things in sight, otherwise they will lose or forget them. The result is a problem with organizing and putting things into some sort of categorical scheme. Among the homes of some of our research participants, we observed rooms filled with piles of seemingly unsorted possessions, while drawers and closets were empty. These organizational problems may reflect more basic information-processing difficulties (see below).

DIAGNOSIS AND CO-MORBIDITY

Hoarding has been reported in a variety of disorders, including organic mental disorders (Greenberg, Witzum & Levy, 1990), psychotic disorders (Luchins, Goldman, Lieb & Hanrahan, 1992), eating disorders (Frankenburg, 1984) and brain injury (Eslinger & Damasio, 1985). In addition, hoarding has been reported in conjunction with aging-related processes, including dementia and self-neglect (Hwang et al., 1998). Although hoarding is one of the diagnostic criteria for obsessive-compulsive personality disorder (OCPD), few empirical findings link hoarding to OCPD. Frost & Gross (1993) failed to find an association between hoarding and a standardized measure of OCPD (Millon Multiaxial Clinical Inventory-II), although hoarding was found to be associated with perfectionism, another symptom of OCPD. Recently, we (Frost et al., 2000c) found that hoarders did not differ from non-hoarding obsessive-compulsive disorder (OCD) patients on the Personality Disorders Questionnaire-4 (PDQ-4) measure of compulsive personality disorder, but they did have higher scores than non-hoarding OCD patients on dependent and schizotypal personality disorder. Examination of the individual items composing the OCPD measure indicated that only on one item, concerning the tendency to get lost in the details and lose sight of the big picture, did hoarders score higher than OCD non-hoarders. This raises questions about the extent to which hoarding belongs in the OCPD category.

Hoarding is most often associated with obsessive-compulsive disorder. It is included on the major measures of OCD, including the Yale–Brown Obsessive Compulsive Scale (Y-BOCS; Goodman et al., 1989b) and the

Anxiety Disorders Interview Schedule (ADIS; Brown et al., 1994b). It has been estimated to occur in 18–33% of individuals with OCD (Frost et al., 1996; Rasmussen & Eisen, 1992). A number of studies have found that subclinical hoarders report more OCD symptoms on most measures than non-hoarders (Frost & Gross, 1993; Frost et al., 1996), as do clinical hoarders (Frost & Gross, 1993; Frost et al., 1996). However, recent work on the distinctiveness of OCD symptoms suggests that although hoarding is a part of OCD, it is somewhat distinct from other OCD symptoms. Factor analyses of the checklist from the Y-BOCS have found hoarding items to load on a distinct factor with symmetry, ordering, repeating and counting compulsions (Baer, 1994) or as a completely separate factor (Leckman et al., 1997; Summerfeldt et al., 1999). Consistent with these findings, Calamari et al. (1999) found that hoarding formed a stable and separate cluster in a cluster analysis of Y-BOCS checklist responses. Recent findings on response to treatment also suggest that hoarding is distinct from other OCD symptoms (Black et al., 1998; Mataix-Cols et al., 1999b).

In a recent study (Hartl et al., 2000), self-identified problem hoarders were given a Structured Clinical Interview for DSM-IV Disorders (SCID; First et al., 1995). Only 18% met criteria for OCD, raising questions about the extent to which hoarding is correctly classified as an OCD symptom. In fact, as many hoarders met criteria for PTSD as they did OCD. However, one cautionary note regarding this study is that the OCD section of the SCID does not ask questions about hoarding as a symptom of OCD, while other structured diagnostic interviews like the ADIS (Brown et al., 1994b) do. Thus, this finding may be an artefact of the assessment method. However, it does raise a question about the extent to which hoarding in the absence of any other OCD symptom should be considered OCD. More research is needed to clarify differences between hoarders with and without other OCD symptoms.

A related question is whether there are different types of hoarders. For instance, hoarding accompanied by self-neglect and living in squalor is considered a hallmark symptom of Diogenes' syndrome, a condition in which older individuals are typically found living among their own garbage and human waste products (Clark, Mankikar, & Gray, 1975). It is possible that hoarding among individuals with dementia or Diogenes' syndrome may represent different processes than those seen in compulsive hoarding. One reason to think so is reflected in the disparity of types of possessions that are typically saved. For example, most hoarders without dementia or self-neglect reportedly save usable items such as paper, clothing, magazines and newspapers (Frost & Gross, 1993, Greenberg et al., 1990). In contrast, it appears that rubbish is most often saved among individuals with Diogenes' syndrome or dementia (Clark et al., 1975; Vostanis & Dean, 1992). These observations are based largely on anecdotal information, however, and we have seen examples of OCD hoarding of rubbish in the absence of dementia. Further research is needed to assess whether subtypes of hoarding may be classified according to the kinds of possessions saved or along other dimensions.

In addition to co-morbidity with other disorders, hoarding has been found to be associated with increased levels of general distress and overall psychopathology. Relative to controls, hoarders are more likely to have had psychiatric treatment (Frost & Gross, 1993) and score higher on a measure of general psychopathology (Frost et al., 1996). Furthermore, individuals who have hoarding symptoms in addition to other OCD symptoms have been found to be significantly more anxious and depressed than controls (Frost et al., 2000b).

The severity of hoarding behaviours ranges from mild forms seen in non-clinical populations to extreme hoarding that threatens the health and safety of the hoarder and those living nearby (Frost et al., 2000b). Hoarding behaviour in non-clinical populations, such as students and community members, shows considerable variability and can be reliably measured (Frost & Gross, 1993; Frost et al., 1998). Furthermore, the relationships observed between hoarding and other constructs, such as indecisiveness and perfectionism, shows the same pattern among non-clinical populations as in clinical ones. Seldom in these samples are the hoarding behaviours problematic. Clinical populations show considerable impairment, however. In one recent study (Frost et al., 2000a), OCD hoarders reported significantly more family and social impairment than OCD non-hoarders. In a study of 5 years' worth of complaints made about hoarding to local health departments in the State of Massachusetts (Frost et al., 2000b), substantial risk to health and safety and several deaths were directly attributed to hoarding that facilitated fires and impeded exit from the burning home. Numerous anecdotes also point to the severity of certain cases, including one description from the daughter of an 80-year-old hoarder who complained that her mother could not walk anywhere in her house, but instead had to 'swim' through the waist-high debris.

Perhaps related to the effect this problem has on the living environment is evidence that people who hoard are more likely to live alone, Frost & Gross (1993) found a smaller percentage of hoarders to be married than non-hoarders. Consistent with this finding, in a study of service workers with elderly hoarding clients, Steketee et al. (2001) found that over half of the hoarders had never been married, far greater than the base rate for never-married elders. Whether differences in marital status are due to the hoarding behaviour, to associated psychopathology or to difficulties forming attachments to others will be apparent only with more research.

Little is known about the age of onset for hoarding. On the basis of a very small number of subjects, Greenberg (1987) concluded the onset was in the early 20s. In contrast, Frost & Gross (1993) found that 66% of hoarding participants reported that their hoarding started in childhood, whereas only 25% said that it started during their teens or early 20s. Only 9% of the participants reported onset of hoarding after age 24. While the age of onset for hoarding may be relatively young, the mean age of hoarders in several studies has been about 50 (Frost et al., 2000a; Hartl et al., 2000). It may be that hoarding tendencies do not reach clinical significance until later in life, while the self-perception is that it has been a consistent pattern since childhood. Hoarding poses a particular problem for community health and housing authorities (Frost et al., 1999) and the largest such group affected is the elderly. In a recent study of health department officers in Massachusetts, we found that more than 40% of complaints about hoarding concerned elderly people. Elderly hoarders faced serious threats to their health and safety, but were rarely insightful about their plight (Frost et al., 2000a).

Frost & Gross (1993) found evidence of a familial link to hoarding; 85% of the hoarders in their sample had first-degree relatives they considered to be 'pack-rats', as compared to 54% of the non-hoarders. Similarly, Winsberg et al. (1999) found that 84% of their hoarding sample reported a family history of hoarding, and 80% grew up in a home with someone who hoarded. It is unclear whether intergenerational transmission of hoarding is learned or genetic, however. Also unclear is the definition of 'pack-rat' used by participants, as evidenced by the high base rate of relatives considered to be pack-rats in the Frost & Gross study.

Information about the aetiology of hoarding is scarce. Some researchers have suggested that hoarding may stem from deprivation earlier in life (Adams, 1973; Shafran & Tallis, 1996), as hoarding symptoms are sometimes present in survivors of the holocaust and periods of economic depression (Adams, 1973; Greenberg, 1987). In some cases, hoarding may arise in response to food deprivation. In the famous Keys study (1946), in which men volunteered to reduce their caloric intake to help research on the effects of starvation, some men began to hoard food items and 'junk' as they lost weight (as cited in Frankenburg, 1984). While some cases of hoarding may certainly be tied to prior financial or food deprivation, Frost & Gross's (1993) investigation failed to find support for an association between hoarding and deprivation. Prior deprivation may therefore account for some, but not a majority of, cases of hoarding behaviour.

Related to the notion of deprivation, some authors have suggested that the early experience of loss may be tied to the disorder (Greenberg et al., 1990). Greenberg et al.'s suggestion was based on a small number of cases ($n = 8$), but other case descriptions have reported similar histories (Shafran & Tallis, 1996). We have noted a somewhat broader theme of loss among the hoarding participants in our studies (Frost & Hartl, 1996). The theme involves the fear of losing opportunities, as well as losing one's personal history and identity when possessions are discarded.

A COGNITIVE-BEHAVIOURAL MODEL OF COMPULSIVE HOARDING

In an effort to provide a framework for understanding hoarding and to facilitate the generation of hypotheses, we have proposed a cognitive-behavioural model of hoarding (Frost & Hartl, 1996; Frost & Steketee, 1998). The model is based on existing research on hoarding, our interviews with hoarders, and our attempts to treat hoarding symptoms. In this model, hoarding is conceptualized as a multifaceted behaviour stemming from four deficits or problems: information-processing deficits; problems in forming emotional attachments; erroneous beliefs about the nature of possessions; and behavioural avoidance of the experience of loss.

Several types of information-processing *deficits* are thought to be associated with hoarding, including deficits in decision-making, deficits in categorization and organization, and difficulties with memory. Several investigations have provided evidence for an association between indecisiveness and hoarding severity (Frost & Gross, 1993; Frost & Shows, 1993). Hoarders often report deep regret when they have thrown a possession away and subsequently find that they could have used it. Frost & Gross (1993) suggest that the indecisiveness comes from a perfectionistic concern over making mistakes. However, some recent evidence suggests there may be more than perfectionism behind hoarders' high levels of indecisiveness (Tarkoff et al., 2000). Hoarders may have trouble making decisions because of a tendency to review every piece of relevant information, however unimportant, before making a decision. For many, they simply do not 'feel' they have enough information on which to base a decision, regardless of the importance of the outcome.

A second type of information-processing deficit pertains to difficulty with categorization and organization. Research has indicated that individuals with OCD have more complex concepts, meaning that they define category boundaries more narrowly (Frost et al., 1988; Persons & Foa, 1984).

Similarly, hoarders seem to have more detailed and elaborate concepts and thus require more information for making decisions. In addition, hoarders tend to be under-inclusive in their category assignments, resulting in an abundance of categories that are very small in size. One of our research participants considered each possession to be worthy of its own category. For example, she was uncertain as to whether she should file a travel brochure containing information about Sturbridge, Massachusetts, under 'travel', 'Sturbridge,' or 'Massachusetts.' Committing the brochure to one category meant that it would be lost to her if she were searching through the other possible categories. Therefore, she felt most comfortable leaving the brochure out in the living space where she could see it, and where it would remain unassigned to one limiting category.

The frequency of complaints by hoarders about poor memory led us to hypothesize it as a potential information-processing deficit. Consistent with this hypothesis, Hartl et al. (2000) found that hoarders had poorer recall of verbal and visual information than non-hoarders. They also confirmed several other hypotheses regarding poorer confidence in memory. Interestingly, the actual memory deficits did not completely account for the lack of confidence hoarders had in their memory, neither did the actual deficits account for their preference for keeping possessions in sight. These beliefs will be discussed below in conjunction with other beliefs associated with compulsive hoarding. For a review of the literature pertaining to neuropsychological deficits in OCD, see Chapter 3.

The second feature of the model consists of problems related to becoming *overly emotionally attached to possessions.* Several case studies and anecdotal reports of hoarding have described strong attachments to possessions (Frankenburg, 1984; Warren & Ostrom, 1988). Hoarders report feeling 'naked' without their possessions and view their possessions as extensions of themselves. Empirically, high levels of hoarding among student and clinical samples have been found to be associated with 'hypersentimentality' about possessions (Frost & Gross, 1993; Frost et al., 1995a). For many hoarders, possessions acquire friend-like or human-like status and provide access to meaningful past events. In addition, possessions become associated with feelings of comfort and safety. They appear to serve as 'safety signals' (Rachman, 1983) that represent comfort and the absence of threat. One hoarder reported eagerly anticipating being close to her possessions as a way to relax after particularly stressful days. Another woman reported arranging her possessions around her bed in a fortress-like manner to protect her from intruders while she was sleeping. Others describe their homes and possessions as 'bunkers' or 'cocoons'. Whether the emotional attachment to possessions influences or replaces attachments to people is unclear. Some evidence indicates that hoarding is associated with insecure, anxious and ambivalent attachments to people (Krause et al., 2000), but this relationship is not due to the overly emotional attachment hoarders have to their possessions.

In addition to the deficits outlined above, a number of *erroneous beliefs about possessions* were proposed in the cognitive-behavioural model. As mentioned above, hoarders endorse several beliefs related to memory, most importantly a belief that they have poor memory. To compensate, hoarders rely on their possessions to serve as visual cues that help them access memories and information. We have gone into several hoarders' homes whose closet and storage spaces were empty, while the bulk of their possessions lay in the middle of the room. In addition, they emphasized the dire consequences of forgetting information and believed that forgetting something would reflect badly on them. These beliefs cannot be accounted for by the actual memory deficits of hoarders (Hartl et al., 2000).

Many of the beliefs about possessions are influenced by a perfectionistic style of thinking. Compulsive hoarders show more concern over mistakes and doubts about actions than non-hoarders do (Frost & Gross, 1993). This perfectionistic pattern leads hoarders to believe they must avoid mistakes, even minor ones, that a perfect solution for disposing of possessions exists, and that they must find that solution before they can do anything with a possession. Part of this perfectionism is reflected in beliefs about acquiring and 'knowing' everything about a possession. A number of hoarders have indicated that they must read and remember everything in a newspaper before discarding it.

A related set of beliefs concerns the issue of loss, particularly the loss of opportunity. Many hoarders believe that information and potential opportunities are contained in their possessions and that if they discard them, these opportunities will be lost forever. This belief also applies to things not yet acquired. This belief remains untested or unchallenged, since most hoarders never discard objects of this sort. Somehow keeping them provides the illusion that they have not forsaken the opportunities they contain.

Consistent with cognitive features related to OCD (Salkovskis, 1985; see Chapter 4 for further information), hoarders have an inflated sense of responsibility that is manifested in several ways. First, hoarders report a strong sense of responsibility for being prepared to meet future needs. Possessions are kept, in part, because of their utility to the owner and to others. Hoarders carry more 'just-in-case' items on them (Frost & Gross, 1993) and are reluctant to discard items that may be useful in the future. In addition, hoarders feel responsible for preventing harm from coming to their possessions (Frost et al., 1995a). Hoarders feel protective toward possessions and wish to preserve their well-being, as if doing so will somehow protect themselves from harm. This may result from the level of emotional attachment to their possessions and from a tendency to bestow human-like properties on their possessions. Hoarders also fear being responsible for wasting a possession. If hoarders can imagine a use for a possession, they often feel they are responsible for making sure the possession is not discarded until it is put to that use. Thus, hoarders will save the cardboard inside of toilet paper rolls for years because they might someday be useful for an art project.

In our research we have found that hoarding is associated with an exaggerated desire for control over possessions (Frost et al., 1995a). Hoarders are less willing to share their possessions or to let others touch or move them, perhaps in part due to their strong sense of responsibility for the well-being of their possessions.

Yet another erroneous belief concerns the role possessions play in making the person feel safe and/or comfortable. Like people who have OCD, people who hoard appear to overestimate threat. They feel safest when they are amongst familiar things. For them, possessions come to be associated with feelings of safety and disposing of them feels like a violation of that safety. The safety signal value of their possessions adds to the emotional turmoil associated with the disposal.

Reflected in all of these beliefs is an underlying assumption about the value of possessions. People who hoard believe in the importance of possessions and the information they contain to a much greater extent than other people. Perhaps they can see more potential for each possession, or perhaps it is an extension of their belief in the necessity of not wasting any opportunity. Whatever the case, from the moment a hoarder recognizes a potential use for a possession, discarding it becomes extremely difficult.

The *avoidance* of categorizing, organizing, throwing things away and making decisions is a feature inevitably tied to the maintenance of hoarding behaviour. As possessions accumulate and piles of clutter thicken, the task of dealing with possessions becomes more daunting. In a sense, saving behaviour begets saving behaviour, because many hoarders attempting to excavate their possessions report looking around their houses and not knowing where to begin. Hoarders may also be avoiding the emotional distress associated with decision-making and throwing things away. One hoarder exclaimed that she felt that she just wanted to die after having thrown away a book that she had not looked at in years. Minutes later, she felt no strong emotion toward the book at all, except for wonderment at her initial reaction to throwing it away (Frost & Hartl, 1996). Hoarders' behaviours may be aimed at avoiding strong emotional states of distress associated with the difficulty of decision-making. As a result, decisions are avoided. This is sometimes associated with a similar approach to organization. Making a decision about where to put something is so distressing that the item is simply tossed on the floor and never thought about again. For some clients, this avoidance is so strong that they will live in what resembles the bottom of a trashcan and never consider trying to get rid of the trash.

TREATMENT OF COMPULSIVE HOARDING

Until recently little has been known about the treatment of compulsive hoarding. This may reflect hoarders' tendency not to seek treatment or to refuse or drop out of treatment (Ball et al., 1996). Other issues may be at play as well. Baer (1994) noted that hoarders seem to have a harder time habituating to exposure relative to other OCD patients. This may be the reason behind several reports of non-responding to cognitive-behavioural therapy (CBT) by patients who have hoarding symptoms (e.g. Basoglu et al., 1988; March et al., 1994). In addition, it has been suggested that complications may arise due to hoarders' perfectionistic behaviours and magical ideas about discarding (Kozak & Foa, 1997).

Several case series have confirmed the poor response to standard OCD treatments among compulsive hoarders. In a sample of 38 non-depressed OCD patients, Black et al. (1998) found that hoarding obsessions and compulsions were the only symptoms to predict poor response to CBT and paroxetine. Similarly, Mataix-Cols et al. (1999b) reported that hoarding symptoms predicted poorer outcome in SSRI treatment for OCD in a sample of 84 non-depressed OCD patients. Also, Winsberg et al. (1999) reported poorer response to SSRIs among a sample of 20 hoarding OCD patients. Shafran & Tallis (1996) reported improvement in one of three hoarding OCD patients following standard CBT for OCD, but only in obsessions and acquiring compulsions, not in degree of clutter. The failure of standard OCD treatments for hoarding has led some to suggest alternative treatments, such as MAOIs or cingulotomy (Mataix-Cols et al., 1999b).

In addition to poor treatment outcome for hoarding symptoms among individuals with OCD, studies suggest that hoarding symptoms in schizophrenia and dementia may also be resistant to pharmacological treatment. Clozapine and risperidone were used to treat hoarding in a 36-year-old female with schizophrenia. The addition of risperidone (6 mg) to the woman's dose of clozapine (200 mg) led to no change in the woman's psychotic symptoms but a worsening of her hoarding symptoms (Chong et al., 1996). Two weeks after discontinuation of risperidone, the woman's hoarding decreased. In cases of dementia, hoarding symptoms, along with symptoms such as poor self-care, hallucinations and delusions, are noted as unresponsive to drug treatments with the newer generation of antipsychotics (Stoppe et al., 1999). Thus, hoarding symptoms, whether in association with OCD or other disorders, appear resistant to many different medications.

Recently, however, investigators have reported some success using CBT specifically designed for the treatment of compulsive hoarding. Hartl & Frost (1999) describe a dramatic reduction in clutter with a protracted in-home treatment focused on decision-making, exposure and response prevention, and cognitive restructuring of hoarding beliefs. Using a multiple baseline experimental design, clutter in specified rooms decreased substantially during the treatment and was maintained through the 17 months of the study. Treatment addressed deficits outlined in the cognitive-behavioural model of compulsive hoarding (Frost & Hartl, 1996). In a similar case report, Cermele et al. (2001) also describe successful treatment of compulsive hoarding using treatment tailored to the cognitive-behavioural model and focusing on the cognitive, emotional and behavioural aspects of the client's hoarding.

Extending this work, Steketee et al. (2000) report the outcome of treatment for seven hoarding patients treated with CBT derived from the cognitive-behavioural model. Six of the patients were treated in a group and one was treated individually. After 20 weeks, noticeable improvement occurred for five of the seven cases, and continued improvement was obtained for three of the four patients remaining in treatment after 1 year. None of the patients was symptom-free at the end of treatment, however.

Clearly, CBT specifically designed for compulsive hoarding shows promise. The treatment program relies on both group meetings and individual sessions in the clients' home (Steketee et al., 2000). The proposed treatment is multifaceted in order to address the multiple difficulties associated with hoarding. Treatment focuses on six general themes—education about hoarding, training of organisational skills, training in decision-making, cognitive restructuring of hoarding-related beliefs, and exposure and response prevention (ERP) for both non-acquisition and discarding. These themes are targeted across three settings/contexts: in a small group of clients (4–6 persons) with hoarding problems, in the client's home with a therapist or helper, and in settings in which the client has trouble controlling his/her acquisition.

Early in treatment the primary goals are the creation of living space and the organization of possessions to improve efficiency. These are goals most clients will readily adopt, which is an important consideration, since discarding is so difficult. Also, some hoarders refuse to accept the premise that they must get rid of some of their possessions. These individuals may more readily accept help with organization. Later in the treatment process, following some success at creating living space, discarding becomes a goal. Another goal of the early phase of treatment is the control of compulsive acquisition. Unless incoming items are curtailed, newly opened living spaces will be cluttered quickly.

Group sessions begin with a review of what is known about hoarding and the cognitive-behavioural model of compulsive hoarding. Following the cognitive-behavioural tradition, we expect clients to learn the model and apply the principles on their own. Group sessions are also used to introduce treatment concepts and exercises such as organizational skills, non-acquisition exposures, and behavioural experiments on discarding.

Several problems complicate the hoarders' attempts to organize possessions, including the need to keep things in sight, problems in categorization, and focusing on too many attributes of the possession. Basic principles of organization are reviewed in the group and clients develop a plan for organization of their possessions. This component is similar to that described in various self-help books and by professional organizers.

Non-acquisition exposures in the group involve visualization of 'non-shopping', where the goal is to learn how to tolerate the urge to acquire. Clients first pick a target store and item, imagine approaching (even handling) the item to increase their urge to acquire. They then imagine walking out of the store without purchasing the item and keep track of their urge and discomfort for the next few days.

Behavioural experiments in the group require clients to bring a bag or box of possessions to each group meeting. Clients select an item from their bag and place it on a table in the middle of the room. The table has been nicknamed the 'purgatory table', since it serves as a way-station between saving and discarding. Behavioural experiments involve making predictions about the consequences (e.g. emotional responses) of discarding, making decisions about the object, identifying beliefs about the loss of the object, and group reinforcement for decisions to discard. A variety of techniques are used in conjunction with these experiments to facilitate the identification and challenging of dysfunctional beliefs. For instance, the 'downward arrow' technique facilitates the identification of core beliefs about the importance and meaning of possessions. For example, one of our downward arrow techniques produced the following:

T 'Why do you save this old newspaper?'
C 'I might need it someday.'
T 'What would happen if you threw it out and later discovered you needed it?'
C 'That would be horrible.'

T   'What would be so horrible about it?'
C   'It would mean I made a mistake.'
T   'So what? Why would that be so bad?'
C   'Because it would mean I'm a bad person, a bad mother if it was something that might have been for my kids.'

Individual sessions in the client's home provide opportunities to extend the behavioural experiments started in the group and to put into practice the organizational skills learned in the first several group sessions. Therapist assistants or helpers with special training for this population conduct these sessions. They are loosely designed to follow a sequence in which an area of the house is identified and each item in the area is reviewed and moved to a more appropriate place (i.e. out of the living area). Individual consideration of these possessions prevents avoidance of emotional discomfort, decision-making, etc. Furthermore, it provides the client with practice at decision-making, organization and eventually discarding. These sessions also provide clients with more opportunities to identify and challenge their hoarding-related beliefs.

Non-shopping exposures outside the group are patterned after the non-shopping visualization described above. Clients identify a store, and if possible, an item in the store that they want to buy. They create a hierarchy of approach behaviours where their urge to acquire escalates. Clients then work up their hierarchy. With particularly difficult stores, the client may begin by driving by, and eventually work their way up to walking in and handling the item. Alternative sites include places where clients pick up free things—at conferences, post offices or even trash dumpsters. In each case the sequence is the same. Emphasis is placed on building tolerance for the urge to acquire.

People with this problem present a significant challenge in treatment, as evidenced by the relatively poor treatment outcomes reported (Black et al., 1998; Mataix-Cols et al., 1999b). Such poor outcomes are due in part to difficulties with motivation for treatment. Levels of motivation vary from those who are willing to work on their hoarding behaviour daily to those who fail to recognize their hoarding as a problem. The latter group pose the most difficulty. Usually these people do not come for treatment, or do so only when forced by family or government officials. Active participation in treatment is not likely to occur with these people unless common goals can be established. For these people, we recommend focusing on life functions that are impeded by clutter by asking, 'What can't you do because of the clutter?'. Usually the answers to this question concern mobility, hygiene, cooking, dining and enjoyment of the living space. Once these dysfunctions are established, we suggest that the goal of treatment will be to re-establish this function, mainly through the reorganization of their possessions. This scenario is the most likely one to produce a goal both therapist and client can share. The necessity of controlling acquisition and increasing discarding can be worked into the treatment once trust has been established and some organizational success achieved. If this approach does not engage the individual, the goal of reducing pressure applied by family members or health officials may be sufficient.

Many hoarders recognize the problem and want to do something about it, but facing a house full of possessions is daunting. Even when people enter therapy enthusiastically, the amount of time necessary for clearing a full house saps their motivation. Contributing to this difficulty is the inability of hoarding clients to work by themselves. We have seen a number of clients who work well when accompanied by a therapist or helper, but seem unable to do anything between sessions. Progress for these people is so slow that their motivation to proceed with treatment begins to lag.

Clients who complete their homework between sessions tend to be the ones who get better. Therefore, understanding variables controlling motivation is crucial. We have observed several things that seem to influence motivation. Group meetings appear to keep clients engaged in treatment. As the end of the group portion of our treatment approached, several clients dropped out of therapy, even though the plan was for them to continue with their therapist assistant (Steketee et al., 2000). Even clients who had little motivation to work on their own between sessions found the group a source of support.

Regarding completion of homework, one phenomenon we observed frequently was the 'visitor effect'. Most of the assigned homework (e.g. organisation, clearing, discarding) was done the day or two before the therapist assistant's visit. In addition, any type of visitor to the home prompted a flurry of cleaning activity. Scheduling frequent visitors may be one way to improve homework compliance. Perhaps even scheduling group meetings at clients' homes may help maintain motivation.

Frequent monitoring of homework compliance may also increase the amount of work done between sessions. We have used a variety of such tactics, including having clients call in every day and report their progress on an answering machine, or bring in weekly pictures of parts of the house that were the targets of homework.

SUMMARY

Only recently has hoarding been the subject of systematic research. Progress has been made in defining the problem and conceptualizing a phenomenological model to guide research and treatment development.

Several hypotheses based on this model have been tested (Frost et al., 1998; Hartl et al., 2000), and more work is ongoing. Many questions remain, however. Are there different types of hoarding based on the nature of the items saved? What is the prevalence of hoarding in the general population? When does hoarding behaviour begin, and when does it develop into a clinical disorder? Does hoarding behaviour cause people to end up living alone? Or does loss of close ties with other people cause closer attachments to possessions? Such questions can only be answered by further research.

Chapter 10

PRIMARY OBSESSIONAL SLOWNESS

Stanley Rachman

INTRODUCTION

Primary obsessional slowness (POS) is a compulsive disorder in which the affected person carries out simple everyday tasks, mainly self-care tasks such as washing and dressing, in an exceedingly meticulous, precise, un-varying manner and sequence. As a result, they take an inordinate amount of time to complete these tasks. It can take between 2 and 6 hours to get prepared in the morning.

The disorder is termed 'primary obsessional slowness' because the slowness is not, as in other types of OCD, secondary to another type of compulsion, such as checking (Rachman, 1974). In other types of compulsions the slowness, if any, is the result of repeatedly carrying out the same action. For example, such persons are slow to leave the house because they repeatedly return to check that each and every electrical device is unplugged, that all the doors and windows are tightly shut, and so forth. Some patients whose main disorder is POS may also display some slowness that is secondary to checking. Lucid case illustrations are provided by Bennun (1980), Bilsbury & Morley (1979) and Clark et al. (1982) and textbook descriptions are given in Gelder et al. (1983), Kendell & Zealley (1983) and Marks (1981). A recent report of cases, which also gives long-term data, is provided by Takeuchi et al. (1997). Further cases have been described by Takeuchi et al. (2001).

NATURE OF THE PROBLEM

The case of a 38-year-old man who suffered from a chronic and severe obsessional disorder provides an illustration of the nature of the problem. At the start of treatment he was taking approximately 3 hours each morning

---

Obsessive-Compulsive Disorder: Theory, Research and Treatment.
Edited by Ross G. Menzies and Padmal de Silva. © 2003 John Wiley & Sons, Ltd.

to prepare himself for work, confining his teeth-brushing to late at night because it took on average 45 minutes to complete. He bathed irregularly because it required 3–5 hours to complete the process. The patient was asked to demonstrate the teeth-cleaning process in front of the therapist and it was evident that the slowness resulted from his wish (need?) to brush each small group of teeth in turn, in an astonishingly meticulous, unchanging manner. The same slowness was apparent in virtually all of his self-care activities.

This meticulous, precise behaviour is self-prescribed. Typically the person will say that it is necessary to do it correctly and that it is not ego-dystonic; there is acceptance rather than the resistance that is found in most other forms of OCD. The form of the behaviour is exact and unvarying, as is the sequence in which the behaviour has to be carried out. Intense attention is paid to precise details, as in the case of the person mentioned above who had to clean each tooth or small group of teeth in a precise manner and in the same sequence. There can be no short cuts and the whole proce- dure is extremely rigid. The activities have perfectionistic and compulsive qualities, in that the person feels that the behaviour *must* be completed correctly and the standard that is set is extremely high. To an outsider it seems an intolerable burden to wake each morning faced with the prospect of spending hours and hours to get dressed and washed, to complete their preparations, but the patients appear to regard these self-care tasks as no different from those carried out by everyone else. They consider their self- care tasks as ordinary preparations that simply are too time-consuming.

This self-prescribed, meticulous and slow behaviour with its compulsive qualities is different from other forms of OCD in a number of respects. There is little or no sign of the cognitive features that are prominent in compulsive checking, compulsive cleaning and obsessions. Unlike these other forms of OCD, patients with POS show little evidence of suffering from an inflated sense of responsibility, neither is there evidence of sig- nificant and persistent cognitive biases. The patients rarely complain of the unwanted intrusive thoughts that indicate the presence of obsessions, there is little or no mention of perceived deficits of memory that are com- mon in compulsive checking, and the patients seldom complain of anxiety or construe their meticulous behaviour as an attempt to reduce or avoid anxiety. The inordinately slow behaviour is hollow and seemingly without significant cognitive content.

POS tends to follow an unfluctuating course over many years. Fortunately it is a rare disorder, and in the survey carried out on the case files of a group of 665 patients with OCD seen at the Maudsley Hospital in London during 1969–1984 there were 21 cases of clinically significant slowness. Nineteen of the 21 cases were male and the mean age of onset was 19 years. Six of the patients had prenatal or delivery problems but only one of these had a developmental delay. In nine patients there was a family history of psychiatric illness.

ISSUES IN CLASSIFICATION

In his comprehensive review of POS, Veale (1993) argued for a different classification of POS and reviewed the various neurological explanations that have been put forward to account for this unusual disorder. The question of classification has not been finally resolved, with some critics urging that it should be maintained within the existing framework of OCD (see for example the Editorial in the *British Medical Journal*, 1974; Veale, 1993; Ratnasuriya et al., 1991). The arguments vary a little, but have in common the view that this disorder should not be separately considered and that other patients with OCD also display slowness. The critics see no advantage in distinguishing between primary slowness and slowness secondary to checking or other compulsions. More neurologically-minded critics feel that POS is indeed distinct and has a different aetiology (see Veale, 1993, for a discussion). Certainly the extraordinarily slow and rigid movements have a neurological flavour but these same patients also display normal motor actions; they walk and talk at normal pace for example. In order to justify a separate classification for primary obsessional slowness, one or a combination of criteria should be met. One needs to have psychometric analyses in order to determine the association and separateness of POS from other forms of OCD, evidence of a different clinical presentation for POS, evidence of differential responsiveness to psychological treatment and/or evidence of differential responsiveness to medication, and—ultimately—evidence of different aetiology. As far as psychometric analyses are concerned, the comparative rarity of cases of POS ensures that they will be severely under-represented in most psychometric studies, thereby precluding full analyses. In an early psychometric analysis of OCD, Hodgson & Rachman (1977; see Rachman & Hodgson, 1980) found some fleeting evidence of a separate factor of slowness but, given the rarity of cases and the fact they had only two psychometric items targeted on slowness, the evidence was weak and difficult to confirm. Later Sanavio & Vidotto (1985) studied a large non-clinical sample of Italian subjects and found evidence of a clear slowness factor among the male subjects but no such factor among the female subjects. This information, plus the disproportionate number of male patients with POS, emphasizes the limitations of a purely psychometric test of the proposed

Table 10.1   Comparative features of primary obsessional slowness

Primary obsessional slowness	Compulsive checking	Compulsive cleaning	Obsessions
Clinical features			
Meticulous self care	Not marked	Often	Not common
Slowness—minimal repetitions	Slowed by repetitions	Slowed by repetitions	Slowed by ruminations
Rigidly self-prescribed self-care	Not common	Often	Not common
Need for symmetry common	Common	Common	Common
Rigidly unvarying routines	Common	Common	Common
Perfectionism elevated	Common	Common	Common
Dependent, very	Not common	Occasional	Not common
Sense of lost time	Occasional	Occasional	Occasional
Sense of memory deficit, nil	Perceived deficits	Not common	Not common
Cognitive biases, nil	Marked	Occasional	Marked
Unwanted intrusive thoughts, nil	Common	Occasional	Universal
Anxiety, minimal/absent	Marked	Marked	Marked
Avoidance, minimal	Marked	Marked	Marked
Course, prevalence			
Unvarying	Can be episodic	Can be episodic	Unvarying
Early onset	Onset range (6–30 years)	Early adulthood	Early adulthood
Natal/prenatal problems?	Uncommon	Uncommon	Uncommon
Family psychiatric history, common	Not uncommon	Not uncommon	Not uncommon
Rare; possibly 3% of all OCD?	Most common OCD	Common OCD	Common OCD
Predominantly male disorder	No gender difference	Slightly more common in women	No gender difference
Response to treatment			
Shaping, prompting, pacing—helpful	Can be helpful	Can be helpful	Not relevant
Exposure and response prevention—irrelevant	Effective	Effective	Can be helpful
Cognitive behavioural treatment—unknown	Effective	Effective	Effective?
Medications—not known	Helpful	Helpful	Minimally helpful

classification of POS. As to clinical presentation, there are a sufficient number of differences between POS and the other forms of OCD to justify the separate classification (see Table 10.1). The very low incidence of POS, and the fact that it is disproportionately common in men, are arguments in favour of a separate classification. There are distinctive clinical features in primary slowness (Table 10.1). In addition, the psychological treatment that seems to be the most practical and promising for helping patients with POS (shaping and pacing) is of little relevance in the treatment of the major forms of OCD (see Foa & Wilson, 1991; Steketee, 1993a; Turner & Beidel, 1988).

A full list of the clinical and epidemiological similarities and differences between POS and other forms of OCD is set out in Table 10.1.

SOME INVESTIGATIONS

In an early investigation of POS, patients gave full accounts of their difficulties and background and carried out a number of simple tests and tasks under standard instructions and then under speeded conditions (Rachman, 1974). In addition, tests were used to assess patients' estimation of time, given the fact that some patients report that time seems to stop and they have difficulty believing that the clocks are accurate. The tasks and tests were also carried out on patients with disorders other than OCD. All of the patients with POS had severe disorders characterized by incapacitating slowness. During the worst phases of their illness none of them were able to function satisfactorily and each had a poor work record. They all required many hours to complete their daily tasks before leaving home. As a rule they rose 1–3 hours before other members of the household and left the house at or between 1 and 2 hours after lunchtime. Some of the most extreme cases had not completed their preparations before 4 or 5 o'clock in the afternoon. Care was taken to exclude those patients in whom slowness was a secondary consequence of repeated checking or other compulsions. All of the patients in the early study carried out some checking behaviour, but in no case was it the major problem. All of the patients had great difficulty in carrying out the simple tasks of daily life, which absorbed a vast amount of their time. They spent many hours each day getting ready in the morning—having a wash, brushing their hair, cleaning their teeth, and so on. They were unable to explain why it took so long to complete these simplest of tasks. In the main it seems to be a desire to do things precisely and correctly, a need to be extraordinarily meticulous. Each task has to be done in the correct manner, in the correct sequence, in an unchanging manner from day to day. Slow motion of the limbs played no part in the overall slowness and they all confirmed that there were many tasks that they could carry out in normal speed, such as walking, talking and eating. The predominant impression was that the major determinant of their slowness was a meticulous concern for the manner in which they carried out their tasks and a compulsion to do it in this rigidly unchanging self-prescribed manner. To take an example, when shaving they would gather their equipment and carefully place each piece in a set position, after which they would carry out a preliminary face wash. A lather would then be worked up using an inflexible regular motion involving a set number of movements. Some lather was then placed on the face and one small region shaved, involving a large number of small and precise movements of the razor. Hereafter, another small region of the face received some lather and was in turn shaved in the precise and ordered manner. At times it seemed as if they were shaving themselves hair by hair. Similar slow meticulousness was observed in tooth cleaning, another common cause of slowness. The toothbrush and paste were prepared very carefully and placed in a set position. A small amount of toothpaste was then carefully squeezed onto one part of the toothbrush, which was then dampened with 3 or 4 drops of water. They then proceeded to clean one or two teeth with precise and regular movements. The mouth was then rinsed, as was the toothbrush, and then the whole process was carried out for the next tooth or group of teeth. Although the patients agreed that some aspects of their behaviour were irrational, including their extraordinary slowness, most of them asserted that their method of carrying out the tasks was correct and that the sole problem was the loss of time. They felt they were doing the job correctly, and with proper regard, but needed to reduce the amount of time taken.

The patients were asked to carry out one real-life task that ordinarily took them a long time to complete, e.g. shaving (Figure 10.1). The time taken to complete the task was recorded and they were asked to give discomfort ratings before and after completing the task. At a later time the patient was asked to carry out the task for a second time but under speeded conditions in which they were asked to cut the time taken by exactly half. They were given frequent time checks in order to monitor their progress during this speeded performance. The second task that had to be completed under standard and then under speeded conditions was a simple digit cancellation task (Figure 10.2). Once again the times and discomfort

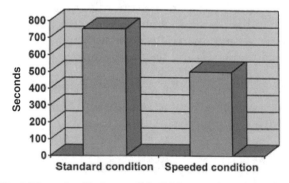

Figure 10.1 Real-life tasks. Patients with POS complete their tasks less slowly under a speeded condition. Their discomfort scores show only a marginal increase during speeded conditions

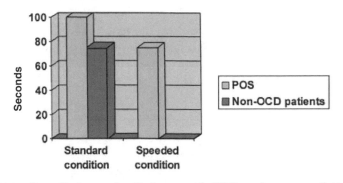

Figure 10.2   Cancellation tasks. Patients with POS perform cancellation tasks normally under speeded conditions

scores were recorded. The third task consisted of a series of arithmetic problems (Figure 10.3) and, as before, the duration of the performance was noted, as were the discomfort scores reported before and after completion. In the time estimation task the patients were asked to close their eyes and estimate the passage of a 2-minute period. Later, the patients were asked to indicate to the experimenter when a period of 3 minutes had elapsed. Finally the patients were asked to estimate how long each particular testing session had taken. The purpose of these little tasks was to gain some idea as to whether or not obsessionally slow patients do indeed have a disturbed sense of time, and it emerged that they do not.

The patients were moderately successful in speeding up their performance on a real-life task when they were given external monitoring and time checks, plus the specific aim of reducing their time by half. However, a few of the patients took slightly longer under the speeded condition than under

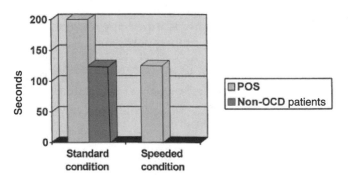

Figure 10.3   Arithmetic tasks. Patients with POS perform arithmetic normally under speeded conditions

the non-speeded instruction. Under the speeded condition a small number of the patients experienced an increase in discomfort. On the cancellation and arithmetic tasks the patients were slower than the comparison patients but were able to decrease their times under instruction and to do so without any notable increase in discomfort.

Most of the patients were excessively dependent on their relations and some had been dependent from an early age. It was not possible to disentangle whether the excessive dependency was a consequence of the slowness or whether the slowness was a product of their excessively dependent relationships. One young adult was still being helped to dress each morning by his mother, even though in hospital he was capable of dressing himself, albeit over a period of 1–2 hours. In most cases the patients were able to recall periods of excessive stress or even trauma, but none of this was noticeably different or more excessive than the accounts given by other OCD patients or patients with other kinds of psychological disorder. There was some evidence, consistent with treatment information described below, that patients with POS are at risk of relapsing if they are subjected to undue stress. There was little evidence of elevated anxiety and very few of the patients felt that meticulous completion of their everyday tasks served to reduce anxiety or some other unpleasant emotional state. It was curiously detached and content-less slow behaviour. There is little evidence at present of any prominent cognitive factors in the form of inflated responsibility, cognitive biases or unwanted intrusive thoughts. Attempts should be made in future work to detect the cognitions involved in this hollow, apparently contentless compulsion.

Before turning to matters of treatment, a number of problems need to be mentioned. In the first place, we have little or no idea why this disorder is so rare, indeed neither have we any clue as to why it should be disproportionately more common among men than among women. Furthermore, it is unclear why this precise, meticulous, slow behaviour should for the most part be confined to self-care. Is it perhaps related to some unusual form of social phobia? This possibility is partly supported by evidence that obsessionally slow patients are excessively dependent and rather isolated people. But against that idea, the meticulous and rigid behaviour is carried out even when they are socially isolated, so it is unlikely to be merely a reaction to stressful social experiences. Of course, self-care implies a social element and the patients are concerned to ensure that their appearance is satisfactory. Despite the common factor of a concern for one's appearance, POS does not resemble body dysmorphic disorder. In the latter disorder, sufferers are falsely convinced that some aspect of their body is distorted or asymmetrical or weird. Accordingly, they go to extreme lengths to correct or disguise the perceived defect (see further, Chapter 13).

The fact that POS is disproportionately preponderant in males, has a fairly early onset and in some minor respects resembles the motor dysfunctions of patients with neurological disorders, inevitably raises the question of whether or not this disorder may indeed be tracked to some dysfunction of the nervous system. As noted earlier, however, the coexistence of normal motor movements (as in walking, talking, etc.) may argue against a neurological disorder.

TREATMENT

Given the apparent absence of major cognitive components in POS and the apparent absence of significant anxiety and associated avoidance, the prevailing methods of treating other forms of OCD, notably cognitive-behavioural therapy (CBT), would not appear to be appropriate. In any event, the concept of POS emerged in 1974, during the pre-cognitive-behavioural era, in which modelling and exposure plus response prevention (ERP) was being established as a standard form of treatment. This particular form of treatment was not found to be of much help for people with POS but a related form of 'learning therapy' was used instead. This treatment became known as 'shaping, monitoring, and pacing' (or 'prompting, pacing and shaping') and is best illustrated by excerpts from the following case studies. There is no evidence that these patients derived much benefit from the medications that were in use in the period 1975–1990 (except perhaps in those instances in which the primary slowness was accompanied by significant depression) and there appear to be no reports about whether or not patients benefit from the current anti-OCD medications. It seems unlikely, except perhaps in the presence of significant depression.

The first case illustration concerns the treatment of the patient T.N., referred to above, who spent up to 3 hours each morning preparing himself and devoted a great deal of attention to cleaning his teeth. Initially he was advised and instructed on how to brush his teeth within a reasonable length of time. This simple instruction produced a small improvement but soon a plateau was reached, and this is not atypical. The patient was then asked to carry out the brushing process in front of the therapist on a few occasions and it became evident that the slowness resulted from his insistence on brushing each tooth or each small group of teeth in turn in an astonishingly meticulous and rigid fashion. He was given demonstrations of brushing at normal speed and then asked to imitate this more conventional method. Some improvement was obtained immediately. Lastly, the patient was asked to brush his teeth on a number of occasions during which the therapist set a speeded goal and provided time checks every 30 seconds.

This produced further improvements but the patient found it hard to break the 5-minute barrier, which had been the agreed goal. Nevertheless, he did make some useful improvement in brushing his teeth and subsequently in washing and dressing (see Figures 10.4 and 10.5 below for the progress of T.N.'s treatment).

Bilsbury & Morley (1979) have given a full and lucid description of their treatment of a patient who was admitted to hospital for his

> extreme slowness and meticulousness...he took about 4 hours to get up in the morning and eventually appeared ready for the day between noon and 1 p.m. Interview and observation indicated that his slowness was not caused by him having to repeat his activities many times, but resulted from them. For instance, he would wash his face in separate sections, each section being washed and dried before taking the next. This procedure took about 35 minutes to complete. Getting out of bed in the morning was particularly difficult, taking approximately 1 hour. During this period he would think about what he had to do to get out... and would plan and prepare his routine in minute detail (p. 405).

Bilsbury & Morley (1979) determined that six of the patient's morning routine activities were responsible for his perpetual lateness: getting out of bed in the morning, going to the toilet, washing, dressing, combing hair, and making the bed. Accordingly, they treated this isolated 29-year-old patient (who until relatively late in his childhood was dressed and washed by his overprotective grandmother) by the 'prompting, pacing and shaping' procedure. The sessions were given each weekday afternoon and lasted for 1 hour. The patient made gratifying reductions in his self-care behaviour and ultimately was considerably better off than when admitted to hospital. Interestingly, Bilsbury & Morley (1979) comment on a common finding reported by therapists who use this procedure. In a curious way the prompting, pacing and shaping procedures appear to have very specific effects that are confined to the target under consideration. It is unusual to find a spontaneous spill-over or generalization from the target activity to non-target activities. So, for example, in the patient described by Bilsbury & Morley, they began helping him to comb his hair more efficiently and succeeded in doing so, but there was little carry-over to his other washing and dressing activities, which had to be dealt with in turn. The reason for this specificity remains unclear. They also make the interesting point that, throughout the treatment, their patient showed very little sign of anxiety or discomfort, even when the pace of his activities was quickened. Unfortunately the patient had two relapses, both occurring after specific stresses. Happily, he recovered from both relapses without undue difficulty.

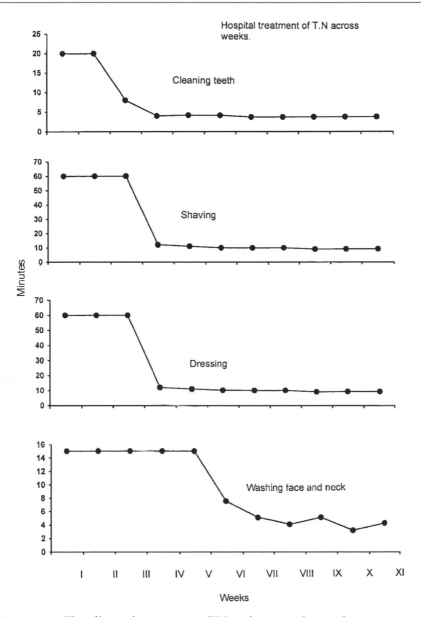

Figure 10.4 The effects of treatment on T.N., a chronic and severely incapacitated obsessional patient. Notice the specificity of treatment effects, reflected in the step-wise sequence of change *and* the size of the early improvements

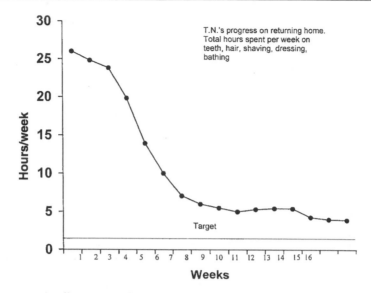

Figure 10.5   An illustration of T.N.'s overall progress after discharge from hospital, with moderate amounts of outpatient supervision

The patient described by Bennun (1980) was a 39-year-old single man, living on his own. Formerly he had stayed with his parents and was very dependent on them for most of his needs. He was initially admitted to hospital at the age of 19 and had been struggling from that time until his admission. He is described as 'being very slow to initiate and complete all tasks relating to self-care. On interview he described himself as very meticulous and careful to do everything right the first time. He took over 3 hours to get up, wash, dress, eat breakfast, and leave for work. Because he had to be at work at 9 a.m. he would wake at 5.15 a.m. in order to get to work on time' (Bennun, 1980, p. 596). The treatment programme was divided into three phases, consisting of the pre-breakfast, breakfast and post-breakfast periods. He was given prompting, shaping and pacing and made useful progress in overcoming the most extreme slowness in his activities. As other therapists have observed, the effects of the treatment were highly specific. Only the particular target behaviour responded to the treatment programme, with very little spontaneous transfer to other activities. Bennun also observed the plateau, which is apparently reached within a few weeks of introducing this type of treatment program. However, the improvements tend to be well maintained, unless the patient is exposed to some significant stress. Exacerbations can be caused by exposure to stress but, curiously, before and during the treatments the patients display and complain of little anxiety. According to Bennun, for example, 'the patient's slow rituals are not generally preceded or accompanied by anxiety and . . . obsessionally slow behaviour may not be directly related to the anxiety reduction view of obsessional behaviour' (Bennun 1980, p. 598).

In 1982, Clark et al. described the treatment of a 13-year-old adolescent who had a 5-year history of POS. 'He is severely slow in all his personal functions, requiring the nurses to dress, wash, bathe and even help him to eat. If left on his own he would take 6–8 hours to dress and often stands motionless for long periods of time' (Clark et al., 1982, p. 289). The treatment programme was directed at four specific targets—dressing, washing, eating and making the bed. He showed improvements in three of the four tasks, but his eating failed to speed up. In the three affected tasks, the treatments produced an increase in response rate but the gains were not maintained when the intervention program was gradually faded. The patient improved with active treatment but relapsed on discharge. Clark et al. (1982) speculate that the patient's obsessional slowness might have helped him to avoid social situations because he was highly dependent and isolated. His mother was extremely overprotective and continued to bathe the patient up to the age of 13. The exact nature of the interplay between excessive dependency and POS remains to be elucidated.

In summary, the prompting-shaping-pacing programme appears to be helpful in reducing the extreme slowness of these patients, but in none of the cases described was there evidence of a return to full normal functioning. At best, and it is a useful best, they were helped to the point where their lives were made easier and in some cases they were able to obtain an occupation or return to part-time or full-time functioning. Another possibility is that their rigid and meticulous behaviour is an attempt to avoid any significant changes in their day-to-day activities. If this were the case, and there is scant evidence to support it at present, then it might be worthwhile to think about treatment programmes designed to help them overcome the putative fear of changes in their simple self-care tasks. For the present, however, that remains no more than a possibility.

CONCLUSIONS

POS is a compulsive disorder in which patients carry out simple everyday self-care tasks in an exceedingly precise, meticulous, unvarying manner and sequence. As a result, they take an inordinate amount of time to complete these everyday tasks. POS is incapacitating and most of the patients displaying the disorder lead dependent and isolated lives. The disorder shows some similarities with other forms of OCD, but there are a significant number of differences and these include the rigidly self-prescribed performance of self-care behaviour, very low incidence, a disproportionate number of male patients, an apparent absence of significant cognitive components and an apparent absence of anxiety and avoidance behaviour. Thus far there is no encouraging evidence that medication is helpful in the treatment of these patients, except perhaps in the presence of significant depression, and the institution of extensive psychological management in the form of prompting, pacing and shaping appears to be the best course available to therapists at the moment. Most patients will derive some benefits from this programme and, in the best of cases, will regain sufficient time each day to enable them to resume a more satisfactory life, including part-time or full-time occupation.

Chapter 11

OBSESSIONS, RUMINATIONS AND COVERT COMPULSIONS

Padmal de Silva

INTRODUCTION

This chapter deals with a specific presentation of obsessive-compulsive disorder (OCD). In Chapter 2 it was noted that some patients with OCD report obsessions only, or obsessions occurring with cognitive, or covert, compulsions. For many years, work on the understanding and treatment of these patients lagged behind the developments in work on patients with overt compulsions. Indeed, in major, pioneering research programmes investigating OCD, the researchers gave priority to overt compulsions. Rachman (1971) stated:

> During the course of a research programme which is directed at the modification of obsessional neuroses ... it was considered best to concentrate on overt compulsive behaviour during the early stages of our investigations. Obsessional patients who suffered from ruminations but displayed little or no compulsive behaviour were not included in the formal systematic studies (p. 229).

The emphasis on studying the clinical features and treatment of OCD patients whose difficulties included prominent overt compulsions led to a relative neglect of the exploration of the problems of those who lacked such compulsions. To make matters worse, many clinicians also took the view that compulsions were necessarily overt (see Chapter 2). The recognition of the covert compulsions (e.g. Rachman, 1976b) was a major impetus to the study of those who lacked overt rituals and to the development of treatment strategies for them.

In this chapter, the focus will be on obsessions, covert compulsions and ruminations. There are OCD patients who present with pure obsessions, i.e. with no compulsions, overt or covert. There is a large sub-group of

Obsessive-Compulsive Disorder: Theory, Research and Treatment.
Edited by Ross G. Menzies and Padmal de Silva. © 2003 John Wiley & Sons, Ltd.

patients presenting with obsessions plus covert compulsions (Rachman, 1976b, 1978). There are, in addition, a small number of cases that have obsessional ruminations (de Silva & Rachman, 1992, 1998).

TERMS AND CONCEPTS

As a first step in the discussions of these presentations and their treatment, however, it is necessary to clarify terms and concepts. For some time in the literature, the term 'obsessional ruminations' was commonly used to refer to obsessional thoughts, images or impulses. Rachman's classic paper published in 1971, which gave the first detailed analysis of obsessions, used the term in this way, as can be seen in the quotation from it in the previous section. In fact, the paper also had the title 'Obsessional Ruminations'. He stated: 'Obsessional ruminations are repetitive, intrusive and unacceptable thoughts. They may be distasteful, shameful, worrying or abhorrent, or a combination of all these characteristics' (Rachman, 1971, p. 229). Many authors still use the term 'rumination' in this sense (e.g. Yaryura-Tobias & Neziroglu, 1997), while some have used it to refer to obsessions and covert compulsions taken together (Salkovskis & Westbrook, 1989). Salkovskis et al. (2000b) have acknowledged the inconsistent way in which the term has been used: 'The term *obsessional rumination* is confusing because it has been used indiscriminately to describe both obsessions and mental neutralising' (p. 213). The same point has been made by de Silva & Rachman (1992, 1998) and de Silva (2000).

One step towards achieving terminological and conceptual clarity is to consider what a 'rumination' is normally taken to be. *Chambers Dictionary* (1993) gives the meaning of 'to ruminate' as 'to meditate (on or upon)' and 'to muse on'. The *Oxford English Dictionary* (1989) gives the following meanings: 'contemplation'; 'meditation' for the word 'rumination'; and 'to ruminate' is explained as 'to revolve, to turn over and over again in the mind', 'meditate upon', etc. The general meaning, reflected in dictionary definitions, emphasises that a rumination is not a passive experience— thus, an obsession cannot be a rumination.

The growing literature on ruminations in depression can also be cited in the endeavour to clarify the meaning of the term. The work of Nolen-Hoeksema and others has thrown valuable light on this phenomenon. Ruminations tend to occur in depression, and some depressed patients use the ruminative response as a coping style (e.g. Lybomirsky & Nolen-Hoeksema, 1995; Nolen-Hoeksema et al., 1994). The term is used to refer, not to the simple occurrence of negative thoughts, but specifically to the self-focused thinking engaged in by the person.

Some of the examples that have been given in the literature on OCD as instances of ruminations also help us to define the concept. Classical descriptions refer to obsessional ruminations about the nature of the universe and other such metaphysical subjects. Scharfetter (1980) gives the examples: 'Why is the tree just there?' 'Why does the world exist?' and 'Why do I exist?' Slater & Roth (1969) cite the examples: 'Why did God make the world?' 'Who created God?' and 'Why are there so many different forms of substance?'. A more recent example given by de Silva & Rachman (1992) is as follows:

> A young man had complicated and time consuming ruminations on the question, 'Is everyone basically good?'. He would ruminate on this for a long time, going over in his mind various considerations and arguments and contemplating what superficially appeared to him to be relevant evidence... (p. 19).

Another example given by the same authors may also be cited:

> A young man had ruminations on the subject of whether he had any hereditary abnormality. The episodes, which were quite frequent, usually began with the thought, "Am I genetically flawed?", which came to his mind intrusively. When this intrusion came, he would start his ruminative thinking, carefully but unproductively trying to think the matter through. This would include thoughts about his parents, grandparents and other relatives, the evidence for their sanity or otherwise, ideas about the heritability of mental illness, what kind of tests could be done to find an answer to these questions, and so on. The thinking was quite time consuming and rather muddled. It never yielded any solution. He would in the end give up, angry and exhausted (de Silva & Rachman, 1992, pp. 36–37).

Barlow (1988) has given the example of a student who ruminated continually on whether his studying and concentration were adequate. This rumination also extended to the appropriateness of his behaviour in social situations.

The active nature of obsessional ruminations and their time-consuming nature are also evident in a case cited by Salkovskis et al. (2000b), a patient who reported that she had thoughts and images about her family dying. 'She would then ruminate about these thoughts for periods of up to 3 hours at a time' (p. 213). Finally, an excellent example recently provided by Albert & Hayward (2002) is worth citing. They have described a young man, a student, who had mathematical ruminations. While studying or listening to lectures in class, he would get the thought that he was not understanding the subject adequately. This would lead to thoughts such as, 'What is the difference between a vector and a point in space?'. He would then ponder, i.e. ruminate, on these questions. This had the effect of, among other things, making his studying time much longer. These ruminations also left him feeling low. The authors characterise this young man's difficulty as feeling himself compelled to worry about problems that he knew he could never resolve.

It is clear then, that the term 'rumination' in the context of OCD should be used to denote a specific kind of phenomenon. In the scheme of the elements or components of obsessive-compulsive phenomena given in Chapter 2, a rumination appears to be a covert or internal compulsive behaviour. It is usually triggered by a preceding obsession. While it is a compulsion, it seems to differ from the more common, well-defined compulsions, such as saying a silent prayer or conjuring up a specific mental image. The obsessional rumination is a compulsion only in the sense that the person engages in it because of a strongly felt compulsive urge. The urge is to think through the question or theme that is raised in the obsession; the actual details of these thoughts, or the sequence, are not predetermined. Neither is there a fixed end-point at which the person feels some satisfaction or relief and so can stop. Thus, an obsessional rumination is a compulsion of a very distinctive nature. It is preferable, therefore, to treat ruminations as a separate category in the phenomenology of OCD.

Clinical data also show that the ruminations may include images as a part of the thinking through. Much of the rumination, however, is made up of thoughts, rather than images.

Close analysis of obsessional ruminations also indicates that the phenomenon may be interspersed with spontaneously arising thoughts and/or images. Within the prolonged ruminative process, spontaneous cognitions may occasionally appear. This is an aspect on which little has been written and much remains to be investigated.

In sum, an obsessional rumination is a compulsive cognitive activity that is carried out in response to an obsessional thought. The content of the intruding thought determines the question or the theme that the person will ruminate about. The obsessional rumination differs from the more common, relatively brief cognitive compulsions which are carried out to fit pre-set requirements. Only the theme is pre-set in ruminations. What goes into the thinking about the topic is open-ended and variable (de Silva & Rachman 1998). Being a prolonged and effortful process, a rumination may allow for the arising of spontaneous thoughts or images, which get interspersed with the compulsive thinking.

Several examples of the themes of ruminations have already been given. Some other examples are: 'What will happen to me after death?', 'Am I going mad?', ' Am I really a woman?' 'Does the universe have a beginning?', 'Is there a supreme God or power?'. It is clear from these and other examples that obsessional ruminations have either a metaphysical or a personal theme.

We have discussed ruminations in some detail in order to highlight their defining features and to distinguish them from the more common covert OCD phenomena—obsessions and cognitive compulsions (see also Chapter 5 for a detailed discussion of the theoretical underpinnings of rumination). Obsessions are repetitive, persistent, intrusive thoughts, images or impulses. Cognitive compulsions are essentially covert compulsive behaviours. They are also referred to as 'covert compulsions', 'internal compulsions', 'mental compulsions' and 'covert/cognitive neutralisations', although the last-mentioned term should strictly be used to denote those covert compulsions that are carried out in order to cancel out or neutralise the assumed harmful effects of a preceding obsession. These phenomena are discussed in some detail in Chapters 1 and 2.

OBSESSIONS AND THEIR TREATMENT

Early Work

The psychological treatment of obsessions has evolved over the years. The technique of thought-stopping was described by Wolpe in 1958, based on a suggestion made by J. G. Taylor. It is now known that the procedure had been described by Alexander Bain 30 years previously (Bain, 1928), and Rosen & Ornstein (1976) have shown that the technique had been used even earlier. Essentially, the unwanted obsession was elicited and interrupted by a loud 'stop' command from the therapist. In subsequent stages of therapy, the stop command was given by the patient himself, and—eventually—this was done sub-vocally. Thought-stopping was also used with a modification: the adding of a mildly aversive stimulus, such as a faradic shock or flicking an elastic band against the wrist. Wolpe (1958, 1970) was enthusiastic about the thought-stopping technique and reported successful case examples. Some other early reports also provided successful case illustrations (e.g. Hackman & Mc Lean, 1975; Yamagami, 1971; Stern, 1970). However, failures were also reported (e.g. Stern et al., 1973). In addition to the limited therapeutic success, the thought-stopping technique, when applied to obsessions, suffered from the absence of a psychological rationale. It was essentially a pragmatic technique, not one derived from a theoretical account of obsessions, although Wolpe (1982) felt that the procedure probably worked though the reinforcement of thought inhibition by the anxiety-reducing consequences of each successful effort at stopping the cognition.

Rachman (1976b), in an influential paper, offered a new formulation for the modification of obsessions. He proposed that, instead of teaching obsessional patients to curtail or control their obsessions, 'we should encourage them to produce the thought' (Rachman, 1976b, p. 437). He had previously (Rachman, 1971) given an analysis of obsessions as internal noxious stimuli that are resistant to habituation. Rachman (1971) argued that the preferred treatment for obsessions should be one that would promote habituation. Habituation training was proposed. This entailed the prolonged and/or repeated exposure of the patient to his unwanted obsession. This was to be combined with another important element—the patient was instructed to refrain from all attempts at neutralising, or 'undoing' the effects of the obsession. These attempts, he pointed out, could be internal or external. They were equivalent to other kinds of compulsive rituals. Rachman (1976b) concluded his paper with this succinct statement of the position he expounded:

> To conclude, it is proposed that the modification of obsessions should follow a new approach—one which conforms with the methods that have proved to be moderately successful in the modification of other forms of obsessional and compulsive problems. It is argued that this can be best achieved by recognising the significance of neutralising rituals and construing them as being functionally equivalent to other kinds of compulsive ritual. The practical consequences of this view are that we should request the affected person to obtain the obsessional thoughts, impulses or images and then to refrain from putting matters right (i.e. refrain from carrying out any internal or external neutralizing activities (pp. 442–443).

This approach to treatment, including prolonged exposure to the target obsessions, was carried out by, among others, Emmelkamp & Kwee (1977), Likeirman & Rachman (1982), Salkovskis (1983) and Stern (1978). In this approach, the patient's exposure to the obsession for prolonged periods of time is ensured in variety of ways: by therapist's prompts, by writing down the thought repeatedly, or listening to audio-taped recordings of the thought (e.g. Headland & MacDonald, 1987).

Recent Developments

Further developments in this exposure-based approach to the treatment of obsessions have come from the work of Salkovskis (e.g. Salkovskis, 1999; Salkovskis & Kirk, 1997; Salkovskis & Westbrook, 1989). It will be useful to give somewhat detailed consideration of the approach of Salkovskis and his colleagues. Several discussions are available in the literature (e.g. Salkovskis, 1999; Salkovskis & Kirk, 1997; Salkovskis et al., 2000b; see further, Chapter 4). The treatment approach is fully integrated into the cognitive theory of OCD formulated initially in Salkovskis (1985), and relates to its key elements, such as inflated sense of responsibility for harm and negative interpretation. It also places emphasis on the fact, empirically well established, that attempts to suppress an unwanted thought in fact have the opposite effect, i.e. they increase the frequency of the thought (e.g. Wegner, 1989). The role of the neutralisation in the persistence of the obsession is also fully taken into account (e.g. Rachman et al., 1996). Another major feature of the approach is the recognition that the intrusion of unwanted cognitions into the mind is a common and normal experience (e.g. Rachman & de Silva, 1978; Salkovskis & Harrison, 1984).

The treatment programme consists of several stages:

Stage 1—Assessment and goal-setting.   In the assessment of stage, the therapist elicits from the patient a description of a recent episode of the experience of the obsession, identifying within that episode the specific sequence of events that occurred. Much emphasis is placed on identifying the way in which the obsession was appraised or interpreted by the patient. The role of an inflated sense of responsibility (for harm) in this interpretation is closely explored. The way the interpretation has led to attempts at suppressing the thought, or neutralising its supposed effects, etc., is enquired into. The impact of such control attempts on the repeated appearance of the obsession is highlighted. Following the assessment, a formulation or shared understanding of the problem is reached and agreed on. Goals of therapy are also negotiated. Salkovskis has pointed out (e.g. Salkovskis & Kirk, 1997) that it should be made clear to the patient that the type of treatment goal being considered does not include getting rid of the obsession entirely.

Stage 2—Normalizing and considering alternative explanations.   This stage involves further clarification. It also includes helping the patient to understand the mechanisms by which his/her problem is being maintained. Many strategies are employed in this phase in order to help the patient to understand the significance of their intrusive thoughts. Salkovskis & Kirk (1997) mention the following: (a) discussing the normal function of intrusive cognitions, including the fact that there are positive, helpful intrusions; (b) considering the links between the content of intrusive cognitions and their appraisal; (c) exploring how those with intrusive cognitions provide their own ideas about what could go wrong; (d) considering how the context of the occurrence of an intrusion can influence its appraisal; (e) examining the issue of who would experience what kinds of intrusive cognitions; and (f) asking the patient to consider the question of what it would be like if he/she had no intrusive cognitions at all. What is expected to be achieved in this stage is for the patient to realise the normality of intrusive cognitions and the valuable role they play in everyday life.

Stage 3—Reconsidering the problem.   The patient is invited to contrast directly the two alternative views of the problem. These are: (a) the problem is one of actual harm and one's responsibility; and (b) the problem is one of worry about that harm and an excessive concern about one's responsibility for preventing it. The differences and similarities are highlighted. The need to be able to experience the obsessional thought without experiencing distress is discussed in detail. It is made clear that the prevention of intrusive thoughts is not desirable. The use of the audiotape procedure and the importance of identifying ideas about responsibility (so they can be modified and any kind of neutralising behaviour prevented) are explained.

Stage 4—Audiotaped exposure and belief modification.   The target obsession is now elicited and recorded on audiotape; a loop tape is used, so that the recorded obsession can be heard repeatedly in playback. The need to refrain from any neutralisation is strongly emphasised. After some habituation work in the session with the aid of the tape, homework instructions are given. Work on changing beliefs is also undertaken. Behavioural experiments are used in this endeavour. The behavioural experiments are chosen carefully, to enable the patient to test directly the processes assumed to be involved in the problem. A widely used experiment involves the demonstration that trying to suppress a thought in fact increases its frequency. For example, the patient may be asked to 'try not to think of white bears' (cf. Wegner, 1989). To give another example, the patient may be encouraged to test the belief that thinking about an action increase the chance of that action being performed (cf. Shafran et al., 1996). A detailed discussion of this kind of experiment is available in Salkovskis & Kirk (1997). The patient is also asked during this phase of therapy what he/she thinks of any changes that occur in the course of the exposure sessions and how they fit with each of the two alternative accounts of the problem previously agreed. The patient is asked to use the tape regularly at home at set times. A portable playback machine with headphones is used to allow the tape to be played over in real life contexts where the obsession tends to occur. Finally, the audiotape is carried and used upon the occurrence of obsession, as and when it happens.

Stage 5—Further behavioural experiments.   The fifth stage consists of using the natural occurrence of intrusive thoughts as a cue for the use of the audiotape. During the latter stages of the tape sequence, self-directed exposure and response prevention for other unwanted thoughts are initiated and recorded. Throughout this period, monitoring of the beliefs with regard to responsibility and interpretation is also carried out. In sessions, further discussion and behavioural experiments, as necessary, are carried out to foster the alternative explanation ('my problem is worry').

> Examples would be imagery or thought restructuring, catastrophising imagery, or verbal exercises as a demonstration of the way in which these ideas worsen discomfort and distress; pie charts which tackle the idea of responsibility; thought experiments in which the person thinks of ways of bringing about the event they fear they may be responsible for; pros and cons of being obsessional and not being obsessional; cumulative probability-downward arrows (Salkovskis & Kirk, 1997, p. 203).

What this treatment aims to achieve is the modification of the *meaning* of obsessions to the kind of level experienced by most people. No direct attempt is made to decrease frequency of the obsession. However, the treatment usually does lead to an actual decrease in intrusions. That is because the patient's appraisal of the thought has changed, and there is no longer a belief that the thought will lead to serious harm or negative consequences.

In this treatment approach, Salkovskis and his colleagues (e.g. Salkovskis & Kirk, 1997) also include a relapse prevention phase. This includes identifying any residual difficulties and helping to modify them with discussion and by using further behavioural experiments as needed. The emphasis at this stage is on the patient's own efforts, with the therapist playing a limited role.

Another cognitive approach to the treatment of obsessions has been developed by Rachman (1997, 1998) in two recent papers. Rachman proposed that obsessions are caused by catastrophic misinterpretations of the significance of one's thoughts, images and impulses. Most people's intrusions do not turn into problematic obsessions. What leads to the transformation of an intrusion into a 'torment' (Rachman, 1997) is its misinterpretation as being very important, personally significant, revealing and threatening, even catastrophic. Rachman (1997) points out that the common themes of obsessions—aggression, sex and blasphemy—are important themes of all moral systems, and are thus open to an exaggerated sense of personal significance. Rachman (1997, 1998) has cited numerous case examples that highlight these misinterpretations. Some of these are as follows: (a) A 25-year-old computer analyst had recurrent thoughts and images of harming the very young children of a close friend. He interpreted this to mean that he was a potential murderer and a fundamentally evil and worthless person. (b) A devoutly religious patient had recurrent obscene images about the Church and Mary, especially when she tried to pray in Church. She interpreted them to mean that she was a vicious, lying hypocrite and her religious beliefs and feelings were a sham. (c) An affectionate grandmother had recurrent images of throwing her beloved grandson over the balcony, which caused very deep distress in her. She interpreted the images to mean that she was a dangerous and uncontrollable psychopath, someone incapable of love or concern for others (Rachman, 1997).

What are the implications of Rachman's account of obsessions for their treatment? Rachman, (1997, 1998) suggests that a comprehensive therapeutic approach should include several components. The first is education regarding the essential normalcy of intrusive thoughts, including the message that such thoughts are not by any means a sign of deep character flaws. As part of the education, the treatment model is also discussed, stating the belief that 'unwanted intrusive thoughts become clinically significant if and when the person interprets them as being of great personal significance' (Rachman, 1998, p. 396). The nature and origins of intrusive thoughts in general are discussed. The nature of thought suppression and neutralization are also explained. These may be illustrated with demonstrations. The role of persistent avoidance is also discussed, as is the role of concealment of the obsession from others. 'Concealment also inadvertently promotes the catastrophic misinterpretations because the person in not exposed to evidence that might disconfirm the interpretation' (Rachman, 1998, p. 397). Other elements of the education component include the notion of inflated responsibility and its role in OCD, and the link between depressed mood and OCD. It is recommended that reading material be given to the patient to supplement the educational steps.

The second stage begins with a description of the treatment. It is explained to the patient that the purpose of treatment is to help him/her to replace the catastrophic misinterpretation with more benign explanations of their obsessions, and to supplement these therapeutic attempts by deliberate and persistent modification of relevant unwanted behaviours (reduction of avoidance, neutralization, suppression and concealment). The active part the patient has to play in the treatment is emphasised. Demonstrations may be undertaken where appropriate, to illustrate key elements of the therapy. These demonstrations are in fact a type of behavioural experiment (cf. Salkovskis & Kirk, 1997).

While the treatment is not explicitly aimed at the reduction of the frequency of the unwanted obsessions, Rachman (1998) states that this will be one of the effects of therapy. It is specifically predicted that a reduction in the catastrophic misinterpretation placed on the obsession, which the treatment aims to achieve, will lead to fewer, and less intense, attempts to fight against the obsession. This, in turn, can be expected to lead to a reduction in the frequency of its occurrence.

Freeston et al. (1996) have described several techniques, which they call 'cognitive corrective strategies', that they have found useful in the treatment of patients with obsessions. They, too, stress the importance of starting treatment with an educational component, which includes giving the patient a detailed cognitive-behavioural account of obsessions. Identifying faulty appraisals is a major part of the work. Once target appraisals are identified, the therapist may use a variety of techniques, as needed, to modify them. Specific interventions are used to deal with several areas: the over-estimation of the importance of thoughts, exaggerated responsibility, perfectionism, over-interpretation of threat, and feared consequences of anxiety. Some examples are given below.

The over-estimation of the importance of thoughts is dealt with by demonstrating the circularity of this thinking ('It must be important because I think about it, and I think about it because it is important'). The role of attempts at suppression in the persistence of obsession is explained, using behavioural experiments as necessary. Thought–action fusion (a feature of over-estimation of the importance of thoughts) is tackled with the use of behavioural experiments. For example, 'a minor household appliance is identified that is found to be in good working order (e.g. a toaster). The patient thinks a hundred times a day that the appliance will break down within the next week. The outcome is then compared to the prediction' (Freeston et al., 1996, p. 438).

Comments on the New Treatment Approaches

As can be seen from the above, there is much overlap in the approaches of Salkovskis, Rachman, and Freeston and colleagues. They all use a primarily cognitive analysis of obsessions, using cognitive concepts. The treatments they propose are cognitive-behavioural and include a strong educational element. All emphasise the need to modify the meaning and significance of the obsession. A range of techniques are suggested for this purpose. They represent a major advance on the early accounts of obsessions and early treatment strategies. Cognitive treatment approaches to OCD are discussed more fully in Chapter 16.

Is there evidence for the efficacy of this overall approach? Not many data are available; given that these developments have taken place only in recent years, this is not surprising. There is, however, some relevant information in the literature.

Ladouceur et al. (1995a) reported a multiple baseline study of three patients with obsessions. The treatment given included education about the nature of obsessional thoughts and the role of neutralisation, exposure with response prevention using looped audiotapes, identification and proscription of activities aimed at controlling the obsessions, and cognitive restructuring focusing on exaggerated responsibility, perfectionistic thinking, overestimation of the importance of thoughts and feared negative consequences. The treatment input was large in each case, but all cases showed much improvement with regard to their obsessions.

In a larger and more ambitious study, Freeston et al. (1997) treated 29 patients who had obsessions but no overt compulsive rituals. They were randomly allocated to two groups. One group ($n = 15$) received CBT and the other ($n = 14$) was placed on a waiting list. The CBT consisted of: an explanation of the occurrence and persistence of obsessional thoughts; loop tape and *in vivo* exposure to obsessional thoughts with response prevention of all neutralising strategies; cognitive restructuring; and relapse prevention. Comparison with the waiting list group showed that the treated group achieved significant improvement. Those on the waiting list were subsequently given the same treatment. The combined group showed significant improvement, and the gains were maintained at 6-months follow-up. The average amount of treatment given was 40.5 hours. Twenty-two of the total group completed therapy. Freeston et al. (1997) point out that there were six drop-outs and two non-responders, and add, 'it is clear that there is still a great deal to be done' (p. 411). Despite this caution, the study has clearly shown the promise of a well-planned CBT package for obsessions unaccompanied by overt compulsions.

TREATMENT OF COVERT COMPULSIONS

When the dominant problem is a covert compulsion, the treatment should, in principle, be similar to that of overt compulsive behaviour (de Silva & Rachman, 1998). This would require exposure to a stimulus (it may be an external object or, more often, an internal one) that will lead to the urge to perform the compulsion, followed by prevention of the compulsive activity. Thus, the paradigm is essentially that of exposure plus response prevention (ERP). Preventing a covert compulsive behaviour is, of course, not nearly as easy as preventing an overt compulsion. In order to achieve this, the therapist needs to consider, with the patient, various possible strategies and use what seems the most suitable in each case. Distraction tasks, such as mental arithmetic or word search puzzles, have been found to be useful (see further de Silva et al., 2003). The thought-stopping technique (e.g. Wolpe, 1958) discussed in a previous section of this chapter can also be used as a means of stopping the mental compulsion. The following example from de Silva & Rachman (1998) illustrates this. A middle-aged woman had the mental compulsion to correct any asymmetrical figure or pattern that she saw by imagining it in perfect, symmetrical form. She had to do this every time she saw an asymmetrical object, or the image of it intruded into her mind, which happened quite frequently and made her quite tense. She often had to work very hard at the 'correcting image' until she got it absolutely symmetrical. The treatment consisted of exposing her to various asymmetrical patterns, which she was instructed to look at carefully, and then blocking her mental compulsive behaviour with self-administered thought-stopping.

The above approach seems appropriate when the prominent feature of the phenomenology is the covert compulsion. When brief internal neutralisations and other covert compulsions follow repetitive, persistent and highly distressing obsessions, the use of a CBT package which includes major cognitive work on the nature of the obsession, and prolonged exposure to it through the use of a loop tape, would be the treatment of choice. This is because the target of the treatment is the obsession in such cases. The prevention of the compulsions is a part of this package, and is usually achieved by continuous loop-tape feedback and detailed prior instruction. This approach has been described in detail in the previous section.

TREATMENT OF RUMINATIONS

In the first part of this chapter, we identified obsessional ruminations as a specific presentation of OCD. We showed that these are a type of covert compulsive behaviour with distinctive features. These elaborate, time-consuming ruminations sometimes present for treatment.

The treatment approach to ruminations is, again, response prevention. The urge to engage in the rumination needs to be provoked, and it must be ensured that the patient does not engage in the ruminative activity. Thought-stopping, or other blocking procedures stated above, are useful in achieving this (de Silva & Rachman 1998). Cognitive work on the obsession that triggers the rumination also needs to be undertaken (see previous section), where relevant. However, many of the ruminations clinically observed do not seem to be linked to the misinterpretation of an obsession; instead, they are attempts to think through a question or theme which the person feels compelled to engage in. Thus, the emphasis in these cases is on the prevention of the compulsion, very much in the way that a checking or washing compulsion is behaviourally treated (see Chapters 7 and 8).

CONCLUSIONS

This chapter has focused on covert OCD phenomena. The need to identify the specific classes of phenomena, and to define the relevant terms and concepts precisely, was emphasised. Special attention was paid to the nature of obsessional ruminations, which were distinguished from the more commonly found obsessions. Their compulsive nature was acknowledged, and it was stressed that they are different from other, more common, covert compulsions. The chapter then considered the nature and treatment of obsessions in some detail, with special reference to recent theoretical formulations and the treatment approaches derived from them. Finally, brief comments were made on the treatment of cognitive compulsions and ruminations.

Chapter 12

ATYPICAL PRESENTATIONS

Danielle Einstein and Ross G. Menzies

Obsessive-compulsive disorder (OCD) is remarkable in that there are seemingly an infinite number of presentations of the disorder. Intrusive thoughts about virtually any topic can become the subject of obsessions and rituals and these may arise in the most unusual circumstances. For example, one woman watched a movie in which a young girl fell pregnant to the devil. She then experienced intrusive thoughts (which subsequently required neutralising) about whether she, herself, had fallen pregnant to the devil. There are an unlimited number of topics that can be perceived to be threatening to an individual. Intrusive thoughts as diverse as killing a loved one with an axe to wondering whether a cough 'sounds right' can become the subject of obsessive thoughts and rituals.

The present chapter will focus on atypical presentations that frequently accompany washing and checking. The effectiveness of exposure and response prevention (ERP) for the treatment of these behaviours has not been extensively documented (Ball, Baer & Otto, 1996). Despite the dominance of studies focused on cleaning and checking rituals, estimates of atypical compulsions reach as high as 56% in clinical samples (Summerfeldt et al., 1997; see further, Table 12.1).

The chapter will examine atypical obsessions and compulsions, including aggressive, sexual and religious obsessions, repeating and counting compulsions, obsessions with a need for symmetry or exactness and associated ordering/arranging compulsions, and symptoms referred to as miscellaneous on the Yale–Brown Obsessive-Compulsive Scale (Y-BOCS; Goodman et al., 1989a, 1989b). The characteristics of these obsessions and compulsions will be reviewed, and case examples will be provided. This will be followed by a brief description of treatment strategies.

Obsessive-Compulsive Disorder: Theory, Research and Treatment.
Edited by Ross G. Menzies and Padmal de Silva. © 2003 John Wiley & Sons, Ltd.

Table 12.1 Frequency of atypical obsessions and compulsions observed in adult clinical samples (percentage of total sample)

	Akhtar et al. (1975) (n = 82)	Rasmussen & Eisen (1989) (n = 200)	Rasmussen & Eisen (1992) (n = 560)	Summerfeldt et al. (1997) (n = 182)	Rasmussen & Tsuang (1986) (n = 44)	Nicolini et al. (1997) (n = 71)
Atypical obsessions						
Sexual	10	26	24	20	32	31
Religion	11	x	x	24	x	7
Symmetry/exactness	27	31	32	53	36	17
Aggressive	29	28	31	69	50	13
Somatic	x	36	33	34	34	3
Others	22	13	x	56	14	x
Atypical compulsions						
Repetitions	x	x	x	56	x	17
Counting	x	36	36	35	x	6
Need to ask or confess	x	31	34	x	x	x
Symmetry	x	28	28	40	x	21

x = subtype was not identified in this study.

AGGRESSIVE OBSESSIONS

Aggressive obsessions are experienced as intrusive and ego-dystonic thoughts, images, sounds or impulses pertaining to harm to oneself or others. Patients usually report alarm at the experience of violent or horrific images. The Y-BOCS lists a number of aggressive obsessions, including:

- Fear might harm self.
- Fear might harm others.
- Fear of blurting out obscenities or insults.
- Fear of doing something else embarrassing.
- Fear will act on an unwanted impulses (e.g. to stab a friend).
- Fear will steal things.
- Fear will harm others because not careful enough (e.g. hit and run motor vehicle accident).
- Fear will be responsible for something else terrible happening (e.g. fire, burglary).

Aggressive obsessions are extremely distressing to individuals with OCD. Rasmussen & Tsuang (1986) reported that 82% of clients with aggressive obsessions engaged in checking rituals.

One 54-year-old woman was preoccupied with a fear that she had mistakenly sewn a knife inside any craft activity that she had completed. Similarly, she believed that a knife may have been absorbed into any item that she had come into contact with. She had difficulty giving items to her partner to take home from hospital and giving presents to her grandchildren.

Another client described a fear of having run over a person every time he felt a bump in his car or perceived a blur at the periphery of his vision. He would retrace his route several times, becoming confused and taking excessive detours as more and more incidents occurred on the one journey. Driving became an onerous task. This type of aggressive obsession is quite common.

A fear of doing something embarrassing refers to actions prompted by intrusive thoughts, which may be observed by others to be abnormal. For example, one client reported fearing that he would write the phrase, 'I'm going to kill you' on a deposit slip at his local bank or in the midst of a letter to a friend. Again, such thoughts are not uncommon in OCD.

Studies of aggressive obsessions are sparse; however, a few reports have found that aggressive obsessions are more common in certain subgroups. Mothers with post-partum OCD experience intrusive thoughts about harming their newborn babies (Maina et al., 2000). Symptoms may include obsessional thoughts and/or checking behaviour or other compulsive rituals.

In a comparison of 10 participants with pure OCD and 15 participants with OCD and co-morbid Gilles de la Tourette's syndrome, patients with the co-morbid disorder reported more violent, sexual and symmetrical obsessions and self-damaging compulsions than pure OCD patients (George et al., 1993). The latter group reported more obsessions and compulsions surrounding the themes of contamination and germs.

Matsunaga et al. (1999) compared the clinical characteristics of 21 female patients with co-morbid anorexia nervosa and OCD and 23 age-matched female patients with OCD alone. Subjects in the dual-diagnosis group, compared to subjects with OCD alone, were more likely to have obsessions with a need for symmetry or exactness and compulsions related to ordering and arranging. However, these subjects were less likely to describe aggressive obsessions and checking compulsions than the pure OCD group.

Finally, Stein et al. (1994) examined impulsivity in a large sample of clients with OCD. Patients with OCD from the DSM-IV field trial ($n = 431$) were rated on the Y-BOCS and completed the Barratt Impulsivity Scale, version 10R. Patients with OCD did not demonstrate different impulsivity scores when compared to a group of student controls. Interestingly, patients with OCD who were impulsive were more likely to report aggressive and sexual obsessive-compulsive symptoms and less likely to report cleaning and checking symptoms.

SEXUAL OBSESSIONS

Sexual obsessions are common, occurring in 32% of the 100 patients studied by Rasmussen & Tsuang (1986). Lensi et al. (1996) found that 27% of men in their sample reported sexual obsessions compared to 12.7% of women. Sexual obsessions often include thoughts or images of engaging in sexual activities with a range of people that one would not expect to have a sexual relationship with. They may include relatives, children, friends and strangers. One client reported experiencing images of having sexual intercourse with every person she met. She was particularly distressed by thoughts pertaining to children or the elderly. Sexual obsessions may also involve themes of violence or homosexuality.

Misinterpretation of physical sensations can trigger fears about one's sexual intentions. For example, one client misinterpreted his arousal with children as indicating his potential to wilfully sexually assault a child.

Freeman & Leonard (2000) described two children who developed OCD after sexual abuse. Both children presented with ruminations about the abuse as well as obsessions that were unrelated to the incident. The first case involved a 10-year-old boy with obsessions about dirt and germs, scrupulosity and images with aggressive and sexual themes. His ritual involved confessing thoughts to his mother. He met diagnostic criteria for OCD but not PTSD. His OCD had started at age 5 after he had been repeatedly abused by an older child. The onset of symptoms occurred after the abuse had ceased. The second case involved a 7-year-old girl who had been involved in an incident of unwanted sex play prior to the onset of OCD symptoms. PTSD was not diagnosed. She described experiencing obsessions about harm to herself and others, sexual images, bodily fluids and needing to say things 'exactly right'. Her compulsions included handwashing and a need to confess.

RELIGIOUS OBSESSIONS

Religious obsessions were reported by 24% of individuals with OCD in a sample examined by Summerfeldt et al. (1997). The Y-BOCS distinguishes two types of religious obsessions, those concerned with sacrilege and blasphemy and those surrounding an excessive concern for morality.

Religious obsessions include doubts about the existence of important religious figures, imagining sexual acts with a religious figure, or intrusive thoughts about objects or actions that nullify a religious ritual or law. For example, Hoffnung et al. (1989) describe two cases. The first was obsessed with red-coloured stimuli. She feared that red stimuli may have contacted blood, which would render her 'unclean' and 'unfit' for many religious rituals. The second case involved a man who believed that if he failed to protect himself from a serious danger and consequently died, this would be tantamount to suicide. He believed that suicide would lead to his forfeiture of his right to share in the 'world to come'. As a result he engaged in excessive checking behaviour and avoided electrical outlets. Another man experienced blasphemous thoughts whilst praying. These thoughts were particularly distressing due to religious teaching that thoughts should be 'pure' at all times, especially during prayers. He believed that his prayers were invalidated by impure thoughts.

While religiosity does not increase the risk of developing OCD, the content of OCD symptoms is more likely to be related to religion in individuals with a strong religious background (Antony et al., 1998a). Religious obsessions are usually distortions and exaggerations of rituals from the individuals' religious subculture (Hoffnung et al., 1989). Greenberg, Witzum

& Levy (1990) examined 34 Jewish outpatients with OCD. Religious symptoms were evident in 13 of 19 extremely religious subjects, and in one of the 15 less religious subjects. Interestingly, the authors reclassified the symptoms and found that, after ignoring religious context, all obsessions fell within the categories of cleanliness, orderliness, aggression and sex. Okasha et al. (1994) examined 90 Egyptian outpatients with OCD. Religious obsessions were as common as contamination obsessions (reported by 60% of the sample). The emphasis on cleanliness or ritual purity was the basis of most of the compulsive rituals reported by Moslem subjects. The number of prayers and their verbal content was also subject to checking and repetition.

NEED FOR SYMMETRY OR EXACTNESS

This obsession relates to a need to have objects in a certain order or position, or to perform actions in a precise fashion (Rasmussen & Eisen, 1992). One man insisted on walking through an office door exactly in the middle and sitting at a 90° angle to the therapist. A second person leant on objects at just the right angle before she completed a motor action. A third man, with Tourette's syndrome, would make sure that the number of involuntary tics exhibited on one side of his body were 'evened up' with the same number of voluntary movements on the other side. Most patients with this symptom also exhibit checking and counting rituals (Rasmussen & Eisen, 1988; 1992).

Goodman et al. (1989a) categorise obsessions with a need for symmetry or exactness into two groups based on the presence or absence of magical thinking. The first group is characterised by a belief that if objects are not in the 'correct' position, negative consequences will occur. At times magical thinking may reach near-delusional proportions. The second group consists of individuals who do not link their need for exactness to magical consequences. These individuals may describe an obsession with symmetry as arising out of 'habit' or perfectionistic tendencies. However, in the absence of cognitive mediational and/or experimental laboratory studies designed to tease out the relative causal roles of potential cognitive constructs, one must take patient accounts of causality with some caution. For example, despite frequent reports from washers/cleaners that their behaviours are due to perfectionistic tendencies, considerable evidence suggests that perfectionism plays little role in this subtype (Jones & Menzies, 1997a, 1998b)

Compared to OCD patients without tics, OCD patients with a co-morbid tic disorder appear to have a greater incidence of symmetry and exactness obsessions accompanied by magical thinking (Leonard et al., 1999;

George et al., 1993). Interestingly, symmetry and ordering obsessions are also correlated with reports of dissociative symptoms. In a sample of 70 patients with OCD, this association was present for symmetry and ordering obsessions and checking compulsions but not for washing, cleaning, touching or aggressive obsessions or compulsions (Grabe et al., 1999).

REPEATING RITUALS

Repeating rituals severely impair functioning. They may be either motoric or mental. Motoric rituals have the capacity to affect every aspect of functioning, including walking, eating, reaching, blinking, reading, writing and moving. They may be specific or general (e.g. walking through doorways, footpaths or corridors in a particular manner, getting up/down). They are idiosyncratic and may vary across time within the individual (see Neziroglu et al., 2000). Mental compulsions include arithomania, mentally checking or patterning objects, ritualistic prayers, mental replay of conversations, and repetition of phrases or nonsense syllables (Neziroglu et al., 2000). Repeating rituals are often combined with counting behaviours.

COUNTING COMPULSIONS

Counting rituals involve the selection of special numbers. A counting ritual may be repeated a certain number of times (e.g. a woman who needed to count from one to seven and repeat this seven times before starting to eat her meal). If interrupted, the individual often feels compelled to start again and is unable to commence or continue with the specified activity until the counting has been completed satisfactorily. Counting may be confined to a restricted number of activities or generalised to apply to most activities. It commonly co-occurs with other obsessions and compulsions, including cleaning, checking and superstitious rituals. Some individuals are unable to articulate particular threats associated with failing to count properly, while others are able to describe specific feared consequences. Counting was observed significantly more frequently in patients with OCD with psychotic features (Eisen & Rasmussen, 1993).

One unusual aspect of counting is the assignment of lucky and unlucky numbers. The selection of numbers to be targeted and avoided can dramatically alter across time. For example, one client reported a long history of counting in threes. If four of an object were present, the client neutralized the 'danger' by a tapping ritual. However, by the time this client presented at our clinic, he reported a complete reversal of this system. He was counting in fours and if he encountered three of an object, he now neutralized that. Such a complete reversal of the stimuli considered harmful is not unusual in counting compulsions but is highly unusual in OCD checkers or washers. Another client reported that threes and multiples of threes were bad, except for nine and twenty-one. The person was unable to explain why nine and twenty-one were not dangerous. With counting rituals, it appears that the system itself is completely arbitrary and the whole system can change within days to weeks. The only crucial feature is that the current belief is adhered to.

MISCELLANEOUS OBSESSIONS

The Y-BOCS lists a group of miscellaneous obsessions. These include:

- Need to know or remember things.
- Fear of saying certain things.
- Fear of not saying just the right thing.
- Fear of losing things.
- Intrusive (non-violent images).
- Intrusive nonsense sounds, words or music.
- Bothered by certain sounds/noises.
- Lucky/unlucky numbers.
- Colours with special significance.
- Superstitious fears.

The majority of these miscellaneous obsessions appear to spring from one central underpinning construct, namely magical thinking. Magical thinking refers to beliefs that defy scientific laws of causality accepted by Western culture (Chapman et al., 1982; Einstein & Menzies, 2000, Obsessive Compulsive Cognitions Working Group, 1997). Large positive correlations between measures of magical thinking and obsessive-compulsive symptomatology have been found in both a clinical population (Norman et al., 1996) and a non-clinical population (Einstein & Menzies, 2000). In the absence of magical thinking tendencies, it is difficult to imagine how individuals would sustain intrusive obsessional concerns about superstitions, nonsense sounds, colours with special significance, lucky and unlucky numbers and needing to touch, tap or rub items. Our data suggests that magical thinking is required for some rituals and not for others. For example, significant correlations were observed between checking and magical thinking but not between washing and magical thinking (Einstein & Menzies, 2000).

TREATMENT SUGGESTIONS

With most of the thoughts described in this chapter, effective interventions will lower the sufferers' threat expectancies, i.e. the interventions will highlight the individuals' appraisals of fear, assist the clients to develop insight into the nature of these appraisals and then provide effective challenges. This approach can be placed within broader cognitive-behavioural conceptions of OCD (see Chapters 4, 11 and 16).

In terms of contemporary cognitive accounts of OCD (or of anxiety more generally), the management of atypical obsessions and compulsions should not be fundamentally different to the management of washing and checking. In our view, the primary goal in each case is to lower estimates of perceived threat (see further, Menzies et al., 2000). Whether the therapist proceeds down a response prevention path or a cognitive therapy path, the principle aim is to modify clients' expectancies of harm. Almost universally, sufferers of atypical obsessions will spontaneously suggest that harm of various sorts may follow a failure to ritualise. For example, one client suggested that hopping in a particular pattern prevented her from being raped. Another client suggested that a failure to repeat certain motoric behaviours in sets of 5 would result in his mother contracting breast cancer. A third client believed that the repetition of a particular mantra upon hearing a blasphemous thought prevented him from suffering eternal damnation. Clearly, while these types of beliefs are maintained, neutralising behaviours would be expected to continue. Thus, the target of contemporary CBT must be to reduce or eliminate these expectancies.

In our view, normalising (see Chapters 4, 11 and 16) is an effective therapeutic technique because (and only because) it lowers the individual's threat expectancy. If a client believes that everyone experiences aggressive thoughts, and that most individuals do not act on them, then it follows that aggressive thoughts are not inherently dangerous. Thus, the essence of normalising is its ability to effectively lower the perceived threat associated with a particular intrusive thought.

In our view, it is for similar reasons that ERP is an effective therapeutic technique for atypical obsessions and compulsions (see also Chapter 15). Many modern theorists argue that the central mechanism through which ERP operates is not habituation (as it was once thought), but through the lowering of threat expectancies. For this reason, exposure activities must have an experimental question underlying them. Behavioural experiments are extremely important in this process, and have been described elsewhere (see Chapters 4, 10 and 16). Asking a person who counts in fives to change and count in fours is effective because noxious events in the world can be shown to be independent of the repetition of a particular number. The following section includes many examples in which the individual is asked to participate in experiments to lower his/her beliefs in harm. Given the coverage of these and related treatment issues in Chapters 15, 16, 18 and 19, the present observations will be kept quite brief.

Aggressive and Sexual Obsessions

Rachman (1998) has shown that fears often relate to beliefs about the individual's basic sense of self. For example, one man in our clinic believed that he was a homosexual, describing intrusive thoughts and images about sexual intercourse with other males. Although these thoughts were superficially repulsive to him, he feared (on the basis of no evidence) that he was denying his true sexual being. He had experienced many vibrant, active and fulfilling heterosexual relationships in the past. Part of the treatment plan for this individual involved procuring homosexual pornography and sending him to gay bars. His prediction that he might approach men for sex in these locations proved to be entirely without foundation. This outcome provided an effective means to begin to dismantle his fears, and the intrusive thoughts soon ceased.

Another male client experienced terrifying images of bestiality. He believed that he had been saved from acting on these thoughts by the absence of opportunity. He dreaded visiting the homes of various friends who had pets for fear of acting on these impulses. One (of several) components of his successful treatment involved the provision of a large dog and a private room. This behavioural experiment dramatically reduced his threat expectancies, since he did not carry out, or attempt to carry out, his feared behaviours.

Naturally, the use of these types of behavioural experiments relies on the therapist making an accurate diagnosis (and feeling confident enough to arrange such tests). Many practitioners feel daunted by the idea of setting tasks that will directly challenge such fears. It must be acknowledged that the procedures are confronting and may require disclosure and informed consent. For example, one young woman (with an extensive history of sexual, aggressive and other obsessions) began to fear throwing her infant nephew off a balcony. In order to conduct the necessary experiments (e.g. placing the child in the sufferer's arms), consent was first obtained from the child's parents. This procedure (along with a raft of other threat-reducing strategies) proved highly effective in reducing anxiety and, subsequently, the woman's obsessionality.

Religious Obsessions

In the case of religious obsessions, clients often report concern with consequences consistent with their religious upbringing. For example, they may believe that they will go to hell (Christian), or not have a place in the 'world to come' (Jewish), as a result of failing to meet strict religious standards. Such fears may be exacerbated when an individual receives advice from a respected religious figure that apparently confirms his/her fear.

Again, in our view, the crux of treatment is to normalise intrusive thoughts and reframe the individuals' understanding of the religious consequences of their obsessions. A 27-year-old male described the repeated intrusive thought (for up to 6 hours a day) that Christ was a false prophet. He believed that he would burn for eternity if he continued to experience this thought. This threat belief was, unfortunately, strengthened after talking to his local priest. Attempts to suppress the thought had simply increased its frequency (see further, Chapters 4, 5, 8 and 10). Components of our successful treatment plan for this patient may surprise many readers. For example, consistent with a threat-expectancy model of OCD, part of this man's treatment involved him searching Old and New Testament passages for clear statements that thoughts (neither solicited nor believed) that were alien and repulsive to him would be punished by eternal damnation. His inability to produce such scripture substantially weakened the threat expectancies (or appraisals) associated with the obsession. The thoughts stopped occurring within 10 sessions of CBT, despite a 5-year history of the problem.

Symmetry, Numbers, Repeating and Miscellaneous Obsessions

Given the potentially important role of magical thinking in these atypical obsessions, lowering threat expectancies may require an intervention that targets general superstitious thinking. We have produced several breakthroughs in individual cognitive therapy that have centred on debunking popular superstitious and mythological notions in order to develop a sense of scientific method in the patient's analyses of the world. The focus of such treatment need not be on the particular magical notion of the sufferer, but more broadly on the spuriousness of magical thinking and superstitious beliefs. For example, one man with a 14-year history of severe OCD and social phobia reported being afraid that the car doors would fall off if he did not balance his internal organs while driving. In addition to the use of ERP, this man was asked to critique popular superstitions that had little to do with his overt problem. For example, he was asked to compare the nature of his belief with the astrological prediction that the third moon of Jupiter would cause a tall, dark (and particularly beautiful) woman to walk down his street. He suggested, after some discussion, that both beliefs were (a) unfalsifiable, (b) made you feel special, and (c) gave you a false feeling of control over the external world. This man reported a dramatic reduction in his belief that car doors and his internal organs were linked. This reduction enabled him to accelerate his exposure program (which further disproved his belief), and he reported an absence of obsessive-compulsive problems within 2 months. This improvement was maintained at 6-month follow up.

CONCLUDING COMMENTS

The above cases are included to illustrate important notions in the contemporary application of CBT for atypical presentations of OCD. Therapeutic effectiveness, in each case, depended on isolating the specific nature of the appraisal (i.e. the threat expected), establishing viable experiments (both behavioural and cognitive) to test these beliefs, and interpreting the results of such tests in a rational manner. These procedures should not be regarded as cure-alls. They are applied within a broad cognitive conceptualisation of the disorder, and are often accompanied by other procedures. Having said this, it is important to again stress that, in our view, recovery from OCD inevitably depends on the elimination of danger expectancies, whether these concern one's physical, social or spiritual safety, or the safety of others (see further, Menzies et al. 2000).

Chapter 13

THE OBSESSIVE-COMPULSIVE SPECTRUM AND BODY DYSMORPHIC DISORDER

David Veale

Are you a 'splitter' or are you a 'lumper'? Do you like to conceptualise psychiatric problems into yet smaller distinct categories or do you like to lump them together into a broad spectrum? Whichever conceptualisation is chosen, does it advance our understanding and treatment of a given mental disorder? In this chapter, I shall give an overview of the concept of obsessive-compulsive spectrum disorders (OCSDs). I shall then discuss some of the concerns about the concept and then highlight one disorder on the spectrum, namely body dysmorphic disorder.

One type of 'lumping' is the OCSDs, introduced by Hollander (1993). One immediate concern is that about a third of DSM-IV is part of the OCS! The spectrum is divided into three broad clusters. The first of these clusters is a *preoccupation with bodily appearance or sensations* and includes body dysmorphic disorder (BDD), hypochondriasis, depersonalisation and anorexia nervosa. These disorders are mainly characterised by beliefs, which are held extremely strongly (usually 'overvalued ideas'; Veale, 2002), and difficulties in engaging patients in treatment. There is a high degree of comorbidity with OCD for most of these disorders. This cluster contains some evidence for a specific treatment response to serotonin reuptake inhibitors (SRIs) for body dysmorphic disorder. Some of the disorders may also respond to cognitive-behavioural therapy (CBT) but there is no evidence that this is a treatment specific response.

The second cluster is *impulse control disorders*, and includes pathological gambling, kleptomania, sexual compulsions, pyromania, trichotillomania and self-injurious behaviour. Compulsive and impulsive behaviours have a common characteristic of an inability to inhibit repetitive behaviour.

Obsessive-Compulsive Disorder: Theory, Research and Treatment.
Edited by Ross G. Menzies and Padmal de Silva. © 2003 John Wiley & Sons, Ltd.

Whereas compulsions are associated with risk avoidance and a reduction in anxiety, impulsive behaviours are associated with risk seeking and maximising pleasure, arousal or gratification (at least in the short term). There is some evidence that SRIs improve compulsive behaviours after a time lag but there is a high rate of relapse when the medication is discontinued. Impulsive disorders may respond to a wider variety of medications, including SRIs, with a more rapid response than compulsions, which then decrease over time. CBT is generally more effective at reducing compulsive rather than impulsive behaviours, although the latter are under-researched.

The third cluster of OCSDs includes *neurological conditions* such as autism, Asperger's syndrome, simple tics, Tourette's syndrome, encephalitis lethargica and Sydenham's chorea. Again, there is frequent co-morbidity with OCD. This cluster includes OCD from an abnormal immune response from Group A β-haemolytic streptococci, in which antibodies bind to the basal ganglia (Swedo et al., 1997); OCD as a consequence of encephalitis lethargica (Marks, 1987); or OCD as part of Tourette's disorder. There is limited evidence for the efficacy of pharmacotherapy or behavioural therapy in these conditions, except for tics and Tourette's syndrome.

Hollander and others have argued that OCSDs share many features with OCD. These include:

1. *Symptom profile*: the pattern of repetitive thoughts, urges or behaviours.
2. *Associated features*: evidence from demographics, family history, co-morbidity and clinical course.
3. *Neurobiology*: evidence from pharmacological challenge studies, neuroimaging and immune factors.
4. *Aetiology*: evidence from genetics and environmental factors.
5. *Treatment*: a specific response to SRIs.

Evidence for inclusion of each disorder in an OCS with these criteria can be argued to a greater or lesser degree. However, the empirical evidence so far is limited, even in conditions such as BDD and hypochondriasis that have a stronger argument for a close relationship with OCD. Conditions such as paedophilia and sexual compulsions have weak evidence for a close relationship to OCD. For example, patients with BDD have a high degree of co-morbidity with OCD, whilst those with sexual compulsions do not. Both BDD and paedophilia may have recurrent intrusive thoughts and repetitive behaviours. BDD patients are unable to resist their 'compulsive' behaviours (such as mirror-checking), which is similar to OCD. However, a paedophile does not usually wish to inhibit his impulsive behaviour.

I have a few concerns about the concept of OCSDs. First, I believe that the concept of OCSD has been pharmacologically driven. A model of aetiology

should be not be influenced by treatment response and OCSDs are characterised by a paucity of randomised controlled trials (RCTs). The argument
is that one of the differences about OCD is that patients respond preferentially to an SRI compared to a noradrenergic reuptake inhibitor (NRI;
e.g. desipramine). This is in contrast to depression, in which patients respond equally well to an SRI or an NRI. Hence it was hypothesised that
OCSDs will also preferentially respond to SRIs compared to NRIs. The
only RCT to confirm this so far has been in BDD, in which clomipramine
(an SRI) was compared to an NRI (e.g. desipramine) (Hollander et al.,
1999). However, are OCD and BDD the only psychiatric disorders that
preferentially respond to an SRI? There have been occasional studies comparing an SRI with an NRI in other anxiety disorders, such as panic or
social phobia, which tend to preferentially respond to an SRI (Zolhar et al.,
2000), suggesting that a preferential response to an SRI is not unique to
OCD.

Second, the OCSD model has little to say about response to psychological
treatments. The model is predominantly a biological one and cognitive-
behavioural theorists have not tended to be quite as enthusiastic for the
concept of OCSD, as they prefer a specific model for each disorder. In this
regard, the treatment model and rationale for CBT are different, although
there are obvious similarities between them. There is very little evidence
comparing different psychological treatments for OCD or OCSDs similar
to the controlled trials comparing CBT and interpersonal therapy (IPT)
in depression (Elkin et al., 1989). Perhaps OCD or OCSDs will respond
preferentially to CBT compared to IPT? This intriguing hypothesis remains
to be evaluated.

Third, the model does not emphasise the heterogeneity of OCD. Some argue that it may be more helpful to split OCD into a number of subtypes. If
you are splitter, then you might want a separate disorder for each of various
subtypes, such as 'hoarding disorder'. There is indeed evidence for three
subtypes of OCD from a factor analysis of symptom subtypes into 'symme-
try/hoarding', 'contamination and washing' and 'pure obsessions' (Baer,
1994). Other subtypes include obsessional slowness, association with an
obsessive-compulsive personality and those with poor insight (see previous chapters). There is some evidence that hoarding is predictive of a poor
response to SRIs (Mataix-Cols et al., 1999b) and cognitive-behavioural therapists have developed a separate model for hoarding (Frost & Hartl, 1996;
see further, Chapter 9).

Last, those with long memories will remember concepts such as
'schizophreniform spectrum' or 'affective disorder spectrum'. Some of
the OCSDs, such as BDD, could also fit a schizophreniform or an affective disorders spectrum (Phillips et al., 1995) or a 'body image spectrum'

(Thompson et al., 1999). I am not therefore entirely convinced that the concept of spectrum disorders has advanced our understanding or treatment of such disorders. Many of the similarities in phenomenology are superficial; for example, mirror gazing in BDD has been compared to the compulsive checking of OCD. Early experimental analysis of compulsions such as washing and checking found that they were maintained because they 'work' by reducing anxiety in the short term (Hodgson & Rachman, 1972; Roper et al., 1973; Roper & Rachman, 1975). More recent analyses of compulsions reveal a more complex picture of safety or neutralising behaviours, which are distinct from compulsions (Rachman, 1998). We compared mirror-gazing behaviour in BDD patients and healthy controls (Veale & Riley, 2001) and found that mirror gazing in BDD does not follow a simple model of a compulsive checking in OCD in terms of anxiety reduction, and is a more complex phenomenon. We now believe that mirror gazing is best conceptualised as a series of idiosyncratic and complex safety behaviours which generally increase distress.

Sometimes there are more differences than similarities in the phenomenology, although these are at the extreme end of a spectrum. For example, the intrusive thoughts of sexual pleasure with a child would cause great distress to a patient with OCD and enormous pleasure to a paedophile. Such diagnoses are at the opposite end of a risk-aversion or pleasure-seeking spectrum and one might argue that there are more differences than similarities between paedophilia and OCD. However, both diagnoses are regarded as opposite ends of the obsessive-compulsive spectrum. I therefore believe that the importance of the concept of OCSD is in the various dimensions of psychopathology that have been proposed by Hollander (1993). I find these dimensions attractive and a novel approach to classifying psychopathology. The symptoms of OCSD can be viewed along several dimensions. First, they can be seen along a spectrum with risk-averse and compulsive behaviours at one end and risk-seeking and impulsive behaviours at the other end. Both compulsive and impulsive behaviours have an inability to delay repetitive behaviours. However, compulsive behaviours may be associated with hyperfrontality and increased serotonergic sensitivity, whilst impulsivity is associated with hypofrontality and low presynaptic receptor sensitivity. Some patients may have features of compulsive and impulsive behaviours and are therefore placed in the middle of the spectrum.

A second dimension is a continuum between pure obsessions to motoric ritualistic behaviour. Some OCD patients have pure obsessions, whilst others have only compulsions and stereotypic or tic-like behaviours, without any obsessions. Disorders with neurological conditions are more likely to be placed at the motoric end of the spectrum.

A third dimension is a continuum of uncertainty (good insight) to certainty (delusional). Most OCD patients accept their obsessions as doubts and have good insight. However, many BDD patients may have an additional diagnosis of a delusional disorder and are convinced about the severity of their defect.

In conclusion, splitting mental disorders into distinct categories can exist alongside lumping them into broad spectra, but perhaps the concept of a spectrum is best confined to the psychopathology and developing treatment strategies (whether pharmacological or psychological) for different ends of the continuum or in the middle.

BODY DYSMORPHIC DISORDER

BDD is the prototypal OCSD. It was first described by an Italian psychiatrist, Morselli, who used the term 'dysmorphophobia' in 1886 (Jerome, 2001). However, the term is now falling into disuse, probably because ICD-10 has discarded it and subsumed it under that of hypochondriacal disorder.

BDD is defined in DSM-IV as a preoccupation with an 'imagined' defect in one's appearance. Phillips (1996) suggests that to make a diagnosis of BDD, the preoccupation with the 'imagined' defect should last at least an hour a day, although most patients report that they are conscious of their perceived defects most of the day. The diagnostic criteria also state that if a minor physical anomaly is present, then the person's concern is regarded as markedly excessive. The preoccupation must also cause significant distress or handicap to distinguish between normal concerns about the appearance (especially during adolescence) and a diagnosis of BDD. The beliefs about appearance (e.g. that 'skin is too wrinkled and puffy') may be held with poor insight (when it is regarded as an overvalued idea) or no insight (when it is delusional). DSM-IV classifies BDD on the strength of such beliefs as to whether there is an additional (or in ICD-10, an alternative) diagnosis of a delusional disorder.

Presentation

The most common preoccupations are around the face (especially the nose, skin, hair, eyes, eyelids, mouth, lips, jaw and chin (Neziroglu & Yaryura-Tobias, 1993b; Phillips et al., 1993; Veale et al., 1996a). However, any part of the body may be involved and the preoccupation is frequently focused on several body parts. Complaints typically involve perceived or slight flaws on the face, body features being too small or too big, hair thinning, acne, wrinkles, scars, vascular markings, paleness or redness of the complexion, asymmetry or lack of proportion. Sometimes the complaint is extremely vague or amounts to no more than the patient believing him/herself generally ugly.

Epidemiology

BDD has never been included in the large catchment area surveys of psychiatric morbidity. There has been one catchment area study of somatoform disorders which found a one-year prevalence of BDD of nearly 1% (Faravelli et al., 1997). The prevalence is higher than expected, as at present many patients do not seek help from a mental health professional. In general BDD is a hidden disorder and many patients do not seek help. In this respect there is a low level of awareness about BDD amongst the public or health professionals. When patients do seek help they are more likely to consult a dermatologist or a cosmetic surgeon, as opposed to a psychiatrist. For example, Phillips et al. (2000) surveyed 268 patients attending a dermatology clinic and found that 11.9% screened positive for BDD. The only reliable data in a cosmetic surgery clinic is from Sarwer et al. (1998), who found that 5% of 100 women had BDD. If BDD patients do seek help from their GPs or mental health professionals, they are often too ashamed to reveal their preoccupation with their appearance and present with symptoms of depression, social phobia or OCD unless they are specifically questioned about symptoms of BDD. Patients are especially secretive about symptoms, such as mirror gazing, probably because they think they will be viewed as vain or narcissistic. Patients are therefore diagnosed, on average, 10–15 years after onset. Surveys of BDD patients attending a psychiatric clinic tend to have an equal sex incidence, an age of onset during adolescence, and to be single or separated (Neziroglu & Yaryura-Tobias, 1993b; Phillips & Diaz, 1997; Phillips et al., 1993; Veale et al., 1996a). They have a quality of life worse than that of depressed patients (Phillips, 2000). Patients are often unemployed or disadvantaged at work, and may be housebound or socially isolated because of their handicap. A risk assessment must be performed, as they are at high risk of committing suicide (Veale et al., 1996a) They may also perform 'DIY' cosmetic surgery if they cannot afford private surgery or if a surgeon refuses their request (Veale, 2000).

Co-morbidity

There is frequent co-morbidity, especially for depression. Phillips et al. (1994) found a rate of 60% of current major depression and a lifetime rate of more than 80% in a survey of 100 patients. Other common co-morbid diagnoses were social phobia, substance abuse and OCD (all with lifetime rates of more than 30%). In our own survey of 50 patients, we found a lower rate of co-morbidity but the same Axis I diagnosis being either a mood disorder (26%), social phobia (16%) or OCD (6%) (Veale et al., 1996a).

Aetiology

There are number of possible aetiological factors in the development of BDD. These include a genetic predisposition and non-specific factors, such as a history of teasing or low self-esteem. An intriguing factor may be aesthetic sensitivity. Harris (1982) first proposed that individuals (not BDD patients) seek cosmetic surgery because they may be more sensitive of aesthetic proportions, which he termed 'aestheticality'. He hypothesised that such individuals were more likely to notice abnormalities of appearance (e.g. being disproportionate, asymmetrical or discoloured) and that this ability to discriminate between a normal and abnormal appearance had survival value. Perhaps BDD patients are also more aesthetically sensitive and this is one reason why it persists?

In a similar vein, Thornhill & Gangestad (1993) have proposed a Darwinian theory of beauty that predicts that sexual selection favours those traits that advertise resistance to infections and healthy genes. There is evidence that humans and animals seek symmetry, perhaps because it advertises biological quality and serves to attract individuals to partners resistant to developmental disruptions and the absence of infections. In humans, for instance, females with evenly matched breasts were more fertile than a less evenly endowed matched control group of females. In another study, males preferred photographs of females with symmetrical facial features, and vice versa. Symmetry was also positively correlated with self-reported age at first copulation and number of lifetime partners (Thornhill & Gangestad, 1993). The size of secondary sexual characteristics that develop during puberty are also important in ratings of attractiveness (Thornhill & Grammer, 1994). High levels will lower immunocompetence and only healthy organisms can cope with the high levels required. Enlarged jaws, chins and cheekbones are examples of secondary sexual facial characteristics that are enlarged by testosterone in males, and largeness of these of features are considered by females as sexually attractive, perhaps because of advertised immunocompetence. Female attractiveness is correlated with the opposite—tiny lower faces, big lips and slender lower jaw. High levels of oestrogen are required for these changes, which also lowers immunocompetence. In a recent study (Veale et al., 2001), we hypothesised that if BDD patients are preoccupied with aesthetics, they are more likely to have had an occupation or education in art and design than comparative groups of psychiatric patients. We extracted the occupation, higher education or training from the case notes of 100 consecutive patients with BDD and compared them to 100 patients with a major depressive episode, 100 patients with OCD and 100 patients with post-traumatic stress disorder (PTSD). We found that 20% of the BDD patients had an occupation or training in art or design compared to 4% in the depressed group, 3% in the OCD group and 0% in the PTSD group, which was highly significant. We concluded that an interest in art and design may be a contributory factor to the development of the disorder in some patients. Patients might develop a more critical eye and appreciation of aesthetics, which is then applied to their own appearance. An equally plausible explanation is that subjects have a selection bias for an interest in aesthetics. It would be interesting to know whether, if we encouraged our BDD patients who do not have a training in art and design to take up such an interest, it would help them focus their attention away from their own appearance, or whether it would make their preoccupation with their appearance worse.

CLINICAL ASSESSMENT

Patients are often dissatisfied with multiple areas of their bodies. For example, a patient believed that his nose was too crooked and big and that it should be straight and small. He also believed that his facial skin was flawed with blackheads, spots and wrinkles and that it should be perfectly smooth with no lines. He also had other concerns about his facial hair not being symmetrical and being ugly, his lips being too big, his ears sticking out, and veins sticking out on his arms. The nature of the preoccupation may also fluctuate over time and may explain why, after cosmetic surgery, a preoccupation may often shift to another area of the body.

It is also important to assess the personal meaning or the assumptions held about the perceived defectiveness or ugliness. Patients may have difficulty in articulating the meaning but a 'downward arrow technique' can usually identify such assumptions. After eliciting the most dominant emotion associated with thinking about the defect, the therapist enquires about what is the most shameful (or anxiety-provoking) aspect about the defect. For example, the patient might believe that being defective in his nose will mean that he will end up alone and unloved. For another person, the most disgusting aspect of the flaws in her skin was being dirty. These assumptions can be challenged within CBT.

Mirror gazing is at the core of BDD and appears to consist of a complex series of safety behaviours. However, mirror gazing is not even described in standard textbooks of psychopathology. Why do some BDD patients spend many hours in front of a mirror when it invariably it makes them feel more distressed and self-conscious? We conducted a study comparing the behaviour of mirror gazing in BDD patients and normal controls (Veale & Riley, 2001). The conclusions were that the main motivation for mirror gazing in BDD patients is the hope that they will look different; the desire to know exactly how they look; a desire to camouflage themselves; and a belief that they will feel worse if they resist gazing (although they actually felt more distressed after gazing). BDD patients were more likely to focus their attention on an internal impression or feeling (rather than their reflection in the mirror) and on specific parts of their appearance. Although BDD patients and the controls used the mirror to put on make up, shave, pick their skin, groom their hair or check their appearance, only BDD patients performed 'mental cosmetic surgery' to change their body image and to practise different faces to pull in the mirror. Suffice to say, a detailed assessment is required of exactly what the patient does in front of a mirror and his/her motivation, as this will be grist to the mill in therapy and the construction of behavioural experiments to test out patients' beliefs. The length of the longest session in the mirror and the frequency of the shorter sessions can be used throughout therapy to monitor the severity of mirror gazing. Other reflective surfaces, such as the backs of CDs or shop window panes, may also be used, which further distort their body image. Patients may also check their appearance by measuring their perceived defect; by feeling the contours of the skin with their fingers or repeatedly taking photos or a video of themselves. Other behaviours include asking others to verify the existence of the defect or their camouflage; making comparisons of their appearance with others or old photos of themselves; wearing make-up 24 hours a day; excessive grooming of their hair; excessive cleansing of the skin; use of facial peelers or saunas, facial exercises to improve muscle tone; beauty treatments (e.g. collagen injections to one's lips); cosmetic surgery or dermatological treatments. There may also be impulsive behaviours, such as skin-picking, which produce a very brief sense of satisfaction or pleasure (similar to trichotillomania), followed by a sense of despair and anger.

Beliefs about being defective and the importance of appearance will drive varying degrees of social anxiety and avoidance. Thus, depending on the nature of their beliefs, patients will tend to avoid a range of public or social situations or intimate relationships. Many patients endure social situations only if they use camouflage or various safety behaviours. These are often idiosyncratic and depend on the perceived defect and cultural norms. Behaviours such as avoidance of eye contact, using long hair or excessive make-up for camouflage are obvious, but others are subtler and are difficult to detect unless the patient is asked how he/she behaves in social situations. For example, a BDD patient preoccupied by his nose avoided showing his profile in social situations and only stood face on to an individual. A patient preoccupied by perceived blemishes under her eye wore a pair of glasses to hide the skin under her eyes. Safety behaviours contribute to the inability to disconfirm beliefs and further self-monitoring in mirrors to determine whether the camouflage is 'working'.

A COGNITIVE-BEHAVIOURAL MODEL OF BDD

The model focuses on the experience of BDD patients especially when they are alone, rather than in social situations, which is likely to follow a model similar to that of social phobia (Clark & Wells, 1995). The model (see Figure 13.1) begins with a trigger that is an external representation of one's body image, typically in front of a mirror. Alternative triggers may include looking at an old photograph when the patient was younger or comparing one's appearance with somebody else. It is proposed that such activities activate idealised values about the importance of appearance, which have become over-identified with the self or 'personal domain' (Veale, 2002). The term 'personal domain' was first used by Beck (1976) to describe the way a person attaches meaning to events or objects around him/her. At the centre of a personal domain are a person's characteristics, his/her physical attributes, goals and values. Clustered around are the animate and inanimate objects in which he/she has an investment, such as family, friends and possessions. An idealised value occurs when one of the values develops to being of such over-riding importance that it defines the 'self' or identity of the individual or becomes at the centre of a personal domain. The thinking error is similar to that described for personalisation, in which the value has over-generalised from one aspect to (almost) the whole of the self and is at the very centre of a personal domain. The idealised value in BDD is usually the importance of appearance but other values may include social acceptance, perfectionism, symmetry or youth. It is hypothesised that the value (in combination with other factors) drives the abnormal beliefs about appearance; for example that one's 'nose looks crooked and too red'. The absence of a value about the importance of appearance is likely to preclude the development of BDD or make it considerably less dysfunctional, for example, a well-known female politician in the UK has said publicly that she views herself as ugly but believes appearance to be an irrelevant and unimportant value (Gerrard, 1999).

The idealised values about the importance of appearance lead to processing of the self as an aesthetic object (and in varying degrees as a social object; see Clark & Wells, 1995). This may lead to a negative aesthetic

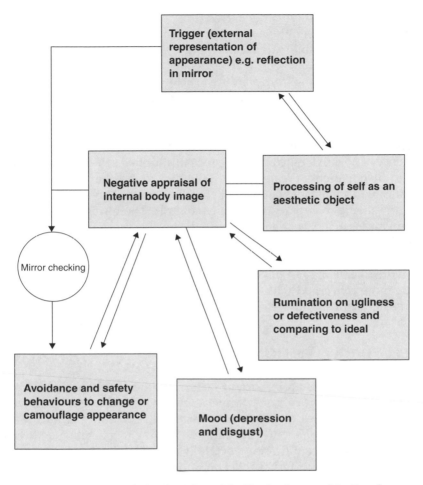

Figure 13.1   A cognitive-behavioural model of body dysmorphic disorder

judgement and comparisons with an internal standard as to how one thinks one should be. There is some evidence for this from self-discrepancy theory. The theory was developed by Higgins (1987), who proposed three basic domains of self-beliefs that are important to understanding emotional experience: (a) *the actual self*—the individual's representation of the attributes that someone (self or significant other) believes the individual actually possesses; (b) *the ideal self*—the individual's representation of the attributes that someone (self or significant other) would ideally hope the individual to possess; (c) *the should or ought self*—the individual's representation of the attributes that someone (self or significant other) believes the individual should, as a sense of duty or moral obligation, possess. The 'ideal' and 'should' selves are referred to as 'self-guides'. It is assumed that a discrepancy between the actual self and the self-guides determines the individual's vulnerability to negative emotional states (Higgins, 1987). For example, in a self-actual:self-ideal discrepancy, the individual is vulnerable to depression resulting from a failure to achieve one's aspirations and ideals (through the absence of positive reinforcement). In a self-actual:other-should discrepancy, the individual is vulnerable to social anxiety or bulimia from the appraisal that he/she has been unable to achieve the expectations of others. In learning theory, one is liable for punishment (the anticipated presence of negative outcomes). We recently applied self-discrepancy theory to BDD patients (Veale et al., 2000) and found that they displayed significant discrepancies between their self-actual and both their self-ideal and self-should, compared to healthy controls. There were no significant discrepancies in BDD patients between their self-actual and other-actual or other-ideal domains. The results suggest that BDD patients have an unrealistic ideal or demand as to how they think they should look. BDD patients are more like depressed patients (rather than social phobics or bulimics), being more concerned with a failure to achieve their own aesthetic standards than with a failure to achieve the demands of others.

SELECTIVE ATTENTION

Selective attention is an important factor in the maintenance of all anxiety disorders. The process of selective attention in BDD might begin when an individual focuses attention on an external reflection in a mirror and on specific aspects of his/her appearance, leading to a heightened awareness and relative magnification of certain aspects. If the focus of attention was entirely on the external reflection, then one might predict that this would lead to increased accuracy of certain aspects of one's body image. Jerome (1992) found that patients on a waiting list for cosmetic rhinoplasty (but not diagnosed as BDD) were more accurate than healthy controls in estimating the size of their nose and spent more time looking at their features in a mirror. This work needs to be replicated in BDD patients who, it is hypothesised, are more likely to selectively attend to an internal mental representation of their body image, similar to social phobia (Clark & Wells, 1995). However, it is also possible that selective attention on specific aspects of one's appearance will contribute to the relative magnification and the development of a distorted body image. The internal body image in BDD is more likely to be unstable and distorted than in controls, as it will be influenced by mood and the values about the importance of appearance to one's identity. The concept of one's body image is also more complex than a pictorial image of our body, such as a photograph or a mirror image

(Ben-Tovim, 1998). Body image has a significant verbal and somatosensory component and is influenced by mood and attitudes. More recent research in the psychology of perception suggests that what we see is largely 'constructed'. Simons & Levin (1998) have found that our impression of seeing everything is just that, an impression. We extract a few details and rely on memory, or perhaps even our imagination, for the rest.

BDD patients may therefore compare three different images: the external representation (e.g. when they first look in a mirror); their ideal body image; and their distorted body image. Not surprisingly, these repeated comparisons result in further uncertainty in the body image and further mirror gazing. The desire to see exactly how one looks is only rewarded whilst looking in front of the mirror. However, the longer a person looks, the worse he/she feels and the more his/her view of being ugly and defective is reinforced. When a patient is not looking in a mirror, he/she may focus attention on his/her internal body image and ruminate and worry on his/her ugliness and assumptions such as being alone and isolated all his/her life.

MOOD AND DYSMORPHIC BELIEFS

Mood changes during mirror gazing are complex and require further research. Patients may experience anticipatory anxiety prior to mirror gazing, when they hope they may see something different or think they will feel worse if they resist gazing. When they look in a mirror, they may experience a depressed mood as they lose their hope that they do not look different. They might feel disgust as they evaluate their body image. During a long session in front of a mirror, they might experience a dissociative state (similar to the experience of self-mutilation or bingeing). After mirror gazing, they might become angry or feel guilty for wasting so much time in front of a mirror. Social avoidance and social isolation will also contribute to a depressed mood.

Depressed mood was noted to be a trigger for looking in a mirror and being caught in a further vicious circle. Interestingly, the link between mood and aesthetic judgements was noted by Beck in his original Depression Inventory (BDI) (Beck et al., 1961). Item 14 in the Inventory asks a patient to pick out one of the following statements that best describe the way they he/she has been feeling: (a) 'I don't feel I look any worse than I used to'; (b) 'I am worried that I am looking old and unattractive'; (c) 'I feel there are permanent changes in my appearance that make me look unattractive'; (d) 'I believe that I look ugly'. The item has unfortunately been dropped from the Revised Version of the Beck Depression Inventory (BDI-II; Beck et al., 1996) on psychometric grounds. However, it was a useful screening item for BDD patients presenting with depression. Ooosthuizen et al. (1998) developed a dysmorphic questionnaire and this also found that concerns about appearance were strongly correlated with cognitive items on the BDI. BDD patients have a high rate of suicide and maintaining a stable mood is important in many cases of BDD.

SOCIAL ANXIETY

Beliefs about being ugly or unattractive and the importance of appearance will drive varying degrees of social anxiety and evaluation of the self as a social object (Clark & Wells, 1995). This refers to the value of conveying a favourable impression of one's self to others. However, there is a marked discrepancy between how a person sees him/herself with how others think he/she should be. Social avoidance and increasing social isolation will lead to increased depressed mood. Safety behaviours contribute to the inability to disconfirm beliefs and further self-monitoring in mirrors to determine whether the camouflage is 'working'.

A few BDD patients are more concerned with the fear of negative evaluation, rather than an internal aesthetic standard. These patients tend to resemble patients with social phobia and may be easier to treat. Most BDD patients process themselves as both an aesthetic and a social object. However, the preoccupation with their own aesthetic standard tends to be proportionally greater than that of social evaluation. A few BDD patients are entirely concerned with meeting an aesthetic standard and have little concern about the impression they give to others. An example of this is a young man who was preoccupied with the shape of his penis, namely the 'flesh' on one side of his frenulum on the underside of his penis being flatter than on the other side. There were no reported concerns about his sexual performance or what his girlfriend would think if she could see it flatter.

THE DRIVE TO CHANGE APPEARANCE

The negative aesthetic judgement, the internal aversion to one's self and the social anxiety will drive the need to change one's appearance. This may be done either physically, by the use of camouflage or make-up, or by cosmetic surgery or a dermatologist. However, this may lead to further disappointment and depression at the failure to achieve an ideal or anger directed against oneself or the surgeon for making one's appearance worse. Patients who cannot afford cosmetic surgery or who are turned down for surgery may resort to 'DIY' cosmetic surgery (e.g. using a stapler to create a face-lift; Veale, 2000). Inevitably, the use of camouflage or cosmetic surgery leads to further mirror checking to see whether it is still working and this feeds the distorted body image in a further vicious circle. Another safety behaviour is 'mental cosmetic surgery', in which patients spend hours trying to change the mental representation of their internal body image.

TREATMENT

Psychiatrists and psychotherapists of whatever persuasion generally have little experience in treating BDD patients or lack an effective treatment model, and there is an unmet need for effective treatment of BDD patients. Published research on the terms 'body dysmorphic disorder' or 'dysmorphophobia' (on Medline, Psychlit, Cochrane database and Evidence-based Mental Health) reveal only three RCTs—two on CBT and one on pharmacotherapy. Rosen et al. (1995) describe group CBT against a waiting list and found significant improvements in the treated group. There is likely to be a selection bias at this centre, as they were all female with a large proportion mainly concerned with their weight and shape. They were less handicapped than other BDD patients described at other centres, who are mainly preoccupied with aspects of their faces. Our own group (Veale et al., 1996b) conducted a pilot RCT of individual CBT against a waiting list in 19 BDD patients. We found significant improvement in the treated group on specific measures of BDD and depressed mood and no differences over time in the waiting list group. The importance of this study was that it was possible to engage BDD patients in CBT and provide an effective treatment. The main criticisms of this study were: that female subjects made up 90% of the subjects; the lack of a non-specific treatment condition; the absence of any follow-up after 15 weeks; and the lack of a measurement of the conviction of belief on a standardized scale (to determine whether or not the cases were regarded as delusional). There have also been a number of case series describing the use of CBT in BDD (Gomez Perez et al., 1994; Neziroglu & Yaryura-Tobias, 1993a, 1993b; Wilhelm et al., 1999). No studies in BDD have demonstrated that CBT contains specific components over and above general factors, such as therapist contact, or that CBT is associated with changes in beliefs and behaviours.

Many psychiatrists still treat BDD patients with an antipsychotic, after an influential case series with pimozide by Riding & Munro (1975). However, the case reports included cases of delusions of infestation, delusions of body odour and dysmorphic delusions. Phillips (1998) reported a clinical observation that selective serotonin reuptake inhibitors (SSRIs) were beneficial in 54% of 113 trials, compared with 2% of 83 trials of anti-psychotic medication. More recent evidence exists for the efficacy of SSRIs in the treatment of BDD, with one randomised crossover trial comparing clomipramine and desipramine (Hollander et al., 1999), one randomised controlled trial of fluoxetine against a placebo (Phillips et al., 2002) and two case series on the use of fluvoxamine (an SSRI; Phillips et al., 1998; Perugi et al., 1996). These studies were associated with modest gains (a 10% reduction on the modified Y-BOCS for BDD). In the study by Phillips et al., fluvoxamine was as effective in 'deluded' and 'non-deluded' cases. However, an SSRI is likely to be associated with a high rate of relapse on discontinuation of the medication (similar to the treatment of OCD) and side effects such as sexual dysfunction. No studies have yet compared SSRIs with CBT or a combination of the two and this needs further evaluation.

SECTION IV

APPROACHES TO ASSESSMENT AND TREATMENT IN OCD

Chapter 14

ASSESSMENT PROCEDURES

Tamsen St. Clare

INTRODUCTION

The importance of using psychometrically sound measures of obsessive-compulsive symptoms in both research and clinical settings is widely recognised. Likewise, it is generally accepted that the assessment measures should evolve in accordance with current theoretical and clinical developments, so that we are able to evaluate contemporary theories and treatments effectively (e.g. Obsessive-Compulsive Cognitions Working Group, 1997; Taylor, 1998). Although there are some reliable and valid instruments available for assessing obsessive-compulsive disorder (OCD), the popular treatment outcome measures have been restricted predominantly to the domains of diagnosis and symptom description.

Current theories of OCD emphasise the importance of cognitive variables in the aetiology and maintenance of the disorder (Foa & Kozak, 1986; Jones & Menzies, 1997a, 1997b; Salkovskis, 1989c; Tallis, 1995a, 1995b; see further, Chapter 4). There appear to be three levels of cognition essential to the disorder: (a) *intrusions* —the unwanted thoughts, impulses and images that sufferers experience; (b) *appraisals* of specific events, particularly appraisals of the significance or meaning of intrusions; and (c) *dysfunctional assumptions or beliefs* that are enduring and relate to many situations (Obsessive Compulsive Cognitions Working Group, 1997). It is therefore important that assessment of OCD incorporate not just measurement of diagnostic symptoms, but also measurement of these cognitive constructs. In brief, a thorough assessment of OCD should include the following:

1. *Diagnosis.* Reliable and valid diagnostic instruments are essential to ensure accurate classification of subjects in research and clinical settings. The availability of psychometrically sound diagnostic measures contributes to the standardisation of diagnostic procedures across studies.

Obsessive-Compulsive Disorder: Theory, Research and Treatment.
Edited by Ross G. Menzies and Padmal de Silva. © 2003 John Wiley & Sons, Ltd.

2. *OCD symptoms and signs.*   The nature and severity of common OCD symptoms should be assessed in detail. Variables of interest would include obsessions, compulsions, avoidance, fear, interference and resistance.

3. *Cognitive appraisal.*   There are several styles of cognitive appraisal thought to be of importance in OCD. These include: (a) overemphasising the importance of thoughts (Rachman, 1998); (b) thought–action fusion (TAF; Rachman, 1993; Salkovskis, 1985), which has two components: considering thoughts to be morally equivalent to actions (moral TAF), and believing that thinking about something increases its chance of occurrence (likelihood TAF); (c) dysfunctional beliefs about the importance of controlling one's thoughts (Clark & Purdon, 1993), and (d) inflated perceived responsibility (Salkovskis, 1985, 1989b).

4. *Related cognitive constructs thought to be significant in OCD.*   Recent theories emphasise a number of additional cognitive constructs that, whilst not exclusive to OCD, are hypothesised to contribute significantly to the aetiology and maintenance of the disorder. 'Perfectionism', 'increased threat expectancy' and 'intolerance of uncertainty' are examples of constructs that feature prominently in current cognitive theories of the disorder (e.g. Carr, 1974; Foa & Kozak, 1986; Frost & Hartl, 1996; Jones & Menzies, 1997a, 1997b; Salkovskis, 1985, 1989b).

In this chapter, I will review a variety of popular assessment measures and evaluate their effectiveness in assessing OCD with respect to the domains listed above. I will discuss recent developments in the assessment of OCD and identify areas requiring further attention. Due to space limitations, this chapter is unable to review all available measures of OCD, and will therefore focus on those that are either widely used or promising. There are several notable omissions, including the obsessive-compulsive subscale from the Symptom Checklist-90-Revised (SCL-90-R; Derogatis, 1977) and the obsessive-compulsive subscale from the Comprehensive Psychopathological Rating Scale (Asberg et al., 1978), both of which have been found to have poor discriminant validity (Steketee & Doppelt, 1986; Woody et al., 1995b) and which are predominantly measures of non-specific distress (Taylor, 1995, 1998). In addition, relatively little coverage will be given to recent measures of cognitive aspects of the disorder, since there is currently little psychometric data available.

I would like to preface the discussion of individual measures with a brief outline of psychometric terminology and recommendations for determining the adequacy of psychometric data. There are three main areas of interest: reliability (the consistency with which a measure performs across testing circumstances); validity (the extent to which a scale actually measures what it purports to measure); and sensitivity to change.

There are several ways in which the *reliability* of a scale can be determined. Internal consistency refers to the degree of homogeneity of items on the scale, test–retest reliability refers to the stability of scores obtained over time by the same subject, and interrater reliability refers to the consistency between scores from different raters for the same subject. It is generally accepted that a coefficient above 0.70 represents adequate reliability, whilst a coefficient above 0.80 indicates good reliability (Feske & Chambless, 2000; Nunnally, 1978; Taylor, 1995, 1998). With regard to interrater reliability, Kappas (κ) of 0.50–0.70 indicate fair agreement, whilst those below 0.50 indicate poor agreement (Fleiss, 1981).

In accordance with other literature in this area (e.g. Feske & Chambless, 2000), correlations of 0.30–0.50 will be taken to indicate acceptable convergence between measures of different modalities (such as a self-report measure and an interview) and correlations over 0.50 will be taken to indicate acceptable convergence between measures of the same modality (such as self-report and self-report). Criterion-related validity will be demonstrated by showing that individuals with OCD score higher than other groups on a given measure. Discriminant validity will be determined by stronger correlations with other measures of OCD symptoms than with measures of different symptoms/disorders. Sensitivity to change will be determined by the degree to which scores change following reported change in symptom severity (particularly following treatments known to be efficacious).

DIAGNOSTIC INTERVIEWS

The most widely used of the standardised diagnostic interviews are the Structured Clinical Interview for DSM, Axis I (SCID-I; First et al., 1995) and the Anxiety Disorders Interview Schedule (ADIS; Di Nardo et al., 1994).

The SCID-I

The SCID-I is a semi-structured interview that provides a broad assessment of all major DSM Axis I disorders. It is economical, in that it provides just enough information to either establish or rule out a diagnosis. The current version is based on DSM-IV (APA, 1994) diagnostic criteria. It is designed to be administered by trained and (ideally) experienced clinicians.

Psychometric data for the SCID-I for DSM-IV have not yet been published. However, to the extent the DSM-IV diagnostic criteria for OCD remain similar to the DSM-IIIR criteria, findings from previous psychometric studies can be generalised to the most recent version. Reliability data for the SCID-I for DSM-IIIR are somewhat variable. Williams et al. (1992) found rather low interrater agreement for both current ($r = 0.59$) and lifetime ($r = 0.67$) diagnoses of OCD. Steketee et al. (1996a) found excellent interrater agreement ($r = 1.0$) on a small sample of 11 OCD patients. The SCID adheres closely to the DSM diagnostic criteria, and therefore has good content validity.

The ADIS

The ADIS is a semi-structured interview designed to diagnose DSM anxiety disorders, common co-morbid disorders (such as major depression), and those disorders commonly used to screen participants from research trials (e.g. substance use disorders). Although the ADIS assesses fewer disorders than the SCID, it provides a more detailed assessment of the anxiety disorders, including OCD. It provides information about severity of obsessive-compulsive fears, insight into obsessive-compulsive symptoms, resistance and avoidance. This additional information can be useful for both research and treatment planning, but may be redundant if the Y-BOCS (Goodman et al., 1989a, 1989b) is also administered. The most recent version is based on DSM-IV (APA, 1994) diagnostic criteria. Like the SCID-I, the ADIS is designed to be administered by trained clinicians, and is best administered by clinicians experienced in the diagnosis of anxiety disorders.

Like the SCID, psychometric data for the latest version of the ADIS have not yet been published. However, both the ADIS and the ADIS-R have shown excellent reliability. Barlow and colleagues found high interrater agreement for current diagnosis of OCD on the ADIS ($r = 0.82$; Barlow, 1987) and the ADIS-R (Di Nardo et al., 1993). Given its close adherence to the DSM diagnostic criteria, the ADIS demonstrates good content validity.

It is important for treatment outcome studies to include a reliable, standardised instrument to diagnose OCD. The ADIS seems the most appropriate, given that it appears psychometrically superior to the SCID, and it accesses a broader range of information about OCD symptoms. As noted by Feske & Chambless (2000), the apparent difference in reliability between the two instruments may be due to the fact that studies on the ADIS have been conducted at a specialist anxiety clinic by clinicians highly trained in the diagnosis of anxiety disorders, whilst the SCID has been primarily administered to a heterogeneous sample by interviewers not specialised in the diagnosis of anxiety states.

OBSERVER-RATED SCALES

Yale–Brown Obsessive-compulsive Scale (Y-BOCS)

The Y-BOCS is a semi-structured interview that was designed to assess OCD symptom severity independent of the number and type of obsessions and compulsions present. It comprises three sections. Section One contains definitions and examples of obsessions and compulsions, and is designed to educate the patient about the meaning of the terms and how to distinguish between them. Whilst this section is crucial for the first rating session, it is generally not required on subsequent administrations. The second section consists of a 64-item target symptom list, which determines past and current obsessions and compulsions. This is used to create an individual symptom profile for each patient. The clinician must rely on his/her judgement to determine the presence or absence of each obsession and compulsion listed, and to decide whether a given symptom is in fact a symptom of OCD, rather than a symptom of a related disorder (such as a paraphilia). The target symptom list is used to determine the most prominent obsessions, compulsions and avoidance behaviours. The third section consists of 10 core items and 11 investigational items. This component is semi-structured —all items are accompanied by standard questions, but additional information provided by the patient during the interview can also be considered, and the clinician is permitted to ask additional questions for clarification. The 10 core items are used to rate the client's prominent obsessions and compulsions on the following five parameters: duration/frequency, interference in social and occupational functioning, associated distress, degree of resistance, and perceived control (over obsessions or compulsions). Each item is rated on a five-point (0–4) scale. Scores from the 10 core items are added to generate scores for the obsessions subscale (items 1–5), the compulsions subscale (items 6–10) and the total Y-BOCS scale (items 1–10). The 11 investigational items assess the following: amount of time free from obsessions/compulsions; insight into irrational nature of the symptoms; avoidance; indecisiveness; inflated personal responsibility; obsessional slowness/inertia; pathological doubting; global symptom severity; treatment response; and reliability of information obtained during the interview. Like the core items, the investigational items are each rated on a five-point scale, where greater scores indicate greater severity.

Psychometric studies of the Y-BOCS have focused predominantly on the Y-BOCS total score. There is little information available for either the symptom list or the investigational items. Psychometric investigations of the Y-BOCS are numerous, and it is generally considered to be the 'gold standard' for assessing the severity of OCD symptoms and signs. There are several studies attesting to the excellent interrater reliability of the Y-BOCS total score. Correlation coefficients have ranged from 0.80 to 0.99 (Goodman et al., 1989b; Jenike et al., 1990b; Price et al., 1987; Woody et al., 1995a). It is possible that some of these indices of interrater reliability have been spuriously inflated, as reliability estimates were based on independent rater's evaluations of the same interview. Whilst this demonstrates that interviewers can reliably rate another's interview, it does not show that they can reliably administer the scale (Taylor, 1998). The Y-BOCS has acceptable internal consistency, with alpha (α) coefficients ranging from 0.69 to 0.91 (Goodman et al., 1989a; Richter et al., 1994; Woody et al., 1995a). Test–retest reliability has been found to be good over a 2 week period ($r = 0.81–0.97$; Kim et al., 1990a; Kim et al., 1992, 1993) but appears to be reduced over extended periods. Woody et al. (1995a) found an intraclass correlation of 0.61 when they administered the Y-BOCS 10–103 days apart, with a mean time interval of 49 days.

The convergent validity of the Y-BOCS is supported by large correlations with other symptom measures, such as the SCL-90-R OC subscale, the Maudsley Obsessional Compulsive Inventory (MOCI; Hodgson & Rachman, 1977), the Compulsive Activity Checklist (CAC; Philpott, 1975) and the symptom scale from the Leyton Obsessional Inventory (LOI; Cooper, 1970; Frost et al., 1995b; Goodman et al., 1989a; Richter et al., 1994; Woody et al., 1995a). Rosenfeld et al. (1992) found the total Y-BOCS score to distinguish people with OCD from those with other anxiety disorders and normal controls, which supports the criterion-related validity of the scale. Content validity is supported by the fact that the Y-BOCS targets a large number of obsessions and compulsions, as well as avoidance and resistance. However, it does not address covert compulsions as adequately as it should (Taylor, 1995, 1998). The addition of the investigational items make the Y-BOCS a more comprehensive measure, overlapping into the assessment of related phenomena thought to be integral to OCD (e.g. inflated personal responsibility). Unfortunately, these items are rarely used in treatment outcome studies.

Studies of discriminant validity have yielded disappointing results, with substantial correlations being demonstrated between the Y-BOCS and measures of anxiety ($Mdn\, r = 0.35$) and depression ($Mdn\, r = 0.48$; Goodman et al., 1989a; Hewlett et al., 1992; Richter et al., 1994; Woody et al., 1995a). These correlations tend to be as large as those demonstrating convergence, and two studies have in fact demonstrated larger correlations with measures of anxiety and depression than measures of OCD (Goodman et al., 1989a; Woody et al., 1995a).

In summary, the Y-BOCS has generally good psychometric properties and is the most comprehensive of the available symptom measures. For this reason it should be used routinely in treatment outcome studies. The Y-BOCS does not have strong discriminant validity, and scores may be spuriously low in individuals presenting with only obsessions or compulsions if the total score is used. Use of the subscale scores is preferable, as it circumvents this problem.

Self-report and Computerised Versions

Several self-report and computerised versions of the Y-BOCS are now in existence (e.g. Rosenfeld et al., 1992). For a more comprehensive review, see Taylor (1998). Overall, the available research suggests that these versions are psychometrically comparable to the clinician-administered interview. Rosenfeld et al. (1992) found a high degree of agreement between their self-administered computerised version and the traditional Y-BOCS interview, with a 97% agreement on the diagnosis (using a cut-off score of 16) and correlations of 0.86–0.88 between the subscale scores. Steketee et al. (1996b) conducted an extensive evaluation of the self-report Y-BOCS in OCD subjects, non-OCD anxiety-disordered subjects and a non-clinical control group, and found a high level of agreement between the two versions.

In sum, the findings to date suggest that self-report and computerised versions of the Y-BOCS produce similar results to the traditional clinician-rated interview. They may therefore provide a more cost-efficient alternative to the time-consuming interview procedure.

National Institute of Mental Health Global Obsessive-compulsive Scale (NIMH-GOCS)

The NIMH-GOCS (Insel et al., 1983b) is a single-item, clinician-administered measure of global severity of OCD symptoms. Scores range from 1 (minimal symptoms) to 15 (very severe obsessive-compulsive behaviour). Scores fall within five clusters of severity (i.e. 1–3, 4–6, 7–9, 10–12, 13–15) and detailed descriptors are provided for each of the five clusters. Scores above 6 indicate clinically significant OCD symptoms.

There is limited psychometric data available for the NIMH-GOCS. Kim and colleagues have reported excellent 2 week test–retest reliability coefficients of 0.98 and 0.87 (Kim et al., 1992, 1993). Several studies have shown good convergence ($r = 0.63$–0.77) with the Y-BOCS (Black et al., 1990; Goodman et al., 1989a; Kim et al., 1992, 1993). There is as yet no data relating to other aspects of the scale's reliability and validity. Several drug treatment studies attest to the fact that the NIMH-GOCS is sensitive to treatment-induced changes in symptom severity—it tends to be more sensitive than some self-report measures and equally sensitive to most observer rated scales, such as the Y-BOCS (Taylor, 1995).

The NIMH-GOCS is brief, and is therefore appealing to use as an outcome measure. However, there is much that remains unknown about its psychometric properties, and it provides very limited information about OCD symptoms. It does not capture information about the nature of the symptoms, neither does it assess the severity of each symptom. It should not be used as a stand-alone measure of OCD, and when used in combination with other measures, such as the Y-BOCS, it may be redundant.

Compulsive Activity Checklist (CAC)

The original CAC is a 62-item, clinician-administered interview, developed to assess the extent to which obsessive-compulsive symptoms interfere with day-to-day activities (Philpott, 1975). Each item lists an activity, and ability to perform that behaviour is rated on a four-point (0–3) scale. Impairment is judged according to four criteria: frequency, duration, avoidance and oddity of behaviour. Impairment can be due to either obsessions or compulsions.

There have been several subsequent versions of the scale (Cottraux et al., 1988; Freund et al., 1987; Marks et al., 1977; Steketee & Freund, 1993), all of which have been found to have similar psychometric properties (Taylor, 1998). Recent versions have demonstrated good internal consistency, with α coefficients for the 28-item, 37-item, and 38-item self-report versions ranging from 0.78 to 0.95 (Cottraux et al., 1988; Frost et al., 1995b; Steketee & Freund, 1993; Sternberger & Burns, 1990a). Similar results were obtained for the 38-item clinician-administered CAC ($r = 0.91$; Freund et al., 1987). Internal consistency for the washing and checking subscales also appears good ($r = 0.89$–0.93; Freund et al., 1987). Studies of interrater and test–retest reliability have yielded mixed results: Marks and colleagues obtained interrater reliability coefficients of 0.95 for two independent raters in separate administrations of the 39-item CAC (Marks et al., 1980), whilst results for the 38-item version were substantially lower ($r = 0.62$; Freund et al., 1987). Marks et al. (1980) found good correlations between their self-report and clinician-rated versions ($r = 0.83$) and Freund et al. (1987) found that the mean total CAC score correlated 0.94 with the 38-item self-report CAC. Studies of test–retest reliability have produced marginal results for both the 1 month test–retest reliability of the 37-item self-report version ($r = 0.62$; Cottraux et al., 1988) and the 37-day test–retest reliability of the 38-item interview version ($r = 0.68$; Freund et al., 1987). Sternberger & Burns (1990b) found adequate ($r = 0.74$) test–retest reliability for the 38-item self-report version over a 6–7 month period.

Convergent validity appears adequate, with reasonable correlations being found between various versions of the CAC and other measures of OCD symptoms, such as the MOCI, PI, SCL-90-R OC subscale, Likert scales of symptom severity and the Y-BOCS (Cottraux et al., 1988; Freund et al., 1987; Frost et al., 1995b; Marks et al., 1980; Steketee & Freund, 1993; Sternberger & Burns, 1990b). With respect to discriminant validity, Freund et al. (1987) found that whilst the 38-item clinician-rated CAC correlated 0.38 with the SCL 90-R OC subscale, it demonstrated only slightly weaker ($r = 0.14$–0.31) correlations with other scales on the SCL-90-R. Foa et al. (1987) found that correlations between the observer-rated CAC and measures of depression ($r = 0.33$–0.47) were almost as large as those with other measures of obsessive-compulsive symptoms. These findings suggest that the clinician-rated CAC has poor discriminant validity. Given the high correlations between clinician-rated and self-report versions of the scale, these findings are also likely to apply to self-report versions of the CAC.

There is some evidence for the criterion-related validity of the CAC. Cottraux et al. (1988) found that OCD subjects obtained higher scores than normal controls, panic-disordered patients and social phobics. Steketee & Freund (1993) reported that 29 of the 38 items on the self-report CAC discriminated people with OCD from those with other anxiety disorders and from normal controls. Data relating to the content validity of the scale is somewhat mixed. Whilst the CAC assesses the degree of interference with day-to-day activities, it confounds slowness, avoidance and oddity of behaviour (Taylor, 1998), rendering high scores somewhat ambiguous. Furthermore, it does not cover the degree of distress, or interference with social relationships (Feske & Chambless, 2000; Goodman & Price, 1998), neither does it address covert rituals or compulsions.

Like the MOCI, the CAC focuses primarily on washing/cleaning and checking rituals. Given the above weaknesses with the CAC, there is little reason to recommend it over the MOCI (Feske & Chambless, 2000; Goodman & Price, 1998).

SELF-REPORT MEASURES

Maudsley Obsessional-compulsive Inventory (MOCI)

The MOCI (Hodgson & Rachman, 1977) is a 30-item true–false question-naire consisting of four subscales: washing, checking, slowness and doubt-ing. The scale generates four subscale scores and a total score. Scores re-flect the amount of time consumed by obsessive-compulsive symptoms. Although all four subscales were originally derived through factor anal-ysis, subsequent analyses have generally failed to replicate the slowness subscale (Chan, 1990; Rachman & Hodgson, 1980; Sanavio & Vidotto, 1985; Sternberger & Burns, 1990a).

Studies on clinical samples have demonstrated good internal consistency for the total MOCI score (Emmelkamp et al., 1999) and adequate inter-nal consistency for the checking, cleaning and doubting subscales, with α coefficients of 0.60–0.87 (Emmelkamp et al., 1999; Hodgson & Rachman, 1977; Rachman & Hodgson, 1980; Richter et al., 1994). Studies on non-clinical samples have yielded lower α coefficients of 0.40–0.62 (Chan, 1990; Sanavio & Vidotto, 1985; Sternberger & Burns, 1990a). This is possibly due to the restricted range of scores obtained from non-clinical samples (Feske & Chambless, 2000; Taylor, 1998). In general, all studies have found very low internal consistency for the slowness subscale, with α coefficients of 0–0.44 (Chan, 1990; Emmelkamp et al., 1999; Rachman & Hodgson, 1980; Sanavio & Vidotto, 1985). The MOCI total score has acceptable test–retest reliability (Emmelkamp et al., 1999; Hodgson & Rachman, 1977).

Several studies attest to the convergent and discriminant validity of the MOCI. It tends to show good convergence with other self-report measures of OCD symptoms ($Mdn\,r = 0.69$), such as the PI, and the LOI symptom scale (Hodgson & Rachman, 1977; Kyrios et al., 1996; Richter et al., 1994; van Oppen, 1992), but correlations with clinician-administered scales, such as the Y-BOCS and the CAC, tend to be lower ($Mdn\,r = 0.54$; Goodman et al., 1989b; Richter et al., 1994; Woody et al., 1995a). The convergent and divergent validity of the washing and checking subscales, but not the doubting and slowness subscales, have also been established. The washing scale correlates highly with the PI contamination subscale but not with the PI checking subscale and the checking subscale correlates highly with the PI checking subscale but not with the PI contamination subscale (Sternberger & Burns, 1990b; van Oppen, 1992; van Oppen et al., 1995c). Correlations between the MOCI subscales and indices of depres-sion tend to be lower than the convergence correlations, which supports the discriminant validity of the subscales. Validity of the doubting and slowness subscales has not yet been comprehensively examined. Studies of criterion-related validity have also generated positive results. The MOCI has been shown to distinguish people with OCD from phobics, those with mixed psychiatric diagnoses, and normal controls (Kraaijkamp et al., 1986).

The studies pertaining to content validity of the MOCI are less encouraging. Whilst the MOCI assesses two of the most common obsessive-compulsive presentations, i.e. washing and checking, there are many other obsessive-compulsive symptoms, such as covert compulsions and aggressive and sexual impulses, that are not addressed. This may result in patients with washing and checking presentations scoring higher on the MOCI than those with other symptoms, regardless of the severity of symptoms. Its use as an index of symptom severity is therefore problematic. The dichotomous response format of the MOCI may further decrease its ability to assess symptom severity. A further problem associated with use of the MOCI is the poor psychometric properties of the slowness and, to a lesser extent, the doubting subscale.

Given these weaknesses, the MOCI should not be used in isolation as an outcome measure. It should, at the very least, be combined with a more comprehensive measure like the Y-BOCS. Given the poor psychometric properties of the slowness and doubting subscales, use of the MOCI should ideally be restricted to the washing and checking subscales.

MOCI–Revised

The revised MOCI (MOCI-R; Rachman et al., 1995) has recently been designed in an attempt to overcome some of the shortcomings inherent in the original version. It addresses a wider range of obsessions and compulsions, includes avoidance behaviours and beliefs commonly found in OCD, and the previous dichotomous response format has been replaced by a five-point scale. The scale consists of 84 items and includes 17 subscales. Rachman et al. (1995) administered the revised MOCI to a non-clinical sample and found evidence of adequate internal consistency, convergent validity and divergent validity. However, there were problems found with the validity of certain subscales (such as the cleaning subscale, which correlated equally with the MOCI cleaning and checking subscales, and which correlated almost as highly with a measure of depression). Furthermore, the revised MOCI was found to be unifactorial. The MOCI-R is still in the process of development (Taylor, 1998) and, despite these significant drawbacks, it may develop into a valid and comprehensive measure of obsessive-compulsive symptoms.

Padua Inventory (PI)

The original version of the Padua Inventory (PI; Sanavio, 1988) is a 60-item self-report measure designed to assess the most common obsessions and compulsions. The PI has four subscales: contamination; checking; impaired control of mental activities; and urges and worries over losing control of motor behaviours. Each item is rated on a five-point (0–4) scale according to the degree of disturbance caused. It yields one total score and four subscale scores. Most psychometric investigations of the PI have been performed on non-clinical samples. One of the two factor-analytic studies to include clinical subjects identified five factors rather than four, and this led to the construction of a 41-item revised version of the scale (PI-R; van Oppen, Hoekstra and Emmelkamp, 1995c). The 41-item PI-R is comprised of five subscales: impulses, washing, checking, rumination, and precision. Interestingly, a second study combining clinical and non-clinical subjects failed to replicate the above finding, with outcome data supporting the original four-factor structure (Macdonald & de Silva, 1999).

Whilst the PI and the 41-item PI-R have both demonstrated excellent internal consistency (Burns et al., 1996; Kyrios et al., 1996; Sanavio, 1988; van Oppen, 1992, van Oppen et al., 1995), reasonable test-retest reliability (Kyrios et al., 1996; Sanavio, 1988; van Oppen, 1992), and good convergence with other self-report measures of OCD such as the MOCI (Kyrios et al., 1996; van Oppen, 1992), discriminant validity appears problematic. In particular, there are strong correlations with neuroticism ($r = 0.60$), trait anxiety ($r = 0.58$), depression ($r = 0.55$–0.61) and worry ($r = 0.57$) (Freeston et al., 1994a; Kyrios et al., 1996; Sternberger & Burns, 1990b; van Oppen, 1992). These high correlations with anxiety and depression are concerning, as they suggest that the PI and the 41-item PI-R are indicators of general emotional distress rather than specific measures of obsessive-compulsive symptomatology.

The PI has been widely criticised for failing to distinguish between obsessions and worries (Freeston et al., 1994a). This prompted Burns and colleagues to introduce a 39-item revised PI, in which all original items that were thought to assess worry were removed (Burns et al., 1996). This version of the scale comprises five subscales: obsessional thoughts about harm to oneself or others; obsessional impulses to harm oneself or others; contamination obsessions and washing compulsions; checking compulsions; and dressing and grooming compulsions. All five subscales of the 39-item PI have shown good internal consistency ($r = 0.77$–0.88), and the measure has demonstrated adequate test–retest reliability ($r = 0.61$–0.84) over intervals of 6–7 months (Burns et al., 1996). There is also preliminary support for the criterion-related validity of the 39-item revised scale, in that 15 people with OCD were found to have significantly higher scores than normal controls on all five subscales (Burns et al., 1996). Discriminant validity of this scale appears superior to that of the other two versions: Burns et al. (1996) found that the total score had only 12% of shared variance with the Penn State Worry Questionnaire (PSWQ; Meyer et al., 1990), compared with 34% for the original PI.

Whilst the 39-item revised PI seems promising as a measure of OCD, there are a number of issues that should be noted. First, all psychometric data to date is from the one original study, and further evaluation is required. Second, there is as yet no data pertaining to convergent validity or sensitivity to change. Third, although the revised version appears to discriminate adequately between obsessions and worry, it is not clear whether the high correlations with other constructs, such as depression, have also been reduced. Fourth, although the PI covers many obsessive-compulsive symptoms, there are several areas that are not addressed, such as neutralising and hoarding (Foa et al., 1998b). Whilst this raises some concerns about content validity, the PI nevertheless addresses a reasonable range of obsessions and compulsions, including some ruminations and impulses that are poorly covered in many other measures.

Leyton Obsessional Inventory (LOI)

The Leyton Obsessional Inventory (LOI; Cooper, 1970) is a 69-item questionnaire designed to assess obsessional symptoms and traits. It is most commonly administered in its original form, as a card sorting, 'post-box', procedure, although a pencil-and-paper version has been developed to facilitate administration (Snowdon, 1980). In addition to 'yes' and 'no' responses for each item, scores are obtained for 'resistance' and 'interference'. These scores range from 0 to 3. The scale yields four subscale scores: symptom, trait, interference and resistance. There is also a total LOI score, although this is rarely used.

The LOI has demonstrated reasonable internal consistency, with α coefficients of 0.75–0.93 for the four subscales (Richter et al., 1994; Stanley et al., 1993). Likewise, the test–retest reliability of these subscales appears satisfactory ($r = 0.79$–0.89, 1–2 weeks; Kim et al., 1990a).

Convergent validity has generally been supported by the available data. The LOI subscales correlate highly with other self-report measures for OCD, such as the MOCI and the PI (Hodgson & Rachman, 1977; Richter et al., 1994; Sanavio, 1988), but correlations with clinician-rated scales such as the Y-BOCS are weaker (Kim et al., 1990a; Richter et al., 1994). Although significant correlations have been found with other constructs, such as depression and neuroticism (Richter et al., 1994, Stanley et al., 1993), these tend to be lower than the correlations with other measures of OCD, indicating that the LOI has reasonable discriminant validity. The LOI has been found to discriminate well between individuals diagnosed with OCD and normal controls (Cooper, 1970; Millar, 1980; Murray et al., 1979). Whilst the interference and resistance scales have been consistently shown to differentiate OCD patients from depressed patients (Millar, 1983; Stanley et al., 1993), there are inconsistent results for the symptom scale. Millar (1983) found that this subscale failed to distinguish between people with OCD and those who were depressed, whilst Stanley et al. (1993) found that the symptom scale was able to discriminate well between these two populations. It should be noted that Stanley et al. (1993) were the only group to employ a reliable standardised interview to diagnose patients. Both of these studies found that the trait scale failed to differentiate between individuals with OCD and those with depression.

There are some concerning findings relating to the content validity of the LOI. First, there are some important aspects of obsessive-compulsive symptomatology that are not well represented in the scale, due to its overwhelming bias towards cleaning and washing-related items. There are very few items relating to other common compulsions, such as checking, or to obsessions. Coverage of aggressive and sexual obsessions is particularly poor. Secondly, the scale confounds symptom severity and resistance (Taylor, 1995). Whilst the LOI considers greater resistance to be related to more severe obsessive-compulsive symptoms, it is in fact related to less severe OCD symptomatology (Feske & Chambless, 2000; Taylor, 1995). Furthermore, the LOI has been shown to be less sensitive to treatment-induced changes in symptomatology than other measures of OCD (Insel et al., 1983b; Thoren et al., 1980). Given that several other measures of OCD assess a wider domain of symptoms (e.g. Y-BOCS, PI) and appear to be psychometrically superior, it is difficult to justify use of the LOI as an outcome measure.

Likert Scales

Likert scales are single-item, continuous scales, designed to assess any of a number of variables. They have numerical anchor-points, which are generally accompanied by a written descriptor. They can be rated by either the interviewer or the patient. A number of nine-point Likert scales have been developed for assessing OCD. The most commonly assessed variables are: global severity of obsessions and compulsions, obsessive-compulsive-related fear, avoidance, time taken up in compulsive activity, and urge to ritualise (e.g. Emmelkamp, 1982; Foa et al., 1992, 1983b).

Likert scales appear to have good interrater reliability. Reasonable correlations have been noted between self-report and observer-rated versions (Cottraux et al., 1990) and between patient-, therapist- and independent observer-rated versions ($r = 0.64$–0.83; Foa et al., 1987). The evidence pertaining to test–retest reliability is less encouraging. Steketee et al. (1988) reported 60-day test–retest reliability coefficients of 0.40–0.87 for self-report ratings and 0.20–0.50 for observer ratings. The degree of variation in these coefficients is concerning, and unfortunately the authors did not state which ratings yielded which coefficients. Freund & Foa (1988) reported significant discrepancies between self-ratings of avoidance ($r = 0.72$–0.87) and fear ($r = 0.35$–0.59). In this study, interviewer ratings of both avoidance and fear were inadequate ($r = 0.16$–0.70). The available data suggests that test–retest reliability is highly variable, and there is little available evidence to suggest which types of rating are more stable over time. Further investigation is warranted.

Convergent validity appears generally acceptable, with moderate correlations being found between Likert scales and other measures of OCD, such as the CAC, Y-BOCS, SCL-90-R OC subscale and the PI (Cottraux et al., 1988; Foa et al., 1983b; Freund et al., 1987; Steketee & Doppelt, 1986; van Oppen et al., 1995a; Woody et al., 1995a, 1995b). As noted by Feske & Chambless (2000), moderate correlations between these measures indicate acceptable convergence, given that Likert ratings tend to assess the most disturbing symptoms, whereas other measures of OCD offer a broader coverage of OCD symptoms. There is little available evidence concerning discriminant validity. Likert ratings tend to have small to medium correlations with Hopkins SCL measures of depression, somatisation, anxiety and interpersonal sensitivity ($r = 0.09$–0.36; Foa et al., 1983b), and self-report measures of depression ($r < 0.30$; Foa et al., 1987). These correlations tend to be lower than those with other obsessive-compulsive measures, suggesting that discriminant validity is adequate.

Likert scales appear to be sensitive to treatment-induced changes in symptomatology, with mean effect sizes of 1.56–3.47 (Taylor, 1995). They tend to be more sensitive to treatment effects than self-report inventories such as the MOCI, and equally sensitive to the Y-BOCS (Taylor, 1995).

In summary, Likert scales are appealing for use in treatment outcome studies because they are simple to administer and score. Although Likert scales have reasonable psychometric properties, test–retest reliability appears highly variable. The absence of standardised instructions makes reliable and valid replication impossible. Standardised instructions would be valuable in overcoming this difficulty. Several precautions should be taken when using Likert scales to measure treatment outcome. As the scales themselves are often unreliable, they should never be used as a sole measure of treatment outcome, but should be used in combination with other Likert scales and with comprehensive measures of obsessive-compulsive symptomatology, such as the Y-BOCS. A further way in which reliability of the measurement can be enhanced is to administer each Likert scale several times at each measurement point and use the average score (Feske & Chambless, 2000).

Obsessive-compulsive Inventory (OCI)

The OCI (Foa et al., 1998b) is a 42-item self-report measure that was specifically designed to address problems inherent in previous measures of OCD symptom severity. It comprises seven subscales: washing, checking, doubting, ordering, obsessing, hoarding and mental neutralising. Each item is rated on a five-point (0–4) scale for both frequency and distress.

To date there are only two published studies evaluating the OCI. Internal consistency for the total score and the subscales was found to be acceptable in both a non-clinical ($r = 0.71$–0.95; Simonds et al., 2000) and a mixed sample ($r = 0.59$–0.96; Foa et al., 1998b). Test–retest reliability over a 1–4 week interval was found to be adequate ($r = 0.68$–0.97; Foa et al., 1998b; Simonds et al., 2000). Convergent validity of the scale is supported by reasonable correlations with the MOCI and the CAC (Foa et al., 1998b; Simonds et al., 2000). The OCI also correlated positively with measures of general anxiety and depression, but these correlations tended to be lower than those with other measures of OCD, supporting the discriminant validity of the scale. Interestingly, whilst the overall distress score has been found to correlate with depression, the overall frequency score has not (Foa et al., 1998b). OCD subjects scored higher than normal controls, individuals with generalised social phobia and those with post-traumatic stress disorder on all scales except the hoarding subscale (Foa et al., 1998b). This supports criterion-related validity for all but the hoarding subscale, which is now under review.

The OCI promises to be one of the most comprehensive self-report measures for use in OCD. It addresses several symptoms that are not adequately represented in other self-report measures, such as hoarding and mental neutralising, and it assesses both frequency of symptoms and the degree of distress caused by them. Psychometric properties appear generally strong, although the hoarding subscale is problematic. Further research into the scale is required (e.g. to ascertain sensitivity to change) but it is a potentially useful measure.

BEHAVIOURAL AVOIDANCE TESTS

Behavioural avoidance tests (BATs) are designed to assess *in vivo* fear and avoidance behaviour. Several types of BAT have been developed for use in OCD. The 'single-task' BAT (e.g. Foa et al., 1984) involves the patient approaching as near as possible to a feared stimulus and reporting his/her subjective units of distress (SUDs). The SUDs rating is an index of fear and distress, measured on a 0–100 scale, where $0 =$ no fear or distress and $100 =$ maximum fear or distress. Avoidance is either assessed by the minimum distance the patient reaches from the feared stimulus or by some other predetermined criterion, such as whether the subject is able to touch the feared object. The 'single-task' BAT is limited by the fact that it assesses avoidance in relation to only one feared object. The 'multitask' BAT (Rachman et al., 1979) requires subjects to complete a number of different anxiety-inducing tasks. Each task is rated according to the level of distress experienced and the degree of avoidance. Steketee et al. (1996a) developed a more sophisticated BAT, in which subjects are required to attempt several anxiety-inducing tasks, each of which is broken down into 3–7 steps according to degree of difficulty. Scores include SUDs, avoidance, percentage of steps completed and degree of ritualising. Steketee and colleagues have developed an instruction guide to aid with the development and implementation of BATs.

There is little known about the psychometric properties of BATs. They are difficult to adapt to the wide variety of obsessive-compulsive symptoms and have therefore not been extensively used or evaluated (Krochmalik et al., 2001). Most of the existing data relate to Steketee et al.'s (1996a) BAT. Woody et al. (1995a) provided support for the convergent validity of the BAT by demonstrating reasonable correlations between pre-treatment fear and avoidance measures from the BAT and the Y-BOCS ($r = 0.38$–0.43). Steketee et al. (1996a) found similar correlations between pre-treatment BAT measures and the Y-BOCS ($r = 0.36$–0.43). Correlations with the MOCI were substantially lower ($r = 0.21$). Discriminant validity of the BAT is supported by the finding that BAT measures of SUDs, avoidance and rituals correlate minimally with the SCL-90-R depression scale ($r = 0.01$–0.20) and with a measure of obsessive-compulsive personality disorder ($r = 0.10$–0.30; Steketee et al., 1996a).

BATs have demonstrated sensitivity to treatment effects (Cottraux et al., 1990; Foa et al., 1984; Rachman et al., 1979). Mean effect sizes for SUDs ratings and avoidance are generally greater that 1.00 SD units (Taylor, 1995).

There are several disadvantages associated with the use of BATs. Whilst they are reasonably well adapted to certain subtypes of OCD, such as contamination/washing, they are very difficult to design for other subtypes (Steketee, 1993a, 1993b). Furthermore, as anxiety and avoidance can be situationally-specific, it can be difficult to generate an appropriate behavioural task within the clinic (Krochmalik et al., 2001). Performance on the BAT has been found to vary according to the perceived demands of the task (Nietzel et al., 1988). This highlights the importance of using standardised instructions. These issues complicate the use of the BATs. However, given that they represent a unique aspect of assessment, they may be useful in certain populations where they can be easily constructed and implemented (such as in OCD washers). They should always be administered with standardised instructions aimed at reducing demand characteristics.

RECENT DEVELOPMENTS AND FUTURE DIRECTIONS

It is apparent that the most widely used and well established of the OCD measures assess predominantly the signs and symptoms of OCD, i.e. obsessions, compulsions, avoidance, fear, interference and resistance. Some instruments are more thorough and psychometrically sound than others, with the Y-BOCS being the most comprehensive. There are also valid and reliable diagnostic measures available, such as the ADIS. However, there are two important domains that mainstream OCD measures have neglected—the assessment of both cognitive appraisal and other cognitive constructs related to OCD. The Y-BOCS does include items relating to inflated personal responsibility and indecisiveness; however, these are among the 'investigational' items, which are poorly researched and seldom used as outcome measures. The majority of the measures reviewed do not address either the metacognitive processes involved in OCD or related cognitive constructs thought to be of theoretical and therapeutic relevance.

In the last decade there has been an increasing awareness of the importance of assessing these constructs, and this, coupled with the recognition that traditional measures fail to adequately do this, has led to the rapid development of a number of cognitive assessment measures (see Obsessive Compulsive Cognitions Working Group, 1997, for a review). Among these are the Multidimensional Perfectionism Scale (Frost et al., 1990), the Lucky Beliefs Questionnaire (Frost et al., 1993), the Responsibility Questionnaire (Kyrios & Bhar, 1995), the Thought–Action Fusion Scale (TAF-Scale; Shafran et al., 1996) and the Overvalued Ideas Scale (OVIS;

Neziroglu et al., 1999). Although few of these measures have been subject to extensive psychometric evaluation, several appear potentially useful, as they target unique aspects of OCD that have been largely ignored by the traditional assessment measures. The next decade will determine the utility of these instruments.

To date, although some promising instruments to assess cognitive aspects of OCD have appeared, a number of problems have also arisen, including multiple overlapping constructs, insufficient psychometric evaluation, and poor consensus between researchers about what types of cognitive content are likely to be integral to OCD (Obsessive Compulsive Cognitions Working Group, 1997). In an attempt to overcome some of these difficulties, a number of researchers have formed the Obsessive Compulsive Cognitions Working Group. This group aims, among other things, to 'engage in a coordinated effort to develop and evaluate assessment strategies, including self-report and laboratory methods' (Obsessive Compulsive Cognitions Working Group, OOCWG, 1997, p. 668.). It is too early to evaluate adequately the assessment measures developed by this group. However, the creation of the OOCWG is an unprecedented initiative, and one that has the potential to improve current OCD assessment procedures significantly. Time will tell.

Chapter 15

EXPOSURE AND RESPONSE PREVENTION FOR OBSESSIVE-COMPULSIVE DISORDER

Michael Kyrios

WHAT IS OCD?

Obsessive-compulsive disorder (OCD) is the fourth most common psychiatric disorder (Rasmussen & Eisen, 1992) and the tenth leading cause of disability in the world (World Health Organization, 1996). With a lifetime prevalence estimated at 2% to 3%, OCD is seen across the lifespan, and remains a significant social and health service concern with high degrees of personal disability, co-morbidity (especially with depression and other anxiety disorders), and relatively poor long-term prognosis (Eisen et al., 1999; Rasmussen & Eisen, 1992; Skoog & Skoog, 1999; Welkowitz et al., 2000).

As discussed at length in Chapters 1 and 2, OCD is characterised by marked distress associated with: (a) recurrent, persistent, and intrusive ideas, thoughts, impulses, or images (obsessions), and/or (b) repetitive or ritualised and often bizarre overt behaviours or mental acts (compulsions) frequently aimed at neutralising distress or alleviating danger concerns caused by obsessions [Diagnostic and Statistical Manual of Mental Disorders, 4th edn (DSM-IV); American Psychiatric Association (APA), 1994]. Obsessions have been found to increase anxiety and physiological reactions such as heart rate and skin conductance, while compulsions are thought to lead to short-term reduction in such discomfort (Boulougouris et al., 1977; Hodgson & Rachman, 1972; Rabavilas & Boulougouris, 1974). On the other hand, neutralisation also leads to long-term increases in anxiety (Salkovskis et al., 1997). Both obsessions and compulsions interfere considerably with

Obsessive-Compulsive Disorder: Theory, Research and Treatment.
Edited by Ross G. Menzies and Padmal de Silva. © 2003 John Wiley & Sons, Ltd.

daily functioning and quality of life in various domains, including social and interpersonal, health, occupational and academic (Hollander et al., 1996).

Most OCD patients present with a mixture of both obsessions and overt compulsions (Foa et al., 1995), although there is a range of classes of symptoms, with various subtypes having been identified (Calamari et al., 1999). Each subtype or class of symptoms presents with distinct clinical features and may require specific clinical attention. For instance, some forms of chronic OCD appear to be associated with seemingly function-ally autonomous compulsions or rituals, often maintained by negative mood states, stress and multiple environmental triggers (Foa et al., 1980a). The obsessional OCD subtype with few or no overt compulsions forms another distinct subgroup (Calamari et al., 1999) and is associated with greater severity of symptoms and depression, more treatment resistance, and worse social outcomes those with a mixed presentation (Arts et al., 1993). Those presenting with contamination fears who wash or clean com-pulsively have received recent clinical attention (Jones & Menzies, 1998a, 1998b), while checking rituals have been associated with safety or harm concerns (Salkovskis et al., 2000a) and memory deficits, possibly associated with poor confidence in memory (MacDonald et al., 1997; Sher et al., 1989). Additional common classes of symptoms include concerns about scrupu-losity, hoarding and concerns about order and symmetry. Other important features of OCD requiring clinical attention include avoidance patterns, the development of depression, increased suicidality and the social and personal consequences of the disorder (e.g. relationship and employment difficulties). The choice of treatment for OCD needs to be considered within the context of the individual patient's clinical presentation. The various subtypes of OCD and contemporary treatment strategies are described in Chapters 7–13.

Various theories have emerged to guide our understanding of the ae-tiology and associated features of OCD, including: (a) neurobiological and neuropsychological theories that explore brain structures and func-tions (Maruff et al., 2000; Purcell et al., 1998; Savage et al., 2000; Saxena et al., 1998; see further, Chapter 5); (b) behavioural theories that focus on early conditioning or modelling experiences and subsequent contingen-cies that maintain the disorder (Dollard & Miller, 1950; Mowrer, 1960; Rachman, 1971, 1977); and (c) cognitive theories that focus on a range of information-processing mechanisms, beliefs, attitudes and metacogni-tive styles (Foa & Kozak, 1986; Obsessive-Compulsive Cognitions Working Group, 1997; Rachman, 1997, 1998; Salkovskis et al., 1998a; see further, Chapter 4). Each aetiological formulation is associated with specific treat-ment approaches.

HOW IS OCD TREATED?

Over the past 30 years, a range of treatments has become available for OCD, including pharmacological and psychological treatments. While a range of minor tranquillisers and augmenting agents have been administered, serotonergic agents are currently the most widely used medications for OCD and, with clomipramine, are regarded as the most effective pharmacological treatments (Rauch & Jenike, 1998). Pharmacological agents are administered alone or in combination with psychological treatments. The use of medication to treat OCD will be discussed more fully in Chapter 17. The most widely used and generally effective psychological interventions for OCD include behavioural and cognitive therapies (Franklin & Foa, 1998).

Behavioural therapy (BT) primarily involves prolonged exposure to distressing stimuli, together with the prevention of their associated compulsive overt and covert responses, rituals or safety and avoidance behaviours (Meyer et al., 1974). This form or aspect of BT is referred to as 'exposure with ritual or response prevention' (ERP). Various strategies are used to accomplish *exposure* to distressing situations and the *prevention* of the compulsive responses. These are discussed in greater detail below. BT has also been associated with a range of other techniques, such as use of aversion, covert sensitisation, contingency management and thought stopping. While these techniques have been found to be useful in many case studies, equivocal results and a lack of group studies have limited their use (Franklin & Foa, 1998; Steketee, 1993a).

More recently, cognitive therapy (CT) strategies have been developed, with the principal aim of changing specific beliefs and assumptions thought to underlie the disorder and its subtypes (Freeston et al., 1996). The extent to which behavioural therapists use techniques from CT varies, although even in cases where CT is combined with BT [i.e. cognitive-behaviour therapy (CBT)], the focus to date in outcome studies has still primarily been on ERP (Franklin & Foa, 1998; Steketee, 1993a). When CT is used alone, it is more detailed and direct in the way that it deals with the cognitive features of OCD and is less likely to rely on ERP techniques (Whittal & McLean, 1999). See Chapter 16 for a detailed account of CT procedures.

WHAT IS ERP?

ERP constitutes the basis of the most common form of BT for OCD, and consists of two components. First, patients undertake prolonged and usually graded *exposure*, whereby they confront anxiety-provoking or otherwise

Table 15.1 Examples of exposure hierarchies and augmentation techniques for two different OCD symptoms

Example 1: Fear of contamination from germs	Example 2: Teacher's distressing intrusive thoughts about sexually abusing student/s
Situation (distress level/100)	*Situation (distress level/100)*
1. Touch rim of own unwashed coffee cup (30)	1. Watch video or listen to audio tape of expert discussing sexual abuse of children (40)
2. Touch rim of partner's unwashed coffee cup (40)	2. Listen to tape of expert while looking at class photo (50)
3. Eat snack from dish in cupboard after touching partner's unwashed coffee cup (45)	3. Listen to loop tape of own distressing thought about sexually abusing students in general (60)
4. Drink water from partner's glass (55)	4. Listen to loop tape about students in general looking at class photo (65)
5. Eat snack straight from unwashed table top (65)	5. Listen to loop tape of distressing thought about sexually abusing specific student (70)
6. Have coffee at café (70)	6. Listen to loop tape about specific student looking at class photo (75)
7. Have meal at restaurant (80)	7. Listen to loop tape holding specific student's homework (80)
8. Touch toilet seat at home without washing hands for 15 minutes (85)	8. Stand in front of class repeating statement on loop tape to self (90)
9. Touch toilet seat at home without washing hands for 30 minutes (90)	9. Stand close to specific student repeating statement on loop tape to self (95)
10. Using public toilet (100)	10. Stand next to specific student repeating statement on loop tape to self (100)

distressing situations or triggers, either directly (*in vivo* exposure) or through imagination (*imaginal* exposure). Hierarchies consist of different situations or objects graded from least to most distressing (on a scale 0–100), or a series of increasingly more difficult or distressing steps leading to a specific situation or object (for examples, see Table 15.1). Hierarchies usually comprise around 10–20 steps. Patients expose themselves to each step in a planned manner, one at a time and repeatedly, until distress levels have decreased to the point at which patients can deal adaptively with the situation (usually, decreases in distress of around 50% or more). It is often best to start with situations rated in the 50–70 out of 100 range, and to work up to the most distressing step. In cases where patients are particularly avoidant or sensitive to anxiety, it is useful to start with exposure to situations in the 30–50 range.

Intrusive thoughts can be dealt with in a similar way through repeated exposure to graded thoughts on a loop tape. Augmentation strategies can be used in such cases, with patients using increasingly more anxiety-producing objects to enhance the experience of the intrusive thought or image (see Table 15.1, e.g. 2). While a strategy of graded exposure through the use of hierarchies is frequently used, flooding strategies can also be administered, although these may not be as conducive to encouraging a sense of self-efficacy and control. Furthermore, stimulus control and activity management can be used in conjunction with exposure, with the aim of regulating the individual patient's environment and activities, respectively, and encouraging naturalistic exposure. For instance, using example 1 from Table 15.1, activity management could include arranging, when appropriate, to go out with friends for coffee or dinner. Stimulus control could include placing the partner's unwashed coffee cups in strategic positions around the kitchen.

The second component, *response prevention*, involves the prevention of compulsive overt and covert responses or rituals that aim to neutralise the distress or threat associated with particular triggers (Meyer et al., 1974). Response prevention strategies need to account for the compulsion being targeted, but may comprise strategies such as competing alternative behaviour and habit reversal, or modification of compulsive rituals (see Table 15.2). Response prevention strategies may be applied in a graded manner, or may lead to the immediate banning of neutralising strategies. Use of response prevention strategies can be incorporated into the development of hierarchies; for instance, before going on to the next item on a hierarchy of concerns about leaving the house, patients could use restricted checking for 10 minutes before leaving, then go on to using more restricted checking for 5 minutes before leaving, and finally without any checking before leaving the house for a planned outing.

Additional strategies, such as paradoxical intention and satiation, can also be used in conjunction. The former aims to instil a sense of control over rituals, while the latter aims to abate the patient's urge to carry out compulsions. It is also useful to incorporate the modification of safety behaviours, which are more subtle forms of compulsion or neutralisation. In the example of a contamination fear, hand washing is commonly preceded by an avoidance of handling any part of oneself or others in an attempt to prevent further contamination. Response prevention strategies can be extended by the elimination of such safety or avoidance patterns (e.g. the purposeful touching of one's face or clothes following exposure to the contamination agent). Furthermore, it is important to encourage the rewarding of appropriate responses.

In BT, therapy sessions are taken up by training in the monitoring of anxiogenic situations, the operationalisation and monitoring of problematic behaviours (particularly, avoidance, overt and covert neutralisation),

Table 15.2 Examples of response prevention and habit reversal strategies for specific OCD symptoms

OCD symptom	Response prevention strategy
Hand-washing or cleaning rituals	Response delay (i.e. extending period between 'contamination' and cleaning or washing); use of ritual restrictions (e.g. decreasing cleaning or washing time; decreasing number or intensity of washing or cleaning;) clenching fists; extension strategies to undermine avoidance (e.g. touch self, clothes, etc.)
Checking lights switches, oven, appliances, etc.	Response delay; use of ritual restrictions (e.g. restrict period or number of checks; restrict what is checked to gradually more difficult items); turning and walking away, extension strategies (whistle a happy tune)
Visual checking	Closing eyes; looking straight ahead; turning back and walking away; distraction techniques using alternative visual imagery that is not related to the content of the checking concern
Mental checking	Refocusing techniques using alternative visual imagery that is not related to the content of the intrusive thought; singing a song; counting backwards by three from 101; going 'blank'; meditational techniques
Counting (e.g. bricks, words, etc.)	Refocusing techniques; singing a song; going 'blank'; meditation
Blocking or suppressing intrusive thoughts	Refocusing techniques; singing a song; counting; going 'blank'; meditation
Intrusive 'bad' thoughts followed by thinking the opposite 'good' thought	Reverting back to original 'bad' thought and then using distraction techniques; extension strategies (imagining the negative outcome happening whilst using relaxation)

the active engagement of the patient using a cognitive-behavioural explanation for his/her problems, the development of exposure hierarchies, identification and practice of adaptive response or ritual prevention strategies, training of strategies to cope with distress resulting from exposure (e.g. anxiety management, relaxation training), and discussion of relapse prevention strategies. In-session therapy work is complimented by set tasks, which are completed between sessions during patients' own time. In more recent times, loop tapes have been used with obsessional patients as a way of exposing them to distressing thoughts or images (Salkovskis et al., 1998a; see also Chapter 11). While response prevention can also focus on mental compulsions and other cognitive neutralisation, such intervention strategies may be more closely aligned with CT and do not always form part of a traditional BT treatment package. Nonetheless, the underlying premise of loop tape exposure, from a behavioural perspective, is the habituation of distress associated with obsessions. A combination of aversive relief and satiation has also been used successfully with taped obsessions (Solyom et al., 1971).

In addition to individual therapy, ERP can be administered in a number of formats, including group (Fals-Stewart et al., 1993; Fischer et al., 1998; van Noppen et al., 1998), self-help (Grayson, 1999), inpatient (Carmin et al., 1998; Wetzel et al., 1999), outpatient (Franklin et al., 2000; Hand, 1998), family therapy (Grunes, 1999; Mehta, 1990; van Noppen, 1999), high-density or intensive (Franklin et al., 1998; Wetzel et al., 1999), self-guided (Fritzler et al., 1997; Nakagawa et al., 2000), therapist-guided (Fischer et al., 1998) and manual- or computer-guided interventions (Baer & Greist, 1997; Clark et al., 1998; Kirkby et al., 2000; Marks et al., 2000; Nakagawa et al., 2000; see also Chapter 20). Future developments in Internet-based and virtual reality interventions are also likely to influence future directions in the behavioural therapies, with particular implications for exposure strategies (Rothbaum et al., 1997).

Various explanations have been proposed for the therapeutic effects associated with ERP. Baer (1996) argues that, on the basis that ERP leads to functional brain changes similar to those seen following serotonergic pharmacotherapy (Baxter et al., 2000), ERP may be an endogenous serotonergic therapy. However, there is little support for such neurobiological explanations for the efficacy of ERP. Behavioural theories focus on the processes of habituation, the disconnection of obsessions from their associated distress, and the elimination of ritualistic behaviours that negatively reinforce fears (Dollard & Miller, 1950; Steketee, 1993a). Reciprocal inhibition focuses on the prolonged and repeated association between situations considered to be threatening and a strong rehearsed relaxation response. On the other hand, according to cognitive perspectives, such as information-processing models (see Eysenck, 1992), the processing of information incompatible with dysfunctional cognitive structures during ERP is directly related to successful outcomes. Treatment failures are seen as resulting from the interference caused by cognitive defences, autonomic arousal, negative mood states and erroneous ideas on the habituation and reprogramming process, such that targeted fear structures remain intact (Foa & Kozak, 1986). In order for fear structures to be modified, they must first be activated. Furthermore, the nature of incoming information must be inconsistent with the nature of the stored erroneous information. The individual must undergo prolonged exposure to the new incoming information without the interference of avoidance, selective bias or cognitive defences. Attention during ERP needs to be focused on the fearful stimuli, in order to maximise habituation (Grayson et al., 1982; Grayson et al., 1986). As such, treatment requires energy and effort, with positive outcomes maximised through a 'shaping' framework. Overall, Steketee (1993a) identified four processes underlying the effectiveness of ERP: (a) the activation of physiological and subjective anxiety during exposure; and (b) the gradual decrease of anxiety within and between exposure sessions; (c) the processing of fear-related information during the exposure; and (d) the generalisation of gains across different anxiogenic situations.

EVALUATION OF TREATMENTS FOR OCD

Pharmacological and psychological treatments, alone or in combination, are considered effective in the treatment of OCD, leading consistently to better outcomes than wait-list and placebo conditions (Abramowitz, 1997; de Haan et al., 1997; van Balkom et al., 1994). That treatments are often combined begs the question of their relative efficacy. While much research has compared pharmacological and psychological treatments, far less research has investigated the relative advantages of different components of psychological treatment, particularly for different OCD subtypes. Nonetheless, ERP has been the most widely evaluated psychological treatment for OCD (Abramowitz, 1997; Cox et al., 1993; Foa & Kozak, 1996; Foa et al., 1985; Franklin et al., 2000; Franklin et al., 1998; Hodgson et al., 1972; Kobak et al., 1998; Lindsay et al., 1997; March, 1995; Marks, 1997; Rachman et al., 1971; van Balkom et al., 1994; van Oppen et al., 1995a). ERP has been found to be effective across the lifespan, with around 75% of those treated with ERP improving significantly and staying so at follow-up (Franklin & Foa, 1998).

A number of researchers have evaluated the relative efficacy of ERP and pharmacotherapy in adults, adolescents and children in direct comparative and meta-analytic studies, with many studies comparing BT with serotonergic antidepressants (SSRIs) and a combination of BT and SSRIs. (Abel, 1993; Cox et al., 1993; Christensen et al., 1987; de Haan et al., 1998; Foa et al., 1992; Hohagen et al., 1998; Kobak et al., 1998; van Balkom et al., 1998). Others have compared outcomes from exposure, anti-exposure and pharmacological treatments (Cottraux et al., 1993b), although subject compliance with anti-exposure therapy has been poor. While most studies report that all treatments are superior to placebo, there are few differences between the various treatments, although this depends on methodological and treatment variations (e.g. type of outcome measure, specific SSRI used).

Van Balkom et al. (1994) concluded that serotonergic antidepressants (SSRIs), BT, CT, combined antidepressants plus BT, and placebo plus BT, were associated with relatively large mean effect sizes for improvements in a range of assessor-rated symptoms (1.63, 1.47, 1.04, 1.99, 1.85, respectively). On clinician ratings of symptom severity, BT alone, SSRIs, and BT in combination with SSRIs were significantly superior to a placebo condition, although no differences were found between the three treatments. Both BT alone and the combined BT/SSRI conditions were superior to SSRIs alone on self-report measures of severity. Follow-up data from 3 months to 6 years indicated stable treatment effects. Larger effect sizes were generally reported for clinician-rated compared to self-rated measures of severity, although this has not been supported consistently (Kobak et al., 1998). Cox et al. (1993) reported relatively larger effect sizes of 3.34, 3.25 and 2.56 for fluoxetine, clomipramine and exposure therapy, respectively. No differences emerged between the different treatments. However, relatively few exposure-based treatments were included in this meta-analysis. Another meta-analysis by Christensen et al. (1987) reported more modest mean effect sizes of 1.22, 1.40, 0.21 and 0.43 for exposure-based therapy, antidepressant medications (primarily clomipramine), non-specific treatment programs and thought-stopping, respectively. Exposure-based and medication treatments did not differ significantly from each other, and were superior to the other treatments.

On the other hand, from a large meta-analytic study, Kobak et al. (1998) reported that ERP exhibited a significantly greater effect size than SSRIs as a class, although there were no differences between ERP and clomipramine. When methodological variables correlating with effect size were controlled (e.g. year of study publication, existence of a control group or random allocation, clinician vs. self-report symptom severity outcomes, method of effect size calculation), differences between ERP, SSRIs and combination treatments disappeared. Some researchers, however, have reported that the combination of CBT and medication is associated with superior response rates compared to CBT plus placebo (Hohagen et al., 1998). Others consider that the addition of CBT when medication has not been effective initially can lead to a further 50% reduction in symptoms (Simpson et al., 1999). It has been further suggested that, when using a combined medication and CBT approach, it is useful to add the CBT after medication has been commenced for a few weeks (O'Connor et al., 1999). It has also been suggested that the concomitant use of SSRIs is particularly useful for depressed OCD cohorts or for essentially obsessional presentations (Hohagen et al., 1998).

As to which variant of psychological treatment is associated with the best outcomes, results have been equivocal. Methodological issues concerning the length, integrity and quality of psychological treatments administered influence results. Nonetheless, the separate effects of exposure (E) and response prevention (RP) have been examined by a number of studies. Foa et al. (1984) concluded that, while the combination leads to superior outcomes on virtually all measures, the two components affect outcomes differently. While E was found to lead to greater decreases than RP in anxiety upon confrontation with the feared stimulus, RP was associated with greater decreases in the urge to ritualise. In addition, a number of researchers have supported the use of imaginal exposure to enhance live exposure (de Araujo et al., 1995; Ito et al., 1995), particularly for the maintenance of treatment outcomes (Foa & Goldstein, 1978; Foa et al., 1980b).

In a meta-analysis, Abramowitz (1996) compared general variations of ERP. With regard to OCD symptom amelioration, it was concluded that therapist-guided exposure was superior to self-controlled exposure, while complete response prevention was better than partial or no response prevention. Furthermore, the addition of imaginal exposure to *in vivo* exposure appeared to improve outcomes for anxiety symptoms. Hiss et al. (1994) also provide support for the efficacy of adding a formal relapse prevention program following ERP, while Amir et al. (2000) have indicated the importance of targeting family accommodation (e.g. participating in the patient's rituals) to treatment outcome.

To date, CT has been associated with smaller effect sizes relative to BT and serotonergic medications in meta-analyses (van Balkom et al., 1994). However, recent developments in cognitive theory have led to more refined cognitive techniques (see Freeston et al., 1996). More recent outcome studies indicate optimistic outcomes in terms of engagement in therapy (i.e. lower drop-out rates), decreased symptom severity and disability (Freeston et al., 1997; Kyrios et al., 2001) and greater improvement in general coping (van Oppen & Arntz, 1994), although CT in group format may not be as effective as BT in the short and medium term (Kyrios et al., 2001; McLean et al., in press). Nonetheless, the distinction and separation of BT and CT remains difficult to operationalise, particularly in light of the use of graded behavioural experiments in CT, which may be seen to be no more than exposure strategies. Furthermore, a number of studies comparing CT or rational emotive therapy (RET) with ERP (Emmelkamp et al., 1988; van Oppen & Arntz, 1994) may have used ERP treatments that do not meet acceptable practice standards (Franklin & Foa, 1998).

The effectiveness of treatments for OCD may not necessarily generalise across all OCD subtypes (Ball, Baer & Otto, 1996). For instance, having a fear of contamination and overt ritualistic behaviour may be predictive of better outcomes from BT (Buchanan et al., 1996). On the other hand, outcomes for obsessional patients with few or no overt rituals have been equivocal.

While some researchers report higher drop-out rates, worst relapse rates and worst outcomes for obsessionals compared to other OCD subtypes (Abel, 1993; Christensen et al., 1987; Hohagen et al., 1998), others consider that differences do not exist (Dar & Greist, 1992; Marks, 1997).

Subtypes of OCD or particular symptom profiles may be better managed through a selection of intervention strategies. For instance, while Hohagen et al. (1998) found no differences on outcomes for compulsions when comparing CBT and placebo with combined medication and CBT, the combined treatment was better for obsessions and for depressed OCD subjects. It has been suggested that the addition of a specific *cognitive* component to treatment leads to decreases in obsessional beliefs associated with vulnerability to OCD (O'Connor et al., 1999), hence aiding in the reduction of relapse and increasing the extent of improvement (van Oppen & Arntz, 1994). This may make CT particularly suitable for the obsessional OCD subtype, although such claims need to be investigated further.

A number of studies have investigated predictors of outcome. Predictor variables can be classified into seven broad categories: symptom and severity factors (e.g. avoidance, presence of hoarding); co-morbidity and associated problems; personality factors; motivational factors, such as treatment expectations; other treatment factors (e.g. compliance, previous treatment); demographic variables; and biological factors. In a review of predictors of outcome from BT, Steketee & Shapiro (1995) concluded that age, gender, marital status, education level, living arrangements, duration and severity of symptoms, and degree of anxiety do not predict outcomes. However, there is no general agreement about such conclusions.

Severity of OCD symptoms has been identified as a predictor of poorer outcome by a number of researchers (de Araujo et al., 1996; de Haan et al., 1997; Keijsers et al., 1994), although this has not been a consistent finding (Foa et al., 1983a). Presence of hoarding has been implicated in poor prognosis (Black et al., 1998), while high avoidance is associated with poorer outcomes (Cottraux et al., 1993a). Likewise, depression has been identified as a predictor of poor outcome by some researchers (Buchanan et al., 1996; Cottraux et al., 1993a; Foa et al., 1983b; Keijsers et al., 1994; Marks et al., 1980) but not by others (Mawson et al., 1982; Zitterl et al., 2000). A co-morbid schizoid personality disorder and the presence of overvalued ideas have also been found to predict poor outcome in OCD (Minichiello et al., 1987; Neziroglu et al., 2001). De Haan et al. (1997) further reported that high scores on the Personality Disorder Questionnaire (revised for cluster A personality disorder) predicted poorer treatment outcome for both medication and CBT, although this may be due to a higher degree of psychopathology in patients with both OCD and personality difficulties.

Treatment expectations for BT have received some attention in the panic disorder literature, although they have not necessarily been predictive of outcome (Lax et al., 1992). While panic has been associated with a notable placebo response, this has not been the case for OCD. On the other hand, baseline motivation and early compliance with treatment have been supported as predictors of better treatment outcome for OCD (Bachofen et al., 1999; de Araujo et al., 1996; de Haan et al., 1997; Keijsers et al., 1994), although not having a prior history of treatment has also been reported as predictive of positive outcome (Buchanan et al., 1996).

Various demographic factors, such as being employed and living with one's family, have been reported as predictive of treatment compliance and outcome (Buchanan et al., 1996), although there appear to be some gender differences in predictors (Castle et al., 1994). Studies of biological and related predictors of response to BT are rare. Kyrios et al. (1999) reported that over half of the variance in outcome following CBT was accounted for by pre-treatment neuropsychological deficits in tasks sensitive to frontostriatal dysfunction. Another recent study indicated that higher normalised metabolism in the left orbitofrontal region was associated with better BT outcome but worse SSRI outcome (Brody et al., 1998). This would suggest that OCD patients with differing patterns of metabolism might preferentially respond to BT or medication. Nonetheless, non-response at the end of treatment may not be a good predictor of longer-term outcome. For example, de Haan et al. (1997) found that one-third of non-responders at the end of treatment were better 6 months later.

While relatively effective psychological and pharmacological treatments have been developed for OCD (Franklin & Foa, 1998; Rauch & Jenike, 1998), their availability and proper implementation is often found wanting. Eisen et al. (1999) reported that while only around 60% of patients achieved partial or full remission, around half relapsed after remission, and less than one-fifth received a full trial of CBT, while around 70% received adequate doses of a serotonergic agent. Longer-term outcomes for OCD may be poor because of the under-utilisation of effective psychological treatments (see further, Chapter 20).

Overall, ERP has been shown to be a highly effective treatment for avoidance, rituals and compulsions, and obsessions, although in the case of those presenting with obsessions alone or with concomitant depression, the use of CT and serotonergic medication may also be warranted. Nonetheless, whatever one's basic approach to the management of OCD, be it psychological or biological, the data is unequivocal in supporting the use of ERP. The following section describes some challenges often encountered in the implementation of ERP.

CHALLENGES IN ERP

Emotional Regulation

Patients subjectively report that ERP is difficult to undertake, even within a graded framework. Under normal circumstances, the OCD patient would deal with distress through avoidance, compulsive responses or even substance use, thus maintaining an (albeit temporary) sense of control over the threatening situation. On the other hand, exposure to feared objects or situations, whilst targeting avoidance, invariably leads to an increased experience of anxiety. RP techniques, which aim to prevent the neutralisation of threat, further exacerbate that experience of anxiety. As patient's levels of anxiety rise, so too will the tendency to deal with the threat in the usual maladaptive manner.

The therapist's challenge is to help the patient deal adaptively with: (a) anticipatory anxiety leading up to the exposure session in order to minimise arousal levels, avoidance patterns and safety behaviours; (b) anxiety during the exposure task to effect habituation; and (c) post-exposure or refractory anxiety, which is likely to increase the urge to neutralise. Of particular concern is the fact that panic attacks can often result from high arousal levels, although in such cases the grading of steps on the patient's hierarchy needs to be re-examined. Furthermore, as the use of substances can interfere with reprogramming processes, clinicians need to minimise their maladaptive use in substance-abuse cases and help patients to develop more adaptive skills in dealing with their distress.

Patients need to maintain their exposure to the relevant anxiogenic stimuli, keeping neutralisation to a minimum, while still attending to the feared outcomes. Many therapists experience a conflict in helping patients to maintain prolonged exposure, often through the use of relaxation and other coping strategies, while still maintaining patients' attendance to the feared stimuli. While anxiety-reduction techniques (e.g. relaxation, breathing control) can help with panic, anticipatory, *in situ* and refractory anxiety, clinicians need to ascertain that such coping strategies do not minimise attendance to fearful outcomes or constitute neutralisation strategies themselves. Nonetheless, relaxation techniques can help in minimising the effects of high arousal levels on cognitive biases, and help patients maintain their exposure and increase their perceived coping capacity. Relaxation strategies are particularly useful for anticipatory and refractory anxiety.

A further step in reducing cognitive biases, as well as maximising the energy levels required to undertake an exposure regime, concerns the use of activity and contingency management to deal with depression.

Contingency and activity management can also be important for maintaining positive motivation and compliance. Patients experiencing anxiety and distress from exposure often need to compensate for their difficulties through the use of activities and rewards, and by expanding their previously limited quality of life.

Following the implementation of ERP and the cessation of compulsive responses, some patients experience a period of dysphoria characterised by perceived loss of control, feeling overwhelmed and feelings of helplessness. However, this is usually only a temporary state, and is often followed by an increased sense of self-efficacy as anxiety extinguishes. The period of dysphoria can be a sign that patients may be progressing too rapidly through their hierarchies. Progress through exposure hierarchies needs to be sustainable, not necessarily rapid. However, there is a case for the use of intensive exposure in individuals who can cope with its demands. In cases where a dysphoric period arises, clinicians can provide support and coping strategies to help patients overcome unrealistic expectations. Nonetheless, as depression is often associated with the severity of OCD symptoms, some patients may need to rapidly decrease their compulsive activity in order to improve their mood. In these cases, clinicians perhaps need to provide a more intensive and supportive BT program (Franklin et al., 1998; Wetzel et al., 1999). Ultimately, clinicians need to pace the progress of therapy with the patient's needs.

Pace and Progress of ERP

After becoming actively engaged in the behavioural approach to the treatment of OCD, patients undertake monitoring of their symptoms, before developing and refining a reasonable graded exposure hierarchy. Each step of the hierarchy is described in detail, and response prevention strategies are agreed upon for each step beforehand. It is important to build in an expectation for change in the hierarchy once exposure is commenced, in order to deal with likely complications. As a starting point, it is often useful to plan, role-play and then undertake initial exposure tasks within therapy sessions. With regard to imaginal exposure, it is important to assess that the patient's imaginal capacity is intact and that he/she remains focused on the task at hand.

For each exposure task, the therapist needs to check that the task was targeted at an appropriate anxiety level. This can be assisted by the monitoring of anxiety levels every 5–10 minutes. It is important that the level of adherence to agreed-on RP strategies is monitored. This can be done as an overall rating over the time of the exposure task, or every 5–10 minutes along with the anxiety ratings. It is also useful to rate the overall extent to which patients could attend to anxiogenic stimuli during the *in vivo* or imaginal exposure task. Having completed an in-session imaginal or *in vivo* exposure task, it is useful to debrief about the patient's experiences during the task, checking on the use of any new neutralisation strategies. The patient can continue with the same task as homework before the next session, depending on his/her response to the initial task. Alternatively, the patient can undertake subsequent steps in his/her hierarchy before the next session with the therapist.

Refinement of RP strategies can encourage broadening of gains. For example, having dealt with direct checking of doors and windows, patients concerned with safety from robbery can be encouraged to cut down on peripheral visual or mental checking. Patients can continue on to the next step on their hierarchies when they feel sufficiently comfortable with the current step. Usually this occurs following a number of prolonged exposures with increasing degrees of response prevention and decrease in safety behaviours and/or neutralisation. However, the pace of progress will depend on the individual and the specific exposure tasks, as will the point at which patients feel confident to go on to the next step in their hierarchies. Therapists need to ensure the use of rewards and encouragement throughout the process of progress through the hierarchy. As OCD patients can have perfectionistic expectations (Frost & Steketee, 1997), making it less likely that they use self-rewards, contingency management needs to target motivation and the degree of patient initiative, rather than just success *per se*.

Often, patients dealing with exposure tasks within a range of difficulty or distress (e.g. 50–70 out of 100) will encounter: (a) situations in their daily lives within that same range of difficulty but not necessarily included in their hierarchies; or (b) situations beyond that range of difficulty. Therapists can encourage patients to deal as rationally as possible with such situations, monitoring their coping strategies and anxiety levels. Should patients see themselves as having 'failed' to deal with a difficult situation, therapists need to restructure these unrealistic expectations, as well as help patients develop alternative coping strategies. Such situations might then be placed on a patient's hierarchy for immediate or future attention.

Lack of progress can often be traced back to a number of factors, including avoidance and use of new or hidden neutralisation strategies, reassurance seeking, secondary gains, handing of responsibility to others, personality difficulties (Minichiello et al., 1987) and overvalued ideas (Neziroglu et al., 2001). It is imperative that therapists deal directly with such situations; for instance, dealing with related psychopathology (e.g. major depression, schizoid personality, overvalued ideas), through either pharmacological and/or psychological treatments, can have a positive impact on OCD outcomes.

Continued monitoring and weekly review of monitoring sheets can often inform about avoidance and new or hidden neutralisation strategies. Within-session or therapist-guided exposure needs to be followed up with naturalistic exposure, so that patients are encouraged to 'avoid avoidance' and so that gains generalize. As covert neutralisation can be a significant impediment to progress, it needs to be targeted directly. For instance, in using BT with obsessions and mental rituals, it is important to hold the content of the obsession in mind (e.g. unwanted sexual image, blasphemous words) whilst using RP techniques to prevent the neutralising compulsion or ritual (e.g. praying, thought suppression).

Building towards a self-directed approach to ERP can help overcome any previous dependency on assurance from others, as well as dependency on therapists and family members. While family sessions can often help to overcome secondary gains, it is also useful to discuss such issues directly with patients, as there may be other examples of secondary gain (e.g. at work, amongst friends, etc.). Progress through the hierarchy needs to maximise the patient's sense of success and self-efficacy. A self-directed approach may further enhance a more functional attributional style, whereby patients increase their sense of self-efficacy by initiating planned and naturalistic exposure.

SUMMARY

Overall, ERP is the most widely supported psychological treatment for OCD, with much evidence for its efficacy across the lifespan and across different treatment settings. ERP compares favourably with serotonergic medications, with some researchers considering ERP to be a superior but under-utilised treatment in most cases. While around 75% of those treated with ERP improve significantly and stay so at follow-up, there are still significant challenges to be met. For instance, ERP can be associated with a significant drop-out rate, relative difficulties in dealing with obsessional presentations where there are few or no compulsions, and a compromised effectiveness in patients with overvalued ideas and personality difficulties. However, there are instances in which the combination of ERP with either pharmacological treatments or cognitive therapy can lead to positive outcomes in some challenging presentations (e.g. co-morbid depression, obsessional patients). The development of ERP treatment programs that engage patients and deal with their idiosyncratic needs will increase the efficacy of treatment. Furthermore, ERP can form part of a management program for those patients presenting with difficulties not necessarily related directly to their OCD symptoms.

Chapter 16

COGNITIVE THERAPY FOR OBSESSIVE-COMPULSIVE DISORDER

Melanie Marks

IMPETUS FOR A COGNITIVE MODEL OF OBSESSIVE-COMPULSIVE DISORDER

Obsessive-compulsive disorder (OCD) is a disabling anxiety disorder that affects about 3% of the population (Wilhelm, 2000). As discussed in Chapters 1 and 2, it is characterised by the presence of obsessions, which increase anxiety, and compulsions, which usually decrease anxiety. Obsessions are intrusive repetitive thoughts, impulses or images that are unacceptable or unwanted and give rise to resistance. Typical themes involve sexuality, religion, harming, contamination and disease. Sufferers normally try to neutralise these thoughts with other thoughts or actions and to avoid situations that trigger the obsession. Compulsions are overt or covert acts that often take the form of checking, cleaning, ordering, repeating, hoarding and counting. Usually sufferers report both obsessions and compulsions, although cases of obsessions only are not uncommon.

Exposure and response prevention (ERP) has been the treatment of choice for OCD since the development of behavioural techniques for anxiety (see Chapter 15 for a detailed description of ERP techniques). Prior to this, OCD was considered largely resistant to psychological intervention. The pioneering work of Rachman, Hodgson and Marks in the 1970s put OCD firmly on the treatment map, and numerous studies have proved the efficacy of ERP (Emmelkamp, 1982; Marks, 1987; Rachman & Hodgson, 1980). Nonetheless, ERP has several clinical limitations. A significant number of patients refuse treatment because they are unable to carry out exposure exercises. About 20% drop out before completing treatment. Of those who do respond to treatment, only about half show more than a 30% improvement.

Obsessive-Compulsive Disorder: Theory, Research and Treatment.
Edited by Ross G. Menzies and Padmal de Silva. © 2003 John Wiley & Sons, Ltd.

At the end of treatment, many are left with continuing symptoms (Wilhelm, 2000). There is clearly a need to offer sufferers of this condition alternative treatment options.

Further, the learning theory model upon which ERP is based is unable to explain much of the data derived from contemporary research on OCD and lacks the theoretical power to distinguish between OCD and other anxiety disorders. The chances of improved outcomes and new treatments being derived from the model are therefore remote. The same inadequate learning theory explanation is provided to account for problems that raise very different concerns for sufferers and which demand a different treatment focus. Learning theory assumes that fears are acquired in a random fashion and entrenched through classical and operant conditioning. Yet fear does not appear to be randomly distributed, and factors other than conditioning predict the nature and intensity of obsessive-compulsive symptoms (Rachman, 1990).

Inspired by the contribution the cognitive model of emotional disorders has made to the conceptualisation and treatment of anxiety, a number of theorists have argued that a cognitive approach to OCD addresses some of the limitations mentioned above and could lead to improved treatment outcome (Emmelkamp et al., 1980; Emmelkamp et al., 1988; Rachman, 1997; Salkovskis, 1989a; Salkovskis & Warwick, 1985; Tallis, 1995a; van Oppen et al., 1995a). Others, however, have cautioned against the 'risk of overgeneralising from the successful application of therapeutic methods in some disorders to other disparate areas when there is as yet no evidence of proven efficacy' (James & Blackburn, 1995). This chapter provides an overview of the cognitive model of OCD (see also Chapter 4), covers what is entailed in cognitive therapy for OCD, evaluates treatment outcome studies, highlights some of the difficulties implementing cognitive therapy and raises issues for further research.

COGNITIVE MODEL OF OCD

Intrusions vs. Obsessions—the Role of Meaning

The key idea behind the cognitive model of OCD is that intrusive thoughts are not abnormal and do not in themselves give rise to OCD. In a classic study, Rachman & de Silva (1978), and later Salkovskis & Harrison (1984), showed that about 90% of the general population report intrusive thoughts in the absence of OCD and that the form and content of normal intrusive thoughts and obsessional thoughts is indistinguishable. The critical factor determining whether intrusions develop into obsessions is how they are appraised, what emotion the appraisal leads to and the subsequent action taken to deal with the emotions generated by the appraisal.

Salkovskis (1999) proposes that OCD develops when intrusive thoughts are interpreted as an indication that the sufferer may be responsible for causing or preventing harm. It is this specific interpretation, in terms of responsibility to oneself or to other people, that is believed to link intrusive cognitions with both the discomfort experienced and the neutralising (compulsive) behaviours, whether overt or covert. Thus, the difference between normal intrusive cognitions and obsessional intrusive cognitions lies 'not in the occurrence or even the (un)controllability of the intrusions themselves, but rather in the interpretation made by the obsessional patients of the occurrence and/or content of the intrusions' (Salkovskis, 1999, p. 531). Indeed, according to Rachman (1997), it is this misinterpretation of intrusive thoughts as being important, personally significant and threatening that has the effect of transforming a commonplace nuisance into a torment.

The kinds of appraisal made by patients with OCD are thought to reflect underlying assumptions acquired in childhood. The negative interpretation of the intrusive thought leads to attempts to suppress and neutralise the thought, image or impulse so as to prevent or mitigate the expected effects. Initially, the effort to neutralise may seem small compared to the perceived consequences of failing to neutralise. However, neutralisation serves to increase the frequency and salience of obsessional thoughts and denies the patient the opportunity to discover that his/her worst fears do not materialise. Cognitive theorists suggest that cognitive factors mediate the effects of neutralisation, e.g. 'I acted on my belief and felt better, therefore my thoughts must be true'; 'The disaster I tried to prevent did not occur, therefore it was reasonable to neutralise'.

Salkovskis (1985) and Rachman (1997) have described some of the assumptions that may characterise patients with OCD:

- Having a thought about an action is like performing the action.
- Failing to prevent (or failing to try to prevent) harm to self or others is the same as having caused the harm in the first place.
- Responsibility is not reduced by other factors, such as something being improbable.
- Not neutralising when an intrusion has occurred is similar or equivalent to seeking or wanting the harm involved in the intrusion to happen.
- One should (and can) exercise control over one's thoughts.
- If I am responsible, things will go wrong.
- These obsessions mean that deep down I am an evil person.

A number of studies have confirmed the role of inflated appraisals of responsibility in OCD (e.g. Freeston et al., 1996; Rachman, 1993). Using a measure of responsibility appraisals, Salkovskis et al. (2000a) was able to discriminate sufferers of OCD from those with other anxiety disorders. Others have found that people with obsessional problems tend to overestimate the likelihood of a negative outcome when they are in a position of responsibility, and that an increased sense of responsibility for an unwanted event can lead to increased estimates of the probability of that event (Lopatka & Rachman, 1995). Work by Freeston et al. (1992) showed that an inflated sense of responsibility was the only factor that predicted compulsive activity and was the strongest predictor of avoidance. Early clinical observations made by Rachman & Hodgson (1980) also corroborate the role of perceptions of responsibility. They noted that checkers who were hospitalised initially did not experience much anxiety because they felt that responsibility was shared with clinical staff on the ward.

Patients with OCD show a particular bias in holding themselves responsible not only for acts they carry out but for acts that they fail to perform. In contrast, non-clinical individuals hold themselves responsible for what they actively do (acts of commission), rather than what they omit to do (acts of omission). According to Salkovskis (1999), if a negative outcome is anticipated, responsibility is assumed. By doing nothing, the person has decided not to prevent the harmful outcome, however improbable that might be. Deciding not to act becomes an active decision, making the person a causal agent in relation to disastrous consequences.

Other theorists have highlighted the role of other kinds of appraisals and beliefs in the genesis of OCD. The Obsessive Compulsive Cognitions Working Group (1997) has identified six belief domains as important, further described below:

- Responsibility appraisals (as discussed before)
- Overimportance of thoughts
- Metacognitive beliefs
- Exaggerated perception of threat
- Intolerance of uncertainty
- Perfectionism

Overimportance of Thoughts

Patients with OCD may believe that because a thought comes into their mind, it is important and deserves attention—it reflects their true desires or underlying nature. Merely by thinking something, it may take place. Patients may frequently express thoughts such as, 'If I have bad thoughts it means I am bad, crazy, dangerous'; 'My thoughts show what kind of person

I really am'; 'If I think something bad it's the same as if I had actually done it'; 'If I think something it feels as if it will occur'. Shafran and others have investigated the role of thought–action fusion (TAF) in OCD (Shafran et al., 1996). They distinguish between *moral* TAF, which reflects the belief that thoughts are morally equivalent to actions (if I think about hurting my child, it must mean I really want to do so) and *likelihood* TAF, which reflects the idea that thinking about something increases the likelihood or probability of it occurring (if I think about my parent dying, it is more likely to happen, so I must suppress these thoughts).

Metacognitive Beliefs

A number of theorists have written about the role of metacognitive beliefs, i.e. beliefs about beliefs, and how these may affect the frequency and intensity of intrusions. Patients with OCD believe it is important to have complete control over their intrusive thoughts and may believe that other people do not have intrusive thoughts. According to Salkovskis (1989a, 1989b) meta-cognitions affect the way in which intrusions are appraised and whether or not an intrusion will be resisted. As this will affect whether intrusions become entrenched, such beliefs need to be taken into account. A detailed consideration of meta-cognitions in OCD has been provided recently by Wells (2000).

Exaggerated Perception of Threat

Patients with OCD have been shown to overestimate the likelihood and severity of aversive events. They may be more likely to regard a situation as threatening until proved safe, whereas most people assume that a situation is safe unless it is proved dangerous.

Intolerance of Uncertainty

Patients with OCD have difficulty making decisions and dealing with uncertain or ambiguous situations. Rhéaume et al. (1995) found a significant correlation between concern over mistakes, doubts about actions and OCD symptoms.

Perfectionism

Perfectionism has been linked to checking, cleaning and hoarding. Excessive concern over mistakes has been found to be elevated in patients with OCD compared to non-clinical controls, and to be correlated with symptoms in non-clinical controls. A recent discussion by Shafran & Mansell (2001) has highlighted the role that perfectionism can play in OCD psychopathology. The Obsessive-Compulsive Cognitions Working Group (1997) considers perfectionism as a risk factor for OCD. Patients with OCD tend to strive for certainty, exactness, for things to be exactly the right way. Failure to get this 'perfect' state can lead to an increase in doubting and thus to checking, etc.

KEY THEMES IN COGNITIVE THERAPY FOR OCD

Distinguishing between Intrusions and Appraisals

In accordance with the cognitive model of OCD (see further, Chapter 4), successful cognitive therapy of OCD hinges on helping the patient to understand that the problem he/she is suffering is not intrusive thoughts *per se*, but his/her interpretation of these thoughts. One of the initial tasks of therapy is to help clients distinguish between their intrusive thoughts and their negative automatic thoughts/appraisals. This is done in the first session or so by asking clients to recall a time when they were last troubled by intrusive thoughts, and to reflect upon their reactions to the obsessional thought. Using Socratic dialogue, the therapist asks the client what effect he/she thought the appraisal had had upon his/her subsequent behaviour, and to consider whether it had led to further obsessional behaviour. This may be followed up by asking the client to keep a thought record of the automatic thoughts that follow intrusions and later by behavioural experiments to test out whether modifying the response to the intrusion affects subsequent symptoms. Some clients may find it difficult to distinguish between intrusions and automatic thoughts. It is crucial to get the distinction right, because trying to modify or challenge the intrusion rather than the appraisal can lead to endless discussion that gets nowhere.

Helping to Identify Appraisals

Therapists need to be careful not to be drawn into conversations about intrusions, which provide reassurance, which can be counter-therapeutic and which can confuse the developing formulation. Thus, Salkovskis (1985, p. 581) proposes that therapy should:

> ...concentrate not on the modification of intrusions...but on automatic thoughts consequent on the intrusions, and on the beliefs which give rise to these. Bland reassurance, often involving detailed discussions of tiny

probabilities, is notoriously ineffective for obsessionals because it functions as a form of neutralising. It is important not to debate the obsessional thought itself, to prevent the unwary, inexperienced and over-enthusiastic therapist from attempting to deal with obsessional disorders by bland refutation of the fears expressed. This caution is particularly necessary, given the avid and subtle way in which such patients seek reassurance.

Over the course of the first few sessions, as patients become more familiar with the model and provided the patient and therapist are working collaboratively, it usually becomes easier for patients to identify their automatic thoughts. Also, as patients start reducing avoidance and ritualising, their feared consequences may become more evident. Where this does not happen, Salkovskis (1999) suggests giving an example of behaviour based on thoughts that are not conscious at the time, such as asking a patient why he/she stops at a red traffic light. Most would agree that they do so because it would be dangerous not to, even though they do not consciously think this every time they approach the traffic light—it is simply automatic. Van Oppen & Arntz (1994) suggest asking patients who do not report having negative automatic thoughts what would happen if they did not perform their rituals.

Some examples of the difference between intrusions and appraisals/ automatic thoughts are given in Table 16.1.

Table 16.1   Examples of intrusions and automatic thoughts

Intrusion	Automatic thought/appraisal
Sexual images about children	I am a sick person
	I must be a paedophile
	I will be rejected by everyone I know
	I have let everyone down
Doubt about turning off the bath taps properly	The bathroom will be flooded and destroy the downstairs flat
	My neighbour's home will be ruined and it will be my fault
	I will not be able to face them again
Thoughts of an ancient curse	If I am exposed to anything from the tomb, I will be as responsible for destroying the holy site as those who originally excavated it, and I will be forever cursed
	I must not think about curse or it will affect me and ruin my life
Thoughts of harming grandchildren when looking after them	I am an evil person
	I do not deserve any happiness
	I must not let myself have these bad thoughts

Normalising Intrusions

Educating clients about the nature of intrusive thoughts, and helping them to discover that intrusions are common occurrences that most people have, is an important focus of treatment and can help dispel feelings of guilt, shame and fear. It is often useful to reinforce this by giving patients literature to read, with a view to normalising intrusions and helping them to develop greater tolerance for the variety of thoughts that are part of normal mental life. For example, patients may be given the paper by Rachman & de Silva (1978) and asked what they make of it. If appropriate, therapists may share intrusive thoughts they themselves have had. Salkovskis (1999) suggests asking patients about whether intrusive, automatic thoughts might perhaps have advantages, and to consider the effect on mental life if every thought were to have to be deliberately conjured. Asking patients to consider what people are more likely to be troubled by, e.g. blasphemous thoughts, sexual thoughts, violent thoughts, may help them to feel less guilty about their intrusions. It may help them to recognise that someone who is religious is more likely to be disturbed by blasphemous thoughts than someone without religious feeling; or that someone who respects children would be more distressed at having sexual thoughts about them than a paedophile would be. A goal of cognitive therapy is to help patients recognise that they are worried about, for example, being contaminated, and that the worry itself is the real problem, rather than their actual state of hygiene. Patients can be asked to consider the pros and cons of believing that the problem is one of worry, and the implication this might have for their behaviour. Salkovskis (1999) suggests asking patients to experiment with adopting theory A, that they are contaminated, and theory B, that they think they are contaminated, and to reflect upon how these different perspectives affect symptoms.

In view of the attempt to help patients to recognise that intrusions are a normal part of mental life, the goal of cognitive therapy is not to try to eliminate all intrusions but to help patients to understand how their reactions to their intrusions contribute to their difficulties. Patients may begin treatment with the aim of eliminating all intrusive thoughts and it is important to set attainable goals collaboratively at the beginning of treatment. It is also useful to distinguish between immediate, short-term and longer-term goals.

The Effects of Thought Suppression and Neutralisation

It is important to help patients understand the effects of thought suppression on subsequent symptoms (cf. Wegner, 1989). Behavioural experiments can be carried out to provide first-hand evidence of this. Patients can be asked to attempt to think about something in the session for a given period of time (e.g. pink elephants) and then to resist thinking about it. The therapist can then explore how easily they were able to keep thoughts about pink elephants out of their minds and whether trying to forget them had had a paradoxical effect. This is a useful technique for helping challenge the idea that one should always try to control one's thoughts, and helps patients understand one of the many processes involved in maintaining their symptoms. This can be extended outside the clinic and patients can be asked to collect data to test whether trying to control their thoughts leads to more symptoms and distress than allowing the thoughts to occur.

It is important that patients understand how avoidance and neutralisation feed obsessive-compulsive symptoms, and that they come to realise how their behaviour may be contributing to the problem. Salkovskis (1999) writes that the principle aim of therapy is to help clients conclude that obsessional thoughts, however distressing, are irrelevant to further action, and that the key to controlling obsessional thoughts is to learn that the exercise of such control is unnecessary. The paper by Rachman et al. (1976), which provides data on the spontaneous decay of urges, can help reinforce this kind of experiment.

STRATEGIES FOR MODIFYING APPRAISALS

Modifying Inflated Risk Appraisals

A wide range of strategies used in standard cognitive therapy is applicable to the treatment of OCD. The particular technique used will depend on the kinds of automatic thoughts being worked with and the formulation. Van Oppen & Arntz (1994) propose that the principal focus of cognitive therapy should be on the alteration of abnormal risk assessment. They suggest a method for assessing the extent to which the probability of danger is overestimated and the extent to which the consequences of danger are overestimated. First, the patient and therapist analyse the sequence of events that lead to the feared outcome. Then the patient estimates the chance of each separate sequence. The probability estimates for single events (e.g. the house flooding) is then compared with probability estimates based on the sequence of events that would be necessary for the feared event to occur. The probability of each event is estimated separately and a cumulative probability calculated. This is compared with the initial estimate and the disparity is discussed. Table 16.2 provides an example of this technique with a patient who was afraid of flooding the flat below, and would constantly check her bath taps.

Table 16.2 Probability of a feared event occuring

Step	Chance (cumulative chance)
Leaving the bath taps dripping	1/10 (1/10)
Leaving the bath plug in	1/100 (1/1000)
Water penetrating the floor	1/5 (1/5000)
Downstairs neighbour, who is housebound, not noticing water dripping from ceiling	1/10 (1/50,000)
Downstairs neighbour being out the whole day	1/100 (1/5,000,000)

Modifying Responsibility Appraisals

Van Oppen & Arntz (1994) recognise that even when the probability of a feared event is low, patients with OCD may still feel compelled to continue their rituals. They believe that this is due to patients overestimating their responsibility for negative events and overestimating the consequences of being responsible. For example: if there are any errors in my work documents I will be shown up and fired; if I do not wash after going out I will bring germs into the house, which will contaminate my whole family, and if they become ill it will be my fault for being careless; if I continue having these blasphemous thoughts, I will be to blame if anything bad happens to my loved ones. They suggest using a pie chart technique for modifying the overestimation of responsibility and helping clients to reattribute responsibility. All the factors contributing to a feared outcome are listed and the patient is asked to divide a pie into segments of different size, reflecting the relative importance of each factor. Percentage values can be assigned to each segment and usually, when viewed in the context of other factors, the patient's own role is re-appraised as being smaller than originally predicted. For example, a mother who washed her hands repeatedly after returning home, for fear of bringing germs into the home and making her child ill, was asked what other factors might contribute to her child becoming ill.

After compiling a chart like this, one asks the patient the following types of question: 'Based solely on the chart, what would the likely cause be if your child became ill?'; 'How strongly would you rate your responsibility for your child having become ill?'. Van Oppen & Arntz (1994) advise that the 'double-standard' technique can also be useful for challenging the overestimation of the perceived consequences of being responsible.

Overestimation of the perceived consequences of being responsible can be modified through exposure exercises and behavioural experiments designed to disconfirm feared consequences. For example testing whether leaving a tap dripping leads to a flood; whether leaving on a switch leads to a fire; whether leaving crumbs on the floor means that friends will not accept future invitations; whether handing in a document containing errors leads to one being sacked from work.

Tallis (1995a) has suggested a technique for helping clients to reduce their estimates of the likelihood of things going wrong and reducing pessimism. Based on findings that patients with OCD may be better at generating reasons for rather than against bad things happening, he suggests working with them to generate reasons for and against bad things happening.

Cognitive Continuum

Another method for modifying responsibility appraisals and the tendency to overestimate the severity of consequences is to ask the client to rate how bad the consequences would be compared to other outcomes on a visual analogue scale. This can also help reduce all-or-nothing thinking. Thus, patients may be asked to rate on a 0–100 scale how bad it would be if they left the tap dripping, if the bath overflowed and they were blamed for being careless. They might then be asked about other things that could be worse than this, and where these would rank on a continuum of severity; e.g. leaving the front door open overnight, not locking the entrance to a communal property, not telling neighbours one has seen an intruder looking into their home, not responding to neighbours' requests for help when they have a problem in their home. Patients with intrusive sexual thoughts might be asked to rank how bad this is compared to acting upon the thoughts, to joining a child pornography ring, to carrying out violent acts, to stealing, to reckless driving, etc. Asking how they would judge someone else who had intrusive thoughts but did not act upon them and had the same record of lawful behaviour might help expose the fact that they may judge themselves more harshly than they would others. Parents who fear bringing germs into the house through not washing after coming home, and thus believe they will cause their families to become ill, may be asked how bad not washing would be compared to not feeding their children, not paying them attention, not helping them to cross the road, not putting them to bed on time, not ensuring they have vaccinations, not sending them to school, and other measures of being a responsible parent.

Behavioural Experiments

Behavioural experiments are a crucial part of cognitive therapy for OCD because they provide patients with first-hand evidence to test their automatic thoughts. This is more effective than trying to modify thoughts solely through verbal persuasion, and throughout therapy behavioural and cognitive strategies need to be closely integrated. Although behavioural experiments may seem similar to exposure tasks, the rationale provided is different, with the emphasis less on habituation and more on testing thoughts. Salkovskis (1999) writes that in cognitive therapy, ERP strategies are used as a way of helping patients to discover how neutralising behaviour acts to maintain their beliefs and to show that stopping such behaviour is beneficial. This leads to a variant of ERP, in which belief change is the guiding principle.

Behavioural experiments are especially useful to test out the prediction that thoughts are tantamount to action. Thus, a patient who avoids being with people in the presence of knives, for fear that he/she will stab them, would be asked to test this out. Similarly, a client who has thoughts of harming young children, and who might therefore avoid them, would be asked to test whether having these thoughts leads to any such acts. A client who fears screaming out his blasphemous thoughts during church would be asked to go to church and to allow such thoughts to occur. Behavioural experiments may be more difficult when one is dealing with consequences that are projected into the future (if I don't carry out these rituals, I may become ill in a few years' time) or are more vague (something bad will happen). It is best if clients can design their own experiments and if the predictions are as specific as possible.

The aforementioned provides a description of some of the techniques used in cognitive therapy of OCD. It is important that these are applied in the context of a sound cognitive case formulation and a good collaborative relationship with the patient.

OUTCOME STUDIES

It is only in the past 6 years that controlled trials of cognitive therapy based on the work of Beck and Salkovskis have been published. Prior to this, the first studies investigating cognitive treatment of OCD were either single case studies or controlled trials, which examined the effects of Meichenbaum's self-instructional training and Ellis's rational emotive therapy (RET). For a review of single case studies, the reader is referred to James & Blackburn (1995). Controlled trials are discussed below.

In a study by Emmelkamp et al. (1980), OCD patients were randomised into two groups. One group ($n = 8$) received exposure *in vivo*, while the other ($n = 7$) had self-instructional training (SIT) plus exposure *in vivo*.

Both groups also had two sessions of relaxation training. Patients assigned to the self-instructional condition were trained to produce fewer negative self-statements and to cognitively rehearse anxiety-provoking situations taken from a hierarchy. Preparing, confronting, coping and reinforcing self-statements were practised. Patients were asked to use their positive self-statements during exposure *in vivo*. At the end of treatment and at follow-up 1 month and 6 months later, there was no difference between the two groups; SIT was no better than exposure. The authors comment, however, that no conclusions can be drawn with respect to the effects of cognitive procedures other than self-instructional training. They point out that several patients said that they did not find their positive self-statements helpful during the exposure tasks, and also questioned whether self-instructional training was the most appropriate cognitive treatment to deal with patients with OCD who already engaged in excessive self-talk and rumination (Emmelkamp & Beens, 1991). They proposed that treatment that focused on the irrational beliefs of patients with OCD might be more appropriate.

To this end, Emmelkamp et al. (1988) investigated the value of RET. Eighteen patients were randomised to 10 sessions of either RET without any behavioural experiments or exposure *in vivo*. Patients in the exposure condition were required to carry out exposure homework and response prevention twice a week for at least 90 minutes at a time. Items were chosen from a fear hierarchy, beginning with the easiest. Progress was discussed at each therapy session and new tasks assigned. Patients who were in the RET condition were required to read *A Rational Counselling Primer* by Young, which explains Ellis's ABC framework. The first phase of therapy involved training patients to observe and record their thoughts on pre-coded homework sheets. The next phase involved rationally disputing irrational cognitions in the sessions and for homework. In the following sessions, patients discussed any problems encountered during the homework tasks. Patients were not instructed to expose themselves to fear-provoking situations. Outcome was measured using, *inter alia*, the Maudsley Obsessional Compulsive Inventory (MOCI), the Irrational Belief Test, a self-rating of depression measure and a social anxiety scale. There was no difference between cognitive therapy and exposure therapy on obsessive-compulsive symptoms or social anxiety. There was a significant improvement on depression scores in the RET condition, but not the exposure condition. Most patients required further treatment in the 6 months following treatment. The authors questioned how representative their sample was, as patients tended to have acute symptoms only, were young and well-educated. Emmelkamp & Beens (1991) overcame this problem in a study where patients had to have suffered from OCD for at least 6 months to enter the study. Emmelkamp and Beens (1991) compared the effects of RET to those of exposure therapy. After a 4 week waiting period, 21 patients were randomised to either RET or exposure *in vivo*. After six sessions and another 4-week waiting period, all patients received six sessions of exposure *in vivo*. The cognitive therapy condition was based on identifying irrational thoughts that mediate feelings of anxiety and modifying them so that anxiety was no longer experienced and the need to ritualise to reduce anxiety was reduced. Treatment was based on Ellis's ABC framework. Patients were trained to monitor their cognitions and taught to challenge their irrational beliefs. They were required to practice analysing their problems, using the ABC model and pre-coded homework sheets, 6 days a week for 30 minutes.

Results showed that cognitive therapy was as effective as exposure therapy and that combining exposure therapy with cognitive therapy was no more effective than cognitive therapy or exposure therapy alone. At the end of treatment, patients who had had cognitive therapy and exposure rather than exposure only showed more change on their scores on the Irrational Beliefs Test. The results were maintained at 6-month follow-up.

Van Oppen et al. (1995b) carried out the first controlled trial to compare the effects of cognitive therapy carried out according to the models of Beck and Salkovskis and developed specifically for OCD. The cognitive therapy was directed at modifying overestimation of danger and inflated responsibility. The aim of the study was to compare the effects of cognitive therapy with those of self-controlled exposure plus response prevention on obsessive-compulsive symptoms and associated psychopathology. Another aim was to compare the effects of six sessions of cognitive therapy without behavioural experiments vs. six sessions of exposure and response prevention, without discussing the expectations of consequences in OCD. Seventy-one patients were randomised to 16 sessions of either cognitive therapy or exposure *in vivo*. Patients had to have had at least a year of OCD, no cognitive or behavioural treatment in the preceding 6 months and not to have been on antidepressants.

Outcome was assessed using the Padua Inventory-Revised (PI-R), the Yale–Brown Obsessive Compulsive Scale (Y-BOCS), the Anxiety Discomfort Scale (ADS), the Symptom Checklist, the Beck Depression Inventory and the Irrational Belief Inventory. In the cognitive therapy condition, patients were instructed to monitor and challenge thoughts in diaries as homework assignments. In the therapy sessions, problems with the diary were discussed and resolved, and in each session at least one automatic thought was challenged. After six sessions, behavioural experiments were included to test out dysfunctional assumptions. In the exposure condition, patients were given information about the rationale of ERP and a hierarchy of obsessive-compulsive situations was constructed. Hierarchy items were assigned as homework tasks and discussed at each session, when new tasks were also agreed upon. All patients determined the speed at which they worked through their hierarchy. Both treatments led to significant improvements. Multivariate but not univariate analyses suggested that cognitive therapy was superior to exposure therapy on the measures of obsessive-compulsive symptoms and on associated psychopathology. Significantly more patients in the cognitive therapy group were rated as recovered, compared to those in the exposure group, and the effect size of cognitive therapy was greater than that of exposure.

CONCLUDING REMARKS

The preceding studies show that cognitive therapy is a promising approach to the treatment of OCD and is at least as effective as exposure therapy, but further studies are needed to confirm this. Currently there is only one controlled trial of the treatment model proposed by Salkovskis (1985), even though there are numerous papers elaborating this model. There are more studies corroborating the cognitive model than the treatment that derives from it. Further research is needed to replicate the findings of van Oppen et al. (1995a) and to evaluate the long-term effects of cognitive therapy and whether or not treatment gains are maintained. It is too early to say whether cognitive therapy can improve upon the effects of exposure and offer an alternative to behavioural treatment. We do not yet know whether the drop-out rate is lower for patients offered this approach compared to exposure, whether the amount of clinical improvement exceeds that of ERP or what the relapse rates are. More research is needed to evaluate the process of change in therapy and whether cognitive change mediates improvement in obsessive-compulsive symptoms. In the study by van Oppen et al. there was a significant time effect on the Irrational Beliefs Inventory in the cognitive group only. Although improvement on the Irrational Beliefs Inventory was correlated with improvement on the Y-BOCS, ADS and PI-R, scores on the Irrational Beliefs Inventory test were not significantly different between the two treatment groups.

It would be useful to know whether there is an optimal number of sessions for treatment and whether some patients are better suited to a cognitive approach than others. Van Oppen et al. (1995a) raise the question of whether patients with certain OCD symptoms (e.g. checkers as opposed to cleaners) respond better to cognitive therapy that focuses on appraisals of responsibility, as these appraisals have been shown to be more relevant to checkers.

This information would help tailor treatment according to particular issues. Tallis (1995b) makes the point that there may be a small group of patients who do not respond to cognitive therapy. He writes that there seems to be a range of obsessional behaviours that are resistant to cognitive analysis in terms of appraisals and beliefs. These include order and symmetry rituals, number rituals and touching rituals (see Chapter 12 for an alternative view of these behaviours). These behaviours are dominated by a desire to repeat until things feel 'right', although the exact nature of 'rightness' remains obscure. He also makes the point that it is not uncommon to find individuals who report cognitions meaningfully related to some symptoms (such as checking), who are unable to report cognitions related to other types of behaviour (such as counting). More outcome studies using larger sample sizes would help clinicians to decide which patients are best suited to which particular approach.

There may be patients who use cognitive therapy as a form of reassurance. Some patients in the author's practice have reported that the impact of cognitive therapy has reduced over time as they use challenges in an increasingly ritualistic way. Ruminators may spend a lot of time asking themselves questions about the likelihood of certain events and considering evidence for and against particular eventualities. It is questionable whether cognitive therapy is appropriate in such cases. Van Oppen & Arntz (1994) suggest that, to prevent patients using cognitive therapy ritualistically, it is important to use a variety of different challenges rather than the same cognitive interventions.

In spite of the above reservations, the cognitive model of OCD has expanded the scientific understanding of the phenomenology and psychology of OCD. The hope is that this understanding will deliver a treatment approach that will offer an effective alternative for those who do not respond to currently-available treatments, and improve the outlook for those who, despite treatment, continue to have symptoms. The results of current studies by the Oxford group (see Salkovskis, 1999) are eagerly awaited and will hopefully answer some of the questions raised above.

Chapter 17

PHARMACOLOGICAL AND NEUROSURGICAL TREATMENT OF OBSESSIVE-COMPULSIVE DISORDER

Michael McDonough

Although pharmacological treatments for OCD are effective, they are not superior to the standard psychological intervention, exposure and ritual prevention (ERP). ERP is at least as effective in the short term, free from side effects and associated with greater long-term gains than current drug regimens (Greist 1998b; Marks 1997; see further, Chapter 15). As will be discussed, drug treatment, when effective, is generally continued indefinitely, as relapse is the norm on discontinuation. It is, however, more rapidly accessed, cheaper (at least initially) and generally more convenient for the patient than pursuing ERP, which involves challenging exposure tasks. One should therefore resist the temptation to prematurely medicate patients presenting for the first time unless they have a particular preference for drug treatment, object to ERP or where ERP is unavailable. Cases of significant co-morbid depression are an exception and are probably best treated with medication initially (Marks, 1997). Although there is some evidence of additional benefit from combining pharmacological treatment and ERP in uncomplicated cases (Greist, 1998b, O'Connor et al., 1999), medication should ideally be reserved for patients inadequately responsive to psychological treatment alone.

SEROTONIN AND SEROTONIN RE-UPTAKE INHIBITORS

As early as 1959, evidence was emerging of the anti-obsessional potential of drugs that enhance the availability of the neurotransmitter serotonin

---

Obsessive-Compulsive Disorder: Theory, Research and Treatment.
Edited by Ross G. Menzies and Padmal de Silva. © 2003 John Wiley & Sons, Ltd.

(Joel, 1959). Iproniazid, the first agent studied (more usually used to treat tuberculosis), inhibits the metabolism of serotonin in the nerve cell via its action on the enzyme monoamine oxidase. Although monoamine oxidase inhibitors (MAOIs) still retain a role in the management of OCD, agents that inhibit the re-uptake of serotonin back into the nerve terminal (the so called *serotonin–reuptake inhibitors* or SRIs) have become the mainstay of drug treatment.

Since its introduction in the late 1960s the efficacy of the original and most widely studied SRI, clomipramine, has been shown in numerous randomised controlled trials (RCTs). Most influential was a multi-centre US collaborative study involving over 500 patients, in which 58% rated themselves as much or very much improved after 10 weeks of clomipramine vs. 3% with placebo (De Veaugh-Geiss et al., 1991). This was matched with a roughly 40% reduction in various standard measures, including the Yale-Brown Obsessive-Compulsive Scale (Y-BOCS). Subsequently each of five *selective* SRIs or SSRIs, which unlike clomipramine do not have any action on noradrenaline re-uptake, were shown to be effective in more than one RCT. These are fluoxetine (e.g. Tollefson et al., 1994), paroxetine (e.g. Wheadon et al., 1993), fluvoxamine (e.g. Greist et al., 1995c), sertraline (e.g. Greist et al., 1995a) and citalopram (Mundo et al., 1997). Although antidepressants without this serotonergic action have occasionally been effective in small, uncontrolled studies and case reports (e.g. Snyder, 1980; Ananth et al., 1975), possibly by alleviating co-morbid depression, they

Table 17.1   Therapeutic profile of SRIs in OCD

1. 40–60% respond ('much improved' or 'very much improved').
2. Complete response is unusual; most have some residual symptoms.
3. Patients who do not responded to an initial SRI are less likely to respond to subsequent ones but further trials *are* worthwhile.
4. The most effective dose is often (but not always) higher than used for depression and patients may well respond to higher doses when lower ones have failed. This is most apparent with clomipramine.
5. Although side-effect rates differ between the SRIs, they are tolerated by the vast majority of patients. Starting at the lowest possible dose, increasing slowly and careful coaching of patients about side effects all can reduce discontinuation rates.
6. Most patients do not experience benefit before 6 weeks and at least 6 weeks at the maximum tolerated dose is required for an adequate therapeutic trial.
7. Improvement may continue for several months after the initial response and lasting benefit is seen with long-term continuation in responders.
8. Although slow reduction to the minimum effective dose should be attempted (Ravizza et al., 1996a) relapse is very likely on full discontinuation (80–90%; Pato et al., 1988, 1991). Implementing exposure and response prevention may prevent or delay relapse during discontinuation (Foa & Kozak, 1996).

have been consistently less effective in numerous controlled comparisons with SRIs (e.g. Goodman et al., 1990). Furthermore, a recent multi-centre RCT found sertraline more effective than desipramine for both depression and OCD in co-morbid patients (Hoehn-Saric et al., 2000).

Despite the unquestioned therapeutic benefit of these drugs, neurochemical and neuroendocrine studies have not led to a coherent aetiological model of serotonin dysfunction in OCD (for a review, see Delgado & Moreno, 1998). It is proposed rather that SRIs, through their effect on serotonin neurotransmission, modulate other brain systems such as dysfunctional neural circuits.

The therapeutic profile of SRIs in OCD differs from that for depression in some important respects. Table 17.1 summarises these differences and other important clinical information gleaned from the myriad of trials to date (see Greist and Jefferson, 1998). An understanding of these points is essential for good prescribing practice.

WHICH SRI?

This important clinical question divides opinion among experts. Table 17.2 summarises the main advantages and disadvantages to be considered when choosing between SRIs. The choice hinges on relative efficacy and tolerability and on some safety issues. There are as yet no clinically useful predictors based on symptom pattern to guide SRI choice (Ackerman et al., 1994), although hoarding has been associated with a poor response (Mataix-Cols et al., 1999b) and for this form psychological treatment may be preferable (Winsberg et al., 1999). Occasionally individual characteristics of the patient will lead one to choose one agent over another. For example in patients at risk of overdose, clomipramine should be avoided. In women of childbearing age, where there is the possibility of unplanned (or future planned) pregnancy, treatment with fluoxetine is appropriate, given its low risk of teratogenesis and record of safety perinatally. More often, however, it is one's own personal preference that will dictate. The research evidence is reviewed below to help inform this choice.

COMPARATIVE EFFICACY

This continues to be a source of debate. The meta-analyses of placebo-controlled RCTs to date have come out clearly in favour of clomipramine and rate all SSRIs equally (Abramowitz, 1997; Greist et al., 1995b; Janicak

Table 17.2 Advantages and disadvantages of individual SRIs in the treatment of OCD

	Advantages	Disadvantages	Recommended dosing regimen*		
			Start dose and increment for subsequent increase (mg)	Usual target dose (mg)	Maximum dose (mg)
Clomipramine	Probably most efficacious; inexpensive; sedative action can help with sleep disturbance; safest SRI during breast feeding	Toxic in overdose; most contraindications and reported side effects; risk of neonatal complications if used in pregnancy	10–25	100–250	250
Fluoxetine	Long half-life of benefit when compliance intermittent; lowest risk of discontinuation syndrome; good safety record in pregnancy; relative safety in overdose	Avoid during breast feeding; slower onset of action; drug interactions due to liver enzyme inhibition	20	40–60	80
Paroxetine	Relative safety in overdose	Drug interactions due to liver enzyme inhibition; highest rate of discontinuation syndrome	10–20	50	60
Fluvoxamine	Relative safety in overdose	Drug interactions due to liver enzyme inhibition	50	200	300
Sertraline	Relative safety in overdose; evidence to support safety during breast feeding	Drug interactions due to liver enzyme inhibition	50	150	225
Citalopram	Relative safety in overdose; drug interactions unlikely		20	40–60	60

* Expert Consensus Guidelines for treatment of OCD, 1997. Note: all the drugs listed, other than clomipramine (i.e. the SSRIs), are felt to have equal efficacy.

et al., 1993; Kobak et al., 1998; Stein et al., 1995b; Van Balkom et al., 1994). The review of four large multi-centre RCTs comparing clomipramine, fluoxetine, sertraline and fluvoxamine with placebo, conducted by Greist and colleagues, rated an approximately 2:1 chance of improvement with any one of the SSRIs compared with a 5:1 chance with clomipramine. Similarly, Piccinelli et al.'s European meta-analysis of 47 RCTs found a 61% reduction in Y-BOCS scores with clomipramine, compared with 22–28% with the same 3 SSRIs. Although this kind of analysis cannot be considered as robust as direct head-to-head comparison, a consistent finding of this nature is not easily dismissed. Fineberg (1996) suggested that recent trials (predominately of SSRIs) recruited milder or atypical cases, where smaller responses were more likely, and that the relative insensitivity of recent measures, such as the Y-BOCS, could have biased against SSRIs. A more convincing argument examined by Rasmussen (1996) points to the fact that many centres conducted more than one trial and that recent SSRI trials inevitably recruited patients who had failed previous treatments. A preliminary re-analysis of data excluding non-naive patients by the same author did not significantly change the effect size.

In contrast, comparative studies have not found clomipramine to be superior to SSRIs. RCTs have been carried out with all SSRIs apart from citalopram–fluoxetine, in 3 trials with 32, 55 and 26 patients (Pigott et al., 1990; Lopez-Ibor et al., 1996; Todorov et al., 1996); fluvoxamine, in 3 trials with 12, 66 and 79 patients (Smeraldi et al., 1992; Freeman et al., 1994; Koran et al., 1996); sertraline in 1 trial with 168 patients (Bisserbe et al., 1997); and paroxetine in 1 trial with 360 patients (Zohar et al., 1996). In Koran and colleagues' well-conducted study with fluvoxamine, a 30% reduction in Y-BOCS scores and a 55% response rate was seen with both drugs. However, they made the calculation based on available data that 150 subjects would be required in each treatment group to adequately test the hypothesis that the 2 drugs are equally efficacious. In the large paroxetine study, the sample size should have been large enough to answer this question but with a mean clomipramine dose of 113 mg (recognised therapeutic maximum in OCD, 250 mg) vs. 37.5 mg for paroxetine (therapeutic maximum 60 mg) it is clear that the clomipramine group did not receive equivalent doses. In Bisserbe et al.'s study, sertraline was in fact superior to clomipramine on intent-to-treat analysis but a higher and earlier drop-out rate in the clomipramine group was probably due to an inappropriately large starting dose of 50 mg—again biasing the comparison. So, taken together, the comparative studies are inconclusive and larger well-conducted trials are required to confirm or refute the findings on meta-analysis of placebo-controlled trials.

TOLERABILITY

Clomipramine has a greater range of side effects than the SSRIs and in studies to date adverse effects have been reported more frequently by clomipramine-treated patients. However in 2 meta-analyses drop-out rates with clomipramine were significantly less than with SSRIs (Greist et al., 1995b: 12% vs. 23–27%; and Cox et al., 1993: 12% vs. 16%) and in 4 of 7 comparative studies where clomipramine was started at the recommended dose of 25 mg, drop-out rates were comparable (Koran et al., 1996; Lopez-Ibor et al., 1996; Pigott et al., 1990; Todorov et al., 1996). So although more likely to cause side effects, clomipramine, if prescribed correctly, is probably no less acceptable to patients than SSRIs.

Todorov et al. (2000), in a recent review, discuss the impact of a shift in attitude to clomipramine from undoubtedly positive around the time of the original studies to a more negative one since the introduction of SSRIs. This, they argue, has led to reluctance on the part of clinicians and patients to persist with therapeutic trials of clomipramine or to use it first line, despite evidence that it is well tolerated and probably most efficacious among anti-obsessional agents. They challenge the Expert Consensus Guidelines (1997) recommendation that clomipramine be considered only after 2 to 3 failed trials of SSRIs, stating that such an approach may delay effective treatment and is unnecessarily costly.

SAFETY

Clomipramine, like all tricyclic antidepressants, can cause fatal cardiac arrhythmias in overdose and should not be prescribed where there is a significant overdose risk. Fortunately this is less common among OCD patients than among primary depressives. It should also be avoided in those with cardiac instability, particularly where conduction defects are present, and used with caution in those at risk of urinary retention, narrow angle glaucoma or where there is significant hepatic or renal impairment. Sedative, anti-cholinergic (e.g. dry mouth, constipation) and anti-adrenergic effects (e.g. postural hypotension) are additive and, on the rare occasions when combination with a neuroleptic is indicated (see below), choice of drug and dosing should reflect this.

By contrast, SSRIs are considered safe for almost all OCD patients except in unusual situations, such as severe hepatic or renal impairment or unstable epilepsy. They need to be used with caution when combined with other medications, as unlike clomipramine they significantly inhibit various iso-enzymes of the cytochrome P450 system, which is central to the hepatic metabolism of many commonly used drugs. Thus they can inhibit breakdown (and increase blood levels of): all tricyclic antidepressants including clomipramine; many antipsychotics, including clozapine, thioridazine, haloperidol and risperidone, β-blockers, opiates and several anti-arrhythmics (type 1C). Citalopram only weakly inhibits cytochrome P450 and as yet no interactions have been reported. It is therefore the best choice when combining SSRI treatment with other medications, especially those with a narrow therapeutic window such as cardiac anti-arrhythmics.

Any drug that enhances serotonin neurotransmission (all SRIs, buspirone, bupropion, mirtazapine, venlafaxine or nefazadone) can precipitate the serotonin syndrome (agitation, confusion, delirium, fever, sweating, nausea, diarrhoea, ataxia and muscle rigidity) when combined with an MAOI. This syndrome, although usually self-limiting, can be fatal. Rapid recovery normally follows discontinuation of the SRI, although supportive care is required during the acute phase (Lane & Baldwin 1997). At least a 14-day washout period should elapse before commencing an MAOI after a course of any of these agents or when switching from an MAOI. In the case of fluoxetine, because of its protracted half-life, a 5-week washout period is required after discontinuation (or longer if doses > 40 mg were used) [BMA, 2000; Koran, 1999].

SAFETY IN PREGNANCY AND DURING BREAST-FEEDING

Given that psychological treatment (PT) is at least as effective as SRIs for OCD, it is difficult to justify drug treatment during pregnancy or breast-feeding. There are of course incidents where PT has failed and symptoms pose a significant risk to the welfare of the mother and child, or where discontinuation of maintenance SRI treatment is very likely to result in relapse. Where drug treatment appears the only option, a careful balancing of the risks and potential benefits is required, informed by the available literature and discussion with the appropriate drug advisory service—a process that should as much as possible involve the mother and her partner/family. From the available data, fluoxetine has the greatest proven safety; clomipramine has been associated with problems in the neonate; and although problems have not been reported, other SSRIs have been studied far less. Sertraline has been associated with adverse effects in animals and the manufacturers recommend it be avoided in pregnancy (BMA, 2000).

Three reports on fluoxetine in 783, 109 and 128 pregnancies, respectively (Chambers et al., 1996; Pastuszak et al., 1993; Rosa, 1994), have found no higher incidences of spontaneous abortion, premature delivery or major anomalies than the general population. Additional data from Chambers et al. (1996) compared 228 pregnant women on fluoxetine with 254 controls who called the same information service. There was an excess of 3 or more minor anomalies in infants exposed to fluoxetine in the third trimester and more frequent premature delivery, admission to special care nurseries and poor neonatal adaptation. However, the comparison group was not controlled for co-existing diseases, including depression, that are independently associated with perinatal problems. Also, 30% of the fluoxetine-treated patients were on additional psychoactive drugs.

Kulin et al. (1998) prospectively compared rates of perinatal problems and neonatal malformation between 2 groups (each comprising 267 pregnancies)—a fluvoxamine, paroxetine or sertraline group and one in which mothers had taken a non-teratogenic drug. No difference was found. Fluvoxamine usage showed low numbers of spontaneous abortion and gross anomalies.

Clomipramine has been associated with neonatal complications due to anticholinergic effects (cardiac arrhythmias, urinary retention and intestinal obstruction) and the discontinuation syndrome (irritability, tremor and unstable temperature), so a slow withdrawal prior to delivery in women who have remained on this drug during pregnancy is considered best practice (Bromiker & Kaplan, 1994; Cowe & Lloyd, 1982; Goldberg & Nissim, 1994; Ostergaard & Pederson, 1982).

Nulman et al. (1997) followed to 86 months 55 children who were exposed to fluoxetine *in utero* and 80 children exposed to a tricyclic antidepressant and compared their development on a range of measures with 84 'normal' controls. Reassuringly, no difference was detected.

Clomipramine, like other tricyclics, does not readily accumulate in breast milk and levels are probably too small to be harmful. Fluoxetine does reach potentially toxic levels in breast milk and is not compatible with breast-feeding. Sertraline has been most studied among other SSRIs and has been shown not to reach significant levels in the infant (Koran, 1999; BMA, 2000).

DOSING

Recommended dosing levels are detailed in Table 17.2. For the elderly or anyone with a history of sensitivity to medication or patients anxious about side effects (as is often the case with OCD sufferers), it is best to start lower (e.g. paroxetine or clomipramine 10 mg) and go slower (e.g. increase the dose every 10–14 days as opposed to every 5–7 days, as is more usual). Most sufferers have been ill for several years before presentation and hasty dose increases are unnecessary and can be counterproductive. It is also crucial to coach the patient regarding the transient and innocuous nature of most side effects prior to commencing the drug, as this greatly reduces the likelihood of non-compliance. Some experts recommend continuing dose increases to the maximum tolerated (or until the upper limit for that drug is reached) (Koran, 1999), while others (Expert Consensus Guidelines, 1997) do not increase beyond a mid-range target dose (Table 17.2) unless no improvement is seen after 6 weeks. Either approach is valid and should achieve the same end result, although for responders a slow reduction to the minimum effective dose should be attempted over subsequent months. As long as the regimen used is flexible enough to allow side effects to subside between dose increases, most drugs will be tolerated by most patients.

SIDE EFFECTS OF SRIs AND THEIR MANAGEMENT

It is beyond the scope of this chapter to discuss in detail the side-effect profiles of each of the SRIs, although some discussion of the main points and topical aspects is warranted. As a general rule, most side effects can be managed by either waiting for tolerance (if occurring shortly after a drug is started or increased), reducing or dividing the dose (if persistent) or by simple measures such as taking the medication with meals to reduce nausea or taking it at night to avoid daytime sedation.

Clomipramine's common side effects relate to its anti-cholinergic (blurred vision, constipation, dry mouth, slowed micturition), anti-adrenergic (postural hypotension) and anti-histamine (sedation) actions. Most of these dissipate with time, although encouraging a high-roughage diet and urging care when standing up after dose increases and night-time dosing can help reduce their impact. Sexual side effects, as with SSRIs, are very common, ranging from delayed orgasm (on as little as 25 mg) to anorgasmia on higher doses to complete loss of libido and, unlike other side effects, generally do not dissipate. It is very important to ask about such effects and to inform patients of the risks before commencement of drug treatment. Brief drug holidays for a few days prior to sexual activity or dose reduction may be effective. Other more experimental solutions, such as oral amntadine, are reviewed by Koran (1999). Seizures are known to occur at doses above 250 mg, so very high doses should be avoided.

As a group, the SSRIs share similar but not identical side effect profiles. Gastrointestinal disturbance is commonest, usually nausea, vomiting or diarrhoea, which normally subside within a few days and can be reduced by taking the SSRI dose with the main meal of the day. Nervousness and agitation is also common but transient and it is particularly important to inform patients that this does not signify a deterioration in their condition. Sexual side effects are estimated to occur in 25–35% (Gitlin, 1994). The approach is as for clomipramine, except in the case of fluoxetine, where drug holidays are not practical given its long half-life.

Slow discontinuation of all SRIs bar fluoxetine is preferable to avoid a discontinuation syndrome characterised by anxiety, dizziness, insomnia, irritability, 'flu-like symptoms and (in the case of SSRIs) strange sensations of detachment and 'electric shock'-like experiences. Withdrawal from paroxetine seems to carry the greatest risk. The frequency has not been established but the syndrome is not uncommon. Symptoms are usually self-limiting and are rapidly relieved by reinstating the drug or by switching to another SSRI. Occasionally very slow reductions are required over weeks, e.g. by dropping the daily dose of paroxetine by 10 mg each week (for a review, see Lejoyeux & Ades, 1997). The serotonin syndrome has been discussed previously.

CO-MORBID CONDITIONS THAT IMPACT ON PHARMACOLOGICAL TREATMENT

OCD with 'Poor Insight', Delusions and Schizophrenia

DSM-IV includes a 'poor insight' subtype of OCD, following fieldwork that revealed that 5% of sufferers have never had insight into the senselessness of their compulsions (Foa & Kozak, 1995). Some of this group have delusional beliefs in the necessity of their behaviours, for whom an additional diagnosis of delusional disorder can be made. However, antipsychotic medication, although it can be tried, is not the mainstay of treatment, as behavioural therapy and/or SRIs are often effective alone (O'Dwyer & Marks 2000).

Obsessions and compulsions are surprisingly common in schizophrenia, with studies suggesting rates of 8–46% (Eisen et al., 1997; Porto et al., 1997). In the latter study, 26% had distinct OCD and in 20% symptoms were variously incorporated with psychotic phenomena. Sasson et al. (1997) suggest trials of anti-obsessional drugs only when psychotic symptoms are stabilised on medication and recommend careful consideration of drug interaction, as many SSRIs increase blood levels of antipsychotics. In 2 open trials and one small double-blind placebo-controlled trial, response was variable and in some cases schizophrenia worsened with SRIs (Berman et al., 1995; Zohar et al., 1994; Sasson et al., 1997).

In a small minority of schizophrenics, OCD symptoms emerge or deteriorate following treatment with the atypical antipsychotic drugs, clozapine, olanzapine and risperidone, possibly as a result of their antagonism of 5-HT_2 receptors (Greist & Jefferson, 1998; Koran, 1999; Panagiotis, 1999). Similar effects have yet to be reported with other atypicals. These symptoms may remit spontaneously within 3 weeks or following dose reduction. Occasionally discontinuation is required, although several cases have responded to the addition of an SRI (e.g. Allen & Tajera 1994). The author has encountered a case where behavioural therapy was effective for clozapine-induced OCD.

Tourette's Syndrome or Tic Disorder

When OCD with co-morbid tic disorder fails to respond to an SRI (studies used fluvoxamine), the addition of haloperidol or pimozide slowly built up to 2–10 mg has been associated with higher response rates than would be expected from changing to another SRI (McDougle et al., 1990, 1994a). In these studies, tics also reduced. Inhibition of excess dopaminergic activity in the basal ganglia via D2 receptor blockade is the putative mechanism of action. Some advocate risperidone for the same role, although the results of controlled trials are awaited (Koran, 1999). More recently, McDougle (1997) has presented evidence for augmentation with dopamine antagonists in SRI-refractory cases and where there is a family history of tics.

Schizotypal Personality Disorder

When patients with schizotypal personality disorder present with OCD, conventional behavioural or pharmacological treatments are frequently ineffective (Jenike et al., 1986; Minichiello et al., 1987). Some patients may benefit from the addition of an antipsychotic agent, although the evidence for this is limited (McDougal et al., 1990, 1994b).

MANAGEMENT OF PARTIAL RESPONDERS TO SRIs

Between 40–60% of patients do not respond adequately to SRI treatment alone (Greist et al., 1995b), so prescribing clinicians need clear strategies for managing partial responders. Unfortunately the literature does not offer any well-validated solutions. After checking that the SRI trial has been adequate (at a therapeutic dose for 12 weeks or more with full compliance) and that there is indeed significant residual handicap, several options can be considered with the patient. First, if exposure and response prevention (ERP) has not been tried, it should be offered next (O'Connor et al., 1999; Simpson et al., 1999). If it has been attempted unsuccessfully in the past, it may still be the best option if the patient has become more willing to comply with exposure tasks or if the previous trial was not carried out with a suitably experienced or proficient therapist. Where adequate ERP has failed, other psychological strategies tackling cognitive aspects described in Chapters 12, 16, 19 and 20 can be offered where available. If further pharmacological treatment is the only viable option or is preferred by the patient, then there are 2 options—change to another SRI (preferable if clinical response is marginal or if side effects have been persistently troublesome) or augment the current SRI with another agent.

AUGMENTATION

Although widely recommended (Greist & Jefferson, 1998; Expert Consensus Guidelines, 1997), none of the augmentation strategies summarised briefly below have been conclusively validated in controlled trials. Considerable further research is needed to clarify the efficacy (against placebo and each other) and safety of these treatments. Several are proposed to act by enhancing SRIs' serotonergic activity (tryptophan, clonazepam, buspirone and fenfluramine). For advice on dosing, consult the British National Formulary or its equivalent. Only controlled or influential studies are listed. For a more detailed literature review see Koran (1999).

Clonazepam

Proposed action: upregulation of 5-HT_1 and 5-HT_2 receptors in the frontal cortex in addition to benzodiazepine effects.
Dose range: 0.5–4 mg daily.
Evidence for efficacy: several reports of anti-obsessional activity when used alone; one placebo-controlled trial as augmentation agent—improvement in one OCD scale vs. placebo but not in 2 others, including the Y-BOCS (Pigott et al., 1992b).
Limitations: side effects may be limiting, including depression, irritability and intoxication.

Buspirone

Proposed action: 5-HT_{1a} partial agonist.
Dose range: 10–90 mg daily.
Evidence of efficacy: four controlled trials: 29% had a clinically meaningful improvement in one (Pigott et al., 1992a); Jenike et al. (1999) found an

additional benefit at 2 months; 2 others found no benefit (Grady et al., 1993; McDougle et al., 1993).
Limitations: irritability and forgetfulness may be dose-limiting.

L-Tryptophan

Proposed action: amino acid precursor of serotonin.
Dose range: 3–9 grams daily.
Evidence of efficacy: no controlled trials; several case reports and one open trial where it was added to an SRI and pindolol with benefit (Blier & Bergeron, 1996).
Limitations: has resulted in the serotonin syndrome when combined with fluoxetine; association with eosinophilia myalgia syndrome, probably due to a contaminant in older preparations—yet to be re-introduced in many countries, including the USA, but available for prescription in the UK.

Lithium

Proposed action: enhances serotonin transmission among other actions.
Dose range: as in mood stabilisation.
Evidence of efficacy: despite promising case reports, lithium was ineffective in 3 double-blind placebo-controlled trials (Pigott et al., 1991; McDougle et al., 1991).
Limitations: toxicity weighs against its use unless there is evidence of concomitant mood disorder.

Atypical anti-psychotics—Risperidone, olanzapine and clozapine

Proposed action: combined D2 and 5-HT$_2$ antagonism. McDougle (1997) has hypothesised that SRI-refractory patients (without tics) have additional abnormalities in dopamine function, which require augmentation with dopamine-blocking agents.
Dose range: as for psychosis but response or side effects usually confined to lower doses. A 4-week therapeutic trial at the maximum tolerated dose is considered sufficient.
Evidence of efficacy: there is most data on risperidone—6 open trials/case series with positive results (e.g. McDougle et al., 1995b; Ravizza et al., 1996b; Stein et al., 1997a). Controlled trials are awaited. The single report on olanzapine found 7 of 10 improved, 4 to 'complete remission', when it was added to SSRIs in partial responders (Weiss et al., 1999). McDougle et al.

(1995b) found none of 10 refractory patients responded to clozapine alone and, given its relative toxicity, use in OCD cannot be justified at present. *Limitations*: the combination is generally well tolerated. SSRIs may reduce breakdown of risperidone, so cautious dosing is required. Additional side effects, such as sedation, weight gain or extra-pyramidal effects (with higher doses of risperidone), may be troublesome. Reports of these agents exacerbating OCD in patients with co-morbid schizophrenia need to be borne in mind (see above).

Inositol

Proposed action: precursor of the second messenger (phosphatidylinositol) for several neurotransmitter systems, including some serotonin receptor subtypes. Is a normal dietary constituent.
Dose range: trials have used 18 g daily dissolved in water or fruit juice.
Evidence of efficacy: 3 of 10 improved on one measure (Clinical Global Impressions Scale) in an open trial when added to SRIs in a treatment-refractory patient group (Seedat & Stein, 1999). 6 of 13 improved on Y-BOCS scores (>25%) when compared as monotherapy against placebo (Fux et al., 1996).
Limitations: well tolerated (commonest side-effect is mild gastro-intestinal disturbance) but in its current form improvement, when evident, is generally modest.

Combining Clomipramine with an SSRI

Proposed action: enhanced inhibition of serotonin re-uptake.
Dose range: lower doses of clomipramine (75–150 mg) than when used alone because of interaction with SSRIs (see above).
Evidence of efficacy: in a randomised open label trial, 9 of 9 SRI refractory patients responded to a combination of citalopram and clomipramine vs. 1 of 7 taking citalopram alone (Pallanti et al., 1998). Another small controlled study found combined clomipramine and sertraline better tolerated but not statistically more effective than clomipramine alone (Ravizza et al., 1996b).
Limitations: risk of toxicity as a result of drug interaction requires careful and slow dose increases, pulse and blood pressure monitoring and serial assays of serum clomipramine and desmethylclomipramine (Koran, 1999).

Gabapentin

Proposed action: anticonvulsant, action unknown.
Dose range: 1800–2400 mg daily in divided doses.

Evidence of efficacy: anecdotal evidence is emerging of possible efficacy in OCD, generalised anxiety and depression (Cora-Locatelli et al., 1998).
Limitations: rebound symptom exacerbation has been reported on discontinuation.

Fenfluramine

Proposed action: releases serotonin and inhibits re-uptake.
Dose range: 20–60 mg daily.
Evidence of efficacy: improvement noted within 4 weeks in 2 small case series (Hollander et al., 1990a; Judd et al., 1991).
Limitations: has been withdrawn from the USA and UK pending investigation of reports of vavular heart disease. Also associated with insidious potentially fatal pulmonary hypertension (BMA, 2000).

Pindolol

Proposed action: as well as blocking adrenergic β-receptors, it may act by inhibiting negative feedback on serotonin nerve firing (by antagonising pre-synaptic 5-HT_{1A}), which is felt to delay the therapeutic response to SRIs.
Dose: 2.5 mg three times daily.
Evidence of efficacy: 4 of 13 improved in an open trial (Blier & Bergeron, 1996) but a small double-blind RCT ($n = 15$) found no difference in efficacy or onset of response between fluvoxamine and pindolol vs. fluvoxamine and placebo (Mundo et al., 1998).

Other agents studied include: the pituitary hormone, oxytocin (Epperson et al., 1996); the antidepressants, trazodone (Hermesh et al., 1990) and desipramine (Barr et al., 1997); and the androgen receptor antagonist flutamide (Altemus et al., 1999). None have shown sufficient promise for inclusion in the list above.

MANAGEMENT OF REFRACTORY CASES

When first- and second-line interventions have been exhausted, both psychological (see above) and pharmacological (adequate trials of each SRI with and without augmentation using the more promising strategies outlined), with minimal or no response, the following options can be considered. As with any treatment-refractory patient, it is prudent to review the diagnosis, optimally treat co-morbid illnesses such as mood disorder, drug

Table 17.3 Summary of management options in OCD

1. Choose between psychological and drug treatments.
2. Choose SRI and continue for 12 weeks at full dose or highest tolerated.
3. No response or not tolerated: change to another SRI and/or start psychological treatment.
4. Partial response: augment with psychological treatment or one of the pharmacological augmentation strategies (PAS)—ideally low-dose neuroleptic or risperidone if co-morbid tic disorder.
5. Inadequate or no response: continue with SRI trials, with and without PAS.
6. Inadequate or no response: try venlafaxine with and without PAS and subsequently an MAOI (after suitable washout period).
7. Review diagnosis and psychosocial aspects; ensure optimal treatment of co-morbid disorders.
8. Consider strategies for refractory cases, e.g. intravenous clomipramine or referral for intensive inpatient psychological treatment.
9. Consider neurosurgery if symptoms remain severe and incapacitating (see Table 17.4).

dependency or psychosis and tackle psychosocial stressors where appropriate before moving away from standard interventions. Table 17.3, loosely based on the management algorithm by the Expert Consensus Guidelines team (1997), lists the options facing the clinician and patient at each stage up to and including this point. It is not intended as a rigid protocol but as a summarising overview. Specialist inpatient treatment centres like the Behavioural Psychotherapy Unit at the Bethlem Hospital in London offer a package of intensive cognitive-behavioural therapy, psychoeducation, family intervention and pharmacological treatment that is frequently effective even in 'end-stage' OCD (Calvocoressi et al., 1993). Where available, such programs should be offered to refractory patients.

Trials of an MAOI and the specific serotonin and noradrenaline re-uptake inhibitor, venlafaxine, are within the prescribing repertoire of most psychiatrists and are usually tried first. The other drug treatments discussed are less familiar to most clinicians but carry few risks when balanced against the handicap of chronic severe OCD. There is mounting evidence for the efficacy and safety of intravenous clomipramine, which is rapidly becoming the optimal strategy in resistant cases. In the tiny minority where symptoms remain incapacitating and life-threatening, psychosurgery can be considered.

Phenelzine and MAOIs

An RCT comparing phenelzine (75 mg daily) with clomipramine (225 mg daily) in 30 patients found that the 2 drugs were equally effective (Vallejo et al., 1992) but a more recent, placebo-controlled comparison with flu-oxetine (80 mg daily) in 64 subjects found fluoxetine treatment signifi-cantly superior. 6 of 7 responders in the phenelzine group ($n = 20$) had obsessions regarding symmetry, which led the authors to conclude that phenelzine may be useful for this subtype or where there are 'atypical' obsessions. There is also a suggestion from the literature that high anxiety or panic predicts a favourable outcome with MAOIs. Although dietary re-strictions to avoid the hypertensive 'tyramine reaction' can be a burden for patients, a trial in refractory cases is worthwhile as a dramatic response is occasionally seen (Jenike, 1981). The importance of leaving an appropriate 'wash-out' period when switching to or from an SRI has been discussed previously.

Venlafaxine

In an open trial, 4 of 10 subjects improved significantly on venlafaxine 375 mg daily (Rauch et al., 1996). This finding, taken with the reported case studies (dose range 150–375 mg), suggest strongly that venlafaxine has anti-obsessional activity, although controlled trials are needed.

Intravenous (i.v.) Clomipramine

The injectable form of clomipramine given as an infusion is available in Europe and Canada but not in the USA outside of specialist centres. The standard regimen involves a test dose of 25–50 mg to gauge tolerance, fol-lowed by daily increases of 25 mg to a target range of 150–250 mg daily. Intravenous treatment usually continues for 14 days and is followed by oral dosing. The initial uncontrolled reports of efficacy in refractory pa-tients (Warneke 1984, 1985, 1989; Fallon et al., 1992) found i.v. clomipramine more rapidly effective (meaningful response within 4 weeks) and better tol-erated than oral treatment, in that several responders had failed to tolerate oral clomipramine. It has been suggested that the ratio of clomipramine to its metabolite desmethylclomipramine (which also inhibits noradrenaline re-uptake), usually 1:2 when given orally, is increased with parenteral treat-ment by reducing first-pass hepatic metabolism, and that this explains its greater tolerability and efficacy (Greist, 1998).

Fallon et al. (1998), in a double-blind RCT, found 9 of 21 refractory patients treated with 14 days of clomipramine infusions and 7 days of oral treat-ment were responders, compared with none of 18 in the placebo group. Improvement continued to the 1-month endpoint and the regimen was well tolerated. This important study requires replication. Koran and colleagues found a 'pulse loading' i.v. regimen, in which 150 mg is administered on day 1 and 150 or 200 mg on day 2 (followed by oral treatment) more rapidly effective (32% drop in Y-BOCS by day 7) in controlled comparisons with oral treatment (Koran et al., 1997) and gradual i.v. dosing (Koran et al., 1998).

Oral Opiates

Warneke (1997) found marked benefit with 20–40 mg morphine every 5–8 days in 5 of 8 intractable cases. Koran (1999) found that one of two refractory patients benefited from 30 mg codeine twice daily in a double-blind crossover comparison with lorazepam. Codeine needed to be stopped for 3–5 days a week to avoid tolerance. The therapeutic response is experienced for 3–4 hours after each dose. Warneke suggests that opiate receptors in the striatal system could mediate this effect and cites previous work in which i.v. naloxone acutely exacerbated OCD in 2 patients.

Neurosurgery

With the advent of effective therapies over the past three decades, psychosurgery has become more than ever an intervention of last resort. Jenike et al. (1998b) have reviewed its place in the treatment of OCD, complimented with a thorough and objective analysis of the literature. They conclude: 'When non-surgical treatments have failed, there is evidence that at least partial, and often significant, relief can be obtained in some OCD patients by surgery'. They emphasise the importance of balancing the risks of non-intervention (social, physical and psychological complications, including suicide) against those of surgery, which they argue are not excessive with current techniques. Unfortunately, in the absence of a controlled comparison with 'sham' surgery, efficacy remains unproven. Follow-up studies from the 1960s and 1970s rating improvement in greater than 80% of patients need to be viewed with caution, as many patients would not meet current criteria for treatment resistance or therapeutic response (Mindus & Jenike, 1992). More recent retrospective (Irle et al., 1998; Jenike et al., 1991a) and prospective (Baer et al., 1995) studies report response in 30–60% (CGI much or very much improved, or > 35% reduction in Y-BOCS score). A 'gamma knife' using cobalt 60 is now used in some centres to create surgical lesions without opening the skull, making a controlled comparison with sham surgery feasible. Jenike et al. (1998b) are undertaking the first such study at Massachusetts General Hospital and aim to correlate clinical response with functional MRI findings.

The procedures favoured across various centres include cingulotomy, subcaudate tractotomy, capsulotomy and limbic leucotomy (cingulotomy plus subcaudate tractotomy). There is no conclusive data on comparative efficacy or safety. A 'stereotactic' frame is used and target sites are visualised on magnetic resonance imaging (MRI). Lesions are made under local anaesthetic or light sedation, either by heating carefully placed electrodes with radio waves or directly with γ-rays. Further research is needed to identify the best target sites. Occasionally surgeons will re-operate if clinically indicated. It is hypothesised that these procedures disrupt dysfunctional neural circuits by severing connections between the orbitomedial frontal lobes and limbic or thalmic structures, although the observation that most patients take weeks or months to improve suggests that secondary effects, such as nerve degeneration, may be important (Jenike et al., 1998b).

Physical complications include infection, haemorrhage, seizures and weight gain. Seizures are estimated to occur in < 1% and are usually responsive to anticonvulsants. Infection and haemorrhage can be contained with prompt intervention. Psychological complications of frontal lobe dysfunction, personality alteration, substance abuse and suicide have been reported, although the risks are estimated to be low.

Table 17.4 lists the indications for neurosurgery in intractable OCD (adapted from Mindus & Jenike, 1992). If the patient appears suitable,

Table 17.4 Neurosurgery for intractable OCD: indications

1. Symptoms fulfil diagnostic criteria for OCD.
2. Illness duration > 5 years.
3. Patient aged 18–65.
4. OCD causing substantial suffering and a considerable impact on psychosocial functioning.
5. The following treatments have failed or were not tolerated: adequate trials of each SRI (some centres insist on only three trials) and an MAOI. Augmentation of at least one SRI with two of lithium, clonazepam or buspirone (a month each) and a low-dose neuroleptic in patients with co-morbid tic disorder; at least 20 hours of behavioural therapy using exposure and response prevention (ERP).
6. Poor prognosis without surgery.
7. Patient gives informed consent and agrees to preoperative evaluation and postoperative rehabilitation.
8. Referring physician is willing to take over postoperative and long-term management.

the next step is to contact the multidisciplinary review committee at an institution that specialises in this form of neurosurgery, such as the Priory Hospital, London, or Massachusetts General Hospital, for further details about their criteria and more detailed information on risks and benefits. It is important to continue or re-start pharmacological and/or psychological treatments post-operatively, as patients may respond to previously unsuccessful interventions.

Chapter 18

OBSESSIVE-COMPULSIVE DISORDER IN CHILDREN AND ADOLESCENTS

Roz Shafran

INTRODUCTION

Obsessive-compulsive disorder (OCD) is estimated to affect 0.5–2% of children and adolescents, and the phenomenology of OCD in children and adults is highly similar (Swedo et al., 1989b). Given the apparent continuum between the forms of OCD across the age range, it is not surprising that similar psychological and pharmacological interventions are used (Franklin et al., 1998). Nevertheless, significant differences exist in terms of the gender distribution of the disorder, co-morbidity, familial contribution, developmental issues and theories of maintenance. These differences have led to some proposals that childhood OCD is a distinct subtype of adult OCD (Geller et al., 1998) and it is argued that it can be viewed within the framework of paediatric auto-immune neuropsychiatric disorder associated with infection (Swedo et al., 1998). The chapter begins by describing the epidemiology and phenomenology of the disorder and assessment techniques. Psychological and neuropsychiatric theories of the disorder are discussed, and treatment outcome studies reviewed. The chapter concludes by calling for a closer integration between the science and practice of treating OCD in young people.

EPIDEMIOLOGY

Early prevalence estimates of OCD from child psychiatric clinics ranged from 0.2% to 1.2% (Berman, 1942; Hollingsworth et al., 1980; Judd, 1965) but more recent studies of adolescents in the community find prevalence rates ranging from 1–4% (Douglass et al., 1995; Flament et al., 1988;

see Zohar, 1999, for a review). Important differences exist between cases identified in the community and the clinic, but taking these studies together, approximately 2% of children and adolescents are estimated to be affected by OCD (Thomsen, 1999; Zohar, 1999).

PHENOMENOLOGY

Obsessions

As with adults, the core characteristic of obsessions in young people is that they are resisted; the patient is usually horrified by the occurrence and/or content of the obsessions (American Psychiatric Association, 1994). The most common obsessions in young people have themes of contamination, harm or death; symmetry/exactness and somatic, religious and sexual obsessions are not uncommon (Flament et al., 1988; Hanna, 1995; Riddle et al., 1990; Swedo et al., 1989b; Toro et al., 1992).

Compulsions

Again, as with adults referred to the clinic, the majority of cases of childhood OCD have both obsessions and compulsions (Hanna, 1995; Last & Strauss, 1989; Riddle et al., 1990; Toro et al., 1992). The compulsions are purposeful and aim to prevent a dreaded event or to reduce distress. Young patients often find the compulsion to engage in this behaviour to be distressing itself, and will often be frustrated by the time that it takes to complete the compulsion 'correctly' and the interference caused to normal social and school functioning. The most common examples of compulsive behaviour are checking, washing, repeating, touching and straightening; symptoms vary greatly over time (Hanna, 1995; Rettew et al., 1992).

In young people who have compulsions without obsessions, it can often be difficult to determine the basis for compulsive behaviour and such patients will often say that the compulsion is driven by a sense that 'it doesn't feel right' unless such compulsive behaviour has been completed. Whether there is an absence of obsessions driving this compulsion or whether young people lack the cognitive ability to articulate their internal mental events remains a topic open to debate.

Co-morbidity and Subtypes

OCD has been associated with a range of other disorders including body dysmorphic disorder, Tourette's syndrome, eating disorders, anxiety disorders and depression (see Hollander, 1993; Chapters 1 and 13, this volume). Indeed, it is considered that OCD is one disorder on an 'obsessive-compulsive spectrum' (Hollander, 1993). A number of factors need to be taken into consideration when drawing conclusions about co-morbidity, including base-rates, phenomenological overlap between the disorders and specificity of assessment measures.

OCD in children and adolescents specifically has been associated with motor tics and Tourette's syndrome (e.g. Leonard et al., 1993; Thomsen & Mikkelson, 1995) and it has been suggested that OCD and Tourette's syndrome may be alternative manifestations of the same underlying illness (Pauls et al., 1995). However, there are important differences between patients with OCD alone and patients with OCD + Tourette's syndrome. Specifically, the latter group tend to have more touching, counting and blinking compulsions and fewer cleaning compulsions than patients with OCD alone (George et al., 1993; Holzer et al., 1994).

There are also treatment differences between patients with OCD + Tourette's syndrome compared to patients with OCD alone. The former group appears to be less responsive to an SSRI alone and, in a study of fluvoxamine-refractory OCD, they were more responsive to a combination treatment (haloperidol and fluvoxamine) (McDougle et al., 1994a). Such findings have led to the view that tic-related and non-tic-related OCD may be different subtypes of the disorder (see Riddle, 1998).

Comorbid affective and anxiety disorders are common comorbid problems. In the NIMH sample of 70 children, only 18 (26%) had OCD as their only diagnosis, with 35% receiving a co-morbid diagnosis of depression, and 40% having a co-morbid anxiety disorder (Swedo et al., 1989b). In other clinical studies of children and adolescents, a similar proportion (60–80%) had other lifetime diagnoses apart from OCD (Hanna, 1995; Last & Strauss, 1989). The episodic course of a substantial number of patients with childhood OCD could be attributed to variability in depression.

Course of the Disorder

As with adults, the course of childhood OCD tends to fluctuate over time and the course is often chronic (Bolton et al., 1995; Thomsen & Mikkelson, 1995; Leonard et al., 1993). For example, in the Danish study of 23 patients, 50% retained a diagnosis of OCD at 1.5–5 years follow-up and the long-term outcome of medication with 54 children and adolescents in the NIMH trial was poor (Leonard et al., 1993). No prognostic indicators have been identified. A recent review has indicated that there is a complete remission rate of approximately 10–15% (Zohar, 1999), although the waxing and waning of symptoms means that long-term follow-up studies are needed. It is important to note that the majority of subclinical cases of OCD in adolescents identified in the community studies do not continue to develop the disorder in adulthood (Berg et al., 1989).

Age of Onset

The average age of onset for childhood OCD ranges from 7.5 to 12.5 years (see Geller et al., 1998), with a mean of 10.3 years. It has been estimated that 30–80% of adults with OCD recall the onset of their symptoms beginning before 18 (Pauls et al., 1995; Rasmussen & Eisen, 1992). The age of onset appears to be earlier in boys than in girls and peaks first in puberty and then in early adulthood (see Zohar, 1999, for a review).

Familial Contribution

Earlier age of onset has been associated with a higher likelihood of OCD in the family of probands (Pauls et al., 1995) and the rate of first-degree relatives of children and adolescents with OCD who have the disorder (or a subclinical form) is higher than for adults. Of interest, parental obsessive-compulsive disorder does not appear to be a prognostic factor in fluvoxamine treatment in offspring with the disorder (Yaryura-Tobias et al., 2000). However, the majority of probands do not have an affected first-degree relative with the disorder (see Hanna, 2000; Pauls et al., 1995; Pauls & Alsobrook, 1999; see Chapter 6 for a comprehensive discussion of the contribution of heredity to OCD).

Gender Distribution

The majority of studies of childhood OCD find an average of 3:2 male: female ratio (Geller et al., 1998) although the gender distribution is found to be approximately equal in adults (Antony et al., 1998a; Rasmussen & Eisen, 1992).

Developmental Issues

It has been argued that the similarities between the phenomenology of OCD and childhood magical thought warrant a developmental account of OCD (Bolton, 1996; Pollock & Carter, 1999). For example, children have 'magical thinking' in which their apparently irrelevant actions can make a difference to reality, and patients with OCD engage in compulsive behaviours that are often unrealistically connected to the dreaded event that they are trying to prevent. Stereotypical superstitious behaviour is a normal part of childhood development and initially appears similar to the compulsive behaviour of OCD. However, compulsions in childhood and adult OCD are characterised by checking, washing and repeating rituals, and are driven by ego-dystonic fears of contamination or danger. Superstitions are concerned with good and bad luck, are not ego-dystonic or resisted and do not cause distress (Leonard, 1990). In addition, superstitions are commonly shared beliefs, whereas obsessions tend to be personal and partly idiosyncratic in content.

Assessment

OCD can be difficult to diagnose in children and adolescents, given the co-morbidity between OCD and other disorders and the lack of insight that the young person might have into the nature of their obsessions. Assessment measures for paediatric anxiety disorders have recently been reviewed (Greenhill et al., 1998; March & Albano, 1998). Standardised interviews include the Schedule for Affective Disorders and Schizophrenia for School-age Children, Present and Lifetime version (K-SADS-PL; Kaufman et al., 1997) and the Diagnostic Interview Schedule (DISC-2.3; Shaffer et al., 1996). Further psychometric data is required for the Anxiety Disorders Interview Schedule—Revised for children (ADIS-R; Silverman & Eisen, 1992). There is no current 'gold standard' on which to base reliable and valid diagnostic procedures (Dulcan, 1996) but the widely-used Children's Yale–Brown Obsessive Compulsive Scale (CY-BOCS; Goodman et al., 1989a, 1989b) is a semi-structured interview with good reliability and validity (de Haan & Hoogduin, 1992; Hanna, 1995; Scahill et al., 1997). Clinical judgement is used to complete the Children's Global Assessment Scale (CGAS; Shaffer et al., 1983), the NIMH Global scale childhood OCD subsection (Murphy et al., 1982) and the four-item Obsessive-Compulsive Rating Scale (OCR; Rapoport et al., 1980).

Self-report questionnaire measures of paediatric anxiety disorders include the Screen for Child Anxiety-related Emotional Disorders (SCARED; Birmaher et al., 1997) and the Multidimensional Anxiety Scale for children (MASC; March et al., 1997b). Both of these measures have good psychometric properties. The Leyton Obsessional Inventory, Child Version (LOI-CV; Berg et al., 1988) is widely used but has a high false-positive rate (see Wolff & Wolff, 1991) and poor test–retest reliability for 8–10-year-olds (King et al., 1995). A new self-report measure is currently under development (Shafran et al., in preparation).

THEORIES

Cognitive-behavioural Approaches

The cognitive-behavioural model of OCD (Salkovskis, 1985; Salkovskis et al., 1998b) considers the behavioural theory and treatment of OCD (Rachman & Hodgson, 1980) within a cognitive framework (Beck, 1976). The theory suggests that OCD is maintained when normal intrusive thoughts (which are experienced by the majority of normal adults and adolescents) (Allsopp & Williams, 1996; Rachman & de Silva, 1978) are appraised in terms of responsibility for harm (see further, Chapter 4; Salkovskis, 1985). Other appraisals concerning the personal significance of intrusive thoughts are also thought to play an important role in the maintenance of the disorder (Obsessive-Compulsive Cognitions Working Group, 1997; Rachman, 1997). A wide variety of evidence supports the addition of the cognitive component to the behavioural model and the role of responsibility in adults (e.g. Abramowitz, 1998; Lopatka & Rachman, 1995; Salkovskis & Campbell, 1994; Shafran, 1997).

Despite the widespread investigation of the cognitive-behavioural theory in adults, there has been relatively little investigation in children and adolescents (see Shafran, 1998, for a review) and the leading researchers in the NIMH group (e.g. Judith Rapoport and Susan Swedo) in childhood OCD are from a psychiatric rather than psychological background. They consider the disorder within a neuropsychiatric framework.

Neuropsychiatric Approaches

A variety of neurobiological and neuropsychological models are proposed to account for OCD (for reviews, see Fitzgerald et al., 1999; Schultz et al., 1999). These models include abnormalities in basal ganglia development and dysfunction of frontal–subcortical brain circuitry (Baxter et al., 1990; Rapoport & Wise, 1988; Saxena et al., 1998) and dysfunction of the serotonergic system (Gross et al., 1998; Rosenberg et al., 2000b). Recent investigations have not shown any neuropsychological dysfunction in children with OCD (Beers et al., 1999) but have shown decreases in caudate glutamatergic concentrations and thalamic volumes in children and adolescents with OCD who were taking paroxetine (Rosenberg et al., 2000b). The authors interpret these findings as indicating that abnormalities in the thalamus and caudate nucleus are central neurobiological deficits in

OCD and that paroxetine treatment reverses this deficit via serotonergic mechanisms (Rosenberg et al., 2000b). Genetic, neuroethological and neuropeptide models have been proposed (see Billet et al., 1998; McDougle et al., 1999; Winslow & Insel, 1991). One model currently receiving a great deal of attention in childhood OCD concerns the immune system (Asbahr et al., 1999; Giedd et al., 2000; Leonard et al., 1999; Swedo et al., 1998).

Paediatric Auto-immune Neuropsychiatric Disorders Associated with Streptococcal Infection (PANDAS)

PANDAS is a novel diagnostic category that has been assigned to children or adolescents who develop, and have repeated exacerbations of, tic disorders and/or OCD following group A β-haemolytic streptococcal infections (Garvey et al., 1998). A large study of 50 children described the clinical characteristics of PANDAS and the authors suggest that abnormal immune responses to the infections might play an aetiological role in the development of OCD and/or tics (Swedo et al., 1998). Specifically, it is suggested that in some cases, as in Sydenham's chorea, the group A β-haemolytic streptococcal bacteria trigger antibodies that cross-react with the basal ganglia of genetically susceptible hosts leading to OCD and/or tics (Garvey et al., 1998). Further to this, the nosological classification of OCD as an anxiety disorder has been called into question. Evidence cited in support of PANDAS includes the increased presence of antibodies directed against the human caudate nucleus in the sera of patients with tics compared with normal controls (Kiessling et al., 1993) and a high prevalence of OC symptoms in Sydenham's chorea (Swedo et al., 1989a). The hypothesis is controversial (Garvey et al., 1998; Kurlan, 1998) and important questions remain. First, are the obsessions in these patients experienced as ego-dystonic and resisted, and do they give rise to purposeful compulsive behaviour that is designed to prevent a dreaded event? Second, does such a nosology have any implications for treatment? The notion of the rationality of immune-modifying therapies for OCD is questionable (Kurlan, 1998). It is also doubtful whether OCD and tic disorders can be regarded as interchangeable, as implied by the first diagnostic criterion for PANDAS.

TREATMENTS

Cognitive-behavioural Treatments

The treatment of OCD in young people has recently been reviewed (Grados & Riddle, 1999) and is a topic of increasing interest. A survey of experts on the treatment of OCD in children and adolescents found that

Cognitive-behavioural therapy (CBT) or CBT + medication is recommended as the initial treatment of choice, with CBT alone preferred in younger patients and/or milder cases (March et al., 1997a). Whether this reflects actual clinical practice is not clear. At present, clinical practice is most likely to be guided by personal clinical experience, since the current evidence base is insufficient to guide CBT reliably, with few outcome studies and only two controlled trials of such treatment (de Haan et al., 1998; Franklin et al., 1998). The CBT used in clinical practice may vary according to whether the therapy is based on the protocol developed by March specifically for OCD in young people (March & Mulle, 1998), or whether the CBT is based on the cognitive theories and treatments used in adults (see Shafran & Somers, 1998).

The CBT that has been most widely investigated in children and adolescents is that of March and colleagues (March, 1995; March & Mulle, 1998; March et al., 1994). March's CBT places OCD in a neurobehavioural framework and comprises three stages: information gathering; exposure and response prevention (ERP); and homework assignments. The cognitive component includes self-statements to 'boss back' or cope with the OCD. Parents are involved in at least two of the twenty sessions (sessions 7 and 12) and family involvement is graded according to the individual clinical needs and family situation (March & Mulle, 1998).

Twelve of the fifteen cases in the first open trial had at least 30% improvement on the Y-BOCS (March et al., 1994). An improvement of 67% was found in a sample of 14 children and adolescents treated with 16 sessions of ERP (Franklin et al., 1998). Additional findings included the maintenance of treatment gains for a short follow-up period, no difference between intensive ERP (18 sessions over one month) and weekly ERP (16 sessions over 4 months), and no difference in outcome between children taking SRIs and those who were medication-free.

Pharmacological Treatments

The pharmacological treatment of OCD in children and adolescents has recently been reviewed (Grados et al., 1999). Serotonin re-uptake inhibitors (SRIs) are effective treatments for OCD in adults and there are some indications that they are beneficial in childhood OCD. Although controlled research trials are again relatively scarce, there is clinical consensus regarding the effectiveness of SSRIs and a double-blind randomised controlled trial was recently conducted with 187 children and adolescents aged 6–17 years. Patients received either sertraline or placebo (March et al., 1998). The maximum dose of 200 mg/day was given for 8–12 weeks; 42% of patients receiving sertraline were 'very much' or 'much' improved, compared with 26% of patients receiving placebo, but the average sertraline-treated patient remained in the mildly ill range on the CY-BOCS at the end of treatment. Age did not predict response to treatment.

Other studies suggest that clomipramine is superior to placebo (DeVeaugh-Geiss et al., 1992) but children remain symptomatic and relapse is likely to follow discontinuation (Leonard et al., 1993). Fluoxetine has also shown benefit in one controlled trial (Riddle et al., 1992) and there is some indication that paroxetine may be efficacious (Rosenberg et al., 1999). Of relevance, a recent double-blind, placebo-controlled study that added a low dose of risperidone to SSRIs in 36 adult patients with OCD who had not responded to SSRIs alone, found that half of the patients had a reduction in their symptoms (McDougle et al., 2000). Although an open-label case series of seven patients found that the combination of CMI and SSRI was more effective compared to either one alone, five of the patients developed side effects, the most common of which were cardiovascular (Figueroa et al., 1998). Of note, there have been some case reports of SSRI-induced mania in children and adolescents with OCD (Diler & Avci, 1999; Grubbs, 1997; Heimann & March, 1996; Kat, 1996).

Comparison of Behavioural and Pharmacological Treatments

Behavioural therapy (BT) has been compared with clomipramine in one controlled trial in childhood OCD (de Haan et al., 1998). In this pilot study, 22 children aged 8–18 years were randomly assigned to BT (ERP) or clomipramine for 12 weeks. In the BT condition, the mean improvement was 60% on the CY-BOCS, compared with improvement of 33% in the clomipramine condition. This study is particularly important, since both medication and BT (or CBT) are often used conjointly in clinical practice (Williams & Allsopp, 1999). Such a research design warrants replication and extension in order to address questions such as how combination treatment (BT + medication) compares to either one alone.

Research investigating how psychological treatments affect the neuropsychiatric mechanisms that are hypothesised to maintain the disorder is also of interest. Initial studies on adults reveal interesting interactions that indicate that psychological interventions can impact on neuropsychiatric functioning (Schwartz et al., 1996), and potential predictors of response to BT vs. medication have been suggested (Brody et al., 1998). However, other studies have failed to find similar interactions (Bolton et al., 2000), with a recent study of 11 children with OCD reporting no change in thalamic volume after an effective intervention of CBT (Rosenberg et al., 2000a).

CONCLUSIONS AND FUTURE DIRECTIONS

In conclusion, the phenomenology of OCD in children and adolescents has been well described and is similar to the phenomenology in adults (see further, Chapter 2). Developmental issues can be related to this phenomenology, but their role remains unclear at this stage. The strong continuity between childhood and adult OCD indicates that such issues are important and need addressing. Another important research issue is the wide range of prevalence rates reported for OCD in adults and young people, leading to confusion about the true prevalence of the disorder. Part of our ignorance may stem from the confusion between OCD and other disorders, such as tics, and the strong association between OCD and anxiety disorders in children and adolescents. This confusion highlights the critical importance of diagnostic precision (McDougle et al., 1999).

There is currently a peculiar desynchrony between cognitive-behavioural theories and treatment of OCD in children and adolescents. The cognitive-behavioural theories that have been most elaborated and supported empirically in adults (Salkovskis et al., 1998b) are not those that have been used to develop the most widely used cognitive-behavioural treatment for the disorder (March & Mulle, 1998). The theoretical basis for CBT in children and adolescents is neurobehavioural. There are several neurological theories that are not incompatible with behavioural ones, but further work is required to integrate them. An increased cohesion between the science and practice of treating childhood OCD will ensure that our patients receive interventions that are both theoretically and therapeutically sound.

Chapter 19

THE MANAGEMENT OF TREATMENT-RESISTANT CASES AND OTHER DIFFICULT CLIENTS

Michael Bruch and Antonio Prioglio

GENERAL ISSUES ON RESISTANCE IN TREATMENT

Resistant cases or difficult clients are issues that were rarely discussed amongst traditional behavioural therapists until interest grew in complex psychiatric cases, often involving both Axis I and II according to DSM classification (APA, 1994). The concept of 'resistance' was traditionally used in psychoanalytic circles to describe personality characteristics and attitudes of a client, rather than aspects of the therapeutic process. Behavioural and cognitive therapists, on the other hand, were more concerned to identify and define problem behaviours that may arise within the therapeutic context. Obviously, this could also involve therapist behaviour.

Turkat & Meyer (1982) have suggested that 'resistance is client behaviour that the therapist labels antitherapeutic' (p. 158) in any given context performed by individuals and evaluated by the therapist subsequently. Clearly, sources of resistant behaviours may be varied, depending on individual circumstances in the therapeutic process, and it is probably futile to attempt a comprehensive list. Turkat & Meyer (1982) have illustrated this with nine specific examples, referring to *reinforcement* and *punishment conditions, avoidance situations, modification methodology, skill deficit, therapeutic relationship, goal discrepancy, client misconceptions, client manipulation* and so on.

When discussing 'difficult' and 'resistant' patients it may also be useful to distinguish between cases which are not understood fully, and individuals who do not adhere to therapeutic recommendations. Accordingly, different strategies may apply to rectify each distinct problem. These issues are

Obsessive-Compulsive Disorder: Theory, Research and Treatment.
Edited by Ross G. Menzies and Padmal de Silva. © 2003 John Wiley & Sons, Ltd.

unfortunately often confused by therapists, who tend to apply such labels in a generalised fashion when treatment does not progress according to expectations.

On the other hand, it may be hypothesised that both aspects are reciprocally related. For example, a problem that is incorrectly formulated is likely to lead to an inappropriate intervention hypothesis and, ultimately, to a treatment programme which either cannot address the main concerns of the patient or is not fully understood and is thus rejected. In any event, from the cognitive-behavioural point of view, it does not appear constructive, or even ethical, to attempt to locate the reasons for resistance or other difficult behaviours predominantly in the personality of the client, as is typically done in psychodynamic approaches.

In view of a broad range of potential difficulties, it seems appropriate to identify and define such behaviours in order to facilitate assessment and treatment according to cognitive-behavioural principles. In other words, the same rules of assessment and conceptualisation as for presenting complaints need to be employed if one wants to understand resistant and difficult behaviours fully. This is illustrated in more detail below, with the case formulation approach for complex and difficult cases.

DIFFICULT AND RESISTANT BEHAVIOURS IN OCD

If one scans the recent literature on OCD, one could be forgiven for believing that once patients understand and accept the rationale of treatment they will be willing and able to commit themselves accordingly (e.g. Salkovskis, 1999). Although success rates of up to 75% have been reported for exposure/response prevention (ERP) treatments (e.g. Salkovskis & Kirk, 1997), most of these cases can only be described as much improved or improved. Our clinical experience suggests that 'complete cures' are much less in evidence and often difficult to sustain. Even successfully treated cases often require long-term follow-up arrangements, including intensive 'booster sessions' from time to time. Therefore it seems hardly surprising that combined drop-out and refusal rates have been estimated at a substantial 50% (e.g. Salkovskis & Kirk, 1997). In view of this, it is astonishing that little can be found in the literature on the issue of difficult and non-compliant patients and how to deal with them in therapy. A notable exception is a recent chapter by Salkovskis et al. (1998b), which attempts to address some of the issues involved.

Can a case be made for resistant or other difficult behaviours relating specifically to OCD? Are there any unique features with OCD clients other than the typical characteristics the clinician is likely to encounter with other anxiety-based problems?

It appears that no differences in principle have been detected; however, the sometimes unique or even bizarre features of OCD may point to some additional features. Clinical observation suggests that OCD sufferers tend to engage in elaborate avoidance strategies, may refuse to engage in confrontational techniques like exposure treatment, and suffer from high levels of chronic anxiety, usually associated with low motivation and doubts about the effectiveness of treatment.

Meyer (1966) has provided a fitting illustration of a difficult case that could be related to inappropriate treatment management. This patient was referred to behavioural therapy after a succession of failed treatments involving ECT, lobotomy and long-term psychoanalytic treatment. The main complaints were intruding blasphemous thoughts eliciting guilt and anxiety. Treatments previously offered were either ineffective or led to further deterioration of symptoms, e.g. after 11 years of psychoanalysis:

> ...not only the intruding sex words and thoughts about the Holy Ghost evoked ritualistic behaviour, but also any activity with sexual meaning, e.g. shutting drawers, putting in plugs, cleaning a pipe, wiping tall receptacles, putting on stockings, eating oblong objects, doing things four times (association with four-letter Anglo-Saxon words), stepping on patterns in the shape of sex organs, entering underground trains, etc. Whenever possible she avoided these activities, e.g. stopped eating bananas and sausages, and her life became a 'misery'. For instance, it took her hours to dress or to travel short distances. She attributed this change to the psychoanalysis, since in it she learned about the extent of sexual symbolisation (p. 276).

In the light of this experience it comes as little surprise that motivation for further treatment was at a low ebb with this patient. This can be a typical attitude and some patients have pointed out that they may do better by applying their own neutralising strategies.

Generally, obsessive-compulsive patients are being judged as difficult to treat, as they often find it difficult to accept a treatment rationale suggesting confrontation with fear-evoking situations. From their point of view, this appears to be undermining their own efforts of neutralising anxiety, which are often perceived as being partially successful, at least in the short term. Furthermore, patients may feel forced to 'jump' into the unknown, which often appears a frightening and unacceptable prospect to them. After all, it has to be acknowledged that elaborate ritualistic behaviours that have developed over many years may provide some temporal relief in reducing anxiety levels, even if coping is ultimately flawed. Such attitudes and experiences may lead to arguments regarding the scope of ERP or to outright refusal to engage in treatment.

Pioneers of ERP such as Meyer et al. (1974) pointed to the difficulties in controlling ritualistic behaviours between sessions, and spoke of 'subjective resistance' as an important predictor in treatment. They did not elaborate on any possible causes, however. There is some evidence that a higher proportion of OCD patients refuse exposure treatment as compared to other anxiety disorders. About 10–20% are not likely to engage in ERP (Salkovskis & Kirk, 1997). At this point in time it is only possible to speculate on possible causes, which may feature inability to tolerate anxiety, inability to anticipate long-term reinforcement regarding treatment outcome, rigidity of thinking that does not allow more flexible ways of adjustment, and finally various forms of secondary gains available to the patient.

In addition, complex long-standing OCD sufferers have often developed maladaptive schemata, which tend to interfere with adaptive self-regulation processes. This is usually manifested in pervasive negative thinking, low self-esteem and related depression and social isolation (Bruch, 1988).

CLINICAL FEATURES WITH DIFFICULT CLIENTS

Lack of Motivation for Treatment

Motivational problems are often associated with an unwillingness to face high levels of anxiety, especially when the outcome is perceived as uncertain. It appears typical for many OCD patients to be oversensitive to anxiety arousal, which in turn affects their motivation adversely. Needless to say, however, strong motivation is required for most individuals to engage in ERP programmes involving high levels of anxiety.

Some patients, especially those who have committed themselves to treatment as a result of external pressures (e.g. a complaining partner), have been observed to develop subtle avoidance strategies (both overt or covert). This can be difficult to detect by the inexperienced therapist. Such tendencies are more typical for the smaller proportion of OCD sufferers who accept their overvalued ideas (e.g. irrational fears) and do not resist ritualistic urges, etc. A good example of this would be cognitive avoidance in an exposure situation, where the patient does not attend to the threatening stimulus. Instead, he may 'switch off' and follow instructions in a passive, disengaged manner. As a result, emotional processing of the therapeutic experience is impaired, thus not allowing habituation to occur.

On an overt level, patients with washing rituals may substitute their hand washing with application of lotion or brushing, etc. In many cases such variations are not immediately recognised as ritualistic behaviours by the patient, let alone by the therapist.

Once patients come to believe that there may be real substance in their fear (e.g. alarmist public debate about AIDS), they may reject any kind of treatment designed to involve perceived risks (e.g. touching a condom).

In summary, the worst-case scenario for lack of motivation would involve low interference of OCD symptoms with general life-style, low tolerance regarding increased anxiety levels (as in ERP), and the expectation that fundamental change is doubtful by therapeutic means.

Unfortunately, all aspects affecting motivation discussed above have the potential to promote vicious cycles, thus undermining treatment motivation even further.

Lack of Understanding of the Treatment Rationale

The treatment of choice for most OCD problems, i.e. ERP, is not immediately plausible and acceptable to all patients. It has frequently been pointed out that this procedure is associated with high drop-out rates or outright refusal to engage in treatment (e.g. Foa et al., 1998a).

Patients who find it difficult to adhere to treatment and who also tend to maintain a safety-seeking attitude often lack proper understanding of the proposed treatment procedure and the underlying rationale. This can be especially true for exposure treatments involving 'overlearning' tasks (e.g. complete prevention of all washing for a limited time). On the face of it, patients may have little confidence in the efficacy of such a procedure, which appears in strong contrast to their acquired neutralising strategies.

Personal Characteristics of the Patient

Anecdotal evidence suggests that certain behavioural tendencies may, at least in part, predispose to the onset of OCD and may also promote non-adherence to treatment or relapse. Typical features have been described as *perfectionism, avoidance of risk, tendency to feel guilty,* and *fear of making mistakes.* Some of these features may point to co-morbidity with *obsessive-compulsive personality disorder* (OCPD).

More specifically, as Rachman & Shafran (1998) have pointed out, selective attention involving frequent scanning of threatening material, loss of confidence in memory and inflated responsibility may all lead to increased resistance in treatment.

SOURCES ASSOCIATED WITH DIFFICULT AND RESISTANT BEHAVIOURS

Difficulties in Assessing the Problem

This refers especially to covert cognitive operations. For example, patients may not be aware of their cognitions and may require special awareness training to achieve this (e.g. behavioural experiments; see below). Otherwise they may not be cooperative in disclosing the nature of intrusive or ritualistic thoughts, due to shame or guilt regarding (intimate or unacceptable) content or feared consequences. For example, an inhibited man developed aggressive and blasphemous intrusions directed at his wife after she had an affair. Feeling embarrassed and fearing that his wife may either punish or leave him, he was unable to disclose the content of his intrusions.

Some other features of OCD behaviours may interfere with the assessment process. For example, patients may not want to disclose obsessional cognitions, as they fear that these may trigger OCD sequences. Other aspects include slowness, indecisiveness, as well as checking and reassurance-seeking manoeuvres. For these reasons it is often not appropriate to employ self-report measures, at least not in an unsupervised form.

Lack of Appropriate Formulation of Problems

A treatment approach focusing solely on neutralising behaviours may not fully address the relation to underlying anxiety. The result of this can be a return of fear or emergence of 'new' responses relating to the same stimulus. In the event, this will have demoralising effects on most patients, who may feel confirmed in their original doubts and worries about the effectiveness of CBT.

Inadequate Therapeutic Relationship

OCD patients suffering from their disorder for a long time can be quite ambivalent or confused about entering a therapeutic relationship. There are often substantial interpersonal problems (related to social avoidance) that make it difficult for many clients to develop trust in the therapist who may encourage confrontation of fears. Their suffering may suggest to them that something needs to be done, but there may be little confidence that something *can* be done.

Often there is great need for emotional support, which may lead to over-reliance and dependence on the therapist. In addition there may be strong urges to seek reassurance in the therapeutic relationship. Such dependencies are likely to prevent self-initiative behaviours, which can be considered as a strong predictor for successful ERP as well as enhancement and maintenance of treatment gains. For example, there is some evidence that self-exposure is more successful than therapist-aided ERP (Steketee and White, 1990).

It is clear, though, that against a background of ambivalent treatment motivation and lack of clarity regarding the treatment rationale, the development of a constructive therapeutic relationship may be crucial, albeit difficult to achieve.

Problems with Environmental Support

It can be considered a bad start when OCD sufferers are coerced into treatment by their partners or other members of the family. In rare circumstances this may also involve employers or even friends. At times patients may feel so desperate about their problems that they are willing to follow any advice, at least initially. However, clinical experience suggests that such extrinsically motivated commitment is hardly a good basis for a constructive therapeutic alliance. Such patients tend to look mainly for support and appear to be less interested in changing their maladaptive behaviours. Typically, they may make pretensions that can be withdrawn at any time, thus undermining any treatment process.

During the course of treatment it is often difficult to assess whether family members ought to get involved and, if so, what form this should take. Clinical evidence suggests that inappropriate support can be more detrimental to the therapeutic effort than no support at all. This is because individuals close to the OCD patient may have developed emotionally strained relations with him/her, and this may jeopardise a constructive and supportive attitude, as suggested by the therapist (see case 1 below). The worst-case scenario can occur if 'old scores' are being settled (i.e. in an acrimonious marital relationship).

Complications Caused by Coexisting Problems

OCD patients tend to have a complex pattern of co-morbidity indicating high levels of suffering. For example, a recent study, using DSM-IV criteria, reports that 29% of patients with a principal OCD diagnosis met criteria for one additional diagnosis, 17% for two additional diagnoses and 18% for three or more diagnoses (Antony et al., 1998a).

According to our clinical data, typical co-morbid problems may involve depression (estimates of up to 50% of all cases), social anxiety/phobia, panic, agoraphobia, maladaptive schemata involving low self-esteem and lack of confidence, marital and family problems, and also alcohol and substance abuse. Such additional problems are likely to promote feelings of hopelessness and helplessness with the patient and will make it difficult for him/her to achieve an appropriate focus in therapy. For example, patients suffering from social phobia may not be able to participate in exposure tasks involving social situations. Generally, clinical experience provides evidence that additional problems interact with OCD symptoms in a reciprocal fashion.

Such complications may be exacerbated by a 'rigid' therapist who may focus exclusively on OCD symptoms, thus overlooking complex co-morbidity and the effect that this may have on the patient. It is questionable whether OCD treatment should proceed in the presence of severe co-morbidity involving psychotic and/or personality disorders.

These sources of resistant and difficult behaviours are listed separately for conceptual reasons. In the clinical reality they are often related to one another, frequently leading to enhancing interactions. In the following section we shall consider suitable management strategies for the problems identified above.

MANAGEMENT STRATEGIES

General Issues

As with most complex and difficult clients, it appears paramount to provide a positive context for the therapeutic process. To facilitate this, the following aspects need to be checked and further explored. As we shall point out later on, the case formulation approach may then be employed to analyse and modify behaviours with an 'antitherapeutic' potential. This should be carried out in preparation for the main therapeutic procedure to follow.

Ideally, the patient who approaches the therapist for help should do so at his/her own volition, as opposed to being coerced by other professionals and/or his/her own social contacts, involving partners, family members, friends and so on. As this type of information is usually not offered in the initial interview, the therapist may want to explore this further. Clearly, the therapist needs to satisfy him/herself that it is the *patient* who is looking for help.

Furthermore, it is important to hear from the patient what his/her concerns are and in what way he/she may want to modify his/her behaviour and/or environment. For example, individuals just seeking non-specific immediate support without long-term objectives may need more encouragement and understanding of the treatment rationale before becoming involved in a sustained therapeutic effort.

Next, it has to be established whether the patient is capable of communicating his/her problems to the therapist and whether he/she possesses appropriate interpersonal skills to develop his/her part of the therapeutic relationship, and if any additional training might be necessary.

Finally, it needs to be explored whether the therapist is perceived as a credible professional and whether the rationale of treatment is sufficiently clear and acceptable to the patient. It is advisable to allow ample time to deal with these issues.

THE CASE FORMULATION APPROACH

In view of the rather complex causes for resistant and difficult behaviours, it becomes clear why standardised technical procedures aiming solely at symptomatic complaints are unlikely to be acceptable to confused and disturbed patients. It is therefore recommended to use a procedure specifically designed for complex cases, referred to as the *case formulation approach* (CF; e.g. Bruch & Bond, 1998). CF is a five-step procedure allowing ideographic assessment of the problem, aiming to achieve a comprehensive *problem formulation.*

CF was originally pioneered by Shapiro (1957) and Meyer (1957) as a clinical–experimental procedure in the psychiatric setting. CF is about developing an individualised 'clinical theory' of the problem under investigation. This should furnish answers to basic questions such as: what are the problems this patient is experiencing?; why have these developed and persisted?; what factors can produce change?; what is the patient's attitude towards his/her problem?; and so on.

CF follows the principles of experimental psychology using the knowledge of cognitive-behavioural principles. Thus, to obtain relevant information, hypotheses of cause are to be generated and subsequently tested in the interview process. Turkat & Maisto (1985) have proposed case formulation as a 'scientific approach to the clinical case'. They emphasise both process and outcome, the former referring to the experimental method requiring hypothesis generation and testing; the latter producing a method to modify the problem behaviour under investigation. This dual aspect approach seems important, as it emphasises the practical implications of a problem formulation, unlike psychiatric diagnosis, which has rather limited relevance in guiding the individual therapeutic process.

In this approach, the initial interview is of pre-eminent importance as one sets out to achieve a plausible framework, the problem formulation, to account for the behaviour in question in terms of its causal history and maintaining factors. This is also expected to enable us to make predictions about specified problem behaviours, thus guiding the design of treatment interventions.

In general, CF is based on the assumption of *individual differences* in problem behaviours. On the level of *psychiatric diagnosis*, presenting complaints might appear identical; however, an ideographic analysis usually reveals differences regarding historical development as well as in response systems, suggesting great variability regarding the cognitive-behavioural mechanism of disorders. Often one can detect complex interactions between presenting complaints and earlier learnt maladaptive behaviours. For example, the underlying mechanism of a social phobia may be understood in terms of lack of social skills or fear of negative evaluation; each would recommend different treatment priorities as well as strategies.

The building of a case formulation is an open and collaborative effort which ought to be fully discussed and explained to the patient. This would also involve outline of an intervention hypothesis and possible treatment options. Such extensive procedures appear justified, as important decisions and interventions are to be made that involve long-term consequences for the patient. Furthermore, an adequate case formulation will be crucial for building motivation and providing insight into the problem for the patient.

The need for an individual formulation of problems for OCD sufferers (Salkovskis et al., 1998b) has been stated elsewhere; however, no clear and specific guidelines were offered as to how this could be achieved in operationalised detail. In our view, it is indispensable to follow the experimental approach in order to be able to identify individual complications involved with difficult clients.

A comprehensive CF may also be instrumental in establishing the beginnings of a constructive therapeutic relationship, by facilitating guidelines regarding the structure of this relationship in consideration of the patient's personality and the nature of the problem (see also AuBuchon & Malatesta, 1998). For example, this allows a decision about whether the therapist should adopt a more supportive role initially or encourage independent, self-controlled behaviour strategies. Furthermore, it is recommended that the therapist's role should be continuously monitored and adjusted to suit the therapeutic process.

We have found that CF is also extremely useful for the understanding and management of resistant and difficult patients, who may have suffered for long periods and may have had a history of failed treatment attempts, leaving them feeling disillusioned. This is often the case when OCD symptoms are treated in an isolated fashion.

In sum, CF aims to achieve a comprehensive understanding of the presenting complaint in terms of aetiology and maintenance. Overall, case formulation encourages innovative and creative psychotherapeutic practice.

It is expected that seemingly similar symptoms will show great ideographic variations, with major implications for respective treatment strategies. In addition, both attitude and motivation of the patient in the therapeutic process will be considered as important moderating variables.

The present format does not allow a comprehensive account of this five-step model. This can be found elsewhere (e.g. Bruch & Bond, 1998).

IDENTIFYING TARGETS WITH DIFFICULT CLIENTS

A comprehensive case formulation should enable us to identify all relevant problems and how they may be related. In the case of difficult and resistant attitudes, we would expect to be able to understand the scope and reasons underpinning such behaviours and may subsequently be able to define targets for intervention. This should not be attempted in isolation and must be guided by the formulation, e.g. resistant behaviours arising in the context of anticipatory anxiety ought to be treated differently from apparently similar behaviours relating to overvalued ideas.

In the remainder of this section we will discuss briefly ideas for management of some of the most common aspects, as introduced earlier. Obviously, this list cannot be exhaustive and ought not be treated as a cookbook. An ideographic, formulation-based approach should always prevail.

Focus on Assessment

As discussed earlier, narrowly focused interviewing may lead to inadequate conclusions and could become major cause for resistant behaviours. For example, anxiety-related cognitions like worry can easily be confused with obsessional ruminations. However, incorrect evidence can also be generated by the patient; for example, there may be discrepancies between verbal reports and observable behaviours in naturalistic settings. This can be due to either an inability to describe problem behaviours or even to attempts to deliberately mislead the therapist. Behavioural tests and experiments should always be employed to confirm verbal reports, especially if inconsistencies are in evidence. Usually this should involve assessments and observations in the home environment or other relevant locations.

Any lack of clarity or ambivalence about treatment goals is also likely to surface during the initial interview. According to the CF philosophy, it is good practice to facilitate the initiative of patients to express their 'ideal' goals, even if these appear unrealistic to start with. As the assessment progresses, and especially when discussing the case formulation, the treatment goals should be revisited and modified if necessary, employing Socratic techniques. This approach avoids confrontation and is more likely to develop a shared concern promoting a realistic outlook of the patient. Under no circumstances should treatment goals be imposed by the therapist.

Focus on Rationale of Treatment

Most difficult and resistant clients have strong doubts that their often long-standing problems can be eliminated or substantially reduced by any form of therapy. Many of these patients may have a history of unsuccessful treatment attempts, sometimes including CBT, which may have promoted pessimistic or even cynical attitudes towards therapy. In the case of cognitive-behavioural attempts involving ERP, one often finds that the procedure was not properly explained and subsequently not adequately supervised. In our experience, perceived failure of poorly designed and executed ERP programmes can have devastating effects on patients' attitudes and expectations toward further attempts. In the worst case, this can mark a point of no return, especially when ERP has been undermined by intermittent reinforcement of the problem behaviour. For these reasons, it seems crucial to take ample time and great care to communicate with the patient all the issues involved in the therapeutic process.

To begin with, an introduction of the cognitive-behavioural 'philosophy' to the patient should instil the belief that change is possible, but that it may require sustained efforts. It needs to be stressed that CBT is a time-limited, active therapeutic approach whereby the patient assumes increasing responsibility for carrying out tasks that have been jointly designed and explained.

In my judgement, it is crucial to give an honest account, especially of the ERP procedure, which usually involves high levels of anxiety to facilitate the habituation process. Treated patients have aptly described this process as 'going through hell' or 'blood, sweat and tears'. Great skill and perseverance on behalf of the therapist is often required to initiate appropriate motivation.

Next, any conclusions reached in the problem formulation should be fully discussed and it ought to be checked that the patient has a full grasp of this. Again, Socratic dialogue techniques may enhance this process. Any treatment options involving all the pros and cons should be fully considered so that the patient's preferences can be established. Finally, the application of clinical experiments, e.g. to confirm the formulation or to demonstrate the ERP procedure, may also be useful to introduce treatment procedures to the patient.

ERP sessions should be planned and operationalised in great detail and a written protocol may be handed to the patient. All discussions about objectives, i.e. stimulus situation, length, mode of application, etc., should take place *before* any session and it should be checked with the patient that everything is being understood and agreed. It needs to be pointed out to the patient that any further clarifications (e.g. reassurance seeking), especially after commencement of ERP, are counterproductive according to the treatment rationale. With some clients, mainly those who appear to have difficulties with honouring verbal agreements, a formal written contract may be envisaged, detailing all task requirements in an operationalised format. This should be signed by all parties concerned. Therapists should also be warned to stand firm when patients are about to undermine any of these agreements. This is more likely to happen with patients who tend to develop anticipatory anxiety and feel unable to tolerate high levels of anxiety. To assist the patient further, taped sessions and explanatory handouts may be provided for further consideration. In addition, patients may be encouraged to compile flashcards, etc. to process and memorise all relevant information.

Despite many such efforts, it is still a possibility that patients neither understand nor accept the treatment rationale fully. This may result in partial or inconsistent involvement or outright refusal to participate. In cases of elaborate and successful avoidance, patients may not see the potential benefits of ERP.

In any such scenario we would not recommend the use of any form of coercion, however subtle, to initiate treatment. Instead, it should be put to the patient to reflect upon further, and if necessary to suspend treatment.

Focus on Relationship

Initially, with many difficult cases it may be approriate (or sometimes necessary) to provide emotional support and to act as a primary reinforcer. Avoidance of emotions and feelings (because of their painful contents) is a common feature with long-term sufferers. Emotional responses should be encouraged and patients should not feel rejected for their seemingly 'weird' ideas and actions. Sometimes a few extra sessions may be needed to build a trusting working relationship. This is time well spent, as it has been shown to enhance patients' treatment motivation greatly.

However, a strongly involved relationship bears a number of risks, thus a balanced and flexible approach (adjusting to progress in therapy) is called for. It is important that the patient is not allowed to rely and depend on the therapist exclusively. For example, it is not a good sign when patients insist on very gradual and small step exposure with the therapist being present at all times. Such 'safe' procedures often do not involve active participation and processing on part of the patient, who may 'cling' to the therapist and follow his/her instructions blindly. At times, the impression can be that patients' efforts are undertaken for the therapist rather than for themselves. Such gradual and safe procedures have been described as graded retraining (e.g. Meyer & Gelder, 1963). Emphasis was placed on relaxing the patient before exposure, but less on processing events. The therapist had to be present at all times. As a result, progress fluctuated considerably and treatment could require up to 140 hours with limited improvement during a 12-month follow-up period. Colluding with the patients' overvalued ideas or providing reassurance are further examples of counterproductive support in the therapeutic interaction.

Finally, how should the therapist deal with mistakes or errors of judgement, which are not uncommon with these frequently complex treatment arrangements? We would recommend openness (which should include the ability for self-criticism) in most cases and also to proceed to explain that a revision of the CF may be necessary. However, any such disclosure should not highlight confusion or even ineptness on the part of the therapist, as this may lead to a serious and sometimes irreversible loss of trust and confidence in the therapist.

In certain circumstances therapeutic relationships may also extend to family members or other individuals in the patient's environment. For example, well-balanced and constructive family support can be a great asset in the therapeutic process, especially when continuous supervision is required in prolonged ERP programmes involving the implementation of 'acceptable' behaviours. This can be a high-risk strategy, however, if the these relationships are strained already. In such cases underlying conflicts have the potential to undermine well-intended co-therapy support completely.

Dealing with Anticipatory Anxiety

How should one deal with patients who refuse to engage, or drop out of treatment prematurely, as they develop the 'fear of fear' syndrome in anticipation of ERP treatment? It appears that some individuals are unwilling or incapable of tolerating increased anxiety levels. This problem has been highlighted by many experts in the field (e.g. Foa et al., 1998a). However, so far no ideal solution to the problem has been offered. In some cases it has been found helpful to reduce anxiety levels by means of medication, or suitable relaxation procedures before and during ERP. A possible disadvantage of this could be a shift toward a perceived external locus of control in the habituation process, which could hinder the processing of self-efficacy during and after exposure.

An excessive need for reassurance is probably related to the inability to tolerate anxiety. This is typically found in difficult and resistant clients. For the therapist, it is most important to remain extremely vigilant, as reassurance seeking can take many different (and subtle) forms that are not always easily detected.

In this context we have also found it helpful to encourage risk-taking attitudes that can be introduced in the form of behavioural experiments. This enables the patient to explore new behaviours and test reality regarding inappropriate expectations and feared consequences.

Failure to Habituate

Adaptive processing during ERP may also be affected when individuals are not attending to fearful stimuli in exposure situations, or engage in mental rituals that may interfere with the habituation process.

In the first case, the therapist ought to check with the patient once more that the ERP rationale and procedure are fully understood. Socratic dialogue techniques may be used for this. For example, we have found it helpful to ask the patient to write an essay about the underlying treatment rationale and his/her tasks during ERP, which can be used for further discussion.

Otherwise, the process may be closely monitored to detect 'anti-therapeutic' behaviours. This may be assisted by asking patients to verbalise their cognitions as well as their anxiety levels before, during and after the event. In particular, patients should be encouraged to focus their cognitions on the exposure situation exclusively.

Often overlooked is the fact that processing and attribution of such coping events may require active guidance. For example, the therapist may prompt patients to reflect upon the activities and experiences, highlighting their thoughts and feelings in particular. They may also be asked to keep a diary of adaptive processing leading to habituation, which should be consulted on a regular basis. It can also be useful to devise flashcards on such topics, which may be used at times when the patient finds it difficult to access positive information about exposure experiences. Obviously, enhanced processing of this kind is likely to strengthen self-efficacy and so promote future coping.

Emergence of New Fears

This is more likely to occur when patients do not disclose the full range of their problems in the initial assessment. Another reason can be limits imposed by patients, especially anxious ones, on the scope of ERP. This may take the form of excluding the higher items on any hierarchy or the attempt to exclude additional problem areas. We have often found that untreated fears, which may not be viewed as important at the time of treatment (e.g. 'we do not need to tackle this now, I am able to do this later by myself'), may later become the nucleus for incubation of new or related fears. Needless to say, the return of fear is rather more likely with individuals who have a history of extensive stimulus generalisation regarding their problems, which can make it an uphill task when trying to discover all relevant triggers.

For all these reasons, we consider it paramount to search with the patient through any suspected areas thoroughly and to explain the necessity of identifying all OCD-related fears. Furthermore, wherever possible, a phase of 'over-learning' (e.g. not to wash at all for a certain period) may be introduced. This usually helps to develop extra confidence and self-efficacy. Patients who are not cooperative with such ideas may reasonably be suspected of being ambivalent about the ERP process.

Complications Arising from Co-morbidity

The presence of other symptomatic complaints and their relationships with OCD are not always easily understood and can resemble the 'chicken and egg' debate. A comprehensive CF is a suitable method to identify the main problem and to develop hypotheses about how this may be related to other presenting complaints. Obviously, the main problem should always receive the principal focus in therapy initially. A possible exception may be considered when strong interference by secondary problems is present (e.g. generalised anxiety may be treated before exposure, by medication or anxiety management).

Salkovskis et al. (1998b) have pointed out that the link with psychosis and OCPDs may be considered as special cases. Psychotic thinking can be easily confused with obsessional thinking, due to the often bizarre and intrusive nature of some thoughts, although genuine co-morbidity is also a possibility. This requires careful investigation. OCPD, on the other hand, may be considered as a predisposing and maintaining factor and should thus be addressed in any relapse prevention programme.

Generally, one finds that successful treatment of OCD symptoms will usually have beneficial effects for related complaints, especially depression and low self-esteem, which are most likely to improve through correct processing and evaluation of perceived achievements in deficient areas (Bruch, 1988). It has to be stressed, however, that most treatment decisions involving co-morbidity are of a hypothetical nature and need to be verified during the ongoing therapeutic process.

Schedule of Treatment Sessions

The way any programme is enacted should also be guided by the problem formulation. We do not believe in standard procedures on a weekly basis, unless there is a good reason for doing so. The following issues ought to be considered carefully. First, if ERP is the treatment of choice, the location of sessions needs to be determined. These will be situations where responsibility issues, urges and ritualistic behaviours are foremost. For example, it has frequently been observed that patients who were taken into a ward setting (safe environment) would not experience any urges, even when exposed to previously feared stimuli.

Second, the frequency and duration of ERP sessions must be experimentally guided, i.e. by clinical experiments as suggested by the formulation. Ideally, patients benefit from prolonged sessions, frequently applied in settings where problems occur. From our point of view, it is regrettable that many clinicians appear unable or unwilling to provide such a service. At a later stage, when self-controlled applications are being introduced, the emphasis may shift to frequent monitoring of this process, e.g. we recommend asking patients to provide frequent feedback on their efforts, which would normally take the form of short telephone calls, if necessary several times a day. This would also serve the purpose of detecting emerging difficulties and assist in the adaptive processing of therapeutic experiences.

Third, the extent of active involvement by the patient needs to be determined. It is clearly not possible for all patients to apply ERP in a self-controlled fashion from the beginning of treatment. Many would need fairly close supervision and perhaps some prompting to begin with. If things progress well, self-control methods may be introduced as soon as possible; however, this should be carefully monitored and guided (see above).

In general, clinical experience clearly points to the usefulness of prolonged exposure in naturalistic settings. Supervision and guidance should be adjusted to the patient's capabilities and progress. It is good practice to encourage patients to explore their problems further (especially when stimulus generalisation is happening) and to apply ERP wherever possible, seeking assistance where necessary.

CONCLUSIONS

Despite converging evidence for highly effective ERP treatments for OCD, the fact remains that a sizeable proportion of sufferers will be too confused or fearful to fully commit themselves to this type of treatment. The reasons for this ought to be further investigated. So far, anecdotal evidence arising from naturalistic settings points to a variety of factors. For these reasons a careful, individualised case formulation should always precede the selection and implementation of treatment procedures. Foa et al. (1998a) are correct in pointing out that, despite an abundance of treatment manuals, access to qualified CBT specialists remains limited. Furthermore, they suggest that apart from an insufficient number of experts, there is growing pressure to rationalise services as demand outstrips provision. This often gives rise to short-term, standardised or group-based treatments. From our perspective, neither option seems appropriate for the more difficult or ambivalent client.

Another concern relates to the growing fashion to rely upon standardised assessment procedures. It appears that this is mainly motivated by research interests and less so by clinical concerns (unfortunately, clinicians seldom write books). For example, in a recent and highly acclaimed textbook, the chapter on assessment (Taylor, 1998) dedicates only about one page to clinical considerations and procedural problems. This is somewhat astonishing, given the complex attitudes of many OCD patients towards their problems. At our unit, we believe that a skilful individualised assessment and formulation is required to address such difficulties appropriately. In our view, structured interviews, checklists and questionnaires are not very helpful in this process. Such tools, however, may rather be used to develop hypotheses, confirm the formulation and establish baselines and measures of change.

Furthermore, the current focus and enthusiasm on the cognitive model of OCD, as promoted by Salkovskis and his group (see Chapter 4), requires some comment. In clinical supervision, when discussing intractable clients, one commonly encounters questions like, 'Would it be useful to try the cognitive model?' (seemingly suggesting that this could be a panacea for all possible difficulties in OCD). Our clinical evidence suggests that highly anxious and resistant patients often find it more difficult to concentrate and focus on primarily cognitive work, not to mention the pitfalls of thought–action fusion. It is often problematic to draw a clear distinction between cognitive work and subtle ways of seeking reassurance. Overall, it seems appropriate to take guidance from Bandura's well-established self-efficacy model (Bandura, 1977), which clearly points to the superiority of performance accomplishments as a source for the building of adaptive cognitive structures. It seems to us that cognitive-behavioural approaches are more effective and successful because of the synergistic enhancement of cognition and behaviour. As always, this requires comprehensive assessment and proper timing of these two aspects in the therapeutic process. No doubt, this is a marriage that should never be divorced!

To date, conclusive evidence about the efficacy of the cognitive approach is still evasive in comparison to well-established ERP procedures. Even combination treatments do not appear to fare better than classic ERP (e.g. Stanley & Averill, 1998), i.e. an enhancement effect appears questionable. In our view, cognitive techniques may be most suitable for enhancement and maximisation of treatment gains, i.e. facilitating the process of self-regulation. At this stage it is premature to pass a final judgement on cognitive approaches until further evidence becomes available. In passing, it seems noteworthy that most scientists involved with the cognitive model would nevertheless apply behavioural experiments to disconfirm feared consequences (e.g. Salkovskis, 1999).

Finally, in discussing sources and features of resistant and difficult behaviours, we would like to stress that the above-listed aspects were addressed separately for reasons of conceptual clarity. Obviously, in the 'clinical reality' one finds that these features are often reciprocally interwoven and should not be considered in isolation. This situation can make it difficult to decide which problems to address and in which order. Again, we believe a comprehensive case formulation will enable us to set priorities appropriately and tackle problems accordingly. On the other hand, resistant and difficult clients who may still not be ready for treatment and may also have developed successful avoidance strategies should not be pushed into treatment under any circumstances. In the following section I shall present two case examples to illustrate difficulties with motivation, high anxiety and the therapeutic relationship.

Case 1: Difficulties with Motivation/Compliance Relating to Low Anxiety Tolerance

Kevin (a pseudonym) is a 32-year-old teacher who has been suffering from OCD for more than 7 years. The problems had started after a former girlfriend was diagnosed as being HIV-positive. At first Kevin was able to reassure himself (that he had not contracted AIDS) by arranging regular tests. However, gradually doubts were 'creeping in' after he had heard about the unreliability of such tests.

The problem soon generalised regarding potential triggers for his fears: traces of real or imagined blood, condoms (either real ones or materials of a similar nature), plastic bits and wrappings, perceived or imagined bandages, body fluids or excrements, and so on. When he was referred for treatment, Kevin was suffering from frequent intrusions regarding possible dangers and consequences of contracting AIDS. These intrusions would make him extremely anxious and his preferred method of neutralising such fears involved frequent and often prolonged showering, which followed a ritualistic pattern. Another strategy, mainly applied with ambiguous objects, would focus on reassuring himself, or seeking reassurance, that the perceived items were harmless. For example, if in doubt he would stand in front of an ambiguous object for long periods trying to identify the object in question. Frequently, this process was not successful and Kevin had to engage in washing rituals.

As neutralising behaviours became increasingly tiring and prolonged, often with little effect (necessitating repetition), Kevin eventually resorted to phobic avoidance and spent most of the time in his room in the family home. Finally he stopped working and even reduced contacts with his girlfriend to a minimum by using the telephone.

Kevin is an intellectually very able person who had embarked on an outstanding academic career which was already evidenced by numerous achievements and prizes. In terms of a formulation, Kevin can be described as an oversensitive and over-responsible person who is hypervigilant regarding perceived environmental hazards with the potential of causing AIDS. Further, it can be hypothesised that this sensitivity is likely to make Kevin more vulnerable to threatening stimuli, thus creating fearful scenarios of possible environmental dangers.

Although Kevin understood the rationale of the treatment very well and had read many books on the subject, he kept pointing out that he felt that he could not face up to the anxiety triggered by AIDS fears, as he found high levels of anxiety intolerable. Despite such uncertainties about his motivation, supervised exposure and response prevention was planned and attempted. However, in the event Kevin would frequently disengage, employing a variety of avoidance strategies. Furthermore, none of these partial achievements could ever be sustained thereafter by self-administered exposure designed as homework between supervised treatments.

Typically, after an intensive supervised treatment phase the patient would be able to maintain progress initially for some weeks (with a tendency to shorten over time) and would then require another intensive supervised period, etc. Also, hypervigilance associated with anticipatory anxiety would promote extensive stimulus generalisation, thus creating related or completely new fears. After several trials treatment became increasingly less effective. At the same time it became clear that Kevin's already weak motivation and belief in the rationale of treatment deteriorated further. In addition, despite a detailed and agreed treatment contract, the patient became increasingly argumentative and avoidant regarding his exposure tasks. He also started to develop reassurance-seeking strategies, which were difficult to detect and slowed or completely undermined exposure exercises.

Another aspect of Kevin's problem behaviours involved 'controlling' his family. He managed to make all family members comply with his ritualistic urges (e.g. priority use of the bathroom and kitchen, keeping all doors shut, controlling the family's whereabouts, etc.). At a later stage he would frequently seek reassurance regarding fearful objects. Despite a therapeutic contract and detailed instructions as discussed with the therapist, family members increasingly complied with Kevin's demands. In turn, this caused great frustration and resentment by the whole family, who felt prevented from living in their house normally. It is easy to see how this turned into a vicious cycle of negative communication with extremely disruptive consequences for the therapeutic process.

Subsequent re-assessment and re-formulation of Kevin's problems highlighted two aspects:

1. Extremely low tolerance of high levels of anxiety, especially in anticipation of events. This was seen to be based on the fact that Kevin's baseline arousal level already appeared elevated, which can be expected to facilitate a steep increase, a long plateau phase and a slow return to baseline levels (Lader & Wing, 1966; Eckman & Shean, 1997). Resultant avoidance behaviour and refusal to engage in exposure fully would clearly impact on his information processing, thus inhibiting habituation to feared objects (in fact Kevin claimed, on the basis of his knowledge of the literature, that 'there must be something wrong with my processing style').

2. Family dynamics in relation to control urges of the patient proved also to be an important intervening variable. After several family conferences, it was decided that Kevin's target behaviours should be outlined in a therapeutic contract, especially as there was growing interference with the needs of other family members (i.e. when spending several hours in the bathroom). Further, it was felt appropriate for his younger brother to act as a co-therapist for home-based response prevention and exposure, as Kevin appeared most at ease with him. Initially, this worked reasonably well; however, it turned out that Kevin found it increasingly difficult to accept 'orders' from his brother or any other member of the family. Partly this appeared to be anxiety-driven, but otherwise arose by a demonstration of 'superiority' at times bordering on arrogance ('I know my treatment best') toward the family. In the end relations deteriorated to such an extent that urges for ritualistic behaviours became the battleground for exerting increasing control over the family, which could involve severe temper tantrums at times. Gradually the family started losing their patience and would retaliate (e.g. angry outburst, attempts to restrict his movements). As a result, Kevin would retire to his room for days.

Despite many ups and downs, Kevin had still managed to maintain a relationship and was able to continue his job as a teacher. This provided him with some structure in his life and thus helped him to survive. However, when fears of AIDS contamination increased and extensive stimulus generalisation prevented him from leaving the house, he rapidly became unable to maintain these aspects of his life, which subsequently created strong feelings of isolation and depression.

In sum, the question arose as to why such massive deterioration occurred at this time, especially as there was plenty of evidence that treatment had worked and as Kevin had previously been able to get 'back on track' whenever setbacks occurred. Two main reasons could be identified. First, Kevin refused to engage in '100%' supervised ERP, claiming that certain aspects were not relevant or could be carried out later by himself. Although this sounded credible to start with, it soon became evident that these pledges were mainly motivated by a strategy of avoidance. It also turned out that Kevin was not able and/or willing to consolidate exposure exercises by applying self-controlled methods and would only engage if prompted repeatedly.

Second, the issue of treatment at home, originally fully supported by all family members, became some sort of competition for power and control in the home. As a consequence of fluctuations in treatment success, several members of the family became resentful about ongoing restrictions in the house. This resulted in outbursts or even bullying behaviours, thus violating previous agreements regarding co-therapy help. In turn, Kevin tended to inflame the situation further by making arrogant and derogatory statements about lack of competence and compassion from some members of the family.

As a result, all constructive treatment efforts came to a halt, which in turn created further negative feelings, creating a vicious cycle within the family relationships. As a consequence of these failings, it appeared sensible to redesign the exposure programme by shifting more responsibility on to Kevin and by encouraging him to describe his difficulties to set up supervised exposure. This was difficult initially, as Kevin was inclined to argue the ethics of certain tasks by pointing out real dangers involved.

On the positive side, Kevin's academic interest in OCD proved helpful. He had started to communicate with other OCD sufferers through the Internet and, because of his growing expertise in CBT methodology, had started to devise sophisticated programmes for some of his contacts which turned out to be very successful. This process began to focus his mind constructively upon his own problems (often reinforced by his Internet partners), thus enabling Kevin to generate cognitions to facilitate motivation and self-control for his own programme. This process was systematically encouraged and enhanced by the therapist and eventually helped shape a self-directed and sustained ERP programme.

With hindsight, we can say that the therapists overestimated the initial motivation and self-control abilities of this patient, who appeared very understanding and articulate about the CBT approach. Further, the dynamics of family relations were not all they seemed to be and served to increasingly undermine the therapeutic process. Only when these two aspects were re-analysed and considered in treatment could substantial and sustained progress become possible.

Case 2: Addressing a Problematic Therapeutic Relationship

The following case illustrates how a comprehensive CF was helpful in guiding the modification of the therapeutic style with a complex case involving a long history and several unsuccessful treatment attempts.

Ben (a pseudonym) is a 36-year-old single man with a 15-year history of severe OCD problems. These included compulsive washing due to fear of chemical substances (up to 8 hours day), compulsive checking (up to 2 hours daily) and hoarding (piles of newspapers and food leftovers), plus a wide spectrum of covert rituals, including counting, neutralising (numbers, letters, words, concepts) and 'magical' rituals (e.g. shaking one hand or gazing in specific ways). The severity of symptoms left him housebound for 7 years and completely isolated from the outside world. For these reasons, Ben had to be admitted as an inpatient twice. Therapy was terminated each time, as he was unable to achieve the set treatment targets. Subsequent private therapy was also terminated early, as he was unable to meet the treatment fees.

Ben's ritualistic behaviours can be understood as a device to reduce anxiety by postponing or avoiding important issues and decisions in his life, which he perceived as impossible to handle, involving high levels of anticipatory anxiety. Over time these ritualistic patterns had developed as a generalised response to deal with environmental stressors involving social situations. In the short term he was able to control his anxiety levels; however, in the long term this led to a significant increase in his general frustration level and lowering of self-esteem.

Ben would try to alleviate this by seeking reassurance in any social interaction. Failure to achieve this would lead to extreme social withdrawal and avoidance as well as self-blaming cognitions. The resulting high levels of anxiety would trigger ritualistic thoughts designed to undo these negative thoughts, e.g. the word 'stupid' would be countered by repeating the word 'clever' a fixed number of times. As this was time consuming, Ben would prefer to avoid any situations which had the potential to trigger these obsessions. It was specifically these behaviours that adversely affected the therapeutic relationship, as he would either continuously seek reassurance or would withdraw completely from any interaction.

Further, because of Ben's oversensitivity to pranks and bullying, it was decided not to employ a directive style in the therapeutic relationship. For example, a previous therapist had tried to convince Ben that there was no danger in handling a feared chemical substance, a strong trigger for obsessional thoughts, by unexpectedly pulling a pill out of a box and eating it in front of him. As a consequence, Ben stormed out of the room and refused to engage in further treatment. The likelihood of such reactions was confirmed by clinical experiments during assessment. This information was further endorsed by the patient's statement that in previous treatment attempts he was never given an understandable account of the nature and causes of his problems.

Instead, it was attempted to enhance treatment motivation by a cooperative–supportive style based on sharing, explaining and discussing all relevant information, especially the problem formulation. This involved going through a detailed functional analysis, response system analysis, historical development, the formulation and intervention hypothesis. This client-focused procedure proved to be a very effective motivator for subsequent treatment.

Furthermore, Ben was given a full account of the cognitive-behavioural model of OCD, to contrast his view that the 'the world is a dangerous place', including a description of the most successful treatment procedures, such as exposure, and their association with high levels of anxiety. This was important, as Ben had not benefited from previous therapies and appeared in an almost permanent state of high arousal. There was even a suspicion that these attempts may have led to further incubation of anxiety as habituation failed to occur. Against this background, which included long-standing avoidance behaviours, it was important, if difficult, to motivate Ben to engage in a treatment approach which would initially lead to a further increase in anxiety levels. On the positive side, it was detected during the initial assessment that the patient was capable of tolerating substantial discomfort (e.g. not taking a shower for months, or not eating properly for weeks). It was decided to emphasise and activate this resourcefulness during the preparation of the ERP programme.

Finally, the patient appeared to have a full grasp of the treatment rationale and was willing to engage in an individually designed ERP programme.

It is clear, however, that the above-described procedure requires a substantially increased amount of time, in terms of both the frequency and duration of sessions. Initially, it was necessary to allow up to 1 hour to enable Ben to 'settle' in, as he was preoccupied by ritualistic thinking arising from the perceived social demand in the therapeutic situation. Thereafter, he became capable of focusing on the therapeutic process. As therapy progressed, this type of support was substantially reduced as Ben became more actively involved, so that weekly one-hour sessions seemed sufficient.

In view of Ben's initial fragile motivation and high levels of anxiety, often in anticipation, it appeared important to design a gradual approach to the ERP programme. This involved intensive support and supervision from the therapist to begin with. This approach was further endorsed in consideration of the previous treatment failures, which did not involve this type of support. At a later stage this was withdrawn stepwise, i.e. the patient was asked to repeat exposure experiments unassisted and was encouraged to process these experiences actively in order to foster an increase in self-efficacy for future tasks.

Eventually Ben was able to engage in the ERP programme successfully and a 40% reduction in the severity of symptoms had been achieved at the time of writing. He also managed to start engaging in work activities again, and was enjoying more satisfactory relationships with his family. He also began to initiate new social interactions, managed to find more suitable accommodation and was planning to resume his studies.

It seems very likely that the CF approach was instrumental in establishing an appropriate therapeutic relationship and overcoming previous difficulties with 'structured and limit-setting' approaches, which were perceived as threatening by the patient.

Obviously, the additional time and cost of individualised CF needs to be taken into account, which amounted in Ben's case to about 10 extra sessions, some of which were prolonged. This effort appears justified considering the 15 year history of severe suffering experienced by this patient. Furthermore, such additional expense appears negligible if compared with two ill-advised admissions to specialised hospitals for periods of up to 4 months. We are also convinced that a further treatment failure would have caused greater damage to his self-esteem and may have led to further depressive episodes, which had previously led to a complete withdrawal from active life.

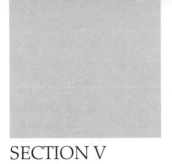

SECTION V

PROFESSIONAL ISSUES

Chapter 20

TRAINING, RESOURCES AND SERVICE PROVISION

Lynne M. Harris and Ross G. Menzies

OVERVIEW

Obsessive-compulsive disorder (OCD) is an objectively distressing condition for the individual and a costly one for the community. People living with OCD are commonly unemployed or underemployed, report relationship problems and social isolation, and have low self-esteem (Hollander et al., 1996). The distress associated with OCD is severe, and in Hollander et al.'s sample of 419 survey respondents, 13% had made suicide attempts secondary to their OCD symptomatology. The financial cost of OCD to the community is also high, and includes direct health care expenditure as well as indirect costs due to the early, occasional, or complete loss of the person with OCD from the workforce (e.g. DuPont et al., 1995; see also Chapter 2). For most people, the onset of OCD occurs early in life, most often between the ages 6–15 years for males and 20–29 years for females. Only 5% of those diagnosed with OCD can expect complete remission between episodes, and the majority experience a chronic course (American Psychiatric Association, 1994). Hollander et al. (1996) reported a 17-year delay between the onset of OCD symptoms and the commencement of effective treatment for OCD. This lag is probably exacerbated by the early age of onset of the disorder, and by the frequent misdiagnosis of OCD as either generalised anxiety disorder or depression.

Chapters 15–17 of this volume discuss the available biological and psychological interventions for OCD in detail and evaluate their usefulness in treating OCD. Of the biological treatments, the serotonin re-uptake inhibitors (SRIs) are useful for management in slightly more than half of cases (e.g. Munford et al., 1994; Hollander et al., 1996). Psychosurgery, a treatment of last resort when all others have failed (e.g. Sachdev & Sachdev, 1998), is helpful in up to 30% of cases unresponsive to other

Obsessive-Compulsive Disorder: Theory, Research and Treatment.
Edited by Ross G. Menzies and Padmal de Silva. © 2003 John Wiley & Sons, Ltd.

treatments (Marks et al., 1998). Of the psychological interventions, the efficacy of behavioural treatments based around the exposure and response prevention (ERP) technique trialled by Rachman and his colleagues (e.g. Rachman et al., 1971) is well established. Foa & Kozak (1996) reported that 76% of individuals who received ERP remained improved at 3 months to 6 years follow-up. More recently, cognitive therapy with OCD has been shown to be useful (for a review, see Salkovskis, 1999), and outcome studies indicate that a large percentage of those diagnosed with OCD respond to behavioural and cognitive-behavioural interventions (see further, Chapters 15 and 16).

Despite the demonstrated effectiveness of behavioural and cognitive-behavioural interventions in the treatment of OCD, many of those meeting criteria for OCD are unable to access these treatment modalities. Several important factors reduce the likelihood that an individual meeting diagnostic criteria for OCD will receive effective treatment.

First, Singleton & Smith (1997) note that an alarming 25–50% of psychiatric cases are not identified by general practitioners. OCD is a poorly recognised condition, even among the psychiatric community, and this increases the likelihood that symptoms of OCD will be missed by general practitioners. As recently as 1992, Black & Blum wrote that within the psychiatric tradition OCD was regarded as 'uncommon and difficult to treat'. Individuals who meet criteria for OCD in terms of symptoms, distress and impairment are known to be over-represented among patients seeking specialist dermatological treatment for skin conditions associated with washing (e.g. Friedman et al., 1993). These individuals generally seek treatment not for their OCD but for the side effects of the condition, and are unlikely to have received a formal OCD diagnosis. Dermatologists are not skilled in the detection and diagnosis of OCD symptomatology and, in a study by Rasmussen (1986), almost universally failed to notice signs of OCD among their patients. This apparently poor detection of OCD signs among medical personnel is of great concern. It clearly restricts access to useful treatments and suggests that the lifetime prevalence rates for OCD may be higher than previously thought (see also Chapter 1).

Second, the cost of delivering effective treatment for OCD is considerable and varies markedly with the experience and skill of the therapist. According to Foa & Kozak (1996), when delivered by specialists, an average of 15 sessions of individually administered behavioural therapy (ERP) is sufficient to achieve effective treatment for OCD. However, Turner et al. (1995) conducted a survey of non-specialist behavioural therapists and found that the average number of sessions reported was 46. As most specialist centres for the treatment of anxiety disorders are located in metropolitan areas, this suggests that for people living with OCD in regional areas, the cost of therapy will be prohibitively high. Calvocoressi et al. (1998) found that people living with OCD had employment characteristics similar to those of people with diagnoses of schizophrenia, i.e. the majority were unemployed (87%) and relied on others for support. Again, this suggests that individual therapy may be beyond the means of many patients.

Previous chapters have discussed evidence concerning the usefulness of behavioural, cognitive, pharmacological and surgical treatment for OCD. This overview has highlighted some of the issues specific to OCD that impact upon access to individual behaviourally-oriented treatment. First, the early age of onset may contribute to the long delay in seeking treatment for OCD symptoms. OCD is associated with significant embarrassment and secretiveness (e.g. Higgins, 1996), and it is not perhaps surprising that general practitioners and specialist physicians do not always detect OCD in their clients. However, there is clearly a need for education directed towards both the general public and health professionals about the signs of OCD, to ensure that those who may benefit from treatment are detected and made aware of what is available. Second, education of health professionals about specialist interventions available for treating OCD may reduce the cost of treatment, by reducing the use of unnecessary and poorly targeted interventions, and therefore increase its affordability. Third, and related to this, the present overview points to a potential gap in the provision of specialist services for those living in regional areas. For people outside metropolitan centres, the likelihood of receiving treatment from a therapist skilled in the delivery of demonstrably effective behavioural therapy for OCD is small. The present chapter examines the availability of information and education about the signs of OCD and about the most effective treatments for the disorder. It also discusses a range of resources available for people with OCD and their families, including support groups and methods of delivering behavioural interventions for OCD by non-traditional methods that reduce therapist involvement.

RECOGNISING THE PROBLEM: EDUCATING GENERAL PRACTITIONERS AND THE COMMUNITY ABOUT OCD

As noted above, there is a very long lag between the time when OCD symptoms first appear and when they are first effectively treated (e.g. Hollander et al., 1996). In addition, people with OCD are over-represented in specialist dermatology practice (e.g. Friedman et al., 1993). This suggests that both general practitioners and the community may be unaware of the symptoms of OCD and of how to gain access to appropriate treatment.

OCD and General Practice

The fact that 25–50% of cases presenting to general practitioners have psychiatric disturbances that are overlooked suggests an urgent need to improve awareness of psychiatric diagnoses among non-psychiatrist medical practitioners. The World Psychiatric Association (WPA) and the World Federation for Medical Education (WFME) emphasise knowledge of the symptoms and syndromes of psychiatric disturbances as an essential feature of core psychiatry curricula for medical students (Gelder, 1999). This recommendation recognises the prevalence of psychiatric problems among patients seen by practitioners in all branches of medicine. In recent years, teaching strategies in medical education worldwide have changed significantly, increasingly incorporating problem-based learning (PBL) approaches. These approaches emphasise skills in acquiring and evaluating new information (e.g. Barrows, 1985). PBL approaches help to reconcile the competing demands of professions whose members need to keep abreast of a rapidly expanding knowledge base and an education system that cannot sustain programs increasing in size to present this knowledge base using traditional methods (Boud & Feletti, 1997). Certainly, the WPA and WFME highlight the importance of PBL in teaching core psychiatry curricula to medical students (Gelder, 1999). It may be suggested that graduates from medical programs using PBL methods of teaching may be better equipped to acquire information about unfamiliar symptoms and syndromes.

As well as emphasising criteria for detecting psychiatric illness in education programs for new doctors, there is a clear need to educate practising general practitioners. In a survey by Ratcliffe et al. (1999) concerning the psychiatric training needs of general practitioners in the UK, respondents listed training in accessing resources and detecting psychiatric illness as their most important requirements, second only to communication skills. A number of methods of continuing education to improve the detection of psychiatric problems have been trialled in the UK. Singleton & Smith (1997) reported a pilot study, in which general practitioners compared their evaluations of patients (based on consultations) with information obtained from patient's self-report responses to the General Health Questionnaire (GHQ). These authors reported that the GHQ was useful as a device for stimulating self-evaluation only if it was linked to a supportive discussion forum. Ratcliffe et al. (1999) reported on the use of workshops, lectures and demonstrations to satisfy the psychiatric training needs of general practitioners. These authors reported only on participants' ratings of their perceived needs before and after the workshops. Although the data were encouraging, the need for more objective evidence concerning the ability to detect psychiatric problems is needed to evaluate the usefulness of programs such as this.

OCD and Community Awareness

Over the last decade, OCD has acquired greater prominence within the general community. The 1990s saw Hollywood actor Jack Nicholson win an Oscar for his role as a writer with OCD in the film *As Good as It Gets*. A brief examination of the Internet reveals a vast number of sites where information about OCD can easily be found, and where people are directed to a range of services available for those who suspect they may have OCD. The percentage of households in developed countries with Internet access is increasing annually at a staggering rate. According to the *Computer Industry Almanac*, 61 million households had Internet access worldwide in 1996 and the equivalent figure for 2000 was 320 million, an increase of more than 500% across 4 years, making this resource increasingly useful (Petska-Juliusen & Juliussen, 1999). The Internet and the many pamphlets and self-help books currently available concerning OCD may, by themselves, be of little use to many OCD sufferers. As Greist (1998a) notes, slightly more than one-fifth of all adult Americans are functionally illiterate and cannot easily access information in printed form. In a similar vein, Kirkby et al. (2000) evaluated the use of a computer-aided treatment for OCD and found that a higher reading test score predicted a greater likelihood that program users would carry out vicarious exposure. The provision of information through audio and videotapes may help to overcome this problem.

The growth of support groups is a further indication of the growing community awareness of OCD, its prevalence and its impact on people with the disorder and their families. The format and goals of support groups are quite varied. They have in common that they seek to address the isolation and sense of being misunderstood commonly reported by those with OCD and/or their families. The majority of support groups about which published information and evaluation is available aim to provide education for members and are facilitated by health professionals (e.g. Black & Blum, 1992; Cooper, 1993; Grayson, 1999; Tynes et al., 1992). However, not *all* support groups place psychoeducation about the condition as their primary aim, and popular 12-step programs modelled on Alcoholics Anonymous encourage reliance on a higher power for support, and are not usually facilitated by health professionals (e.g. Obsessive-Compulsive Anonymous, 1999). A survey carried out by Cooper (1996) among family members of people with OCD suggested that education and information, whether presented in lectures or in pamphlets, books and manuals, were among the most important resources needed by families living with OCD.

Some support groups offer circumscribed time-limited programs (e.g. Tynes et al., 1992), while others offer programs that are not time-limited in any sense, and where at any one time the group is likely to comprise people at very different stages of the course of their OCD (e.g. Grayson, 1999; Obsessive-Compulsive Anonymous, 1999). Time-limited approaches emphasise education and may be more helpful in the early stages of accepting a diagnosis of OCD. The support groups that are not time-limited place greater emphasis on the interactions between group members, and may be particularly useful in the period before people are ready to undertake intensive therapy and in dealing with relapse, reducing the demand for specialist therapists (Grayson, 1999).

Family members of those with OCD require support that addresses their unique concerns, for several reasons. First, family members may have an impact on the expression of the OCD or on the willingness of the person with OCD to seek treatment by participating in, or accommodating, the compulsive behaviours and rituals (Calvocoressi et al., 1993, 1998). Second, apart from the influence of family members and carers on the expression of the OCD, a large literature attests to the burden of care experienced by people supporting a mentally ill relative (e.g. Baronet, 1999). This burden can be seen in 'objective' areas, such as work, leisure, income and relations with extended family, friends and neighbours, as well as in 'subjective' areas (see further, Maurin & Boyd, 1990). Steketee (1993b) reported that poor family functioning and critical or angry interactions with family members were associated with poorer treatment outcome, emphasising the importance of addressing family members' distress directly.

The burden of caring for a family member with OCD tends to fall largely on a single family member (Cooper, 1996). Magliano et al. (1996) investigated burden among a sample of 32 key relatives of people with OCD and reported moderate to severe levels of distress among the sample. In this sample, depression and disruption of social relationships affected the majority. Cooper (1996) surveyed 225 relatives of people with OCD about the resources that they found most helpful. Family members reported gaining most help from information about OCD (lectures and readings), family and group therapy and self-help groups. While information about OCD symptomatology and treatment may be equally useful for family members and for people with OCD, family members confront many issues that are unique to the experience of caring for and supporting a relative with a mental illness. These include financial concerns, social relationship problems and negative emotional states, such as anger and grief (Cooper, 1996).

For this reason, most organisations running OCD support groups favour establishing separate groups for people with OCD and for their family or supporters. The family support groups usually provide information about OCD, supportive environments for normalising emotional reactions to the symptoms, and suggestions for strategies to deal with the OCD symptoms and other problems (e.g. Black & Blum, 1992; Cooper, 1993; Grayson, 1999). Apart from data on satisfaction with the groups obtained from self-selected people who attend or continue to attend group meetings, there is no published evaluation of the extent to which groups influence objective or subjective burden among family members of people with OCD.

ALTERNATIVE MODES OF TREATMENT DELIVERY

Alternatives to traditional face-to-face individual or group psychotherapy for OCD have a number of advantages. First, they reduce the costs to the individual and to the health system. These costs are likely to be exacerbated if therapists are not experts in delivering exposure-based treatment to people with OCD, and require many more sessions of treatment than expert therapists to achieve clinically significant improvement (e.g. Turner et al., 1995). Cost audits of behavioural treatments for OCD reveal that, after inpatient accommodation costs, therapist time and particularly percentage improvement per therapist hour is the major variable impacting on treatment cost (e.g. McKenzie et al., 1995). Second, alternative modes of delivery have the potential to make specialised, effective treatment available to a much larger number of people in a broader geographical area. Third, many people with OCD are embarrassed about their symptoms and try to hide the signs of their disorder (Steketee, 1997). For these people, treatment that does not require direct contact with a therapist may be more acceptable.

A number of alternatives to face-to-face individual therapy exist. These include the delivery of therapy to groups of clients, bibliotherapy, the use of interactive computer software run on personal computers, and the use of computer programs controlled by touch-tone telephone. Recently, Graham et al. (2000) conducted a postal survey of respondents to a teletext article on self-help treatments for OCD and agoraphobia. The survey examined preferred modes of delivery of treatment, as well as the amount people were willing or able to pay for this service. Of those contacted, 35% responded to the survey. The most preferred mode of delivery was via a book, followed by telephone linked to a computer, and then a range of modes of delivery with direct computer interaction. A small percentage favoured audio- or video-taped presentation, and only 9% said that they definitely did not want access through a computer system. The sample was not randomly selected, and the applicability of its findings to the broader population with OCD may be limited. For example, the respondents were accessed through a means that required reading, and therefore it may be implied that the sample had reasonably accurate reading ability as well as competence in interacting with technology. Nevertheless, the findings imply that modes of treatment delivery that do not rely on direct therapist interaction will be acceptable to many people with OCD.

Group Therapy

One means of reducing the cost of treatment for OCD is to offer behavioural therapy in groups (e.g. Krone et al., 1991). Fals-Stewart et al. (1993) randomly assigned people with mild to moderate OCD symptomatology to behavioural group therapy ($n = 10$ per group), individual behavioural therapy, or individual progressive muscle relaxation. Participants did not have co-morbid depression or Axis II diagnoses. Although the people in the individual therapy condition made faster initial gains, the authors reported that group and individual behavioural therapy led to equivalent reductions in distress due to OCD symptoms at the conclusion of treatment, and that treatment gains were maintained at 6-month follow-up. The number of staff hours required for the group compared to individual therapy was, however, markedly different. Staff reported spending 48 hours in total on the group intervention over 12 weeks, compared to 720 hours for the individual condition. Apart from the direct saving in hours of staff time, Fals-Stewart et al. (1993) note that only one staff member was required to run groups. This suggests the possibility of significant savings in specialist staff levels to implement therapy in a group format, at least for those whose problem is at most of moderate severity.

March et al. (2001) emphasise the problems of delivering specialised, effective treatment for OCD to the large population of children and adolescents with OCD. Clinicians frequently complain about difficulties in achieving compliance in younger clients. Fischer et al. (1998) proposed that behavioural group therapy may be particularly useful for enhancing treatment compliance among children and adolescents with OCD by making use of heightened susceptibility to peer influences in this age group. Fischer et al. evaluated the usefulness of a 7-week group program for 15 children 12–17 years of age. Not only did the group improve in obsession, compulsion and total scores from the Children's Yale–Brown Obsessive-Compulsive Scale (CY-BOCS) from pre-test to post-test, but further improvement over post-test scores was observed at 6 month follow-up. Participants in this study were referred for group therapy based on clinical judgement of suitability, and there was no control condition. In the light of the economies to be derived from delivering group therapy in terms of specialized staff time, the results of Fischer et al. (1998) certainly encourage further evaluation of the suitability of a group treatment format for young people with OCD.

Bibliotherapy

The survey conducted by Graham et al. (2000) suggests that many people with OCD prefer to have treatment information provided in book form, and a range of behaviourally-oriented self-help guides for children, adolescents, and adults with OCD are available (e.g. March & Mulle, 1996; Steketee & White, 1990). It is difficult to evaluate the extent to which people with OCD benefit from the use of these books without any therapist intervention, as such people may not come to the attention of health professionals. However, Fritzler et al. (1997) evaluated the usefulness of bibliotherapy with minimal therapist contact in a group of nine people who met DSM-IIIR criteria for OCD. The treatment involved the provision of chapters from Steketee & White's (1990) self-help book, *When Once is not Enough*, across a 12-week period interspersed with five planned meetings with a therapist (weekly for the first 3 weeks, and then at 6 and 7 weeks). The meetings were designed to provide an outline of treatment, ensure that participants were reading and comprehending assigned materials, plan hierarchies and exposure exercises and carry out assessment. No therapeutic exercises or therapist modelling occurred during the meetings. All participants showed statistically significant improvement after the intervention and for one-third of the group improvement was clinically significant. These findings derived from a small sample suggested that bibliotherapy with minimal therapist involvement may be useful for people with less severe OCD. As noted previously, therapies that require extensive reading will only be useful for people with good reading abilities. All participants accepted into Fritzler et al.'s study had a minimum reading level of sixth grade, although two-thirds of the group had a reading level higher than twelfth grade. Interestingly, no-one with the minimum reading level actually completed treatment. Fritzler et al. suggest that this manual-assisted intervention may be particularly useful in rural areas, where access to specialised therapy may not be possible or practical. It may also be suggested that this kind of approach may alleviate problems associated with non-specialist therapists delivering 'behavioural' treatment for OCD, discussed earlier (e.g. Turner et al., 1995). However, despite the minimal therapist interaction with the clients in Fritzler et al.'s report, it was noted that therapeutic outcome was better for people treated by a therapist with experience in treating anxiety disorders.

Interactive Computer Program

Clark et al. (1998) describe an interactive computer program, designed to provide vicarious exposure to scenarios involving contamination and instruction about the principles of ERP. Clark et al. evaluated the usefulness of three sessions of the program with 13 respondents to an advertisement to undertake a computer-based treatment program. The participants with OCD had average IQs slightly more than 113, based on National Adult Reading Test scores. These authors report changes in Padua Inventory (PI) obsessional, checking and total scores, as well as Beck Depression Inventory (BDI) scores between pre-test and post-test, although scores on the commonly used Yale–Brown Obsessive-Compulsive Scale did not change. While the changes in PI and BDI scores were statistically significant, they did not meet the criteria for clinical significance. As noted previously, the success of the computer intervention was related to reading test scores, with those with higher scores carrying out more vicarious exposure (Kirkby et al., 2000). The authors proposed that the program may be a useful introduction to behavioural therapy, but not that it would take the place of therapist-mediated treatment. However, the usefulness of the computer-based package in reducing staff time required to implement standard behavioural treatment for OCD remain to be demonstrated.

Telephone Controlled Computer Program

The BT STEPS computer program uses interactive voice responses accessed by touch tone telephone to present behavioural assessment and individualized treatment for OCD, with little input from a live therapist (Baer & Greist, 1997). In previous computer-aided behavioural treatment for panic and agoraphobia (e.g. Ghosh & Marks, 1987), information was presented in printed form on a personal computer and respondents interacted with the program through the keyboard. Touch-tone telephones are much more readily available compared to personal computers, and are familiar to a much greater proportion of the population. They are also accessible at a much lower cost than a personal computer. These factors suggest that BT STEPS may provide a preferable means of presenting computer-aided treatment to people with OCD. The presentation of information through the spoken voice may also reduce limitations on access due to restricted rapid reading ability (although the program requires participants to work through a basic, printed treatment manual concurrently, and so requires some reading skills).

Marks et al. (1998) report an evaluation of the self-assessment component of BT STEPS in a sample of 63 people with OCD at sites in the USA and in the UK. Participants met DSM-IIIR criteria for OCD and had no co-morbid depression, psychotic disorder, substance use disorder or personality disorder. Of the selected subjects who commenced the trial, more than 80% completed the assessment stage of the program. Less than half of those who began the trial undertook self-treatment following assessment. Importantly, the authors found that all participants who completed at least two ERP tasks significantly improved in their total score on the Yale–Brown Obsessive-Compulsive Scale, and the more tasks that were completed, the greater the improvement.

The findings of a second study in the UK with a more severely impaired sample of people on a waiting list for clinician-guided therapy closely replicated these findings (Bachofen et al., 1999). Again, all of those who completed at least two ERP tasks showed significant improvement in their total score on the Yale–Brown Obsessive-Compulsive Scale. The advantages of a computer-mediated treatment are clear. As Bachofen et al. (1999) note, there is a saving of 80% of the time required per person for a clinician to deliver behavioural therapy.

CONCLUDING COMMENTS

This chapter has examined a number of issues that restrict access to effective treatment for those with OCD, including problems with identifying the disorder and issues associated with the delivery of effective treatment, particularly the cost of therapy. The chapter highlights the need for general practitioners to be educated about psychiatric diagnoses generally and OCD in particular. It also presents recent developments in the provision of resources and services for those with OCD beyond traditional, individual behavioural therapy. There can be little doubt that the computer age offers great opportunities for the cheaper delivery of effective psychotherapy. The advantages of computer-delivered treatment and the World Wide Web have yet to be fully exploited.

REFERENCES

Abel J (1993) Exposure with response prevention and serotonergic antidepressants in the treatment of obsessive compulsive disorder: a review and implications for interdisciplinary treatment. *Behav Res Ther* **31**:463–478.

Abramowitz JS (1996) Variants of exposure and response prevention in the treatment of obsessive-compulsive disorder: a meta-analysis. *Behav Ther* **27**:583–600.

Abramowitz JS (1997) Effectiveness of psychological and pharmacological treatments for obsessive-compulsive disorder. A quantitative review. *J Consult Clin Psychol* **65**:44–52.

Abramowitz JS (1998) Does cognitive-behavioral therapy cure obsessive-compulsive disorder? A meta-analytic evaluation of clinical significance. *Behav Ther* **29**:339–355.

Abramowitz JS & Foa EB (1998) Worries and obsessions in individuals with obsessive-compulsive disorder with and without comorbid generalized anxiety disorder. *Behav Res Ther* **36**:695–700.

Ackerman DL, Greenland S & Bystritsky A (1994) Predictors of treatment response in obsessive compulsive disorder: multivariate analyses from a multicentre trial of clomipramine. *J Clin Pharmacol* **14**:247–254.

Adams PL (1973) *Obsessive Children*. New York, Brunner/Mazel.

Akhtar S, Wig NH, Verma VK, Pershod D & Verma SK (1975) A phenomenological analysis of the symptoms of obsessive-compulsive neuroses. *Br J Psychiat* **127**:342–348.

Alarcon RD, Libb JW & Boll TJ (1994) Neuropsychological testing in obsessive-compulsive disorder, a clinical review. *J Neuropsychiat* **6**:217–228.

Albert A & Hayward P (2002) Treatment of intrusive ruminations about mathematics. *Behav Cogn Psychother* **30**:223–226.

Alighieri D (1998) *Inferno* (Zappulla E, trans). New York, Pantheon.

Allen L & Tegera C (1994) Treatment of clozapine induced obsessive compulsive symptoms with sertraline (letter). *Am J Psychiat* **151**:1096–1097.

Allsopp M & Williams T (1996) Intrusive thoughts in a non-clinical adolescent population. *Eur Child Adolesc Psychiat* **5**:25–32.

Alsobrook JP & Pauls DL (1997) The genetics of Tourette syndrome. *Neurol Clin* **15**(2):381–393.

Altemus M, Greenberg BD & Keuler D (1999) An open trial of flutamide in the treatment of obsessive-compulsive disorder. *J Clin Psychiat* **16**(7):442–445.

APA (American Psychiatric Association) (1952) *Diagnostic and Statistical Manual of Mental Disorders*. Washington, DC, APA.

APA (American Psychiatric Association) (1980) *Diagnostic and Statistical Manual of Mental Disorders*, 3rd edn. Washington, DC, APA.

APA (American Psychiatric Association) (1994) *Diagnostic and Statistical Manual of Mental Disorders*, 4th edn. Washington, DC, APA.

Amir N, Freshman M & Foa EB (2000) Family distress and involvement in relatives of obsessive-compulsive disorder patients. *J Anxiety Disord* **14**:209–217.

Ananth J, Solyom L & Solyom C (1975) Doxepin in the treatment of obsessive-compulsive neurosis. *Psychosomatics* **16**:185–187.

Andrews G, Crino R, Hunt C, Lampe L & Page A (1994) *The Treatment of Anxiety Disorders: Clinician's Guide and Patient Manuals*. Melbourne, Cambridge University Press.

Andrews G, Slade T & Peters L (1999) Classification in psychiatry: ICD-10 versus DSM-IV. *Br J Psychiat* **174**:3–5.

Andrews G, Stewart G, Allen R & Henderson AS (1990) The genetics of six neurotic disorders: a twin study. *J Affect Disord* **19**:23–29.

Antony MM, Downie F & Swinson RP (1998a) Diagnostic issues and epidemiology in obsessive-compulsive disorder. In RP Swinson, MM Antony, S Rachman & MA Richter (eds), *Obsessive Compulsive Disorder: Theory, research and treatment*. New York, Guilford, pp 3–32.

Antony MM, Roth D, Swinson RP, Huta V & Devins GM (1998b) Illness intrusiveness in individuals with panic disorder, obsessive compulsive disorder, or social phobia. *J Nerv Ment Dis* **186**:193–197.

Aronowitz GE, Hollander E & DeCaria C (1994) Neuropsychology of obsessive-compulsive disorder: preliminary findings. *Neuropsychiat Neuropsychol Behav Neurol* **7**:81–86.

Arts W, Hoogduin K, Schaap C & de Haan E (1993) Do patients suffering from obsessions alone differ from other obsessive-compulsives? *Behav Res Ther* **31**:119–123.

Asbahr FR, Ramos RT, Negrao AB & Gentil V (1999) Case series: increased vulnerability to obsessive-compulsive symptoms with repeated episodes of Syndenham chorea. *J Am Acad Child Adolesc Psychiat* **38**:1522–1525.

Asberg M, Montgomery SA, Perris C, Schalling D & Sedvall G (1978) The Comprehensive Psychopathological Rating Scale. *Acta Psychiat Scand* **271**(suppl): 5–27.

Aubuchon P & Malatesta V (1998) Managing the therapeutic relationship: the need for a case formulation. In MH Bruch & FW Bond (eds), *Beyond Diagnosis: Cognitive-behavioural Case Formulation*. Chichester, Wiley.

Bachofen M, Nakagawa A, Marks I, Park J, Greist J, Baer L, Wenzel K, Parkin J & Dottl S (1999) Home self-assessment and self-treatment of obsessive-compulsive disorder using a manual and a computer-conducted. Replication of a UK–US study. *J Clin Psychiat* **60**:545–549.

Baer L (1994) Factor analysis of symptom subtypes of obsessive compulsive disorder and their relation to personality and tic disorders. *J Clin Psychiat* **55**:18–23.

Baer L (1996) Behavior therapy: endogenous serotonin therapy? *J Clin Psychiat* **57**(suppl 6): 33–35.

Baer L & Greist JH (1997) An interactive computer-administered self-assessment and self-help program for behavior therapy. *J Clin Psychiat* **58**(suppl 12):23–28.

Baer L, Rauch SL & Ballantine HT (1995) Cingulotomy for intractable obsessive compulsive disorder: long-term follow-up of 18 patients. *Arch Gen Psychiat* **52**:384–392.

Bain A (1928) *Thought Control in Everyday Life*. New York, Funk and Wagnalls.

Baker RW, Ames D & Umbricht DSG (1996) Obsessive compulsive symptoms in schizophrenia: a comparison of olanzapine and placebo. *Psychopharmacol Bull* **32**:89–93.

Ball SG, Baer L & Otto MW (1996) Symptom subtypes of obsessive-compulsive disorder in behavioral treatment studies: a quantitative review. *Behav Res Ther* **34**:47–51.

Bandura A (1977) Self-efficacy: toward a unifying theory of behavioural change. *Psychol Rev* **84**(2):191–215.

Barlow DH (1987) The classification of anxiety disorders. In GL Tischler (ed.), *Diagnosis and Classification in Psychiatry: A Critical Appraisal of DSM-III*. Cambridge, Cambridge University Press.

Barlow DH (1988) *Anxiety and Its Disorders—the Nature and Treatment of Anxiety and Panic*. New York, Guilford.

Baronet AM (1999) Factors associated with caregiver burden in mental illness: a critical review of the research literature. *Clin Psychol Rev* **19**:819–841.

Barr LC, Goodman WK & Anan DA (1997) Addition of desipramine to serotonin re-uptake inhibitors in treatment-resistant obsessive-compulsive disorder. *Am J Psychiat* **154**:1293–1295.

Barrows H (1985) *How to Design a Problem-based Curriculum for the Preclinical Years*. New York, Springer.

Barsky AJ (1992) Hypochondriasis and obsessive compulsive disorder. *Psychiat Clin N Am* **15**:791–801.

Basoglu M, Lax T, Kasvikis & Marks IM (1988) Predictors of improvement in obsessive-compulsive disorder. *J Anxiety Disord* **2**:299–317.

Baxter LR, Ackermann RF, Swerdlow NR, Brody A, Saxena S, Schwartz JM, Gregortich JM, Stoessel P & Phelps ME (2000) Specific brain system mediation of obsessive-compulsive disorder responsive to either medication or behavior therapy. In WK Goodman, MV Rudorfer & JD Maser (eds) *Obsessive-compulsive Disorder: Contemporary Issues in Treatment*. Personality and Clinical Psychology Series. Mahwah, NJ, Erlbaum, pp 573–609.

Baxter LR, Phelps ME & Mazziotta JC (1987) Local cerebral glucose metabolic rates in obsessive-compulsive disorder: a comparison with rates in unipolar depression and in normal controls. *Arch Gen Psychiat* **44**:211–218.

Baxter LR, Schwartz JM, Guze BH, Bergman K & Szuba MP (1990) Neuroimaging in OCD: seeking the mediating neuro-anatomy. In MA Jenike, L Baer & WE Minichiello (eds), *OCD: Theory and Management*, 2nd edn. New York, Year Book Medical Publishers.

Bebbington PE (1998) Epidemiology of obsessive compulsive disorder. *Br J Psychiat* **35**(suppl):2–6.

Beck AT (1976) *Cognitive Therapy and the Emotional Disorders*. New York, International Universities Press.

Beck AT, Emery G & Greenberg G (1985) *Anxiety Disorders and Phobias: A Cognitive Perspective*. New York, Basic Books.

Beck AT, Steer RA & Brown GK (1996) *Beck Depression Inventory*. San Antonio, TX, The Psychological Corporation.

Beck AT, Ward CH & Mendelson M (1961) An inventory for measuring depression. *Arch Gen Psychiat* **41**:53–63.

Beech, HR (1971) Ritualistic activity in obsessional patients. *J Psychosom Res* **15**:417–422.

Beers SR, Rosenberg DR & Dick EL (1999) Neuropsychological study of frontal lobe functioning in psychotropic-naïve children with obsessive-compulsive disorder. *Am J Psychiat* **15**:777–779.

Behar D, Rapoport JL & Berg CJ (1984) Computerised tomography and neuropsychological test measures in adolescents with obsessive-compulsive disorder. *Am J Psychiat* **141**:363–369.

Bellodi L, Sciuto G, Diaferia G, Ronchi P & Smeraldi E (1992) Psychiatric disorders in the families of patients with obsesssive compulsive disorder. *Psychiat Res* **42**:111–120.

Bengel D, Greenberg BD, Cora Locatelli G, Altemus M, Heils ALQ & Murphy DL (1999) Association of the serotonin transporter promoter regulatory polymorphism and obsessive compulsive disorder. *Mol Psychiat* **4**(5):463–466.

Bennun I (1980) Obsessional slowness: a replication and extension. *Behav Res Ther* **18**:595–598.

Ben-Tovim D (1998) Body image and the experienced body. In CB Tuschen & I Florin (eds), *Recent Research in Eating Disorders*. Mannheim, Springer-Verlag, pp 1–9.

Berg CZ, Rapoport JL, Whitaker A, Davies M, Leonard H, Swedo SE, Braiman S & Lenane M (1989) Childhood obsessive-compulsive disorder: a two year prospective follow-up of a community sample. *J Am Acad Child Adolesc Psychiat* **28**:528–533.

Berg CZ, Whitaker A, Davies M, Flament MF & Rapoport JL (1988) The survey form of the Leyton Obsessional Inventory—Child Version Norms from an epidemiological study. *J Am Acad Child Adolesc Psychiat* **27**:759–763.

Berman I, Sapero BH & Chang HHG (1995) Treatment of obsessive compulsive symptoms in schizophrenic patients with clomipramine. *J Clin Pharmacol* **15**:206–210.

Berman L (1942) Obsessive-compulsive neurosis in children. *J Nerv Ment Dis* **95**: 26–39.

Berrios, GE (2000) *The History of Mental Symptoms*. Cambridge, Cambridge University Press.

Bhar SS & Kyrios M (1999) Cognitive personality styles associated with depressive and obsessive compulsive phenomena in a non-clinical sample. *Behav Cogn Psychother* **27**(4):329–343.

Biccinelli M, Pini S, Bellantuono C et al. (1995) Efficacy of drug treatment in obsessive compulsive disorder: a meta-analytic review. *Br J Psychiat* **166**, 440–443.

Billet EA, Richter MA & Kennedy JL (1998) Genetics of obsessive-compulsive disorder. In RP Swinson, MM Antony, S Rachman & M Richter (eds), *Obsessive-Compulsive Disorder: Theory, Research and Treatment*. New York, Guilford.

Billett EA, Richter MA, King N, Heils A, Lesch KP & Kennedy JL (1997) Obsessive compulsive disorder: response to serotonin reuptake inhibitors and the serotonin transporter gene. *Mol Psychiat* **2**:403–406.

Bilsbury C & Morley S (1979) Obsessional slowness: a meticulous replication. *Behav Res Ther* **17**:405–408.

Birmaher B, Khetarpal S, Brent D, Cully M, Balach L, Kaufman J & Neer SM (1997) The screen for child anxiety related emotional disorders (SCARED): scale construction and psychometric characteristics. *J Am Acad Child Adolesc Psychiat* **36**:545–553.

Bisserbe JC, Lane RM & Flament MF (1997) A double-blind comparison of sertraline and clomipramine in outpatients with obsessive compulsive disorder. *J Assoc Eur Psychiat* **12**:82–93.

Black A (1974) The natural history of obsessional states. In HR Beech (ed.), *Obsessional States*. London, Methuen, pp 20–54.

Black DW & Blum NS (1992) Obsessive-compulsive disorder support groups: the Iowa model. *Compr Psychiat* **33**:65–71.

Black DW, Kelly M, Myers C & Noyes R (1990) Tritiated imipramine binding in obsessive-compulsive volunteers and psychiatrically normal controls. *Biol Psychiat* **27**:319–327.

Black DW, Monahan P, Gable J, Blum N, Clancy G & Baker P (1998) Hoarding and treatment response in 38 non-depressed subjects with obsessive-compulsive disorder. *J Clin Psychiat* **59**:420–425.

Black DW, Noyes R, Goldstein RB & Blum N (1992) A family study of obsessive compulsive disorder. *Arch Gen Psychiat* **49**:362–368.

Blagden JC & Craske MG (1996) Effects of active and passive rumination and distraction: a pilot replication with anxious mood. *J Anxiety Disord* **10**:243–252.

Bland RC, Orn H & Newman SC (1988) Lifetime prevalence of psychiatric disorders in Edmonton. *Acta Psychiat Scand* **77**(suppl 338):24–32.

Bleuler E (1955) *Dementia Praecox or Group of Schizophrenias.* New York, International Universities Press.

Blier P & Bergeron R (1996) Sequential administration of augmentation strategies in treatment resistant obsessive compulsive disorder: preliminary findings *Int J Clin Pharmacol* **11**:37–44.

Bolton D (1996) Developmental issues in obsessive compulsive disorder. *J Child Psychol Psychiat* **37**:131–137.

Bolton D, Luckie M & Steinberg D (1995) Long-term course of obsessive-compulsive disorder treated in adolescence. *J Am Acad Child Adolesc Psychiat* **34**:1441–1450.

Bolton D, Raven P, Madronal-Lugue R & Marks IM (2000) Neurological and neuropsychological signs in obsessive-compulsive disorder: interaction with behavioural treatment. *Behav Res Ther* **38**:695–708.

Boone KB, Ananth J, Philpott L, Kaur A & Djenderedjian A (1991) Neuropsychological characteristics of nondepressed adults with obsessive-compulsive disorder. *Neuropsychiat Neuropsychol Behav Neurol* **4**:96–109.

Borkovec TD (1994) The nature, functions and origins of worry. In GCL Davey & F Tallis (eds), *Worrying: Perspectives on Theory, Assessment and Treatment.* Chichester, John Wiley & Sons, Ltd, pp 5–33.

Borkovec TD & Roemer L (1995) Perceived functions of worry among generalized anxiety disorder subjects: distraction from more emotionally distressing topics. *J Behav Ther Exp Psychiat*, **26**:25–30.

Boswell J (1904) *Life of Johnson.* Oxford University Press, Oxford (originally published in 1791).

Bouchard C, Rhéaume J & Ladouceur R (1999) Responsibility and perfectionism in OCD: an experimental study. *Behav Res Ther* **37**:239–248.

Boud D & Feletti GI (1997) *The Challenge of Problem-based Learning.* London, Kogan Page.

Boulougouris JC, Rabavilas AD & Stefanis C (1977) Psychophysiological responses in obsessive-compulsive patients. *Behav Res Ther* **15**:221–230.

Braconi L (1970) La psiconevrosi ossessiva nei gernelli. *Acta Genet Med Gemel* **19**:318–321.

Editorial (1974) Editorial. *Br Med J* **122**:685–686.

BMA (2000) *British National Formulary (BNF).* London, British Medical Association and Royal Pharmaceutical Society of Great Britain.

Brody AL, Saxena S, Schwartz JM, Stoessel PW, Maidment K, Phelps ME & Baxter LR (1998) FDG–PET predictors of response to behavioral therapy and pharmacotherapy in obsessive compulsive disorder. *Psychiat Res Neuroimag* **84**:1–6.

Bromiker R & Kaplan M (1994) Apparent intra-uterine foetal withdrawal from clomipramine hydrochloride. *J Am Med Assoc* **272**:1722–1723.

Brown HD, Kosslyn SM, Breiter HC, Baer L & Jenkite MA (1994a) Can patients with obsessive-compulsive disorder discriminate between percepts and mental images? A signal detection analysis. *J Abnorm Psychol* **103**:445–454.

Brown TA, DiNardo PA & Barlow DH (1994b) *Anxiety Disorders Interview Schedule for DSM-IV.* San Antonio, TX, The Psychological Corporation.

Brown TA (1998) The relationships between obsessive-compulsive disorder and other anxiety-based disorders. In R Swinson, M Antony, S Rachman & M Richter (eds), *Obsessive-Compulsive Disorder—Theory, Research and Treatment*. New York, Guilford.

Bruce BK & Stevens VM (1992) AIDS-related obsessive compulsive disorder: a treatment dilemma. *J Anxiety Disord* **6**:79–88.

Bruch MH (1988) *The Self-schema Model of Complex Disorders*. Regensburg, S Roederer.

Bruch MH & Bond FW (1998) *Beyond Diagnosis: Cognitive Behavioural Case Formulation*. Chichester, John Wiley & Sons, Ltd.

Bryden MP (1982) *Laterality: Functional Asymmetry in the Intact Brain*. London, Academic Press.

Buchanan AW, Meng KS & Marks IM (1996) What predicts improvement and compliance during the behavioral treatment of obsessive compulsive disorder? *Anxiety* **2**:22–27.

Burns LG, Keortge SG, Formea GM & Sternberger LG (1996) Revision of the Padua inventory of obsessive compulsive disorder symptoms: distinctions between worry, obsessions, and compulsions. *Behav Res Ther* **34**:163–173.

Calamari JE, Wiegartz PS & Janeck AS (1999) Obsessive-compulsive disorder subgroups: a symptom–base clustering approach. *Behav Res Ther* **37**:113–125.

Calvocoressi L, Libman D, Vegso S, McDougle C & Price L (1998) Global functioning of inpatients with obsessive-compulsive disorder, schizophrenia and major depression. *Psychiatr Serv* **49**:379–381.

Calvocoressi L, McDougle C & Wasylink S (1993) Inpatient treatment of patients with severe obsessive compulsive disorder. *Hosp Commun Psychol* **44**:1150–1154.

Carey G (1978) A Clinical Genetic Twin Study of Obsessive and Phobic States. PhD Thesis, University of Minnesota.

Carey G & Gottesman II (1981) Twin and family studies of anxiety, phobic and obsessive disorders. In DF Klein & J Rabkin (eds), *Anxiety: New Research and Changing Concepts*. New York, Raven, pp 117–136.

Carey G, Gottesman II & Robins E (1980) Prevalence rates for the neuroses: pitfalls in the evaluation of familiality. *Psychol Med* **10**:437–443.

Carmin CN, Pollard CA & Ownby RL (1998) Obsessive-compulsive disorder: cognitive behavioral treatment of older versus younger adults. *Clin Gerontol* **19**:77–81.

Carr AT (1974) Compulsive neurosis: a review of the literature. *Psychol Bull* **81**:311–318.

Cartwright-Hatton S & Wells A (1997) Beliefs about worry and intrusions: the metacognitions questionnaire and its correlates. *J Anxiety Disord* **11**:279–296.

Castle DJ, Deale A, Marks IM, Cutts F, Chadhoury Y & Steward A (1994) Obsessive-compulsive disorder: prediction of outcome from Behav Psychother. *Acta Psychiat Scand* **89**:393–398.

Castle KJ, Deale A & Marks IM (1995) Gender differences in obsessive compulsive disorder. *Aust NZ J Psychiat* **29**:114–117.

Cawley R (1974) Psychotherapy and obsessional disorders. In HR Beech (ed.), *Obsessional States*. London, Methuen.

Cermele JA, Melendez-Pallitto L & Pandina GJ (2001) Intervention in compulsive hoarding: a case study. *Behav Modif* **25**:214–232.

Chacko RC, Corbin MA & Harper RG (2000) Acquired obsessive-compulsive disorder associated with basal ganglia lesions. *J Neuropsychiat Clin Neurosci* **12**:269–272.

Chambers CD, Johnson KA & Dick LM (1996) Outcomes in pregnant women taking fluoxetine. *N Engl J Med* **335**:1010–1015.

Chambers Dictionary (1993) Edinburgh, Chambers Harrap.

Chan DW (1990) The Maudsley Obsessional-Compulsive Inventory: a psychometric investigation on Chinese normal subjects. *Behav Res Ther* **28**:413–420.

Chapman LJ, Chapman JP & Miller EN (1982) Reliabilities and intercorrelations of eight measures of proneness to psychosis. *J Consult Clin Psychol* **50**:187–195.

Chong SA, Tan CH & Lee HS (1996) Hoarding and clozapine-resperidone combination. *Can J Psychiat* **41**:315–316.

Christensen H, Hadzi-Pavlovic D, Andrews G & Mattick R (1987) Behaviour therapy and tricyclic medication in the treatment of obsessive-compulsive disorder: a quantitative review. *J Consult Clin Psychol* **55**:701–711.

Christensen KJ, Kim SW & Dysken MW (1992) Neuropsychological performance in obsessive-compulsive disorder. *Biol Psychiat* **3**:14–18.

Claparede M (1911) Recognition et moiite. *Arch Psychol Geneve* **11**:79–90.

Clark A, Kirkby KC, Daniels BA & Marks IM (1998) A pilot study of computer-aided vicarious exposure for obsessive-compulsive disorder. *Aust NZ J Psychiat* **32**:268–275.

Clark ANG, Mankikar GD & Gray 1 (1975) Diogenes syndrome: a clinical study of gross neglect in old age. *Lancet* L:366–368.

Clark DA & Purdon C (1993) New perspectives for a cognitive theory of obsessions. *Aust Psychol* **28**:161–167.

Clark DA, Sugrim I & Bolton D (1982) Primary obsessional slowness: a nursing treatment program with a 13-year-old male adolescent. *Behav Res Ther* **20**:289–292.

Clark DM (1985) A cognitive approach to panic. *Behav Res Ther* **24**:461–470.

Clark DM (1988) A cognitive model of panic attacks. In S Rachman & J Maser (eds), *Panic: Psychological Perspectives*. Hillside, NJ, Erlbaum.

Clark DM (1997) Panic disorder and social phobia. In DM Clark & CG Fairburn (eds), *Science and Practice of Cognitive Behaviour Therapy*. Oxford, Oxford University Press.

Clark DM (1999) Anxiety disorders: why they persist and how to treat them. *Behav Res Ther* **37**(suppl):5–28.

Clark DM & Wells A (1995) A cognitive model of social phobia. In R Heimberg, M Liebowitz, DA Hope & FR Schneier (eds), *Social Phobia: Diagnosis, Assessment and Treatment*. New York: Guilford, pp 69–93.

Clark DM, Ball S & Pape D (1991) An experimental investigation of thought suppression. *Behav Res Ther* **29**:253–257.

Clayton IC, Richards JC & Edwards C (1999) Selective attention in obsessive-compulsive disorder. *J Abnorm Psychol* **108**:171–175.

Clifford CA (1982) Twin studies of drinking behaviour and obsessionality. Unpublished PhD thesis, University of London.

Clifford CA, Murray RM & Fulker DW (1984) Genetic and environmental influences on obsessional traits and symptoms. *Psychol Med* **14**:791–800.

Cohen LJ, Hollander E & DeCaria CM (1996) Specificity of neuropsychological impairment in obsessive-compulsive disorder: a comparison with social phobic and normal control subjects. *J Neuropsychiat* **8**:82–85.

Constans JI, Foa EB, Franklin ME & Mathews A (1995) Memory for actual and imagined events in OC checkers. *Behav Res Ther* **33**:665–671.

Cooper J (1970) The Leyton Obsessional Inventory. *Psychol Med* **1**:48–64.

Cooper JE (1983) Obsessional illness and personality. In GFM Russell & LA Hersov (eds), *The Neuroses and Personality Disorders*. Cambridge, Cambridge University Press.

Cooper M (1993) A group for families of obsessive-compulsive persons. *Fam Soc* **74**:301–307.

Cooper M (1996) Obsessive-compulsive disorder: effects on family members. *Am J Orthopsychiat* **66**:296–304.

Cora-Locatelli, Greenberg AD & Martin JD (1998) Rebound psychiatric and physical symptoms after gabapentin discontinuation (letter). *J Clin Psychiat* **59**:131.

Cottraux J, Bouvard M, Defayolle M & Messy P (1988) Validity and factorial structure study of the Compulsive Activity Checklist. *Behav Ther* **19**:45–53.

Cottraux J, Messy P, Marks IM, Mollard E & Bouvard M (1993a) Predictive factors in the treatment of obsessive-compulsive disorders with fluvoxamine and/or behaviour therapy. *Behav Psychother* **21**:45–50.

Cottraux J, Mollard E, Bouvard M & Marks I (1993b) Exposure therapy fluvoxamine or combination treatment in obsessive-compulsive disorder: one-year follow-up. *Psychiat Res* **49**:63–75.

Cottraux J, Mollard E, Bouvard M, Marks IM, Sluys M, Nury AM, Douge R & Cialdella P (1990) A controlled study of fluvoxamine and exposure in obsessive-compulsive disorder. *Int Clin Psychopharmacol* **5**:17–30.

Cowe L & Lloyd J (1982) Convulsions caused by maternal clomipramine. *Br Med J* **284**:1837–1838.

Cox BJ, Swinson RP, Morrison B & Lee PS (1993) Clomipramine, fluoxetine, and behavior therapy in the treatment of obsessive-compulsive disorder, a meta-analysis. *J Behav Ther Exp Psychiat* **24**:149–153.

Cox C (1997) Neuropsychological abnormalities in obsessive compulsive disorder and their assessments. *Int Rev Psychiat* **9**:45–59.

Cox CS, Fedio P & Rapoport JL (1989) Neuropsychological testing of obsessive-compulsive adolsecents. In JL Rapoport (eds), *Obsessive-Compulsive Disorder in Children and Adolescents*. Washington, DC, American Psychiatric Press.

Craske MG (1999) *Anxiety Disorders: Psychological Approaches to Theory and Treatment*. Boulder, CO, Westview.

Crino RC, Andrews G (1996) Obsessive-compulsive disorder and axis I comorbidity. *J Anxiety Disord* **10**:37–46.

Dar R & Greist JH (1992) Behaviour therapy for obsessive-compulsive disorder. *Psychiat Clin N Am* **15**:885–894.

Davey GCL (1995) Rumination and the enhancement of fear: some laboratory findings. *Behav Cogn Psychother* **23**:203–215.

Davey GCL (1997) A conditioning model of phobias. In GCL Davey (ed.), *Phobias: a Handbook of Theory, Research and Treatment*. Chichester, John Wiley & Sons, Ltd.

Davey GCL & Levy S (1998a) Catastrophic worrying: personal inadequacy and a perseverative iterative style as features of the catastrophising process. *J Abnorm Psychol* **107**:576–586.

Davey GCL & Levy S (1998b) Internal statements and catastrophic worrying. *Pers Indiv Differ* **26**:21–32.

Davey GCL & Matchett G (1994) UCS rehearsal and the retention and enhancement of differential 'fear' conditioning: effects of trait and state anxiety. *J Abnorm Psychol* **103**:708–718.

Davey GCL & Tallis F (eds) (1994) *Worrying: Perspectives on Theory, Assessment and Treatment*. Chichester, John Wiley & Sons, Ltd.

Davey GCL, Field AP & Peerbhoy D (2000a) UCS rehearsal and the enhancement of self-reported fear in spider fearful and non-fearful individuals (unpublished manuscript).

Davey GCL, Field AP, Peerbhoy D, Gouksos S & Ritcheson A (2000b) UCS rehearsal and the enhancement of self-reported fear over successive rehearsal trials (unpublished manuscript).

Davey GCL, Jubb M & Cameron C (1996) Catastrophic worrying as a function of changes in problem-solving confidence. *Cogn Ther Res* **20**:333–344.

Davey GCL, Startup HM & Zara A (2002) Mood-as-input and obsessive checking (submitted).

De Araujo LA, Ito LM & Marks IM (1996) Early compliance and other factors predicting outcome of exposure for obsessive-compulsive disorder. *Br J Psychiat* **169**:747–752.

De Araujo LA, Ito LM, Marks IM & Deale A (1995) Does imagined exposure to the consequences of not ritualising enhance live exposure for OCD? A controlled study—main outcome. *Br J Psychiat* **167**:65–70.

De Haan E & Hoogduin CA (1992) The treatment of children with obsessive compulsive disorder. *Acta Paedopsychiat* **55**:93–97.

De Haan E, Hoogduin KAL, Buitelaar JK & Keijsers GPJ (1998) Behavior therapy versus clomipramine for the treatment of obsessive-compulsive disorder in children and adolescents. *J Am Acad Child Adolesc Psychiat* **7**:1022–1029.

De Haan E, van Oppen P, van Balkom AJ, Spinhoven P, Hoogduin KA & van Dyck, R (1997) Prediction of outcome and early vs late improvement in OCD patients treated with cognitive-behaviour therapy and pharmacotherapy. *Acta Psychiat Scand* **96**:354–361.

De Silva P (1986) Obsessional-compulsive imagery. *Behav Res Ther* **24**:333–350.

De Silva P (2000) Obsessive-compulsive disorder. In L Champion & M Power (eds), *Adult Psychological Problems: An Introduction*, 2nd edn. Hove, Psychology Press.

De Silva P & Marks M (2001) Traumatic experiences, post-traumatic stress disorder and obsessive-compulsive disorder. *Int J Psychiat* **13**:172–180.

De Silva P & Rachman S (1992) *Obsessive Compulsive Disorder: the Facts*. Oxford, Oxford University Press.

De Silva P & Rachman S (1998) *Obsessive-Compulsive Disorder: the Facts*, 2nd edn. Oxford, Oxford University Press.

De Silva P, Rachman S & Seligman MEP (1977) Prepared phobias and obsessions: therapeutic outcome. *Behav Res Ther* **15**:65–77.

De Silva, P, Menzies, RG & Shafran, R (2003) Spontaneous decay of compulsive urges: the case of covert compulsions. *Behav Res Ther* (in press).

De Veaugh-Geiss J, Katz R & Landau P (1991) Clomipramine in the treatment of patients with obsessive compulsive disorder: the Clomipramine Collaborative Study Group. *Arch Gen Psychiat* **49**:730–738.

De Veaugh-Geiss J, Moroz G, Biederman J, Cantwell D, Fontraine R, Greist JH, Reichler R, Katz R & Landau P (1992) Clomipramine hydrochloride in childhood and adolescent obsessive-compulsive disorder: a multicenter trial. *J Am Acad Child Adolesc Psychiat* **31**:45–49.

Delgado PL & Moreno FA (1998) Different roles for serotonin in anti-obsessional drug action and the pathophysiology of obsessive compulsive disorder. *Br J Psychiat*, **35**(suppl):21–25.

Derogatis LR (1977) *SCL-90-R: Administration, Scoring and Procedures Manual*. Baltimore, MD, Clinical Psychometrics Research.

Di Nardo P, Brown TA & Barlow DH (1994) *Anxiety Disorders Interview Schedule for DSM-IV (ADIS-IV)*. Albany, NY, Graywind.

Di Nardo PA, Moras K, Barlow DH, Rapee RM & Brown TA (1993) Reliability of DSM-III-R anxiety disorder categories: using the Anxiety Disorders Interview Schedule-Revised (ADIS-R). *Arch Gen Psychiat* **50**:251–256.

Diler RS & Avci A (1999) SSRI-induced mania in obsessive-compulsive disorder. *J Am Acad Child Adolesc Psychiat* **38**:6–7.

Dirson S, Bouvard M, Cottraux J & Martin R (1995) Visual memory impairment in patients with obsessive-compulsive disorder: a controlled study. *Psychother Psychosom* **63**:22–31.

Dollard J & Miller NE (1950) Personality and Psychotherapy: an Analysis in Terms of Learning, Thinking and Culture. New York, Springer.

Douglass HM, Moffitt TE, Dar R, McGee R & Silva P (1995) Obsessive-compulsive disorder in a birth cohort of 18-year-olds: prevalence and predictors. *J Am Acad Child Adolesc Psychiat* **34**:1424–1431.

Dowson JH (1977) The phenomenology of severe obsessive-compulsive neurosis. *Br J Psychiat* **131**:75–78.

Dulcan MK (1996) Epidemiology of child and adolescent mental disorders. *J Am Acad Child Adolesc Psychiat* **35**:852–854.

DuPont R, Rice D, Shiraki S & Rowland C (1995) Economic costs of obsessive-compulsive disorder. *Med Interface* **8**:102–109.

Ecker W & Engelkamp J (1995) Memory for actions in obsessive-compulsive disorder. *Behav Cogn Psychother* **23**:349–371.

Eckman PS & Shean GD (1997) Habituation of cognitive and physiological arousal and social anxiety. *Behav Res Ther* **35**:1113–1121.

Edelmann RJ (1992) *Anxiety: Theory, Research and Intervention in Clinical and Health Psychology*. New York, John Wiley & Sons, Ltd.

Edwards JG, Inman WHW & Wilton L (1994) Prescription event monitoring of 401 patients treated with fluvoxamine. *Br J Psychiat* **164**:387–395.

Edwards S & Dickerson M (1987) On the similarity of positive and negative intrusions. *Behav Res Ther* **25**:207–211.

Ehlers A (1993) Interoception and panic disorder. *Adv Behav Res Ther* **15**:3–21.

Ehlers A & Clark DM (2000) A cognitive model of posttraumatic stress disorder. *Behav Res Ther* **38**:319–345.

Einstein DA & Menzies RG (2000). The role of magical thinking in obsessive-compulsive disorder. Poster presented at the National Conference of the British Association of Behavioural Cognitive Psychotherapies, London.

Eisen JL & Rasmussen SA (1993) Obsessive compulsive disorder with psychotic features. *Clin Psychiat* **54**:373–379.

Eisen JL, Beer EA & Pato MT (1997) Obsessive compulsive disorder in patients with schizophrenia or schizoaffective disorder. *Am J Psychiat* **154**:271–273.

Eisen JL, Goodman WK, Keller MB, Warshaw MG, De Marco LM, Luce DD & Rasmussen SA (1999) Patterns of remission and relapse in obsessive-compulsive disorder: a 2-year prospective study. *J Clin Psychiat* **60**:346–351.

Elkin I, Shea MT & Watkins JT (1989) National Institute of Mental Health Treatment of Depression Collaborative Research Program. General effectiveness of treatments. *Arch Gen Psychiat* **46**:971–982.

Emmelkamp PMG (1982) *Phobic and Obsessive-compulsive Disorders: Theory, Research and Practice*. New York, Plenum.

Emmelkamp PMG (1983) Phobic and Obsessive-compulsive Disorders: Theory, Research and Practice. New York, Plenum Press.

Emmelkamp PMG (1987) Obsessive-compulsive disorders. In L Michelson & LM Ascher (eds), *Anxiety and Stress Disorders: Cognitive Behavioral Assessment and Treatment*. New York, Guilford.

Emmelkamp PMG & Beens H (1991) Cognitive therapy with obsessive-compulsive disorder: a comparative evaluation. *Behav Res Ther* **29**:293–300.

Emmelkamp PMG & Kwee KG (1977) Obsessional ruminations: a comparison between thought-stopping and prolonged exposure in imagination. *Behav Res Ther* **15**:441–444.

Emmelkamp PMG, de Haan E & Hoogduin C (1990) Marital adjustment and obsessive-compulsive disorder. *Br J Psychiat* **156**:55–60.

Emmelkamp PMG, Kraaijkamp HJM & van den Hout MA (1999) Assessment of obsessive-compulsive disorder. *Behav Modif* **23**:269–279.

Emmelkamp PMG, van der Helm MBL, van Zanten & Ploch G (1980) Treatment of obsessive-compulsive patients: the contribution of self-instructional training to the effectiveness of exposure. *Behav Res Ther* **18**:61–66.

Emmelkamp PMG, Visser S & Hoekstra RJ (1988) Cognitive therapy vs exposure *in vivo* in the treatment of obsessive-compulsives. *Cogn Ther Res* **12**:103–114.

England SL & Dickerson M (1988) Intrusive thoughts: unpleasantness not the major cause of uncontrollability. *Behav Res Ther* **26**:279–282.

Enright SJ & Beech AR (1990) Obsessional states: anxiety disorders or schizotypes? An information processing and personality assessment. *Psychol Med* **20**:621–627.

Enright SJ & Beech AR (1997) Schizotypy and obsessive-compulsive disorder. In G Claridge (ed), *Schizotypy: Implications for Illness and Health*. New York, Oxford University Press, pp 202–223.

Epperson CN, McDougle CJ & Price LH (1996) Intranasal oxytocin in obsessive compulsive disorder. *Biol Psychiat* **40**:547–549.

Eslinger PJ & Damasio AR (1985) Severe disturbance of higher cognition after bilateral frontal lobe ablation: patient EVR. *Neurology* **35**:1731–1741.

Esquirol JED (1838) *Des Maladies Mentales*, vol 2. Paris, Baillière.

Evans M, Bradweijn J, Dunn L (eds) (2000) *Guidelines for the Treatment of Anxiety Disorders in Primary Care*. Anxiety Review Panel, Queen's Printer, Toronto.

Expert Consensus Guidelines: treatment of obsessive-compulsive disorder (1997) *J Clin Psychiat* **58**(suppl):3S–72S.

Eysenck HJ (1985) *The Decline and Fall of the Freudian Empire*. London, Penguin. Books.

Eysenck M (1992) *Anxiety: the Cognitive Perspective*. Hove, Lawrence Erlbaum.

Faber RJ & O'Guinn TC (1992) A clinical screener for compulsive buying. *J Consumer Res* **19**:459–469.

Falcouer DS (1965) On the inheritance of liability to certain diseases, estimated from the incidence among relatives. *Annals Hum Gen* **29**:51–76.

Fallon BA, Campeas R & Schneier FR (1992) Open trial of intravenous clomipramine in five treatment refractory patients with obsessive compulsive disorder. *J Neuropsychiat Clin Neurosci* **4**:70–75.

Fallon BA, Liebowitz MR & Campeas R (1998) Intravenous clomipramine for obsessive compulsive disorder refractory to oral clomipramine: a placebo-controlled study. *Arch Gen Psychiat* **55**(10):918–924.

Fals-Stewart W, Marks I & Schafer B (1993) A comparison of behavioural group therapy and individual behaviour therapy in treating obsessive-compulsive disorder. *J Nerv Ment Dis* **181**:189–193.

Faravelli C, Guerini-Degl'Innocenti B & Giardinelli L (1989) Epidemiology of anxiety disorders in Florence. *Acta Psychiat Scand* **79**:308–312.

Faravelli C, Salvatori S & Galassi F (1997) Epidemiology of somatoform disorders: a community survey in Florence. *Soc Psychiatry Psychiat Epidemiol* **32**:24–29.

Fenichel O (1946) *The Psychoanalytic Theory of Neurosis.* London, Routledge and Keegan-Paul.

Feske U & Chambless DL (2000) A review of assessment measures for obsessive-compulsive disorder. In WK Goodman, MV Rudorfer et al. (eds), *Obsessive-compulsive Disorder: Contemporary Issues in Treatment.* Mahwah, NJ, Erlbaum.

Field AP (1999) The role of cognitive rehearsal in the maintenance of phobias. British Psychological Society Annual Conference, Belfast, 8–11 April.

Field AP & Davey GCL (2001) Conditioning models of childhood anxiety. In WK Silverman & PA Treffers (eds) *Anxiety Disorders in Children and Adolescents: Research, Assessment and Intervention.* Cambridge, Cambridge University Press.

Field AP, St-Leger E & Davey GCL (2000) Past- and future-based rumination and its effect on catastrophic worry and anxiety (manuscript under review).

Figueroa Y, Rosenberg DR, Birmaher B & Keshavan MS (1998) Combination treatment with clomipramine and selective serotonin re-uptake inhibitors for obsessive-compulsive disorder in children and adolescents. *J Child Psychol Psychiat* **8**:61–67.

Fineberg N (1996) Refining treatment approaches in obsessive compulsive disorder. *Int Clin Psychopharmacol* **11**(suppl):13S–22S.

First MB, Spitzer RL, Gibbon M & Williams JBW (1995) *Structured Clinical Interview for DSM-IV Axis I Disorders—Patient Edition* (SCID-I/D, version 20). New York, Biometrics Research Department, New York Psychiatric Institute.

Fischer DJ, Himle JA & Hanna GL (1998) Group behavioural therapy for adolescents with obsessive-compulsive disorder: preliminary outcomes. *Res Soc Work Pract* **8**:629–636.

Fitzgerald KD, MacMaster FP, Paulson LD & Rosenberg DR (1999) Neurobiology of childhood obsessive-compulsive disorder. *Child Adolesc Psychiat Clin N Am* **8**:533–575.

Flament MF, Whitaker A, Rapoport JL, Davies M, Berg CZ, Kalikow K, Sceery W & Shaffer D (1988) Obsessive-compulsive disorder in adolescence: an epidemiological study. *J Am Acad Child Adolesc Psychiat* **27**:764–771.

Fleiss JL (1981) *Statistical Methods for Rates and Proportions*, 2nd edn. New York, John Wiley & Sons, Ltd.

Flor-Henry P, Yeudall LT, Koles ZJ & Howarth BG (1979) Neuropsychological and power spectral EEG investigations of the obsessive compulsive syndrome. *Biol Psychiat* **14**:119–129.

Foa EB (1979) Failure in treating obsessive-compulsives. *Behav Res Ther* **17**:169–176.

Foa EB & Goldstein A (1978) Continuous exposure and complete response prevention of obsessive-compulsive disorder. *Behav Ther* **9**:821–829.

Foa EB & Kozak MJ (1986) Emotional processing of fear: exposure to corrective information. *Psychol Bull* **99**:20–35.

Foa EB & Kozak MJ (1995) DSM-IV field trial: obsessive compulsive disorder. *Am J Psychiat* **152**:90–96.

Foa EB & Kozak MJ (1996) Psychological treatment for obsessive compulsive disorder. In MR Mavissakalian & RF Prien (eds), *Long Term Treatments for Anxiety Disorders.* Washington DC, American Psychiatric Press, pp 285–309.

Foa EB & Wilson R (1991) *Stop Obsessing!* New York, Bantam.

Foa EB, Franklin ME & Kozak MJ (1998a) Psychosocial treatments for obsessive-compulsive disorder. In RP Swinson, MM Antony, S Rachman & MA Richter (eds), *Obsessive-compulsive Disorder: Theory, Research and Treatment*. New York, Guilford.

Foa EB, Grayson JB, Steketee GS, Doppelt HG, Turner RM & Latimer PR (1983b) Success and failure in the behavioral treatment of obsessive-compulsives. *J Consult Clin Psychol* **51**:287–297.

Foa EB, Kozak MJ, Goodman WK, Hollander E, Jenike MA & Rasmussen SA (1995) DSM-IV field trial: obsessive-compulsive disorder. *Am J Psychiat* **152**:90–96.

Foa EB, Kozak MJ, Salkovskis PM, Coles ME & Amir N (1998b) The validation of a new obsessive-compulsive disorder scale: the Obsessive-Compulsive Inventory. *Psychol Assess* **10**:206–214.

Foa EB, Kozak MJ, Steketee GS & McCarthy PR (1992) Treatment of depressive and obsessive-compulsive symptoms in OCD by imipramine and behaviour therapy. *Br J Clin Psychol* **31**:279–292.

Foa EB, Steketee GS, Grayson JB & Dobell HG (1983a) Treatment of obsessive-compulsives: when do we fail? In EB Foa & PMG Emmelkamp (eds), *Failures in Behavior Therapy*. New York, Wiley.

Foa EB, Steketee GS, Grayson JB, Turner RM & Latimer P (1984) Deliberate exposure and blocking of obsessive-compulsive rituals: immediate and long-term effects. *Behav Ther* **15**:450–472.

Foa EB, Steketee G, Kozak M & Dugger D (1987) Effects of imipramine on depression and obsessive-compulsive symptoms. *Psychiat Res* **211 987**, 123–136.

Foa EB, Steketee GS & Milby JB (1980a) Differential effects of exposure and response prevention in obsessive-compulsive washers. *J Consult Clin Psychol* **48**:71–79.

Foa EB, Steketee GS & Ozarow BJ (1985) Behavior therapy with obsessive-compulsives. In M Mavissakalian (ed.), *Obsessive-compulsive Disorders: Psychological and Pharmacological Treatments*. New York, Plenum, pp 49–129.

Foa EB, Steketee GS, Turner RM & Fischer SC (1980b) Effects of imaginal exposure to feared disasters in obsessive-compulsive checkers. *Behav Res Ther* **18**: 449–455.

Frankenburg F (1984) Hoarding in anorexia nervosa. *Br J Med Psychol* **57**:57–60.

Franklin ME & Foa E (1998) Cognitive-behavioral treatments for obsessive-compulsive disorder. In PE Nathan & JM Gordon (eds), *A Guide to Treatments that Work*. Oxford, Oxford University Press, pp 339–357.

Franklin ME, Abramowitz JS, Kozak MJ, Levitt JT & Foa EB (2000) Effectiveness of exposure and ritual prevention for obsessive-compulsive disorder: randomized compared with non-randomized samples. *J Consult Clin Psychol* **68**:594–602.

Franklin ME, Kozak MJ, Cashman LA, Coles ME, Rheingold AA & Foa E (1998) Cognitive-behavioural treatment of pediatric obsessive-compulsive disorder: an open clinical trial. *J Am Acad Child Adolesc Psychiat* **37**:412–419.

Freeman C, Trimble MR & Deakin JFW (1994) Fluvoxamine versus clomipramine in the treatment of obsessive compulsive disorder: a multicentre double-blind parellell group comparison. *J Clin Psychiat* **55**:301–305.

Freeman CP (1992) What is obsessive compulsive disorder? The clinical syndrome and its boundaries. *Int Clin Psychopharmacol* **7** (suppl 1):11–17.

Freeman JB & Leonard HL (2000) Sexual obsessions in obsessive compulsive disorder. *J Am Acad Child Adolesc Psychiat* **39**:141–142.

Freeston MH & Ladouceur R (1993) Appraisal of cognitive intrusions and response style: replication and extension. *Behav Res Ther* **31**:185–191.

Freeston MH & Ladouceur R (1997) What do patients do with their obsessional thoughts? *Behav Res Ther* **35**:335–348.

Freeston MH, Ladouceur R, Gagnon F, Thibodeau N, Rheaume J, Letarte H & Bujold A (1997) Cognitive-behavioural treatment of obsessive thoughts: a controlled study. *J Consult Clin Psychol* **65**:405–413.

Freeston MH, Ladouceur R, Rheaume J, Letarte H, Gagnon F & Thibodeau N (1994a) Self-report of obsessions and worry. *Behav Res Ther* **32**:29–36.

Freeston MH, Rhéaume J, Letarte H & Dugas MJ (1994b) Why do people worry? *Pers Indiv Differ* **17**:791–802.

Freeston MH, Ladouceur R, Thibodeau N & Gagnon F (1992) Cognitive intrusions in a nonclinical population: response style, subjective experience and appraisal. *Behav Res Ther* **29**:585–597.

Freeston MH, Rhéaume J & Ladouceur R (1996) Correcting faulty appraisals of obsessional thoughts. *Behav Res Ther* **34**:433–446.

Freud S (1896) Early psycho-analytic publications. In J Strachey (ed.), *The Standard Edition of the Complete Psychological Works of Sigmund Freud*, vol 3. London, Hogarth Press and the Institute of Psychoanalysis, pp 121–145.

Freud S (1908) Character and Anal Eroticism. In J Stachey (ed.), *The Standard Edition of the Complete Psychological Works of Sigmund Freud*, vol 9. London, Hogarth Press and the Institute of Psychoanalysis, pp 167–176.

Freud S (1909) Notes upon a case of obsessional neurosis. In J Strachey (ed.), *The Standard Edition of the Complete Psychological Works of Sigmund Freud*, vol 10. London, Hogarth Press and the Institute of Psychoanalysis, pp 153–318.

Freund B & Foa EB (1988) Reliability of symptomatology and mood state measures in the assessment of obsessive-compulsive disorder. Poster session presented at the Annual Meeting of the Association for the Advancement of Behavior Therapy, New York.

Freund B, Steketee GS & Foa, EB (1987) Compulsive Activity Checklist (CAC): psychometric analysis with obsessive-compulsive disorder. *Behav Assess* **9**:67–79.

Friedman S, Hatch M, Paradis C & Shalita A (1993) Obsessive compulsive disorder in two black ethnic groups: incidence in an urban dermatology clinic. *J Anxiety Disord* **7**:343–348.

Frijda NH (1988) The laws of emotion. *Am Psychol* **43**:349–358.

Fritzler BK, Hecker JE & Losee MC (1997) Self-directed treatment with minimal therapist contact: Preliminary findings for obsessive-compulsive disorder. *Behav Res Ther* **35**:627–631.

Fromm E (1947) *Man for Himself. An Inquiry into the Psychology of Ethics*. New York, Rinehart.

Frost RO & Gross RC (1993) The hoarding of possessions. *Behav Res Ther* **31**:367–381.

Frost RO & Hartl TL (1996) A cognitive-behavioural model of compulsive hoarding. *Behav Res Ther* **34**:341–350.

Frost RO & Shows DL (1993) The nature and measurement of compulsive indecisiveness. *Behav Res Ther* **31**:683–692.

Frost RO & Steketee G (1997) Perfectionism in obsessive-compulsive disorder. *Behav Res Ther* **35**:291–296.

Frost RO & Steketee G (1998) Hoarding: clinical aspects and treatment strategies. In MA Jenike, L Baer & WE Minichiello (eds), *Obsessive-Compulsive Disorder— Practical Management*, 3rd edn. St Louis, MO: Mosby.

Frost RO, Hartl TL, Christian R & Williams N (1995a) The value of possessions in compulsive hoarding. *Behav Res Ther* **33**:897–902.

Frost RO, Steketee GS, Krause MS & Trepanier KL (1995b) The relationship of the Yale–Brown Obsessive Compulsive Scale (YBOCS) to other measures of obsessive compulsive symptoms in a nonclinical population. *J Pers Assess* **65**:158–168.

Frost RO, Kim H-J, Morris C, Bloss C, Murray-Close M & Steketee G (1998) Hoarding, compulsive buying and reasons for saving. *Behav Res Ther* **36**:657–664.

Frost RO, Krause M & Steketee G (1996) Hoarding and obsessive compulsive symptoms. *Behav Modif* **20**:116–132.

Frost RO, Krause MS, McMahon MJ, Peppe J, Evans M, McPhee AE & Holden M (1993) Compulsivity and superstitiousness. *Behav Res Ther* **31**:423–425.

Frost RO, Lahart CM, Dugas KM & Sher KJ (1988) Information processing among non-clinical compulsives *Behav Res Ther* **26**:275–277.

Frost RO, Marten P, Lahart C & Rosenblate R (1990) The dimensions of perectionism. *Cogn Ther Res* **14**:449–468.

Frost RO, Meagher BM & Riskind JH (2001) Obsessive-compulsive features in pathological lottery and scratch ticket gamblers. *J Gambling Studies*.

Frost RO, Steketee G & Williams LF (2000b) Hoarding: a community health problem. *Health Soc Care* **8**:229–234.

Frost RO, Steketee G, Williams L & Warren R (2000c) Mood, disability and personality disorder symptoms in hoarding, obsessive compulsive disorder and control subjects. *Behav Res Ther* **38**:1071–1082.

Frost RO, Sher KJ & Green T (1986) Psychopathology and personality characteristics of non-clinical compulsive checkers. *Behav Res Ther* **24**:133–143.

Frost RO, Steketee G, Youngren VR & Mallya GK (1999a) The threat of the housing inspector: a case of hoarding. *Harvard Rev Psychiat* **6**:270–278.

Frost RO, Steketee G & Williams L (2002) Compulsive buying, compulsive hoarding and obsessive compulsive disorder. *Behav Ther* **333**:201–214.

Furby L (1978) Possessions: toward a theory of their meaning and function throughout the life cycle. In PB Bates (ed.), *Life Span Development and Behavior*, vol 1. New York, Academic Press.

Fux M, Levine J & Aviv A (1996) Inositol treatment of obsessive compulsive disorder. *Am J Psychiat* **153**:1219–1221.

Garvey MA, Giedd J & Swedo SE (1998) PANDAS: the search for environmental triggers of pediatric neuro-psychiatric disorders. Lessons from rheumatic fever. *J Child Neurol* **13**:413–423.

Gelder M, Gath D & Mayou R (1983) *Oxford Textbook of Psychiatry*. Oxford, Oxford Medical Publications.

Gelder MG (1999) Core curriculum in psychiatry for medical students. *Med Educ* **33**:204–211.

Geller D, Biederman J, Jones J, Park K, Schwartz S, Shapiro S & Coffey B (1998) Is juvenile obsessive-compulsive disorder a developmental subtype of the disorder? A review of the pediatric literature. *J Am Acad Child Adolesc Psychiat* **37**:420–427.

George MS, Trimble MR, Ring HA, Sallee FR & Robertson MM (1993) Obsessions in obsessive-compulsive disorder with and without Gilles de la Tourette's syndrome. *Am J Psychiat* **150**:93–97.

Gerrard N (1999) Iron maiden—an interview with Ann Widdecombe. *The Observer Magazine*, 3 October, 14–18.

Gershuny BS & Sher KJ (1995) Compulsive checking and anxiety in a non-clinical sample: differences in cognition, behavior, personality and affect. *J Psychopathol Behav*, **17**, 19–38.

Ghosh A & Marks I (1987) Self-treatment of agoraphobia by exposure. *Behav Ther* **18**:3–16.

Gibbs NA & Oltmanns TF (1995) The relation between obsessive-compulsive personality traits and subtypes of compulsive behavior. *J Anxiety Disord* **9**:397–410.

Giedd JN, Rapoport JL, Garvey MA, Perlmutter S & Swedo SE (2000) MRI assessment of children with obsessive-compulsive disorder or tics associated with streptococcal infection. *Am J Psychiat* **157**:281–283.

Gitlin M (1994) Psychotropic medications and their effects on sexual function: diagnosis, biology and treatment approaches. *J Clin Psychiat* **55**:406–413.

Goldberg HL & Nissim R (1994) Psychotropic drugs in pregnancy and lactation. *Int J Psychiat Med* **24**:129–147.

Goldberger E & Rapoport JL (1991) Canine acral lick dermatitis: response to the anti-obsessional drug clomipramine. *Am Animal Hospital Assoc* **27**:179–182.

Goldman-Rakic PS (1988) Topography of cognition: parallel distributed networks in primate association cortex. *Ann Rev Neurosci* **11**:137–156.

Goldsmith T, Shapira NA, Phillips KA & McElroy SL (1998) Conceptual foundations of obsessive-compulsive spectrum disorders. In RP Swinson, MM Antony, S Rachman & MA Richter (eds), *Obsessive-Compulsive Disorder: Theory, Research and Treatment*. New York, Guilford.

Gomez Perez JC, Marks IM & Gutierrez Fisac JL (1994) Dysmorphophobia: clinical features and outcome with behavior therapy. *Eur Psychiat* **9**:229–235.

Goodman R & Yude C (1996) IQ and its predictors in childhood hemiplegia. *Dev Med Child Neurol* **38**:881–890.

Goodman WK & Price LH (1998) Rating scales for obsessive-compulsive disorder. In MA Jenike, L Baer & WE Minichiello (eds), *Obsessive Compulsive Disorders: Practical Management*, 3rd edn. St Louis, MO: Mosby.

Goodman WK, Price LH & Delgado PL (1990) Specificity of serotonin reuptake inhibitors in the treatment of obsessive-compulsive disorder. Comparison of fluvoxamine and desipramine. *Arch Gen Psychiat* **47**:577–585.

Goodman WK, Price LH, Rasmussen SA, Mazure D, Delgado P, Heninger GR & Charney DS (1989a) The Yale–Brown Obsessive-Compulsive Scale: Part II, Validity. *Arch Gen Psychiat* **46**:1012–1016.

Goodman WK, Price LH, Rasmussen SA, Mazure D, Fleischmann RL, Hill CL, Heninger GR & Charney DS (1989b) The Yale–Brown Obsessive-Compulsive Scale: Part I, Development, use and reliability. *Arch Gen Psychiat* **46**:1006–1011.

Grabe HJ, Goldschmidt F, Lehmkuhl L, Gansicke M, Spitzer C & Freyberger HJ (1999) Dissociative symptoms in obsessive compulsive dimensions. *Psychopathology* **32**:319–324.

Grados MA & Riddle MA (1999) Obsessive-compulsive disorder in children and adolescents: treatment guidelines. *CNS Drugs* **12**:257–277.

Grados MA, Scahill L & Riddle MA (1999) Pharmacotherapy in children and adolescents with obsessive-compulsive disorder. *Child Adolesc Psychiat Clin N Am* **8**:617–634.

Grady T, Pigott TA & L'Heureux F (1993) Double-blind study of adjuvant buspirone for fluoxetine treated patients with obsessive compulsive disorder. *Am J Psychiat* **150**:819–821.

Graham C, Kenwright M & Marks, I (2000) Psychotherapy by computer: a postal survey of responders to a teletext article. *Psychiat Bull*, **24**:331–332.

Gray JA (1982) *Psychology of Fear and Stress*. London, Weidenfield.

Grayson JB (1999) GOAL: a behavioral self-help group for obsessive-compulsive disorder. *Crisis Inter Time-L* **5**:95–107.

Grayson JB, Foa EB & Steketee GS (1982) Habituation during exposure treatment:. Distraction versus attentioan focussing. *Behav Ther Res* **20**:323–328.

Grayson JB, Steketee GS & Foa EB (1986) Exposure *in vivo* of obsessive-compulsives under distracting and attention-focusing conditions: replication and extension. *Behav Ther Res* **24**:475–479.

Greenberg D (1987) Compulsive hoarding. *Am J Psychother* **41**:409–416.

Greenberg D, Witzum E & Levy A (1990) Hoarding as a psychiatric symptom. *J Clin Psychiat* **51**:417–421.

Greenhill LL, Pine D, March J, Birmaher B & Riddle M (1998) Assessment issues in treatment research of pediatric anxiety disorders: what is working, what is not working, what is missing, and what needs improvement. *Psychopharmacol Bull* **34**:155–164.

Greist J (1998a) Clinical computing: treatment for all: the computer as a patient assistant. *Psychiat Serv* **49**:887–889.

Greist JH (1998b) The comparative effectiveness of treatments for obsessive compulsive disorder (review). *B Menninger Clin* **62**(4, suppl A):65–81.

Greist JH & Jefferson JW (1998) Pharmacotherapy for obsessive compulsive disorder. *Br J Psychiat* **173**(suppl 35):64–70.

Greist JH, Chouinard G & Duboff E (1995a) Double blind parallel comparison of three doses of sertraline and placebo in outpatients with obsessive compulsive disorder. *Arch Gen Psychiat* **52**:289–295.

Greist JH, Jefferson JW & Kobak KA (1995b) Efficacy and tolerability of serotonin transport inhibitors in obsessive compulsive disorder: a meta-analysis. *Arch Gen Psychiat* **52**:53–60.

Greist JH, Jenike MA & Robinson D (1995c) Efficacy of fluvoxamine in obsessive compulsive disorder: results of a multi-centre double blind placebo controlled trial. *Eur J Clin Res* **7**:195–204.

Gross R, Sasson Y, Chopra M & Zohar J (1998) In RP Swinson, MM Antony, S Rachman & M Richter (eds), *Obsessive-Compulsive Disorder: Theory, Research and Treatment*. New York, Guilford.

Grubbs JH (1997) SSRI-induced mania (letter). *J Am Acad Child Adolesc Psychiat* **36**:445.

Grunbaum A (1984) *The Foundations of Psychoanalysis*. Los Angeles, CA, University of California Press.

Grunes M (1999) Family Involvement in the Behavioral Treatment of Obsessive Compulsive Disorder. Unpublished Dissertation, Hofstra University, USA. *Diss Abstr Int B Sci Eng* **59**(9-B):5083.

Hackman A & Mc Lean C (1975) A comparison of flooding and thought-stopping. *Behav Res Ther* **13**:263–270.

Hand I (1998) Out-patient, multi-modal behaviour therapy for obsessive-compulsive disorder. *Br J Psychiat* **173**(suppl 35):45–52.

Hanna GL (1995) Demographic and clinical features of obsessive-compulsive disorder in children and adolescents. *J Am Acad Child Adolesc Psychiat* **34**:19–27.

Hanna GL (2000) Clinical and family-genetic studies of childhood obsessive-compulsive disorder. In WK Goodman, MV Rudorfer & JD Maser (eds), *Obsessive-Compulsive Disorder: Contemporary issues in Treatment*. Personality and Clinical Psychology Series. New York, Erlbaum.

Hanna GL, Himle JA, Curtis GC, Koram DQ, Veenstra-VanderWeele J, Leventhal BL & Cook EH Jr (1998) Serotonin transporter and seasonal variation in blood serotonin in families with obsessive-compulsive disorder. *Neuropharmacology* **18**(2):102–111.

Harris DL (1982) Cosmetic surgery—where does it begin? *Br J Plast Surg* **35**:281–286.

Hartl TL & Frost RO (1999) Cognitive-behavioral treatment of compulsive hoarding: a multiple baseline experimental case study. *Behav Res Ther* **37**:451–461.

Hartl TL, Savage CR, Frost RO, Allen GJ, Deckersbach T, Steketee G & Duffany SR (2000) Actual and perceived memory deficits among compulsive hoarders (unpublished manuscript).

Hartson HJ & Swerdlow NR (1999) Visuospatial priming and Stroop performance in patients with obsessive-compulsive disorder. *Neuropsychology* **13**:447–457.

Harvey JM, Richards JC, Dziadosz T & Swindell A (1993) Misinterpretation of ambiguous stimuli in panic disorder. *Cogn Ther Res* **17**:235–248.

Harvey NS (1987) Neurological factors in obsessive-compulsive disorder. *Br J Psychiat* **150**:567–568.

Head D, Bolton D & Hymas N (1989) Deficit in cognitive set shifting ability in patients with obsessive-compulsive disorders. *Biol Psychiat* **25**:929–937.

Headland K & MacDonald B (1987) Rapid audio-tape treatment of obsessional ruminations: a case report. *Behav Psychother* **15**:188–192.

Heimann SW & March JS (1996) SSRI-induced mania (letter). *J Am Acad Child Adolesc Psychiat* **35**:4.

Henderson JG & Pollard CA (1988) Three types of obsessive compulsive disorder in a community sample. *J Clin Psychol* **44**:747–752.

Hermesh H, Aizenberg D & Munitz H (1990) Trazadone treatment in clomipramine resistant obsessive compulsive disorder. *Clin Neuropharmacol* **13**:322–328.

Hewlett WA, Vinogradov S & Agras WS (1992) Clomipramine, clonazepam, and clonidine treatment of obsessive-compulsive disorder. *J Clin Pharmacol* **12**:420–429.

Higgins E (1987) Self-discrepancy: a theory relating self and affect. *Psychol Rev* **94**:319–340.

Higgins E (1996) Obsessive-compulsive spectrum disorders in primary care: the possibilities and pitfalls. *J Clin Psychiat* **57**:7–10.

Hirt ER, Melton RJ, McDonald HE & Harackiewicz JM (1996) Processing goals, task interest, and the mood-performance relationship: a mediational analysis. *J Pers Soc Psychol* **71**:245–261.

Hiss H, Foa EB & Kozak MJ (1994) Relapse prevention program for treatment of obsessive-compulsive disorder *J Consult Clin Psychol* **62**:801–808.

Hoaken PCS & Schnurr R (1980) Genetic factors in obsessive-compulsive neurosis? A rare case of discordant monozygotic twins. *Can J Psychiat* **25**:167–172.

Hodgson RJ & Rachman S (1972) The effects of contamination and washing in obsessional patients. *Behav Res Ther* **10**:111–117.

Hodgson RJ & Rachman S (1977) Obsessional-compulsive complaints. *Behav Res Ther* **15**:389–395.

Hodgson RJ, Rachman S & Marks IM (1972) The treatment of chronic obsessive-compulsive neurosis: follow-up and further findings. *Behav Ther Res* **10**:181–189.

Hoehn-Saric R, Ninan B & Black DW (2000) Multicentre double-blind comparison of sertraline and desipramine for concurrent obsessive compulsive and major depressive disorder. *Arch Gen Psychiat* **57**:76–82.

Hoekstra R (1989) Treatment of obsessive-compulsive disorder with rational-emotive therapy. Paper presented at the First World Congress of Cognitive Therapy, Oxford, 28 June–2 July, 1989.

Hoffnung R, Aizenberg D, Hermesh H & Munitz H (1989) Religious compulsions and the spectrum concept of psychopathology. *Psychopathology* **22**:141–144.

Hohagen F, Winkelmann G, Rasche-Ruchle H, H& I, Konig A, Munchau N, Hiss H, Geiger-Kabisch C, Kuppler C, Schramm P, Rey E, Aldenhoff J & Berger M

(1998) Combination of behaviour therapy with fluvoxamine in comparison with behaviour therapy and placebo. *Br J Psychiat* **35**(suppl):71–78.

Hollander E (1993) *Obsessive-compulsive Related Disorders.* Washington DC, American Psychiatric Press.

Hollander E & Benzaquen S (1997) The obsessive-compulsive spectrum disorders. *Int Rev Psychiat* **9**:99–110.

Hollander E, Allen A & Kwon J (1999) Clomipramine vs desipramine crossover trial in body dysmorphic disorder: selective efficacy of a serotonin reuptake inhibitor in imagined ugliness. *Arch Gen Psychiat* **56**:1033–1042.

Hollander E, Cohen L, Richards M, Mullen L, DeCaria C & Stern Y (1993) A pilot study of the neuropsychology of obsessive-compulsive disorder and Parkinson's disease: basal ganglia disorders. *J Neuropsychiat Clin Neurosci* **5**:104–106.

Hollander E, DeCaria CM & Schneier FR (1990a) Fenfluramine augmentation of serotonin re-uptake blockade anti-obsessional treatment. *J Clin Psychiat* **51**:119–123.

Hollander E, Schiffman E, Cohen B, Rivera-Stein MA, Rosen W, Gorman JM, Fryer AK, Papp L & Liebowitz MR (1990b) Signs of central nervous system dysfunction in obsessive compulsive disorder. *Arch Gen Psychiat* **47**:27–32.

Hollander E, Kwon JH, Stein DJ & Broatch J (1996) Obsessive-compulsive and spectrum disorders: overview and quality of life issues. *J Clin Psychiat* **57**(suppl 8):3–6.

Hollander HC (1974) Displacement activity as a form of abnormal behavior in animals. In HR Beech (ed.), *Obsessional States.* London, Methuen, pp 161–173.

Hollingsworth CE, Tanguay PE, Grossman L & Pabst P (1980) Long-term outcome of obsessive-compulsive disorder in childhood. *J Am Acad Child Adolesc Psychiat* **19**:134–144.

Holzer JC, Goodman WK, McDougle CJ, Baer, L, Boyarsky BK, Leckman JF & Price LH (1994) Obsessive-compulsive disorder with and without a chronic tic disorder: a comparison of symptoms in 70 patients. *Br J Psychiat* **164**:469–473.

Honjo S, Hirano C, Murase S & Kaneko T (1989) Obsessive-compulsive symptoms in childhood and adolescence. *Acta Psychiat Scand* **80**:83–91.

Horowitz M (1969) Psychic trauma: return of images after a stress film. *Arch Gen Psychiat* **20**:552–559.

Horowitz M (1975) Intrusive and repetitive thoughts after experimental stress. *Arch Gen Psychiat* **32**:1457–1463.

Hwang J-P, Tsai S-J, Yang C-H, Liu K-M & Lirng J-F (1998) Hoarding behavior in dementia—a preliminary report. *Am J Geriat Psychiat* **6**:285–289.

Hymas N, Lees A, Bolton D, Epps K & Head D (1991) The neurology of obsessional slowness. *Brain* **114**:2203–2233.

Ingram IM (1961a) Obsessional personality and anal-erotic character. *J Ment Sci* **107**:1035–1042.

Ingram IM (1961b) The obsessional personality and obsessional illness. *Am J Psychiat* **117**:1016–1019.

Inouye E (1965) Similar and dissimilar manifestations of obsessive-compulsive neurosis in monozygotic twins. *Am J Psychiat* **121**:1171–1175.

Insel TR (1988) Obsessive-compulsive disorder: a neuroethological perspective. *Psychopharmacol Bull* **24**:365–369.

Insel TR, Donnelly EF, Lalakea ML, Alterman IS & Murphy DL (1983a) Neurological and neuropsychological studies of patients with obsessive-compulsive disorder. *Biol Psychiat* **18**:741–751.

Insel TR, Murphy DL, Cohen RM, Alterman I, Kilton C & Linnoila M (1983b) Obsessive-compulsive disorder: a double-blind trial of clomipramine and clorgyline. *Arch Gen Psychiat* **40**:605–612.

Irle E, Exner C & Thielen K (1998) Obsessive compulsive disorder and ventromedial frontal leisions: clinical and neuropsychological findings. *Am J Psychiat* **155**:255–263.

Ito LM, Marks IM, de Araujo LA & Hemsley D (1995) Does imagined exposure to the consequences of not ritualising enhance live exposure for OCD? A controlled study. II. Effect on behavioural v. subjective concordance of improvement. *Br J Psychiat* **167**:71–75.

Jakes I (1996) *Theoretical Approaches to Obsessive-Compulsive Disorder*. Cambridge, Cambridge University Press.

James IA & Blackburn IM (1995) Cognitive therapy with obsessive-compulsive disorder. *Brit J Psychiat* **166**:444–450.

Janet P (1903) *Les Obsessions es la Psychasthénie*. Paris, Alcan.

Janet P (1904) *Les Obsessions et la Psychasthenie*, 2nd edn. Paris, Ballière.

Janicak PG, Davis JM & Preskorn SH (1993) Assessment and treatment of other disorders. In PG Janicak, JM Davis, SH Preskorn et al. (eds), *Principles and Practice of Psychopharmacotherapy*. Baltimore, MA, Williams and wilkins, pp 449–490.

Jardine R, Martin NG & Henderson AS (1984) Genetic co-variation between neuroticism and symptoms of anxiety and depression. *Genet Epidemiol* **1**:89–107.

Jaspers K (1913) *Allgemeine Psychopathologie*. Heidelberg, Springer.

Jenike MA (1981) Rapid response of severe obsessive compulsive disorder to tanylcypromine. *Am J Psychiat* **138**:1249–1250.

Jenike MA (1989) Obsessive-compulsive and related disorders. A hidden epidemic. *N Engl J Med* **321**:539–541.

Jenike MA (1991) Obsessive-compulsive disorders: a clinical approach. In W Coryell & G Winokur (eds), *The Clinical Management of Anxiety Disorders*. New York, Oxford University Press, pp 101–124.

Jenike MA, Baer L & Ballantine HT (1991a) Cingulotomy for refractory obsessive compulsive disorder. *Arch Gen Psychiat* **48**:548–555.

Jenike MA, Baer L & Buttol PH (1991b) Buspirone augmentation of fluoxetine in patients with obsessive compulsive disorder. *J Clin Psychiat* **1**:13–14.

Jenike MA, Baer L & Minichiello WE (1986) Concomitant obsessive compulsive disorder and schizotypal personality disorder. *Am J Psychiat* **143**:530–532.

Jenike MA, Baer L & Minichiello WE (1997) Placebo controlled trial of fluoxetine and phenelzine for obsessive compulsive disorder. *Am J Psychiat* **154**:1261–1264.

Jenike MA, Baer L & Minichiello WE (1998a) An overview of obsessive-compulsive disorder. In MA Jenike, L Baer & WE Minichiello (eds), *Obsessive Compulsive Disorders: Practical Management*, 3rd edn. St Louis, MO. Mosby.

Jenike MA, Rauch SL, Baer L, Rasmussen SA (1998b) Neurosurgical treatment of obsessive compulsive disorder. In MA Jenike, L Baer, WE Minichiello (eds), *Obsessive Compulsive Disorder: Practical management*, 3rd edn. London, Mosby, Boston and Harcourt-Brace, pp 592–610.

Jenike MA, Baer L & Minichiello WE (ed) (1990a) *Obsessive Compulsive Disorders: Theory and Management*, 2nd edn. Chicago, Year Book Medical Publishers.

Jenike MA, Hyman S, Baer L, Holland A, Minichiello WE, Buttolph L, Summergrad P, Seymour R & Ricciardi J (1990b) A controlled trial of fluvoxamine in obsessive-compulsive disorder: implications for serotonergic theory. *Am J Psychiat* **147**:1209–1215.

Jerome L (1992) Body dysmorphic disorder: a controlled study of patients requesting cosmetic rhinoplasty (letter). *Am J Psychiat* **149**:577–578.

Jerome L (2001) Dysmorphophobia and taphephobia: two hitherto undescribed forms of insanity with fixed ideas. A new translation of Enrico Morselli's original article. *Hist Psychiat* **12**:103–114.

Joel SW (1959) Twenty month study of iproniazid therapy. *Dis Nerv Syst* **20**:11–14.

Johnston WM & Davey GCL (1997) The psychological impact of negative TV new bulletins: the catastrophizing of personal worries. *Br J Psychol* **88**:85–91.

Jones E (1912) Anal erotic character traits. In E Jones, *Papers on Psychoanalysis*. London, Tindall and Cox.

Jones MK & Menzies RG (1995) The etiology of fear of spiders. *Anxiety Stress Coping* **8**:227–234.

Jones MK & Menzies RG (1997a) The cognitive mediation of obsessive-compulsive handwashing. *Behav Res Ther* **35**:843–850.

Jones MK & Menzies RG (1997b) Danger Ideation Reduction Therapy (DIRT): Preliminary findings with three obsessive-compulsive washers. *Behav Res Ther* **35**:955–960.

Jones MK & Menzies RG (1998a) Danger Ideation Reduction Therapy (DIRT) for obsessive-compulsive washers. A controlled trial. *Behav Res Ther* **36**:959–970.

Jones MK & Menzies RG (1998b) Role of perceived danger in the mediation of obsessive-compulsive washing. *Depress Anxiety* **8**:121–125.

Jones MK & Menzies RG (1998c) The relevance of associative learning pathways in the development of obsessive-compulsive washing. *Behav Res Ther* **36**:273–283.

Jones T & Davey GCL (1990) The effects of cued UCS rehearsal on the retention of differential 'fear' conditioning: an experimental analogue of the worry process. *Behav Res Ther*, **28**:159–164.

Judd FK, Chua P & Lynch C (1991) Fenfluramine augmentation of clomipramine treatment of obsessive compulsive disorder. *Aust NZ J Psychiat* **25**:412–414.

Judd L (1965) Obsessive-compulsive neurosis in children. *Arch Gen Psychiat* **12**:136–143.

Kaplan HS (1995) *The Sexual Desire Disorders*. New York, Brunner/Mazel.

Karayiorgou M, Sobin C, Blundell ML, Galke BL, Malinova L, Goldberg P, Ott J & Gogos JA (1999) Family-based association studies support a sexually dimorphic effect of COMT and MACIA on genetic susceptibility to obsessive-compulsive disorder. *Biol Psychiat* **45**:1178–1189.

Karno M, Golding JM, Sorenson SB & Burman MA (1988) The epidemiology of obsessive compulsive disorder in five US Communities. *Arch Gen Psychiat* **45**:1094–1099.

Kat H (1996) More on SSRI-induced mania (letter). *J Am Acad Child Adolesc Psychiat* **35**:975.

Kaufman J, Birmaher B, Brent D, Rao U, Flynn C, Moreci P, Williamson D & Ryan N (1997). Schedule for affective disorders and schizophrenia for school-age children—present and lifetime version (K-SADS-PL): initial reliability and validity data. *J Am Acad Child Adolesc Psychiat* **36**:554–565.

Keijsers GPJ, Hoogduin CAL & Schaap CPDR (1994) Predictors of treatment outcome in the behavioural treatment of obsessive-compulsive disorder. *Br J Psychiat* **165**:781–786.

Kelley AE, Lang CG & Gauthier AM (1988) Induction of oral stereotypy following amphetamine microinjection into a discrete subregion of the striatum. *Psychopharmacology* **95**:556–559.

Kendall PC & Ingram RE (1987) The future for cognitive assessment of anxiety: Let's get specific. In L Michaelson & LM Ascher (eds), *Anxiety and Stress Disorders: Cognitive-behavioural Assessment and Treatment*. New York, Guildford.

Kendell RE & Zealley AK (eds) (1983) *Companion to Psychiatric Studies*. Edinburgh, Churchill Livingstone.

Khanna S & Mukherjee D (1992) Checkers and washers: valid subtypes of obsessive compulsive disorder. *Psychopathology* **25**:283–288.

Khanna S, Kaliapercomal VG & Channabasavanna SM (1990) Clusters of obsessive-compulsive phenomena in obsessive-compulsive disorder. *Br J Psychiat* **156**: 51–54.

Kiessling LS, Marcotte AC & culpepper L (1993) Antineuronal antibodies in movement disorders. *Pediatrics* **92**:39–43.

Kim SW, Dysken MW & Kuskowski M (1990a) The Yale–Brown Obsessive-Compulsive Scale: a reliability and validity study. *Psychiat Res* **34**:99–106.

Kim SW, Dysken MW & Kline MD (1990b) Monozygotic twins with obsessive compulsive disorder. *Br J Psychiat* **156**:435–438.

Kim SW, Dysken MW & Kuskowski M (1992) The Symptom Checklist-90 obsessive-compulsive subscale: a reliability and validity study. *Psychiat Res* **41**:37–44.

Kim SW, Dysken MW, Kuskowski M & Hoover KM (1993) The Yale–Brown Obsessive-Compulsive Scale and the NIMH Global Obsessive-Compulsive Scale (GOCS): a reliability and validity study. *Int J Method Psychiat Res* **3**:37–44.

King N, Inglis S, Jenkins M, Myerson N & Ollendick T (1995) Test–retest reliability of the survey form of the Leyton Obsessional Inventory—Child Version. *Percept Motor Skill* **80**:1200–1202.

Kirkby K, Berrios G, Daniels B, Menzies RG, Clark A & Romano A (2000) Process–outcome analysis in computer-aided treatment of obsessive-compulsive disorder. *Compr Psychiat* **41**:259–265.

Kobak KA, Greist JH, Jefferson JW et al. (1998) Behavioural versus pharmacological treatments of obsessive compulsive disorder: a meta-analysis. *Psychopharmacology* **135**:205–216.

Koran LM (1999) *Obsessive Compulsive and Related Disorders in Adults: a Comprehensive Clinical Guide*. Cambridge, Cambridge University Press, pp 3–119.

Koran LM, McElroy SL & Davidson JRT (1996) Fluvoxamine versus clomipramine for obsessive compulsive disorder: a double-blind comparison. *J Clin Pharmacol* **16**:121–129.

Koran LM, Pallanti S & Paiva RS (1998) Pulse loading versus gradual dosing of intravenous clomipramine in obsessive compulsive disorder. *Eur Neuropsychopharmacol* **8**:121–126.

Koran LM, Sallee R & Pallanti S (1997) Rapid benefit of intravenous pulse loading of clomipramine in obsessive compulsive disorder. *Am J Psychiat* **154**:396–401.

Kozak MJ & Foa EB (1997) *Mastery of Obsessive-compulsive Disorder: A Cognitive-behavioral Approach. Therapist Guide*. New York, Psychological Corporation.

Kozak MJ, Liebowitz MR & Foa EB (2000) Cognitive behaviour therapy and pharmacotherapy for obsessive-compulsive disorder: the NIMH-sponsored collaborative study. In WK Goodman, MV Rudorfer & JD Maser (eds). *Obsessive-Compulsive Disorder: Contemporary Issues in Treatment*. Mahwah, NJ, Erlbaum

Kraaijkamp HJM, Emmelkamp PMG & van den Hout MA (1986) The Maudsley Obsessional-Compulsive Inventory: reliability and validity. Unpublished manuscript, University of Groningen, The Netherlands.

Krause EMS, White LE, Frost RO, Steketee G & Kyrios M (2000) Attachment deficits among compulsive hoarders: implications for theory and treatment. Paper to be presented at the Annual Meeting of the Association for the Advancement of Behavior Therapy, New Orleans, November.

Krochmalik A, Jones MK & Menzies RG (2001) Danger Ideation Reduction Therapy (DIRT) for treatment-resistant compulsive washing. *Behav Res Ther* **39**:897–912.

Krone K, Himle J & Nesse R (1991) A standardized behavioural group treatment program for obsessive-compulsive disorder: preliminary outcomes. *Behav Res Ther* **29**:627–631.

Kulin NA, Pastuszak A & Sage SR (1998) Pregnancy outcome following maternal use of the new selective serotonin reuptake inhibitors: a prospective controlled multi-centre study. *J Am Med Assoc* **279**:609–610.

Kurlan, T (1998) Tourette's syndrome and 'PANDAS': will the relation bear out? *Neurology* **50**:5130–5134.

Kyrios M & Bhar SS (1995) A measure of inflated responsibility: its development and relationship to obsessive-compulsive phenomena. Paper presented at the World Congress of Behavioural and Cognitive Therapies, Copenhagen, Denmark, July.

Kyrios M, Bhar S & Wade D (1996) The assessment of obsessive-compulsive phenomena: psychometric and normative data on the Padua Inventory from an Australian non-clinical student sample. *Behav Res Ther* **34**:85–95.

Kyrios M, Hordern C & Bhar S (2001) Specific and non-specific changes in cognition associated with cognitive-behavioural treatment of OCD. Paper presented at World Congress of Behavioural and Cognitive Therapies, Vancouver.

Kyrios M, Wainwright K, Purcell R, Pantelis C & Maruff P (1999) Neuropsychological predictors of outcome following cognitive-behaviour therapy for OCD. A pilot study. Paper presented to the Association for the Advancement of Behaviour Therapy, Toronto.

Lader MH & Wing L (1966) *Physiological Measures, Sedative Drugs and Morbid Anxiety*. London, Oxford University Press.

Ladouceur R, Freeston MH, Gagnon F, Thibodeau N & Dumont J (1995a) Cognitive-behavioral treatment of obsessions. *Behav Modif* **19**:247–257.

Ladouceur R, Rheaume J, Freeston MH & Aublet F (1995b) Experimental manipulations of responsibility: an analogue test for models of obsessive-compulsive disorder. *Behav Res Ther* **33**:937–946.

Ladouceur R, Rhéaume J & Aublet F (1997) Excessive responsibility in obsessional concerns: a fine-grained experimental analysis. *Behav Res Ther* **35**:423–427.

Lane R & Baldwin D (1997) Selective serotonin inhibitor induced serotonin syndrome: review. *J Clin Pharmacol* **17**:208–221.

Langlois F, Freeston MH & Ladouceur R (2000) Differences and similarities between obsessive intrusive thoughts and worry in a non-clinical population: study 1. *Behav Res Ther* **38**:157–173.

Laplane D, Levasseur M & Pillon B (1989) Obsessive compulsive and other behavioural changes with bilateral basal ganglia lesions. *Brain* **112**:699.

Last CG & Strauss CC (1989) Obsessive-compulsive disorder in childhood. *J Anxiety Disord* **3**:295–302.

Lax T, Basoglu M & Marks IM (1992) Expectancy and compliance as predictors of outcome in obsessive-compulsive disorder. *Behav Psychother* **20**:257–266.

Leckman JF & Mayes LC (1998a) Understanding developmental psychopathology: how useful are evolutionary accounts? *J Am Acad Child Adolesc Psychiat* **37**:1011–1021.

Leckman JF & Mayes LC (1998b) Maladies of love: an evolutionary perspective on some forms of obsessive-compulsive disorder In DH Hann, L Huffman, I Lederhendler, D Meinecke (eds), *Advancing Research in Developmental Plasticity: Integrating the Behavioural Science and Neuroscience of Mental Health*. Rockville, MD, NIMH, US Department of Health and Human Services.

Leckman JF, Grice DE, Boardman J, Zhang H, Vitale A, Bondi C, Alsobrook J, Peterson BS, Cohen DJ, Rasmussen SA, Goodman WK, McDougle CJ & Pauls DL (1997) Symptoms of obsessive-compulsive disorder. *Am J Psychiat* **154**:911–917.

Lejoyeux M & Ades J (1997) Antidepressant discontinuation: a review of the literature. *J Clin Psychiat* **58**(suppl 7):11–16.

Lensi P, Cassano GB, Correddu G, Ravagli S & Kunovac JJ (1996) Obsessive-compulsive disorder: familial-developmental history, symptomatology, co-morbidity and course with special reference to gender-related differences. *Br J of Psychiatry* **169**:101–107.

Lelliott PT, Noshirvani HF, Basoglu M, Marks IM & Monteiro WO (1988) Obsessive-compulsive beliefs and treatment outcome. *Psychol Med* **18**:697–702.

Leonard HL (1990) Childhood rituals and superstitions: developmental and cultural perspective. In J Rapoport (ed.), *Obsessions and Compulsions in Children and Adolescents*. Washington, DC, American Psychiatric Press.

Leonard HL, Goldberger EL & Rapoport JL (1990) Childhood rituals: normal development or obsessive-compulsive symptoms? *J Am Acad Child Adolesc Psychiat* **29**:27–38.

Leonard HL, Swedo SE, Garvey M, Beer D, Perlmutter S, Lougee L, Karitani M & Dubbert B (1999) Postinfectious and other forms of obsessive-compulsive disorder. *Child Adolesc Psychiat Clin N Am* **8**:497–511.

Leonard HL, Swedo SE, Lenane MC, Rettew DC, Hamburger SD, Bartko JJ & Rapoport JL (1993) A 2–7 year follow-up study of 54 obsessive-compulsive children and adolescents. *Arch Gen Psychiat* **50**: 429–439.

Leonard HL, Swedo SE, Rapoport JL et al. (1989) Treatment of obsessive-compulsive disorder with clomipramine and desipramine in children and adolescents: a double blind cross-over comparison. *Arch Gen Psychiat* **46**:1088–1092.

Levenkron S (1991) *Obsessive Compulsive Disorders: Treating and Understanding Crippling Habits*. New York, Warner.

Lewis A (1936) Problems of obsessional illness. *Proc R Soc Med* **29**:325–336.

Lewis A (1938) The diagnosis and treatment of obsessional states. *Practitioner* **141**:21–30.

Lewis S, Chitkara B & Reveley AM (1991) Obsessive-compulsive disorder and schizophrenia in three identical twin pairs. *Psychol Med* **21**:135–141.

Lezak MD (1995) *Neuropsychological Assessment*. Oxford, Oxford University Press.

Likeirman H & Rachman S (1982) Obsessions: an experimental investigation of thought-stopping and habituation training. *Behav Psychother* **10**:324–338.

Lindsay M, Crino R & Andrews G (1997) Controlled trial of exposure and response prevention in obsessive-compulsive disorder. *Br J Psychiat* **171**:135–139.

Livingston-Van Noppen B, Rasamussen SA, Eisen J & McCartney L (1990) Family function and treatment in obsessive-compulsive disorders. In MA Jenike, L Baer & WE Minichiello (eds), *Obsessive-Compulsive Disorders: Theory and Management*, 2nd edn. Chicago, Year Book Medical Publications.

Lopatka C & Rachman S (1995) Perceived responsibility and compulsive checking: an experimental analysis. *Behav Res Ther* **33**:673–684.

Lopez-Ibor JR, Saiz J, Cottraux J et al. (1996) Double-blind comparison of fluoxetine versus clomipramine in the treatment of obsessive compulsive disorder. *Eur Neuropsychopharmacol* **6**:111–118.

Lucey JV, Burness CE, Costa DC et al. (1997) Wisconsin Card Sorting Task errors and cerebral blood flow in obsessive-compulsive disorder. *Br J Med Psychol* **70**:403–411.

Luchins DJ, Goldman MB, Lieb M & Hanrahan P(1992) Repetitive behaviors in chronically institutionalized schizophrenic patients. *Schizophr Res* **8**:119–123.

Luxenberg JS, Swedo SE & Flament M (1988) Neuroanatomical abnormalities in obsessive-compulsive disorder detected with quatitative X-ray computed tomography. *Am J Psychiat* **145**:1089–1093.

Lybomirsky S & Nolen-Hoeksema S (1995) Effects of self-focused ruminations on negative thinking and interpersonal problem solving. *J Pers Soc Psychol* **69**:176–190.

Macdonald AM (1996) An Epidemiological and Quantitative Genetic Study of Obsessionality. Unpublished PhD Thesis, Kings College, University of London.

Macdonald AM & de Silva P (1999) The assessment of obsessionality using the Padua inventory: its validity in a British non-clinical sample. *Pers Indiv Differ* **27**:1027–1046.

Macdonald AM & Murray RM (1989) A twin study of obsessive-compulsive neurosis. Paper presented at 6th International Congress on Twin Studies, Rome.

MacDonald PA, Antony MM, Macleod CM & Richter MA (1997) Memory and confidence in memory judgements among individuals with obsessive compulsive disorder and non-clinical controls. *Behav Res Ther* **35**:497–505.

Macdonald AM, Murray RM & Clifford CA (1991) The contribution of heredity to obsessional disorder and personality: a review of family and twin study evidence. In K Kendler, M Tsuang & M Lyons (eds), *Genetic Issues in Psychosocial Epidemiology*. New Brunswick, NJ, Rutgers University Press.

Mackie DM & Worth LT (1989) Processing deficits and the mediation of positive affect in persuasion. *J Pers Soc Psychol* **57**:1–14.

Magliano L, Tosini P, Guarneri M & Marasco C (1996) Burden on families of patients with obsessive-compulsive disorder: a pilot study. *Eur Psychiat* **11**:192–197.

Mahgoub OM, Mirghani AM, Al-Suhaibani MO (1988) Identical Saudi twins concordant for obsessive compulsive disorder. *Saudi Med J* **19**:641–643.

Maina G, Albert U, Bogetto F, Vaschetto P & Ravizza L (2000) Recent life events and obsessive-compulsive disorder (OCD): the role of pregnancy / delivery. *Psychiat Res* **89**:49–58.

March J & Mulle K (1996) Banishing obsessive-compulsive disorder. In E Hibbs & P Jensen (eds), *Psychosocial Treatments for Child and Adolescent Disorders*. Washington, DC, American Psychological Press.

March JS (1995) Cognitive-behavioral psychotherapy for children and adolescents with OCD: a review and recommendations for treatment. *J Am Acad Child Adolesc Psychiat* **34**:7–18.

March JS & Albano AM (1998) New developments in assessing pediatric anxiety disorders. *Adv Clin Child Psychol* **20**:213–241.

March JS & Leonard HL (1998) Obsessive-compulsive disorder in children and adolescents. In RP Swinson, MM Antony, S Rachman & MA Richter (eds), *Obsessive-Compulsive Disorder: Theory, Research, and Treatment*. London, Guilford, pp 367–394.

March JS & Mulle K (1998) *OCD in Children and Adolescents: a Cognitive-Behavioral Treatment Manual.* New York, Guilford.

March JS, Biederman J, Wolkow R, Safferman A, Mardekian J, Cook EH, Cutler NR, Dominguez R, Ferguson J, Muller B, Reisenberg R, Rosenthal M, Sallee FR & Wagner KD (1998) Sertraline in children and adolescents with obsessive-compulsive disorder: a multicenter randomized controlled trial. *J Am Med Assoc* **280**:1752–1756.

March JS, Frances A, Kahn D & Carpenter D (1997a) Consensus guidelines: treatment of obsessive-compulsive disorder. *J Clin Psychiat* **58**:1–72.

March JS, Franklin M, Nelson A & Foa E (2001) Cognitive-behavioural psychotherapy for pediatric obsessive-compulsive disorder. *J Clin Child Psychol* **30**:8–18.

March JS, Mulle K & Herbel B (1994) Behavioral psychotherapy for children and adolescents with obsessive-compulsive disorder: An open trial of a new protocol-driven treatment package. *J Am Acad Child Adolesc Psychiat* **33**: 333–341.

March JS, Parker JD, Sullivan K, Stallings P & Conners CK (1997b) The multidimensional anxiety scale for children (MASC): factor structure, reliability and validity. *J Am Acad Child Adolesc Psychiat* **36**:554–565.

Marks IM (1981) *Cure and Care of Neurosis: Theory and Practice of Behaviour Psychotherapy.* New York, Wiley.

Marks IM (1987) *Fears, Phobias and Rituals.* New York, Oxford University Press.

Marks IM (1997) Behaviour therapy for obsessive compulsive disorder a decade of progress (review). *Can J Psychiat* **42**:1021–1027.

Marks IM(1969) *Fears and Phobias.* London, Heineman.

Marks IM, Baer L, Greist J, Park J, Bachofen M, Nakagawa A, Wenzel K, Parkin J, Manzo A, Dottl S & Mantle J (1998) Home self-assessment of obsessive-compulsive disorder. Use of a manual and a computer-conducted telephone interview: Two UK–US studies. *Br J Psychiat* **172**:406–412.

Marks IM, Crowe M, Drewe E, Young J & Dewhurst WG (1969) Obsessive compulsive neurosis in identical twins. *Br J Psychiat* **115**:991–998.

Marks IM, Hallam RS, Connolly J & Philpott R (1977) *Nursing in Behavioural Psychotherapy.* London, Royal College of Nursing of the United Kingdom.

Marks IM, O'Dwyer AM, Meehan O, Greist J, Baer L & McGuire P (2000) Subjective imagery in obsessive-compulsive disorder before and after exposure therapy: pilot randomised controlled trial. *Br J Psychiat* **176**:387–391.

Marks IM, Stern RS, Mawson D, Cobb J & McDonald R (1980) Clomipramine and exposure for obsessive-compulsive rituals: I. *Br J Psychiat* **136**:1–25.

Martin LL & Davies B (1998) Beyond Hedonism and associationism: a configural view of the role of affect in evaluation, processing, and self-regulation. *Motiv Emotion* **22**:33–51.

Martin LL & Tesser A (1989) Toward a motivational and structural theory of ruminative thought. In JS Uleman & JA Bargh (eds), *Unintended Thought.* New York, Guilford, pp 306–326.

Martin LL & Tesser A (1996) Some ruminative thoughts. In RS Wyer (ed.), *Advances in Social Cognition.* Hillsdale, NJ, Erlbaum.

Martin LL, Ward DW, Achee JW & Wyer RS (1993) Mood as input: people have to interpret the motivational implications of their moods. *J Pers Soc Psychol* **63**:317–326.

Martinot JL, Allilaire JF & Mazoyer BM (1990) Obsessive-compulsive disorder: a clinical, neuropsychological and positron emission tomography study. *Acta Psychiat Scand* **82**:233–242.

Maruff P, Purcell R & Pantelis C (2000) Neuropsychological deficits in obsessive-compulsive disorder: In JE Harrison & AM Owen (eds), *Cognitive Deficits in Brain Disorders*. New York, Martin Dunitz.

Mataix-Cols D, Junque C & Sanchez-Turet M (1999a) Neuropsychological functioning in a subclinical obsessive-compulsive sample. *Biol Psychiat* **45**:898–904.

Mataix-Cols D, Rauch SL, Manzo PA, Jenike MA & Baer L (1999b) Use of factor-analyzed symptom dimensions to predict outcome with serotonin reuptake inhibitors and placebo in the treatment of obsessive-compulsive disorder. *Am J Psychiat* **156**:1409–1416.

Mathews A (1990) Why worry? The cognitive function of anxiety. *Behav Res Ther* **28**:455–468.

Matsunaga H, Kirike N, Iwasaki Y, Miyata A, Yamagami S & Kaye WH (1999) Clinical characteristics in patients with anorexia nervosa and obsessive-compulsive disorder. *Psychol Med* **29**:407–414.

Maurin J & Boyd C (1990) Burden of mental illness on the family: a critical review. *Arch Psychiat Nurs* **6**:99–107.

Mawson D, Marks IM & Ramm L (1982) Clomipramine and exposure for chronic obsessive-compulsive rituals: two-year follow-up and further findings. *Br J Psychiat* **140**:11–18.

McDougle CJ (1997) Update on pharmacologic management of OCD: agents and augmentation. *J Clin Psychiat* **58**(suppl 12):11–17.

McDougle CJ, Barr LC & Goodman WK (1995a) Lack of efficacy of clozapine monotherapy in refractory obsessive compulsive disorder. *Am J Psychiat* **152**:1812–1814.

McDougle CJ, Fleischmann RL & Epperson CM (1995b) Risperidone addition to fluvoxamine refractory obsessive compulsive disorder: three cases. *J Clin Psychiat* **56**:526–528.

McDougle CJ, Barr LC, Goodman WK & Price LH (1999) Possible role of neuropeptides in obsessive compulsive disorder. *Psychoneuroendocrinology* **24**:1–24.

McDougle CJ, Epperson CN, Pelton GH, Wasylink S & Price L H (2000) A double-blind placebo-controlled study of risperidone addition in serotonin reuptake inhibitor-refractory obsessive-compulsive disorder. *Arch Gen Psychiat* **57**:794–801.

McDougle CJ, Epperson CN, Price LH & Gelernter J (1998) Evidence for linkage disequilibrium between serotonin transporter protein gene (SLC6A4) and obsessive-compulsive disorder. *Mol Psychiat* **3**(3): 270–273.

McDougle CJ, Goodman WK & Leckman JF (1993) Limited therapeutic effect of the addition of buspirone in fluvoxamine refractory obsessive compulsive disorder. *Am J Psychiat* **150**:647–649.

McDougle CJ, Goodman WK & Leckman JF (1994a) Haloperidol addition in fluvoxamine refractory obsessive compulsive disorder: a double-blind placebo controlled study in patients with and without tics. *Arch Gen Psychiat* **51**:302–308.

McDougle CJ, Goodman WK & Price LH (1994b) Dopamine antagonists in tic related and psychotic spectrum obsessive compulsive disorder. *J Clin Psychiat* **55** (suppl 3):24–31.

McDougle CJ, Goodman WK & Price LH (1990) Neuroleptic addition in fluvoxamine refractory obsessive compulsive disorder. *Am J Psychiat* **147**:652–654.

McDougle CJ, Price LH & Goodman WK (1991) A controlled trial of lithium augmentation in fluvoxamine refractory obsessive compulsive disorder: lack of efficacy. *J Clin Pharmacol* **11**:175–184.

McElroy SL, Phillips KA & Keck PE Jr (1994) Obsessive compulsive spectrum disorder. *J Clin Psychiat* **5**:33–51.

McGuffin P & Mawson D (1980) Obsessive-compulsive neurosis: two identical twin pairs. *Br J Psychiat* **137**:285–287.

McGuire PK (1995) The brain in obsessive-compulsive disorder. *J Neurol Neurosurg Psychiat* (editorial) **59**:457–459.

McGuire PK, Bench CJ & Frith CD (1994) Functional anatomy of obsessive compulsive phenomena. *Br J Psychiat* **164**:459–468.

McKenzie N, Blanes T & Marks I (1995) Computerised clinical benefit–cost audit of mental health care II: time input, costs, patient satisfaction. *J Ment Health* **1**:71–78.

McKeon JP, McGuffin P & Robinson P (1984) Obsessive compulsive neurosis following head injury: a report of four cases. *Br J Psychiat* **144**:190–192.

McKeon P & Murray RM (1987) Familial aspects of obsessive-compulsive neurosis. *Br J Psychiat* **151**:528–534.

McLean PD, Whittal ML, Thordarson DS, Taylor S, Sochting I, Koch WJ, Paterson R & Anderson KW (2001). Cognitive versus behavior therapy in the group treatment of obsessive compulsive disorder. *J Consult Clin Psychol* **69**:205–214.

McNally RJ & Kohlbeck PA (1993) Reality monitoring in obsessive-compulsive disorder. *Behav Res Ther* **31**:249–253.

Mehta M (1990) A comparative study of family-based and patient-based behavioural management in obsessive-compulsive disorder. *Br J Psychiat* **157**:133–135.

Menzies RG (1995) The uneven distribution of fears and phobias: a non-associative account. *Behav Brain Sci* **18**:305–306.

Menzies RG (1996) The origins of specific phobias in a mixed clinical sample: classificatory differences between two origins instruments. *J Anxiety Dis* **10**:347–354.

Menzies RG (1997a) Height phobia. In GCL. Davey (ed.), *Phobias: Description, Treatment and Theory*. London, John Wiley & Sons, Ltd pp 139–153.

Menzies RG (1997b) Water phobia. In GCL Davey (ed.), *Phobias: Description, Treatment and Theory*. London, John Wiley & Sons, Ltd pp 129–139.

Menzies RG & Clarke JC (1993a) The etiology of fear of heights and its relationship to severity and individual response patterns. *Behav Res Ther* **31**: 355–365.

Menzies RG & Clarke JC (1993b) The etiology of childhood water phobia. *Behav Res Ther* **31**: 499–501.

Menzies RG & Clarke JC (1994) Retrospective studies of the origins of phobias: a review. *Anxiety, Stress and Coping*, **7**:305–318.

Menzies RG & Clarke JC (1995a) The etiology of phobias: a non-associative account. *Clin Psychol Rev* **15**:23–48.

Menzies RG & Clarke JC (1995b) The etiology of acrophobia and its relationship to severity and individual response patterns. *Behav Res Ther* **33**:795–805.

Menzies RG & Clarke JC (1995c) Danger expectancies and insight in acrophobia. *Behav Res Ther* **33**:215–221.

Menzies RG & Harris LM (1997) Mode of onset in evolutionary-relevant and evolutionary-neutral phobias: evidence from a clinical sample. *Depression Anxiety* **5**:134–136.

Menzies RG & Harris LM (2001) Non-associative factors in the development of phobias. In MW Vasey & MR Dadds (ed.), *The Developmental Psychopathology of Anxiety*. Oxford, Oxford University Press, pp 183–204.

Menzies RG & Parker L (2001) The origins of height fear: an evaluation of neoconditioning explanations. *Behav Res Ther* **39**:897–912.

Menzies RG, Harris LM, Cumming, S & Einstein DA (2000). The relationship between inflated personal responsibility and exaggerated danger expectancies in obsessive-compulsive disorder. *Behav Res Ther* **38**:1029–1037.

Meyer TJ, Miller ML, Metzger RL & Borkovec TD (1990) Development and validation of the Penn State Worry Questionnaire. *Behav Res Ther* **28**:487–495.

Meyer V (1957) The treatment of two phobic patients on the basis of learning principles. *J Abnorm Psychol* **55**:261.

Meyer V (1966) Modification of expectancies in cases with obsessional rituals. *Behav Res Ther* **4**:273–280.

Meyer V & Gelder MG (1963) Behaviour therapy and phobic disorders *Br J Psychiat* **109**:19–28.

Meyer V, Levy R & Schnurer A (1974) The behavioural treatment of obsessive-compulsive disorders. In HR Breech (ed.), *Obsessional States*. London, Methuen.

Miguel EC, Rauch SL & Jenike MA (1997) Obsessive-compulsive disorder. *Psychiat Clin N Am* **20**:863–883.

Millar DG (1980) A repertory grid study of obsessionality: distinctive cognitive structure or distinctive cognitive content? *Br J Med Psychol* **53**:59–66.

Millar DG (1983) Hostile emotion and obsessional neurosis. *Psychol Med* **13**:813–819.

Mills HL, Agras WS, Barlow DH & Mills FR (1973) Compulsive rituals treated with response prevention. *Arch Gen Psychiat* **28**:524–529.

Mindus P & Jenike MA (1992) Neurosurgical treatment of malignant obsessive compulsive disorder. *Psychiat Clin N Am* **15**:921–938.

Minichiello WE, Baer L & Jenike MA (1987) Schizotypal personality disorder: a poor prognostic indicator for behaviour therapy in the treatment of obsessive compulsive disorder. *J Anxiety Disord* **1**:273–276.

Modell J, Mountz J, Curtis G & Greden JF (1989) Neurophysiologic dysfunction in basal ganglia/limbic striatal and thalamocortical circuits as a pathogenic mechanism of obsessive-compulsive disorder. *J Neuropsychiat Clin Neurosci* **1**:27–36.

Money J (1976) *A Standarized Road Map Test of Directional Sense: Manual*. San Rafael, CA, Academic Therapy Publications.

Montgomery S (1993) Obsessive compulsive disorder is not an anxiety disorder. *Int Clin Psychopharmacol* **8**(suppl 1):57–62.

Moore K & Burrows GD (1991) Hypnosis in the treatment of obsessive compulsive disorder. *Aust J Clin Exp Hypn* **19**:63–75.

Mowrer OH (1939) A stimulus response theory of anxiety. *Psychol Rev* **46**:553–565.

Mowrer OH (1960) *Learning Theory and Behavior*. New York, Wiley.

Mundo E, Bianchi L & Bellodi L (1997) Efficacy of fluvoxamine, paroxetine and citalopram in the treatment of obsessive compulsive disorder: a single blind study. *J Clin Psychiat* **17**:267–271.

Mundo E, Guglielmo E & Bellodi L (1998) Effect of adjuvant pindolol on the anti-obsessional response to fluvoxamine: a double-blind placebo controlled study. *Int Clin Psychopharmacol* **13**:219–224.

Munford P, Hand I & Liberman R (1994) Psychosocial treatment for obsessive-compulsive disorder. *Psychiatry* **57**:142–152.

Muris P, Merckelbach H & Clavan M (1997) Abnormal and normal compulsions. *Behav Res Ther* **35**:249–252.

Murphy DL, Pickar D & Alterman IS (1982) Methods for the quantitative assessment of depressive and manic behaviour. In EL Burdock, A Sudilvsky & S Gershon (eds), *The Behaviour of Psychiatric Patients*. New York, Marcel Dekker, pp 355–392.

Murray RM, Cooper JE & Smith A (1979) The Leyton Obsessional Inventory: an analysis of the responses of 73 obsessional patients. *Psychol Med* **9**:305–311.

Musaph H (1968) Psychodynamics in itching states. *Int J Psychoanal* **48**:336–339.

Nakagawa A, Marks IM, Park JM, Bachofen M, Baer L, Dottl SL & Greist JH (2000) Self-treatment of obsessive-compulsive disorder guided by manual and computer conducted telephone interview. *J Telemed Telecare* **6**:22–26.

Neale MC (1991) *Mx: Statistical Modelling Box 3*. Richmond VA, MCV.

Neale MC & Cardon LR (1992) *Methodology for Genetic Studies of Twins and Families*. Dordrecht, Kluwer Academic.

Nelson E & Rice J (1997) Stability of diagnosis of obsessive-compulsive disorder in the Epidemiologic Catchment Area Study. *Am J Psychiat* **154**:826–831.

Nestadt G, Bienvenu OJ, Cai G, Samuels J & Eaton WW (1998) Incidence of obsessive-compulsive disorder in adults. *J Nerv Ment Dis* **186**:401–406.

Nestadt G, Romanoski AJ, Brown CH & Chahal R (1991) DSM-III compulsive personality disorder: an epidemiological survey. *Psychol Med* **21**:461–471.

Nestadt G, Samuels J, Riddle M, Bienvenu OJ, Liang KY, LaBuda M, Walkup J, Grados M & Hoehn Saric R (2000) A family study of obsesive-compulsive disorder. *Arch Gen Psychiat* **57**:358–363.

Neziroglu F & Yaryura-Tobias JA (1993a) Body dysmorphic disorder: phenomenology and case-descriptions. *Behav Psychother* **21**:27–36.

Neziroglu F & Yaryura-Tobias JA (1993b) Exposure, response prevention, and cognitive therapy in the treatment of body dysmorphic disorder. *Behav Ther* **24**:431–438.

Neziroglu F, Stevens KP, Liquori B & Yaryura-Tobias JA (2000) Cognitive and behavioural treatment of obsessive-compulsive spectrum disorders. In WK Goodman, MV Rudorfer & JD Maser (eds), *Obsessive Compulsive Disorder: Contemporary Issues in Treatment*. Mahwah, NJ, Erlbaum, pp 233–255.

Neziroglu F, Stevens KP, McKay D & Yaryura-Tobias J (2001) Predictive validity of the overvalued ideas scale: outcome in obsessive-compulsive and body dysmorphic disorders. *Behav Res Ther* **39**:745–756.

Neziroglu FA, McKay D, Yaryura-Tobias JA, Stevens KP & Todaro J (1999) The Overvalued Ideas Scale: development, reliability and validity in obsessive-compulsive disorder. *Behav Res Ther* **37**:881–902.

Nicolini H, Orozco B, Giuffra L, Paez F, Mejia J, Sanchez de Carmona M, Sidenberg D, Ramon de la Fuente J (1997) Age of onset, gender and severity in obsessive-compulsive disorder: study of a Mexican population. *Salud Mental* **20**(2):1–4.

Nietzel MT, Bernstein DA & Russell RL (1988) Assessment of anxiety and fear. In AS Bellack & M Hersen (eds), *Behavioural Assessment*, 3rd edn. New York, Pergamon.

Nisbett R & Ross L (1980) Human Inference: Strategies and Shortcomings of Social Judgement. Englewood Cliffs, NJ, Prentice Hall.

Nolen-Hoeksema S & Morrow J (1993) Effects of rumination and distraction on naturally occurring depressed mood. *Cogn Emotion* **7**:561–570.

Nolen-Hoeksema S, Parker L & Larson J (1994) Ruminative coping with depressed mood following loss. *J Pers Soc Psychol* **67**:92–104.

Norman RMG, Davies F, Malla K, Cortese L & Nicholson IR (1996) Relationship of obsessive-compulsive symptomatology to anxiety, depression and schizotypy in a clinical population. *Br J Clin Psychol* **35**:553–566.

Noshirvani HF, Kasvikis Y, Marks IM, Tsakiris F & Monteiro WO (1991) Gender-divergent aetiological factors in obsessive-compulsive disorder. *Br J Psychiat* **158**:260–263.

Nulman I, Rovet J & Stewart DE (1997) Neurodevelopment of children exposed *in utero* to antidepressant drugs. *N Engl J Med* **336**:258–263.

Nunnally JC (1978) *Psychometric Theory*, 2nd edn. New York, McGraw-Hill.

O'Connor K, Torodov C, Robillard S, Borgeat F & Brault M (1999) Cognitive-behaviour therapy and medication in the treatment of obsessive-compulsive disorder: a controlled study. *Can J Psychiat* **44**:64–71.

O'Dwyer AM & Marks IM (2000) Obsessive compulsive disorder and delusions revisited. *Br J Psychiat* **176**:281–284.

Obsessive Compulsive Anonymous (1999) *OCA: Recovering from Obsessive Compulsive Disorder*. New York, Obsessive Compulsive Anonymous Inc.

Obsessive Compulsive Cognitions Working Group: Amir N, Bouvard M, Carmin C, Clark DA, Cottraux J, Eisen J, Emmelkamp P, Foa E, Freeston M, Frost R, Hoekstra R, Kozak M, Kyrios M, Ladouceur R, March J, McKay D, Neziroglu F, Pinard A, Pollard CA, Purdon C, Rachman S, Rheaume J, Richards C, Salkovskis P, Sanavio E, Shafran R, Sica C, Simos G, Sookman D, Steketee G, Tallis F, Taylor S, Thordarson D, Turner S, van Oppen P, Warren R & Yaryura-Tobias J (1997) Cognitive assessment of obsessive-compulsive disorder. *Behav Res Ther* **35**:667–681.

Okasha A, Kamel M & Hassan AH (1968) Preliminary psychiatric observations in Egypt. *Am J Psychiat* **114**:949–954.

Okasha A, Saad A, Khalil AH, El-Dawla AS & Yehia N (1994) Phenomenology of obsessive-compulsive disorder: a transcultural study. *Compr Psychiat* **35**:191–197.

Ooosthuizen P, Lambert T & Castle D (1998) Dysmorphic concern: prevalence and associations with clinical variables. *Aust NZ J Psychiat* **32**:129–132.

Ostergaard GZ & Pedersen S (1982) Neonatal effects of maternal clomipramine treatment. *Paediatrics* **69**:233-234.

Otto MW (1990) Neuropsychological approaches to obsessive-compulsive disorder. In MA Jenike, L Baer & WE Miniciello (eds), *Obsessive-Compulsive disorder: Theory and Management*, 2nd edn. St Louis, MO, Mosby.

Overton S & Menzies RG (2001) The cognitive mediation of compulsive checking. Paper presented at the 24th National Conference of the Australian Association of Cognitive Behaviour Therapy Association, Sydney, Australia.

Ownby RL (1983) A cognitive behavioral intervention for compulsive handwashing with a thirteen year-old boy. *Psychol Schools* **20**:219–222.

Oxford English Dictionary, 2nd edn (1989) Oxford, Clarendon Press.

Pallanti S, Quercioli L & Paiva RS (1998) Citalopram plus clomipramine for treatment-resistant obsessive compulsive disorder. *Eur Psychiat* **8**:121–126.

Panagiotis B (1999) Development of obsessive and depressive symptoms during resperidone treatment (letter). *Br J Psychiat* **174**:559.

Parker N (1964) Twins: a psychiatric study of a neurotic group. *Med J Australia* **2**:735–742.

Parkin R (1997) Obsessive-compulsive disorder in adults. *Int Rev Psychiat* **9**:73–81.

Pastuszak A, Schick-Boschetto B & Zuber C (1993) Pregnancy outcomes following first trimester exposure to fluoxetine. *J Am Med Assoc* **269**:2246–2248.

Pato MT, Murphy DL & Devane CL (1991) Sustained plasma concentrations of fluoxetine and/or norfluoxetine 4 and 8 weeks after fluoxetine discontinuation. *J Clin Pharmacol* **11**:224–225.

Pato MT, Zohar-Kadouch R & Zohar J (1998) Return of symptoms after discontinuation of clomipramine in patients with obsessive compulsive disorder. *Am J Psychiat* **145**:1521–1522.

Pauls DL & Alsobrook JP (1999) The inheritance of obsessive-compulsive disorder. *Child Adolesc Psychiat Clin N Am* **8**:481–496.

Pauls DL, Alsobrook JP, Goodman W, Rasmussen S & Leckman JF (1995) A family study of obsessive-compulsive disorder. *Am J Psychiat* **152**:76–84.

Pennington BF & Ozonoff S (1996) Executive functions and developmental psychopathology. *J Child Psychol Psychiat* **37**:51–87.

Perse TL (1988) Obsessive-compulsive disorder: a treatment review. *J Clin Psychiat* **49**:48–55.

Persons J & Foa E (1984) Processing of fearful and neutral information by obsessive compulsives. *Behav Res Ther* **22**:259–265.

Perugi G, Giannotti D & Di Vaio S (1996) Fluvoxamine in the treatment of body dysmorphic disorder (dysmorphophobia). *Int Clin Psychopharmacol* **11**:247–254.

Petska Juliussen K & Juliussen E (1999) *The Computer Industry Almanac*, 8th edn. New York, Brady.

Phillips KA (1996) *The Broken Mirror—Understanding and Treating Body Dysmorphic Disorder*. New York, Oxford University Press.

Phillips KA (1998) Body dysmorphic disorder: clinical aspects and treatment strategies. *B Menninger Clin* **62**:A33–A48.

Phillips KA (2000) Quality of life for patients with body dysmorphic disorder. *J Nerv Ment Dis* **188**:170–175.

Phillips KA & Diaz SF (1997) Gender differences in body dysmorphic disorder. *J Nerv Ment Dis* **185**:570–577.

Phillips KA, Albertini RS & Rasmussen SA (2002) A randomised placebo-controlled trial of fluoxetine in body dysmorphic disorder. *Arch Gen Psychiat* **59**(4):381–388.

Phillips KA, Dufresne RG Jr & Wilkel CS (2000) Rate of body dysmorphic disorder in dermatology patients. *J Am Acad Dermatol* **42**:436–444.

Phillips KA, Dwight MM & McElroy SL (1998) Efficacy and safety of fluvoxamine in body dysmorphic disorder. *J Clin Psychiat* **59**:165–171.

Phillips KA, McElroy SL & Hudson, JI (1995) Body dysmorphic disorder: an obsessive-compulsive spectrum disorder, a form of affective spectrum disorder, or both? *J Clin Psychiat* **56**(suppl 4):41–51.

Phillips KA, McElroy SL & Keck PE Jr (1993) Body dysmorphic disorder: 30 cases of imagined ugliness. *Am J Psychiat* **150**:302–308.

Phillips KA, McElroy SL & Keck PE Jr (1994) A comparison of delusional and non-delusional body dysmorphic disorder in 100 cases. *Psychopharmacol Bull* **30**:179–186.

Philpott R (1975) Recent advances in the behavioural assessment of obsessional illness: difficulties common to these and other measures. *Scot Med J* **20**(suppl1):33–40.

Pigott TA (1998) Obsessive-compulsive disorder: symptom overview and epidemiology. *B Menninger Clin* **62**:A4–A32.

Pigott TA, L'Heureux F & Hill JL (1992a) A double-blind study of adjuvant buspirone hydrochloride in clomipramine-treated patients with obsessive compulsive disorder. *J Clin Pharmacol* **12**:11–18.

Pigott TA, Pato MT & Rubenstein CS (1992b) A controlled trial of clonazepam augmentation in OCD patients treated with clomipramine or fluoxetine. *APA Annual Meeting New Research Abstracts*, **82**.

Pigott TA, Pato MT & Bernstein SE (1990) Controlled comparisons of clomipramine and fluoxetine in the treatment of obsessive compulsive disorder. *Arch Gen Psychiat* **40**:926–932.

Pigott TA, Pato MT & L'Heureux F (1991) A controlled comparison of adjuvant lithium carbonate or thyroid hormone in clomipramine-treated patients with obsessive compulsive disorder. *J Clin Pharmacol* **11**:242–248.

Pitman RK (1984) Janet's obsessions and psychasthenia: a synopsis. *Psychiat Qu* **56**: 291–314.

Pollak JM (1979) Obsessive-compulsive personality: a review. *Psychol Bull* **86**:225–241.

Pollak JM (1987) Relationship of obsessive-compulsive personality to obsessive-compulsive disorder: a review of the literature. *J Psychol* **12**:137–148.

Pollock RA & Carter AS (1999) The familial and developmental context of obsessive-compulsive disorder. *Child Adolesc Psychiat Clin N Am* **8**:461–479.

Porto M, Bermanzohn EC and Pollack S (1997) A profile of obsessive compulsive symptoms in schizophrenia. *CNS Spectrums* **2**:21–25.

Poulton, R (2000) Personal communications.

Pratt P, Tallis F & Eysenck M (1997) Information processing, storage characteristics and worry. *Behav Res Ther* **35**:1015–1023.

Price LH, Goodman WK, Charney DS, Rasmussen SA & Heninger GR (1987) Treatment of severe obsessive-compulsive disorder with fluvoxamine. *Am J Psychiat* **144**:1059–1061.

Purcell R, Maruff P, Kyrios M & Pantelis C (1998) Neuropsychological deficits in obsessive-compulsive disorder: a comparison with unipolar depression, panic disorder and normal controls. *Arch Gen Psychiat* **55**:415–423.

Rabavilas AD & Boulougouris JC (1974) Physiological accompaniments of ruminations, flooding and thought-stopping in obsessive patients. *Behav Res Ther* **12**:239–243.

Rachman S (1971) Obsessional ruminations. *Behav Res Ther* **9**:229–235.

Rachman S (1974) Primary obsessional slowness. *Behav Res Ther* **12**:463–471.

Rachman S (1976a) Obsessional-compulsive checking. *Behav Res Ther* **14**:269–277.

Rachman S (1976b) The modification of obsessions: a new formulation. *Behav Res Ther* **14**:437–443.

Rachman S (1977) The conditioning theory of fear acquisition: a critical examination. *Behav Res Ther* **15**:375–387.

Rachman S (1978) An anatomy of obsessions. *Behav Anal Modif* **2**:253–278.

Rachman S (1982) Obsessional-compulsive disorder. In AS Bellack, M Hersen & AE Kazdin (eds), *International Handbook of Behavior Modification and Therapy*. New York, Plenum.

Rachman S (1983) The modification of agoraphobic avoidance behaviour: some fresh possibilities. *Behav Res Ther* **21**:567–574.

Rachman S (1990) *Fear and Courage*, 2nd edn. San Francisco, CA, Freeman.

Rachman S (1993) Obsessions, responsibility and guilt. *Behav Res Ther* **31**:149–154.

Rachman S (1994) Pollution of the mind. *Behav Res Ther* **32**:311–314.

Rachman S (1997) A cognitive theory of obsessions. *Behav Res Ther* **35**:793–803.

Rachman S (1998) A cognitive theory of obsessions: elaborations. *Behav Res Ther* **36**:385–401.

Rachman S (2001) *The treatment of obsessions* (in press).

Rachman S (2002) A cognitive theory of compulsive checking. *Behav Res Ther* **40**:625–639.

Rachman S & de Silva P (1978) Abnormal and normal obsessions. *Behav Res Ther* **16**:233–238.

Rachman S & Hodgson R (1980) *Obsessions and Compulsions*. Englewood Cliffs, NJ, Prentice Hall.

Rachman S & Shafran R (1998) Cognitive and behavioral features of obsessive-compulsive disorder. In RP Swinson, MM Antony, S Rachman & MA Richter (eds), *Obsessive-Compulsive Disorder: Theory, Research, and Treatment*. New York, Guilford.

Rachman S & Shafran R (1999) Cognitive distortions: thought–action fusion. *Cogn Psychol Psychother* **6**:80–85.

Rachman S & Wilson (1980) *The Effects of Psychological Therapy*. Oxford, Pergamon.

Rachman S, Cobb J, Grey B, McDonald D, Mawson D, Sartory G & Stern R (1979) The behavioral treatment of obsessive-compulsive disorders, with and without clomipramine. *Behav Res Ther* **17**:467–478.

Rachman S, de Silva P & Roper G (1976) The spontaneous decay of compulsive urges. *Behav Res Ther* **14**:445–453.

Rachman S, Grüter-Andrew J & Shafran R (2000) Post-event processing in social anxiety. *Behav Res Ther* **38**:611–617.

Rachman S, Hodgson R & Marks I (1971) The treatment of chronic obsessional neurosis. *Behav Res Ther* **9**:237–247.

Rachman S, Marks IM & Hodgson R (1971) The treatment of obsessive-compulsive neurosis. *Behav Res Ther* **9**:237–247.

Rachman S, Shafran R, Mitchell D, Trant J & Teachman B (1996) How to remain neutral: an experimental analysis of neutralization. *Behav Res Ther* **34**:889–898.

Rachman S, Thordarson DS & Radomsky AS (1995) A revision of the Maudsley Obsessional-Compulsive Inventory. Poster presented at the World Congress of Behavioural and Cognitive Therapies, Copenhagen, Denmark, July.

Rado T (1999) Fractionating Executive Functioning: Evidence from Childhood Obsessive Compulsive Disorder. Unpublished doctoral dissertation, Institute of Psychiatry, University of London.

Radomsky AS & Rachman S (1999) Memory bias in obsessive-compulsive disorder (OCD). *Behav Res Ther* **37**:605–618.

Radomsky AS, Rachman S & Hammond D (2001) Memory bias, confidence and responsibility in compulsive checking. *Behav Res Ther* (in press).

Rangaswamy K (1994) Behavioural management of a mentally retarded individual with obsessive compulsive disorder. *Ind J Clin Psychol* **21**:38–39.

Rapoport JL (1989) *The Boy Who Couldn't Stop Washing—The Experience and Treatment of OCD*. New York, Dutton.

Rapoport JL (1990) Editorial: obsessive compulsive disorder and basal ganglia dysfunction. *Psychol Med*, **20**:465–469.

Rapoport JL & Wise SP (1988) Obsessive-compulsive disorder: evidence for a basal ganglia dysfunction. *Psychopharmacol Bull* **24**:380–384.

Rapoport JL, Elkins R & Langer DM (1981) Childhood obsessive-compulsive disorders. *Am J Psychiat* **138**:1545–1554.

Rapoport JL, Elkins R & Mikkelson E (1980) A clinical controlled trial of cholorimipramine in adolescents with obsessive-compulsive disorder. *Psychopharmacol Bull* **16**:62–63.

Rapoport JL, Swedo SE & Leonard HL (1992) Childhood obsessive compulsive disorder. *J Clin Psychiat* **53**(4, suppl):11–16.

Rasmussen SA (1986) Obsessive-compulsive disorder in dermatologic practice. *J Am Acad Dermatol* **13**:965–967.

Rasmussen SA (1996) The meta-analytic saga of serotonin re-uptake inhibitors in an obsessional world. *CNS Spectrums* **1**:2–9.

Rasmussen SA & Eisen JL (1988) Clinical and epidemiologic findings of significance to neuropharmacologic trials in OCD. *Psychopharmacol Bull* **24**:466–470.

Rasmussen SA & Eisen JL (1992) The epidemiology and clinical features of obsessive compulsive disorder. *Psychiat Clin N Am* **15**:743–758.

Rasmussen SA & Tsuang M (1986) Clinical characteristics and family history in DSM-III obsessive compulsive disorder. *Am J Psychiat* **143**:317–322.

Rassin E, Merckelbach H, Muris P & Spaan V (1999) Thought–action fusion as a causal factor in the development of intrusions. *Behav Res Ther* **37**:231–237.

Ratcliffe J, Gask L, Creed F & Lewis B (1999) Psychiatric training for family doctors: what do GP registrars want and can a brief course provide this? *Med Educ* **33**:434–438.

Ratnasuriya RH, Marks IM, Forshaw DC & Hymas NFS (1991) Obsessional slowness revisited. *Br J Psychiat* **159**:273–274.

Rauch SL & Jenike MA (1998) Pharmacological treatment of obsessive-compulsive disorder. In PE Nathan & JM Gordon (eds), *A Guide to Treatments that Work*. Oxford, Oxford University Press, pp 358–376.

Rauch SL & Savage CR (1997) Neuroimaging and neuropsychology of the striatum: bridging basic science and clinical practice. *Psychiat Clin N Am* **20**:741–768.

Rauch SL & Savage CR (2000) Investigating cortico-striatal pathophysiology in obsessive-compulsive disorders: procedural learning and imaging probes. In WK Goodman, MV Rudorfer & JD Maser (eds), *Obsessive Compulsive Disorder: Contemporary Issues in Treatment*. Mahwah, NJ, Erlbaum.

Rauch SL, O'Sullivan RL & Jenike MA (1996) Open treatment of obsessive compulsive disorder with venlafaxine: a series of 10 cases (letter). *J Clin Pharmacol* **16**:81–83.

Ravi K, Smith-Seemillier L & Duffy JD (1996) Obsessive-compulsive disorder after closed head injury: review of literature and report of four cases. *Brain Injury* **10**:55–63.

Ravizza L, Barzega G & Bellino S (1996a) Drug treatment of obsessive compulsive disorder. Long-term trial with clomipramine and selective serotonin reuptake inhibitors. *Psychopharmacol Bull* **32**:167–173.

Ravizza L, Barzega G & Bellino S (1996b) Therapeutic effect and safety of adjunctive risperidone in refractory obsessive compulsive disorder. *Psychopharmacol Bull* **32**:677–682.

Reed G (1985) *Obsessional Experience and Compulsive Behaviour: a Cognitive–Structural Approach*. London, Academic Press.

Rettew DC, Swedo SE, Leonard HL, Lenane MC & Rapoport JL (1992) Obsessions and compulsions across time in 79 children and adolescents with obsessive-compulsive disorder. *J Am Acad Child Adolesc Psychiat* **31**:1050–1056.

Rhéaume J, Freeston MH, Dugas MJ, Letarte H & Ladouceur R (1995) Perfectionism, responsibility and obsessive-compulsive symptoms. *Behav Res Ther* **33**:785–794.

Rhéaume J, Ladouceur R & Freeston MH (2000) The prediction of obsessive-compulsive tendencies: Does perfectionism play a significant role? *Personality & Individual Differences* **28**(3): 583–592.

Rhéaume J, Ladouceur R, Freeston MH & Letarte H (1994) Inflated responsibility and its role in OCD. II Psychometric studies of a semi-idiographic measure. *J Psychopathol Behav* **16**:265–276.

Richter MA, Cox BJ & Direnfeld DM (1994) A comparison of three assessment instruments for obsessive-compulsive symptoms. *J Behav Ther Exp Psychiat* **25**:143–147.

Riddle MA (1998) Obsessive-compulsive disorder in children and adolescents. *Br J Psychiat* **173** (suppl 35):91–96.

Riddle MA, Scahill L, King RA, Hardin MT, Anderson GM, Ort SI, Smith JC, Leckman JF & Cohen DJ (1992) Double-blind, crossover trial of fluoxetine and placebo in children and adolescents with obsessive-compulsive disorder. *J Am Acad Child Adolesc Psychiat* **31**:1062–1069.

Riddle MA, Scahill L, King RA, Hardin MT, Towbin KE, Ort SI, Leckman JF & Cohen DJ (1990) Obsessive-compulsive disorder in children and adolescents: phenomenology and family history. *J Am Acad Child Adolesc Psychiat* **29**:766–772.

Riding J & Munro A (1975) Pimozide in the treatment of monosymptomatic hypochondriacal psychosis. *Acta Psychiat Scand* **53**:23–30.

Riggs DS & Foa EB (1993) Obsessive compulsive disorder. In DH Barlow (ed), *Clinical Handbook of Psychological Disorders*, 2nd edn. New York, Guilford, pp 189–239.

Riggs DS, Hiss H & Foa EB (1992) Marital distress and the treatment of obsessive-compulsive disorder. *Behav Ther* **23**:585–597.

Roberts JE, Gilboa E & Gotlib IH (1998) Ruminative response style and vulnerability to episodes of dysphoria: gender, neuroticism, and episode duration. *Cogn Ther Res* **22**:401–423.

Robins L, Helzer J, Weissman M, Orvashel H, Gruenberg E, Burke J & Regier D (1984) Lifetime prevalence of specific psychiatric disorders in three sites. *Arch Gen Psychiat* **41**:949–958.

Rodrigues TA & Del Porto JA (1995) Comorbidity of obsessive-compulsive disorder and personality disorders: a Brazilian controlled study. *Psychopathology* **28**:322–329.

Roger D & Najarian B (1997) The relationship between emotional rumination and cortisol secretion under stress. *Pers Indiv Differ* **24**:531–538.

Romans SM (1997) Executive functions in girls with Turner syndrome. *Dev Neuropsychol* **13**:23–40.

Roper G & Rachman S (1975) Obsessional-compulsive checking: replication and development. *Behav Res Ther* **14**:25–32.

Roper G, Rachman S & Hodgson R (1973) An experiment on obsessional checking. *Behav Res Ther* **11**:271–277.

Rosa F (1994) Medicaid antidepressant pregnancy exposure outcomes. *Reprod Toxicol* **8**:444.

Rosen GM & Ornstein H (1976) A historical note on thought stopping. *J Consult Clin Psychol* **44**:1016–1017.

Rosen JC, Reiter J & Orosan P (1995) Cognitive-behavioral body image therapy for body dysmorphic disorder [published erratum appears in *J Consult Clin Psychol* (1995) Jun 63:437]. *J Consult Clin Psychol* **63**:263–269.

Rosenberg CM (1967) Familial aspects of neurosis. *Br J Psychiat* **113**:405–413.

Rosenberg DR, Averbach DH & O'Hearn KM (1997) Oculomotor response inhibition abnormalities in pediatric obsessive-compulsive disorder. *Arch Gen Psychiat* **54**:831–838.

Rosenberg DR, Benazon NR, Gilbert A, Sullivan A & Moore GJ (2000a) Thalamic volume in pediatric obsessive-compulsive disorder patients before and after cognitive behavioural therapy. *Biol Psychiat* **48**:294–300.

Rosenberg DR, MacMaster FP, Keshavan MS, Fitzgerald KD, Stewart CM & Moore GJ (2000b) Decrease in caudate glutamatergic concentrations in pediatric obsessive-compulsive disorder patients taking paroxetine. *J Am Acad Child Adolesc Psychiat* **39**:1096–1103.

Rosenberg DR, Stewart CM, Fitzgerald KD, Tawile V & Carroll E (1999) Paroxetine open-label treatment of pediatric outpatients with obsessive-compulsive disorder. *J Am Acad Child Adolesc Psychiat* **38**:1180–1185.

Rosenfeld R, Dar R, Anderson D, Kobak KA & Greist JH (1992) A computer-administered version of the Yale–Brown Obsessive Compulsive Scale. *Psychol Assess* **4**:329–332.

Rothbaum B, Hodges L & Kooper R (1997) Virtual reality exposure therapy. *J Psychother Pract Res* **6**:219–226.

Rubenstein CF, Peyniricioglu ZF, Chambless DL & Pigott TA (1993) Memory in sub-clinical obsessive-compulsive checkers. *Behav Res Ther* **27**:65–69.

Rüdin E (1953) Ein beitrag zur frage der zwangskrankheit. *Archiv Psychiat Zeitschr Neurol* **191**:14–51.

Sachdev P & Sachdev J (1998) Response to White's comments on 'Sixty years of psychosurgery: its present status and its future'. *Aust NZ J Psychiat* **32**:462–463.

Salkovskis PM (1983) Treatment of an obsessional patient using habituation to audiotaped ruminations. *Br J Clin Psychol* **22**:311–313.

Salkovskis PM (1985) Obsessional-compulsive problems: a cognitive-behavioural analysis. *Behav Res Ther* **23**:571–583.

Salkovskis PM (1988) Phenomenology, assessment and the cognitive model of panic. In SJ Rachman & J Maser (eds), *Panic: Psychological Perspectives*. Hillsdale, NJ, Erlbaum.

Salkovskis PM (1989a) Obsessions and compulsions. In J Scott, JMG Williams & AT Beck (eds), *Cognitive Therapy—A Clinical Casebook*. London, Croom Helm.

Salkovskis PM (1989b) Obsessive and intrusive thoughts: clinical and non-clinical aspects. In PMG Emmelkamp, WTAM Everaerd & MJM van Son (eds), *Fresh Perspectives on Anxiety Disorders*. Amsterdam, Swets and Zeitlinger.

Salkovskis PM (1989c) Cognitive-behavioural factors and the persistence of intrusive thoughts in obsessional problems. *Behav Res Ther* **27**:677–682.

Salkovskis PM (1991) The importance of behaviour in the maintenance of anxiety and panic: a cognitive account. *Behav Psychother* **19**:6–19.

Salkovskis PM (1996a) The cognitive approach to anxiety: threat beliefs, safety seeking behaviour, and the special case of health anxiety and obsessions. In PM Salkovskis (ed.), *Frontiers of Cognitive Therapy*. New York, Guilford.

Salkovskis PM (1996b) Cognitive-behavioural approaches to the understanding of obsessional problems. In R Rapee (ed.), *Current Controversies in the Anxiety Disorders*. New York, Guilford.

Salkovskis PM (1996c) Resolving the cognition–behaviour debate. In PM Salkovskis (ed.), *Trends in Cognitive-behaviour Therapy*. Chichester, John Wiley & Sons, Ltd.

Salkovskis PM (ed.) (1996d) *Frontiers of Cognitive Therapy*. New York, The Guilford Press.

Salkovskis PM (1998) Psychological approaches to the understanding of obsessional problems. In RP Swinson, MM Antony, S Rachman & MA Richter (eds), Obsessive-Compulsive Disorder: Theory, Research and Treatment. New York, Guilford.

Salkovskis PM (1999) Understanding and treating obsessive-compulsive disorder. *Behav Res Ther* **37**:529–552.

Salkovskis PM & Bass C (1997) Hypochondriasis. In DM Clark & CG Fairburn (eds), *The Science and Practice of Cognitive-Behaviour Therapy*. Oxford, Oxford University Press.

Salkovskis PM & Campbell P (1994) Thought suppression in naturally occurring negative intrusive thoughts. *Behav Res Ther* **32**:1–8.

Salkovskis PM & Freeston MH (in press) Obsessions, compulsions, motivation and responsibility for harm. *Aust J Psychol*.

Salkovskis PM & Harrison J (1984) Abnormal and normal obsessions—a replication. *Behav Res Ther* **22**:549–552.

Salkovskis PM & Kirk J (1997) Obsessive-compulsive disorder. In DM Clark & CG Fairburn (eds), *Science and Practice of Cognitive Behaviour Therapy*. Oxford, Oxford University Press.

Salkovskis PM & Warwick HMC (1985) Cognitive therapy of obsessive-compulsive disorder: treating treatment failures. *Behav Psychother* **13**:243–255.

Salkovskis PM & Warwick HMC (1988) Obsessional problems. In C Perris, IM Blackburn & H Perris (eds), *The Theory and Practice of Cognitive Therapy*. Berlin, Springer Verlag.

Salkovskis PM & Westbrook D (1987) Obsessive-compulsive disorder: clinical strategies for improving behavioural treatments. In HR Dent (ed.), *Clinical Psychology: Research and Developments*. London, Croom Helm.

Salkovskis PM & Westbrook D (1989) Behaviour therapy and obsessional ruminations: can failure be turned into success? *Behav Res Ther* **27**:149–160.

Salkovskis PM, Forrester E & Richards C (1998a) Cognitive-behavioural approach to understanding obsessional thinking. *Br J Psychiat* **173**(suppl 35):53–63.

Salkovskis PM, Forrester E, Richards HC & Morrison N (1998b) The devil is in the detail: conceptualising and treating obsessional problems. In N Tarrier, A Wells & G Haddock (eds), *Treating Complex Cases: the Cognitive-Behavioural Therapy Approach*. Chichester, John Wiley & Sons, Ltd.

Salkovskis PM, Wroe A, Richards HC, Morrison N, Gledhill A, Thorpe S, Forrester E & Reynolds M (1998c) Responsibility assumptions and appraisals in obsessive-compulsive disorder (submitted for publication).

Salkovskis PM, Rachman S, Ladouceur R, Freeston M, Taylor S, Kyrios M & Sica C (1996) Defining responsibility in obsessional problems. First meeting of Obsessive-compulsive Cognitions Working Group, Smith College, Boston, USA.

Salkovskis PM, Wroe A, Gledhill A, Morrison N, Forrester E, Richards HC, Reynolds M and Thorpe S (2000a) Responsibility attitudes and interpretations are characteristic of obsessive-compulsive disorder. *Behav Res Ther* **38**:347–372.

Salkovskis PM, Richards C & Forrester E (2000b) Psychological treatment of refractory obsessive-compulsive disorder. In WK Goodman, MV Rudorfer & JD Maser (eds), *Obsessive-Compulsive Disorder: Contemporary Issues in Treatment*. Mahwah, NJ, Elbaum.

Salkovskis PM, Shafran R, Rachman S & Freeston MH (1999) Multiple pathways to inflated responsibility beliefs in obsessional problems: possible origins and implications for therapy and research. *Behav Res Ther* **37**:1055–1072.

Salkovskis PM, Westbrook D, Davis J, Jeavons A & Gledhill A (1997) Effects of neutralizing on intrusive thoughts: an experiment investigating the etiology of obsessive-compulsive disorder. *Behav Res Ther* **35**:211–219.

Salzman L (1973) *The Obsessive Personality: Origins, Dynamics and Therapy*. New York, Jason Aronson.

Salzman L & Thaler F (1981) Obsessive-compulsive disorders: a review of the literature. *Am J Psychiat* **138**:286–296.

Sanavio E (1988) Obsessions and compulsions: the Padua Inventory. *Behav Res Ther* **26**:169–177.

Sanavio E & Vidotto G (1985) The components of the Maudsley Obsessional-Compulsive Questionnaire. *Behav Res Ther* **23**:659–662.

Sandler J & Hazari A (1960) The 'obsessional': on the psychological classification of obsessional character traits and symptoms. *Br J Med Psychol* **33**:113–122.

Sanna CJ, Turley KJ & Mark MM (1996) Expected evaluation, goals, and performance: mood as input. *Pers Soc Psychol B* **22**:323–335.

Sarwer DB, Wadden TA, Pertschulk MJ et al. (1998) Body image dissatisfaction and body dysmorphic disorder in 100 cosmetic surgery patients. *Plast Reconstr Surg* **101**:1644–1649.

Sasson Y, Bermanzohn PC & Zohar J (1997) Treatment of obsessive compulsive syndromes in schizophrenia. *CNS Spectrums* **2**:34–36.

Savage CR, Baer L & Keuthen NJ (1999) Organisational strategies mediate nonverbal memory impairment in obsessive-compulsive disorder. *Biol Psychiat* **45**:905–916.

Savage CR, Deckersbach T, Wilhelm S, Rauch SL, Baer L, Reid T & Jenike MA (2000) Strategic processing and episodic memory impairment in obsessive-compulsive disorder. *Neuropsychology* **14**:141–151.

Saxena S, Brody AL, Schwartz JM & Baxter LR (1998) Neuroimaging and frontal–subcortical circuitry in obsessive-compulsive disorder. *Br J Psychiat* **173**(suppl 35):26–37.

Scahill L, Riddle M, McSeiggin-Hardin M, Ort SI, King RA, Goodman WK, Cicchetti D & Leckman JF (1997) Children's Yale–Brown obsessive-compulsive scale: reliability and validity. *J Am Acad Child Adolesc Psychiat* **36**:844–852.

Scarrabelotti MB, Duck JM & Dickerson MM (1995) Individual differences in obsessive-compulsive behaviour: the role of the Eysenckian dimensions and appraisals of responsibility. *Pers Indiv Differ* **18**:413–421.

Schaffetter C (1980) *General Psychopathology* (translated by Helen Marshall). Cambridge, Cambridge University Press.

Schultz RT, Evans DW & Wolff M (1999) Neuropsychological models of childhood obsessive-compulsive disorder. *Child Adolesc Psychiat Clin N Am* **8**:513–531.

Schwartz JM, Stoessel PW, Baxter LR Jr, Martin KM & Phelps ME (1996) Systematic changes in cerebral glucose metabolic rate after successful behaviour modification treatment of obsessive-compulsive disorder. *Arch Gen Psychiat* **53**:109–113.

Schwarz N & Bless H (1991) Happy and mindless, but sad and smart? The impact of affective states on analytic reasoning. In J Forgas (ed), *Emotion and Social Judgements*. London, Pergamon, pp 55–71.

Seedat S & Stein DG (1999) Inositol augmentation of serotonin re-uptake inhibitors in treatment refractory obsessive compulsive disorder: an open trial. *Int Clin Psychopharmacol* **14**: 353–356.

Seligman MEP (1970) On the generality of the laws of learning. *Psychol Rev* **77**:406–418.

Seligman MEP (1971) Phobias and preparedness. *Behav Ther* **2**:307–320.

Shaffer D, Fisher P, Dulcan MK, Davies M, Piacentini J, Schwab-Stone M, Lahey BB, Bourdon K, Jensen P, Bird HR, Canino G & Regier DA (1996) The NIMH diagnostic interview schedule for children, version 2.3 (DISC-2.3): description, acceptability, prevalence rates and performance in the MECA study. *J Am Acad Child Adolesc Psychiat* **35**:865–855.

Shaffer D, Gould MS, Brasic J, Ambrosini P, Fisher P, Bird H & Alawahlia SA (1983) Children's Global Assessment Scale (CGAS). *Arch Gen Psychiat* **40**:1228–1231.

Shafran R (1997) The manipulation of responsibility in obsessive-compulsive disorder. *Br J Clin Psychol* **36**:397–407.

Shafran R (1998) Childhood obsessive-compulsive disorder. In P Graham (ed), *Cognitive-Behaviour Therapy for Children and Families*. Cambridge, Cambridge University Press.

Shafran R & Mansell W (2001) Perfectionism and psychopathology. *Clin Psychol Rev* **21**:879–906.

Shafran R & Rachman S (2002) OCD in childhood (submitted for publication).

Shafran R & Somers J (1998) Treating adolescent obsessive-compulsive disorder: applications of the cognitive theory. *Behav Res Ther* **36**:93–97.

Shafran R & Tallis F (1996) Obsessive-compulsive hoarding: a cognitive-behavioural approach. *Behav Cogn Psychother* **24**:209–221.

Shafran R, Frampton I, Heyman I, Reynolds M, Teachman B & Rachman S (in press) The preliminary development of a new self-report measure for OCD in young people. *Journal of Adolescence*.

Shafran R, Thordarson DS & Rachman S (1996) Thought–action fusion in obsessive-compulsive disorder. *J Anxiety Disord* **10**:379–391.

Shallice T (1988) *From Neuropsychology to Mental Structure.* New York, Cambridge University Press.

Shallice T & Burgess P(1998) The domain of supervisory processes and the temporal organization of behaviour. In AC Roberts & TW Robbins (eds), *The Prefrontal Cortex: Executive and Cognitive Functions.* New York, Oxford University Press.

Sham PC (1998) *Statistics in Human Genetics.* New York, Edward Arnold.

Shapiro M B (1957) Experimental methods in the psychological description of the individual psychiatric patient. *Int J Soc Psychiat* **111**:89–102.

Sher KJ, Frost RO, Kushner M, Crews TM & Alexander JE (1989) Memory deficits in compulsive checkers: replication and extension in a clinical sample. *Behav Res Ther* **27**:65–69.

Sher KJ, Frost RO & Otto R (1983) Cognitive deficits in compulsive checkers: an exploratory study. *Behav Res Ther* **21**:357–363.

Sher KJ, Mann B & Frost RO (1984) Cognitive dysfunction in compulsive checkers: further explorations. *Behav Res Ther* **22**:493–502.

Sher KJ, Martin ED, Raskin G & Perrigo R (1991) Prevalence of DSM-III-R disorders among nonclinical compulsive checkers and noncheckers in a college student sample. *Behav Res Ther* **29**:479–483.

Silverman WK & Eisen AR (1992) Age difference in the reliability of parent and child reports of child anxious symptomatology using a structured interview. *J Am Acad Child Adolesc Psychiat* **31**:117–124.

Simonds LM, Thorpe SJ & Elliott SA (2000) The Obsessive Compulsive Inventory: psychometric properties in a nonclinical student sample. *Behav Cogn Psychother* **28**:153–159.

Simons DJ & Levin DT (1998) Failure to detect changes to people during real-world interaction. *Psychonom Bull Rev* **4**:644.

Simpson HB, Gorfinkle KS & Liebowitz MR (1999) Cognitive behavioural therapy as an adjunct to serotonin reuptake inhibitors in obsessive compulsive disorder: an open trial. *J Clin Psychiat* **60**:584–590.

Singleton A & Smith FR (1997) Education in primary care psychiatry: research-based audit. *Med Educ* **31**:380–385.

Skoog G & Skoog I (1999) A 40-year follow-up of patients with obsessive-compulsive disorder. *Arch Gen Psychiat* **56**:121–127.

Slater E & Roth M (1969) *Mayer–Gross Slater and Roth's Clinical Psychiatry,* 3rd edn. London, Ballière, Tindall and Cassell.

Smeraldi E, Erzegovesi S & Bianchi Y (1992) Fluvoxamine versus clomipramine treatment in obsessive compulsive disorder: a preliminary study. *New Trends Exp Clin Psychiat* **8**:63–65.

Snowdon J (1980) A comparison of written and postbox forms of the Leyton Obsessional Inventory. *Psychol Med* **10**:165–170.

Snyder S (1980) Amitriptyline therapy for of obsessive-compulsive neurosis. *J Clin Psychiat* **41**:286–289.

Solyom L, Zamanzadeh D, Ledwidge B & Kenny F (1971) A comparative study of aversion relief and systematic desensitization in the treatment of phobias. *Br J Psychiat* **119**:299–303.

Spitzer M & Sigmund D (1997) The phenomenology of obsessive-compulsive disorder. *Int Rev Psychiat* **9**:7–13.

Spitzer RL, Williams JBW, Gibbon M & First MB (1992) The Structured Clinical Interview for DSM-III-R (SCID): I History, rationale and description. *Arch Gen Psychiat* **49**:624–629.

Stanley MA & Averill PM (1998) Psychosocial treatments for obsessive-compulsive disorder In RP Swinson, MM Antony, S Rachman & MA Richter (eds), *Obsessive-Compulsive Disorder: Theory, Research and Treatment*. New York, Guilford.

Stanley MA, Prather RC, Beck GJ, Brown TC, Wagner AL & Davis ML (1993) Psychometric analyses of the Leyton Obsessional Inventory in patients with obsessive-compulsive and other anxiety disorders. *Psychol Assess* **5**:187–192.

Startup HM & Davey GCL (2002) Inflated responsibility and the use of stop rules for catastrophic worrying (submitted for publication).

Startup HM & Davey GCL (2001) Mood-as-information and catastrophic worrying. *J Abnorm Psychol* **110**:83–96.

Stein DJ, Bouwer C & Hawkridge S (1997a) Risperidone augmentation of serotonin re-uptake inhibitors in obsessive compulsive and related disorders. *J Clin Psychiat* **58**:119–122.

Stein M, Forde D, Anderson G & Walker J (1997b) Obsessive-compulsive disorder in the community: an epidemiologic survey with clinical reappraisal. *Am J Psychiat* **154**:1120–1126.

Stein DJ, Hollander E, Simeon D & Cohen L (1994) Impulsivity scores in patients with obsessive-compulsive disorder. *J Nerv Ment Dis* **182**:240–241.

Stein DJ, Shoulberg N, Helton K & Hollander E (1992) The neuroethological approach to obsessive-compulsive disorder. *Compr Psychiat* **33**:274–281.

Stein DJ, Simeon D, Cohen LJ & Hollander E (1995a) Trichotillomania and obsessive-compulsive disorder. *J Clin Psychiat* **56**(suppl 4):28–34.

Stein DJ, Spadaccini E & Hollander E (1995b) Meta-analysis of pharmacotherapy trials for obsessive compulsive disorder. *Int Clin Psychopharmacol* **10**:11–18.

Steingard R, Dillon-Stout D (1992) Tourette's syndrome and obsessive compulsive disorder: clinical aspects. *Psychiat Clin N Am* **15**:849–860.

Steketee GS (1993a) *Treatment of Obsessive Compulsive Disorder*. New York, Guilford.

Steketee GS (1993b) Social support and treatment outcome of obsessive-compulsive disorder at 9 month follow-up. *Behav Psychother* **21**:81–95.

Steketee GS (1997) Disability and family burden in obsessive-compulsive disorder. *Can J Psychiat* **42**:919–928.

Steketee GS & Doppelt H (1986) Measurement of obsessive-compulsive symptomatology: utility of the Hopkins Symptom Checklist. *Psychiat Res* **19**:135–145.

Steketee GS & Freund B (1993) Compulsive Activity Checklist (CAC): further psychometric analyses and revision. *Behav Psychother* **21**:13–25.

Steketee GS & Frost R (eds, Obsessive and Compulsive Cognitions Working Group) (2001) Development and initial validation of the obsessive beliefs questionnaire and the interpretation of intrusions inventory. *Behav Res Ther* **8**:987–1006.

Steketee GS & Pruyn NA (1998) Families of individuals with obsessive-compulsive disorder. In RP Swinson, M Antony, S Rachman & MA Richter (eds), *Obsessive-Compulsive Disorder: Theory, Research, and Treatment*. New York, Guilford.

Steketee GS & Shapiro LJ (1995) Predicting behavioral treatment outcome for ago-raphobia and obsessive-compulsive disorder. *Clin Psychol Rev* **15**:317–346.

Steketee GS & White K (1990) *When Once Is Not Enough: Help for Obsessive-Compulsives*. Oakland, CA, Harbinger.

Steketee GS, Chambless DL, Tran GQ, Worden H & Gillis MM (1996a) Behavioral Avoidance Test for obsessive compulsive disorder. *Behav Res Ther* **34**:73–83.

Steketee GS, Frost R & Bogart K (1996b) The Yale–Brown Obsessive-Compulsive Scale: interview versus self-report. *Behav Res Ther* **34**:675–684.

Steketee GS, Foa EB & Grayson JB (1982) Recent advances in the behavioral treat-ment of obsessive-compulsives. *Arch Gen Psychiat* **39**:1365–1371.

Steketee GS, Freund B & Foa EB (1988) Likert scaling. In M Hersen & AS Bellack (eds), *Dictionary of Behavioral Assessment Techniques*. New York, Pergamon, pp 289–291.

Steketee GS, Frost RO & Cohen I (1998a) Beliefs in obsessive-compulsive disorder. *J Anxiety Disord* **12**:525–537.

Steketee GS, Frost RO, Rheaume J & Wilhelm S (1998b) Cognitive theory and treatment of obsessive-compulsive disorder. In MA Jenike, L Baer & WE Minichiello (eds), *Obsessive-Compulsive Disorders: Practical Management*. St Louis, MO, Mosby.

Steketee GS, Frost RO, Wincze J, Greene KAI & Douglass, H (2000) Group and in-dividual treatment of compulsive hoarding: a pilot study. *Behav Cogn Psychother* **28**:259–268.

Steketee GS, Frost RO & Kim H-J (2001) Hoarding by elderly people. Health Soc Work **26**:176–184.

Steketee GS, Grayson JB & Foa EB (1985) Obsessive-compulsive disorder: Differ-ences between washers and checkers. *Behav Res Ther* **23**:197–201.

Steketee GS, Grayson JB & Foa EB (1987) A comparison of obsessive-compulsive characteristics and other anxiety disorders. *J Anxiety Disord* **1**:325–335.

Stern RS (1970) The treatment of a case of obsessional neurosis using a thought-stopping technique. *Br J Psychiat* **117**:441–442.

Stern RS (1978) Obsessive thoughts: the problems of therapy. *Br J Psychiat* **132**:200–205.

Stern RS & Cobb, JP (1978) Phenomenology of obsessive-compulsive neurosis. *Br J Psychiat* **132**:233–239.

Sternberger LG & Burns GL (1990a) Compulsive Activity Checklist and the Maud-sley Obsessional-Compulsive Inventory: psychometric properties of two mea-sures of obsessive-compulsive disorder. *Behav Ther* **21**:117–127.

Sternberger LG & Burns GL (1990b) Obsessions and compulsions: psychometric properties of the Padua Inventory with an American college population. *Behav Res Ther* **28**:341–345.

Sternberger LG & Burns GL (1991) Obsessive-compulsive disorder: symptoms and diagnosis in a college sample. *Behav Ther* **22**:569–576.

Stober J (1998) Worry, problem elaboration and suppression of imagery: the role of concreteness. *Behav Res Ther* **36**:751–756.

Stoll AL, Tohen M & Baldessarini RJ (1992) Increasing frequency of the diagnosis of obsessive compulsive disorder. *Am J Psychiat* **149**:638–640.

Stoppe G, Brandt CA & Staedt JH (1999) Behavioural problems associated with dementia: the role of newer antipsychotics. *Drugs Aging* **14**:41–54.

Strauman TJ (1989) Self-discrepancies in clinical depression and social phobia: cog-nitive structures that underlie emotional disorders? *J Abnorm Psychol* **98**:14–22.

Sullivan MJL & Neish NR (1998) Catastrophizing, anxiety and pain during mental hygiene treatment. *Common Dentistry Oral Epidemiol* **26**:344–349.

Sullivan MJL, Bishop SR & Pivik J (1995) The pain catastrophizing scale: development and validation. *Psychol Assessm* **7**(4):524–532.

Summerfeldt LJ, Antony M, Downie F, Richter M & Swinson R (1997) Prevalence of particular obsessions and compulsions in a clinical sample. In R Swinson, M Antony, S Rachman & M Richter (eds), *Obsessive-compulsive Disorder: Theory, Research and Treatment*. New York, Guilford, pp 79–119.

Summerfeldt LJ, Richter MA, Antony MM & Swinson RP (1999) Symptom structure in obsessive-compulsive disorder: a confirmatory factor-analytic study. *Behav Res Ther* **37**:297–311.

Swedo SE, Leonard HL, Garvey M, Mittleman B, Allen AJ, Perlmutter S, Dow S, Zamkoff J, Dubbert BK & Lougee L (1998) Pediatric autoimmune neuropsychiatric disorders associated with streptococcal infections: clinical descriptions of the first 50 cases. *Am J Psychiat* **155**:264–271.

Swedo SE, Leonard HL & Miffleman BB (1997) Identification of children with pediatric autoimmune neuropsychiatric disorders associated with streptococcal infections by a marker associated with rheumatic fever. *Am J Psychiat* **154**:110–112.

Swedo SE, Rapoport JL, Cheslow DL, Leonard HL, Ayoub EM, Hosier DM & Wald ER (1989a) High prevalence of obsessive-compulsive symptoms in patients with Sydenham's chorea. *Am J Psychiat* **146**:246–249.

Swedo SE, Rapoport JL, Leonard HL, Lenane M & Cheslow D (1989b) Obsessive-compulsive disorder in children and adolescents. *Arch Gen Psychiat* **46**:335–341.

Swedo SE, Schapiro MB, Grady CL et al. (1989c) Cerebral glucose metabolism in childhood-onset obsessive-compulsive disorder. *Arch Gen Psychiat* **46**:518—523.

Swerdlow NR (1995) Obsessive compulsive disorder and the basal ganglia. *Int Rev Psychiat* **7**:115–129.

Swerdlow NR, Benbow CH & Zisook S (1993) A preliminary assessment of sensorimotor gating in patients with obsessive compulsive disorder. *Biol Psychiat* **33**:298–301.

Swinson RP, Antony MM, Rachman S & Richter MA (1998) *Obsessive-Compulsive Disorder: Theory, Research and Treatment*. New York, Guilford.

Takeuchi T, Nakagawa A, Harai H, Nakatani E, Fujikawa S, Yoshizato C & Yamagami T (1997) Primary obsessional slowness: long-term findings. *Behav Res Ther* **35**:445–449.

Takeuchi T, Shibata S & Yamagami T (2001) Some new findings on primary obsessional slowness. Poster presented at the World Congress of Behavioural and Cognitive Therapies, Vancouver, July.

Tallis F (1993) Doubt reduction using distinctive stimuli as a treatment for compulsive checking: an exploratory investigation. *Clin Psychol Psychother* **1**:45–52.

Tallis F (1995a) *Obsessive-Compulsive Disorder: a Cognitive and Neuropsychological Perspective*. Chichester, John Wiley & Sons, Ltd.

Tallis F (1995b) The characteristics of obsessional thinking: difficulty demonstrating the obvious. *Clin Psychol Psychother* **2**:24–39.

Tallis F (1996) Compulsive washing in the absence of phobic and illness anxiety. *Behav Res Ther* **34**:361–362.

Tallis F (1997) The neuropsychology of obsessive-compulsive disorder: a review and consideration of clinical implications. *Br J Clin Psychol*.

Tallis F, Eysenck MW & Matthews A (1991) Elevaved evidence requirements and worry. *Pers Indiv Diff* **12**(1): 21–27.

Tallis F, Rosen K & Shafran R (1996) Investigation into the relationship between personality traits and OCD: a replication employing a clinical population. *Behav Res Ther* **34**:649–653.

Tarkoff A, Owen-Smith A, Cramer M, Gebhart S, Hood S, Skoglund K & Frost R (2000) The mediative qualities of perfectionism in the relationship between hoarding and indecisiveness. Paper presented at the Annual Meeting of the Association for the Advancement of Behavior Therapy, New Orleans, Nov.

Tarsh MJ (1978) Severe obsessional illness in dizygotic twins treated by leucotomy. *Compr Psychiat* **39**(suppl):171.

Taylor HG, Barry CT & Schatschneider CW (1993) School-age consequences on *Haemophilus influenzae* Type B meningitis. *J Clin Child Psychol* **22**:196–206.

Taylor S (1995) Assessment of obsessions and compulsions: reliability, validity and sensitivity to treatment effects. *Clin Psychol Rev* **15**:261–296.

Taylor S (1998) Assessment of obsessive-compulsive disorder In RP Swinson, MM Antony, S Rachman & MA Richter (eds), *Obsessive-compulsive disorder: Theory, research and treatment*. New York, Guilford.

Temple CM (1997) Cognitive neuropsychology and its application to children. *J Child Psychol Psychiat* **38**:27–52.

Thompson JK, Heinberg LJ & Altabe M (1999) *Exacting Beauty Theory, Assessment, and Treatment of Body Image Disturbance*. Washington DC, American Psychological Association.

Thomsen PH (1999) *From Thoughts to Obsessions: Obsessive-compulsive Disorder in Children and Adolescents*. London, Jessica Kingsley.

Thomsen PH & Mikkelson HU (1995) Course of obsessive-compulsive disorder in children and adolescents: a prospective follow-up study of 23 Danish cases. *J Am Acad Child Adolesc Psychiat* **34**:1432–1040.

Thoren P, Asberg M, Cronholm B, Jörnestedt L & Träskman L (1980) Clomipramine treatment of obsessive-compulsive disorder: a controlled clinical trial. *Arch Gen Psychiat* **37**:1281–1285.

Thornhill R & Gangestad SW (1993) Human facial beauty—averageness, symmetry and parasite resistance. *Hum Nature* **4**:237–269.

Thornhill R & Grammer K (1994) Human (*Homo sapiens*) facial attractiveness and sexual selection: the role of symmetry and averageness. *J Comp Psychol* **108**:233–242.

Toates F (1990) *Obsessional Thoughts and Behaviour*. Wellingborough, Thorsons.

Todorov C, Brassard M & Fontaine R (1996) Fluoxetine versus clomipramine in obsessive compulsive disorder. 10th World Congress of Psychiatry, August 23–28, Abstracts 2, 296.

Todorov C, Freeston MH & Borgeat F (2000) On the pharmacotherapy of obsessive compulsive disorder: is a consesus possible? *Can J Psychiat* **45**:257–262.

Tolin DF, Abramowitz JS, Bartholomew BD, Nader A, Street GP & Foa EB (2001) Memory and memory confidence in obsessive-compulsive disorder. *Behav Res Ther* (in press).

Tollefson G, Rampey AH, Potvin JH et al. (1994) A multi-centre investigation of fixed-dose fluoxetine treatment of obsessive-compulsive disorder. *Arch Gen Psychiat* **51**:559–567.

Torgersen S (1980) The oral, obsessive, and hysterical personality syndromes. A study of hereditary and environmental factors by means of the twin method. *Arch Gen Psychiat* **37**:1272–1277.

Torgersen S (1983) Genetic factors in anxiety disorders. *Arch Gen Psychiat* **40**:1085–1089.

Torgersen S (1987) Sampling problems in twin research. *J Psychiat Res* **21**:385–390.

Toro J, Cervera M, Osejo E & Salamero M (1992) Obsessive-compulsive disorder in childhood and adolescence: a clinicalstudy *J Child Psychol Psychiat*, **33**:1025–1037.

Trinder H & Salkovskis PM (1994) Personally relevant intrusions outside the laboratory: long-term suppression increases intrusion. *Behav Res Ther* **32**:833–842.

Trivedi MH (1996) Functional neuroanatomy of obsessive-compulsive disorder. *J Clin Psychiat* **57**(suppl 8):26–35.

Turkat ID & Maisto SA (1985) Application of the experimental method to the formulation and modification of personality disorders. In DH Barlow (ed.), *Clinical Handbook of Psychological Disorders*. New York, Guilford.

Turkat ID & Meyer V (1982) The behaviour-analytic approach. In P Wachtel (ed.), *Resistance Psychodynamic and Behavioural Approaches*. New York, Plenum.

Turner SM & Beidel DC (1988) *Treating Obsessive Compulsive Disorder*. New York, Pergamon.

Turner SM, Beidel DC & Spaulding T (1995) The practice of behavior therapy: a national survey of costs and methods. *Behav Ther* **18**:1–4.

Turner SM, Beidel DC & Stanley MA (1992) Are obsessional thoughts and worry different cognitive phenomena? *Clin Psychol Rev* **12**:257–270.

Tynes L, Salins C, Skiba W & Winstead D (1992) A psychoeducational and support group for obsessive-compulsive disorder patients and their significant others. *Compr Psychiat* **33**:197–201.

Vallejo J, Olivares J & Marcus T (1992) Clomipramine versus phenelzine for obsessive compulsive disorder: a controlled trial. *Br J Psychiat* **161**:665–670.

Van Balkom A, de Haan E, van Oppen P, Spinhoven P, Hoogduin K & van Dyck R (1998) Cognitive and behavioral therapies alone versus in combination with fluvoxamine in the treatment of obsessive-compulsive disorder. *J Nerv Ment Dis* **186**:492–499.

Van Balkom A, van Oppen P, Vermeulen A, Nauta M, Vorst H & van Dyck, R (1994) A meta-analysis on the treatment of obsessive compulsive disorder: a comparison of antidepressants, behavior, and cognitive therapy. *Clin Psychol Rev* **14**:359–381.

Van Noppen BL (1999) Multi-family behavioral treatment (MFBT) for obsessive-compulsive disorder (OCD). *Crisis Inter Time Ltd* **5**:3–24.

Van Noppen BL, Pato MT, Marsland R & Rasmussen SA (1998) A time-limited behavioral group for treatment of obsessive-compulsive disorder. *J Psychother Pract Res* **7**:272–280.

Van Oppen P (1992) Obsessions and compulsions: dimensional structure, reliability, convergent and divergent validity of the Padua Inventory. *Behav Res Ther* **30**:631–637.

Van Oppen P & Arntz A (1994) Cognitive therapy with obsessive-compulsive disorder. *Behav Res Ther* **32**:79–87.

Van Oppen P, de Haan E, van Balkom AJL, Spinhoven P, Hoogduin K & van Dyck R (1995a) Cognitive therapy and exposure *in vivo* in the treatment of obsessive compulsive disorder *Behav Res Ther* **33**:379–390.

Van Oppen P, Emmelkamp PMG, van Balkom A & van Dyck R (1995b) The sensitivity to change of measures for obsessive-compulsive disorder. *J Anxiety Disord* **9**:241–248.

Van Oppen P, Hoekstra RJ & Emmelkamp PMG (1995c) The structure of obsessive-compulsive symptoms. *Behav Res Ther* **33**:379–390.

Vasey M & Borkovec TD (1992) A catastrophising assessment of worrisome thoughts. *Cogn Ther Res* **16**:505–520.

Veale D (1993) Classification and treatment of obsessional slowness. *Br J Psychiat* **162**:198–203.

Veale D (2000) Outcome of cosmetic surgery and 'DIY' surgery in patients with body dysmorphic disorder. *Psychiat Bull* **24**:218–221.

Veale D (2002) Overvalued ideas: a conceptual analysis. *Behav Res Ther* **40**:383–400.

Veale D, Boocock A & Gournay K (1996a) Body dysmorphic disorder. A survey of fifty cases. *Br J Psychiat* **169**:196–201.

Veale D, Gournay K & Dryden W (1996b) Body dysmorphic disorder: a cognitive behavioural model and pilot randomised controlled trial. *Behav Res Ther* **34**:717–729.

Veale D, Ennis M & Lambrou C (2001) Body dysmorphic disorder is associated with an occupation or education in art and design. *Am J Psychiat* (in press).

Veale D, Kinderman P & Riley S (2000) Self-discrepancy and body dysmorphic disorder. *Br J Clin Psychol* (in press).

Veale D & Riley S (2001) Mirror, mirror on the wall, who is the ugliest of them all? The psychopathology of mirror gazing in body dysmorphic disorder. *Behav Res Ther* **39**:1381–1393.

Vostanis P & Dean C (1992) Self-neglect in adult life. *Br J Psychiat* **161**:265–267.

Warneke L (1997) A possible new treatment to obsessive compulsive disorder. *Can J Psychiat* **42**:667–668.

Warneke LB (1984) The use of intravenous clomipramine in the treatment of obsessive compulsive disorder. *Can J Psychiat* **29**:135–141.

Warneke LB (1985) Intravenous clomipramine in the treatment of obsessive compulsive disorder in adolescence: case report. *J Clin Psychiat* **46**:100–103.

Warneke LB (1989) Intravenous clomipramine in obsessive compulsive disorder. *Can J Psychiat* **34**:853–859.

Warren LW & Ostrom JC (1988) Pack rats: world class savers. *Psychol Today* **22**:58–61.

Wegner DM (1989) *White Bears and Other Unwanted Thoughts*. New York, Viking.

Wegner DM & Gold DB (1995) Fanning old flames—emotional and cognitive effects of suppressing thoughts of a past relationships. *J Pers Soc Psychol* **68**:782–792.

Wegner DM, Schneider DJ, Carter SR & White TL (1987) Paradoxical effects of thought suppression. *J Pers Soc Psychol* **53**:5–13.

Weilberg JB, Mesulam MM & Weintraub S (1989) Focal striatal abnormalities in a patient with obsessive compulsive disorder. *Arch Neurol* **46**:223.

Weiss EL, Potenza MN & McDougle CJ (1999) Olanzapine addition in obsessive compulsive disorder refractory to selective serotonin re-uptake inhibitors: an open-label case series. *J Clin Psychiat* **60**:524–527.

Weissman MM, Bland RC, Canino GJ & Greenwald S (1994) the cross national epidemiology of obsessive compulsive disorder: the Cross National Collaborative Group. *J Clin Psychiat* **55**(suppl 3):5–10.

Welkowitz L, Struening E, Pittman J, Guardino M & Welkowitz J (2000) OCD and comorbid anxiety problems in a national screening sample. *J Anxiety Disord* **14**:471–482.

Wells A (2000) *Emotional Disorders and Metacognition*. Chichester, John Wiley & Sons. Ltd.

Wells A and Papageorgiou C (1998) Relationships between worry, obsessive-compulsive symptoms and meta-cognitive beliefs. *Behav Res Ther* **36**:899–913.

Welsh MC, Pennington BF & Groisser DB (1991) A normative–developmental study of executive function: a window on prefrontal functioning in children. *Dev Neuropsychol* **7**:131–149.

Westphal K (1878) Ueber zwangsvorstellungen. *Arch Psychiat Nervenkr* **8**:734–750.

Wetzel C, Bents H & Florin I (1999) High-density exposure therapy for obsessive-compulsive inpatients: a 1 year follow-up. *Psychother Psychosom* **68**:186–192.

Wheadon DE, Bushnell WD & Steiner M (1993) A fixed dose comparison of 20, 40 or 60 mg paroxetine to placebo in the treatment of obsessive compulsive disorder. Abstracts of panels and posters, 32nd annual meeting Honolulu, Hawaii. Nashville, TN, American College of Neuropsychopharmacology, p 194.

Whittal ML & McLean PD (1999) Cognitive-behavior therapy for obsessive-compulsive disorder. *Cogn Behav Pract* **6**:383–396.

Wilhelm S (2000) Cognitive therapy for obsessive compulsive disorder. *J Cogn Psychother* **14**:245–259.

Wilhelm S, Ofto MW & Lohr B (1999) Cognitive behavior group therapy for body dysmorphic disorder: a case series. *Behav Res Ther* **37**:71–75.

Williams JBW, Gibbon M, First MB, Spitzer RL, Davies M, Borus J, Howes MJ, Kane J, Pope HG Jr, Rounsaville B & Wittchen H-U (1992) The Structured Clinical Interview for DSM-III-R (SCID) II: multisite test-retest reliability. *Arch Gen Psychiat* **49**:630–636.

Williams TI & Allsopp M (1999) Obsessional compulsive disorder in adolescent populations. Experiences of offering a combined pharmacological–psychological approach. *Child Psychol Psychiat Rev* **4**:162–169.

Wilner A, Reich T, Robins I, Fishman R & van Doren T (1976) Obsessive-compulsive neurosis. *Compr Psychiat* **17**:527–539.

Wilson KA & Chambless DL (1999) Inflated perceptions of responsibility and obsessive-compulsive symptoms. *Behav Res Ther* **37**:325–335.

Winsberg ME, Cassic KS & Koran LM (1999) Hoarding in obsessive-compulsive disorder—A report of 20 cases. *J Clin Psychiat* **60**:591–597.

Winslow JT & Insel T (1991) Neuroethological models of obsessive-compulsive disorder. In J Zohar, TR Insel & SA Rasmussen (eds), *The Psychobiology of Obsessive-Compulsive Disorder*. New York, Springer.

Wise SP & Rapoport JL (1988) Obsessive-compulsive disorder: is it a basal ganglia dysfunction? *Psychopharmacol Bull* **24**:380–384.

Wolff RD & Wolff R (1991) Assessment and treatment of obsessive-compulsive disorder in children. *Behav Modif* **15**:372–393.

Wolpe JR (1958) *Psychotherapy by Reciprocal Inhibition*. Stanford, CA, Stanford University Press.

Wolpe JR (1970) *The Practice of Behavior Therapy*. New York, Pergamon.

Wolpe JR (1982) *The Practice of Behaviour Therapy*, 3rd edn. New York, Pergamon.

Woodruff R & Pitts FN (1964) Monozygotic twins with obsessional illness. *Am J Psychiat* **120**:1075–1078.

Woody SR, Steketee GS & Chambless DL (1995a) Reliability and validity of the Yale-Brown Obsessive-Compulsive Scale. *Behav Res Ther* **33**:597–605.

Woody SR, Steketee GS & Chambless DL (1995b) The usefulness of the obsessive compulsive scale of the Symptom Checklist-90, Revised. *Behav Res Ther* **33**:607–611.

World Health Organization (1992) *International Clarification of Diseases*, 10th edn (ICD-10). Geneva, WHO.

World Health Organisation (1996) *The Global Burden of Disease*. Geneva, WHO.

Wroe A & Salkovskis PM (2000) Causing harm and allowing harm: a study of beliefs in obsessional problems. *Behav Res Ther* **38**:1141–1162.

Wroe AL, Salkovskis PM & Richards HC (2000) 'Now I know it could happen, I have to prevent it': a clinical study of the specificity of intrusive thoughts and the decision to prevent harm. *Behav Cogn Psychother* **28**:63–70.

Wykes T, Reeder C & Corner J (1999) The effects of neurocognitive remediation on executive processing in patients with schizophrenia. *Schizophren Bull* **25**:291–307.

Yamagami T. (1971) The treatment of an obsession by thought-stopping. *J Behav Ther Exp Psychiat* **2**:135.

Yaryura-Tobias JA & Neziroglu FA (1997) *Obsessive-Compulsive Disorder Spectrum: Pathogenesis, Diagnosis, and Treatment*. Washington DC, American Psychiatric Press.

Yaryura-Tobias JA, Grunes MS, Walz J & Neziroglu F (2000) Parental obsessive-compulsive disorder as a prognostic factor in a year long fluvoxamine treatment in childhood and adolescent obsessive-compulsive disorder. *Int Clin Psychopharmacol* **15**:163–168.

Zald DH & Kim SW (1996) Anatomy and function of the orbital frontal cortex. II: function and relevance to obsessive-compulsive disorder. *J Neuropsychiat Clin Neurosci* **8**:249–261.

Zielinski CM, Taylor MA & Juzwin KR (1991) Neuropsychological deficits in obsessive-compulsive disorder. *Neuropsychiat Neuropsychol Behav Neural* **4**:110–126 .

Zitterl W, Demal U, Aigner M, Lenz G, Urban C, Zapotoczky HG & Zitterl-Eglseet K (2000) Naturalistic course of obsessive-compulsive disorder and comorbid depression: longitudinal results of a prospective follow-up study of 74 actively treated patients. *Psychopathology* **33**:75–80.

Zohar AH (1999) The epidemiology of obsessive-compulsive disorder in children and adolescents. *Child Adolesc Psychiat Clin N AM* **8**:445–460.

Zohar J, Judge R & the OCD Paroxetine Study Investigators (1996) Paroxetine versus clomipramine in the treatment of obsessive compulsive disorder. *Br J Psychiat* **169**:468–474.

Zohar J, Kaplan Z & Benjamin J (1994) Clomipramine treatment of obsessive compulsive symptomatology in schizophrenic patients. *J Clin Psychiat* **54**:385–388.

Zolhar I, Westenberg HGM & Judge R (2000) Anxiety disorders: a review of tricyclic antidepressants and selective serotonin reuptake inhibitors. *Acta Psychiat Scand* **101**:39–49.

AUTHOR INDEX

SUBJECT INDEX

The Wiley Series in

CLINICAL PSYCHOLOGY